PLENISHMENT IN THE EARTH

PLENISHMENT IN THE EARTH

An Ethic of Inclusion

STEPHEN DAVID ROSS

State University
of New York
Press

Published by
State University of New York Press, Albany

Production by Susan Geraghty
Marketing by Bernadette LaManna

For information, address State University of New York Press, State University Plaza, Albany, N.Y., 12246

10 9 8 7 6 5 4 3 2 1

Library of Congress Cataloging-in-Publication Data

Ross, Stephen David.
Plenishment in the earth : an ethic of inclusion / Stephen David Ross.
p. cm.
Includes bibliographical references and index.
ISBN 0-7914-2309-3 (alk. paper). — ISBN 0-7914-2310-7 (pbk. : alk. paper)
1. Sex role—Philosophy. 2. Sex differences—Moral and ethical aspects. 3. Ecological heterogeneity. 4. Irigaray, Luce. Ethique de la différence sexuelle. I. Title.
HQ1075.R67 1995
305.3—dc20 94-9881
CIP

CONTENTS

CHAPTER 1

Prelude

This book undertakes an ethics of inclusion, a responsibility toward the good everywhere, a love, a *cherishment,* of heterogeneous creatures and things throughout human life and nature. It pursues an ethical rethinking of natural kinds in memory of the repeated movements in Western thought that sort and order nature's and humanity's kinds into superiors and inferiors, dominants and subordinates, pure and impure, setting some to rule over others, excluding some from the good: men over women, humans over animals, Europeans over non-Europeans, pureblood over mixed. The difficult thought at the heart of this endeavor, giving voice to the music in which this work resounds, is the possibility that Western reason has been from the beginning a participant in this struggle of superiority and inferiority, demanding from us other notes to echo the good.[1] A related and demanding thought is that every ethical and political task bears a debt in memory of past injustices, struggling against their endless repetition. The moving thought at the core of this venture is that writings on gender, race, and culture mark our time with the possibility of a profound ethical response to this archaic debt.

This book undertakes a thought in memory of the impossibility of caring for all things together in a harmony in which none are hurt. Heterogeneous things come together by selection and exclusion; in human life by judgment, in representation. To live in memory of the good is to experience endless joys and sorrows, fulfillments and injustices, carried out in the name of the good. To undertake the good is to face unceasing *sacrifice* and loss: the deaths of some that others may live, the suffering of some that others may know joy. Sacrifice knows the holiness of cherishment, works within the good, but never becomes sacred, never brings us to safety. Sacrifice never escapes from the contaminations of injustice. Responsibility for sacrifice refuses every comfort in the name of the good.

Plenishment is the crossing of cherishment and sacrifice, inhabiting their borders: an inexhaustible concern for heterogeneous things and kinds together with endless impossibilities of fulfillment, producing boundless possibilities of love and joy, still haunted by memories of disaster. An ethic of plenishment includes the different things of the earth in their heterogeneous plenitude, none excluded from the good, but knows sorrow at the inevitability of loss, mourns the suffering and passing away of creatures and kinds, and knows joy at the goods that emerge from this painful place, a joy bearing unlimited responsibility for the good.

Cherishment, sacrifice, and plenishment speak together in an archaic voice of an inescapable call to the good that ethics can neither resist nor fulfill, expressing something immemorial. This immemoriality is older than any law, the call of things and kinds to us from where we find ourselves together, in kin and kind. From its immemoriality, it repeatedly asks us to wonder who we are. From its memories of injustices, it repeatedly calls upon us to exceed ourselves in the earth, to reach out beyond ourselves to others.

Cherishment is inclusion, includes the heterogeneous things and kinds of the earth, expresses the call of the good. Sacrifice is exclusion, the work of the good in time, dividing the world into good and bad, right and wrong, excluding some that others may thrive, expressing the impossibility of accomplishing the good without qualification. Plenishment is a life, a practice of cherishment joined with this impossibility. Plenishment is judgment guided by the call that every work remain haunted by memories of contamination. This book undertakes the difficult thought of cherishment and sacrifice together, of ethics as inclusion joined with the inescapability of injustice.

All this is said within a certain hesitation. Not a procrastination, not a delay before we work to save ourselves and the earth from injustices, but hesitation in the face of others, called to us in the name of the good. It is a hesitation we bear in being responsible for knowing and pursuing ethical tasks haunted by past and future injustices, including our own.

This book undertakes the task of resisting the division of kinds of things into good and bad, superior and inferior, and asks us to think of heterogeneous ways to relate to heterogeneous kinds. It undertakes the task of thinking of heterogeneous kinds of creatures, human and otherwise, against histories of domination and subordination, of injustice and harm. This task begins here with what Irigaray calls "the question of sexual difference,"[2] with the thought of gender,[3] of men and women composing two kinds of creatures in difficult relations, constituting the human world, instituting a social contract, a social world composed by regulations and laws, domination and subordination; a collective world that includes some and excludes others. This book returns repeatedly to the question of sexual difference to ask whether we can know the limits of sexual difference, or whether something enigmatic, before which we pause, echoes within the ideas of men and women, gender and desire, that compose the thought of sexual difference. This hesitant movement around the question of sexual difference opens onto thoughts of heterogeneity, leading from gender through the social world of race and culture, to the natural world, and on to multiple and heterogeneous natural kinds. This book proceeds from such thoughts of gender and world to consider: first, what such a thought might entail; and second, what kind of measure we can bring to the difficult thought of gender, divided in two into men and women, suffused by a profusion of creatures and kinds and by endless desires. This thought of two genders joined with the immeasurable heterogeneity of the natural and social world leads to animals and other natural creatures and things, to ecological feminism and other ecologies and feminisms, and thereupon to thoughts of multiple kinds emerging from other cultures and subcultures. These tracings and movements echo a thought, a life, a relation to heterogeneities and multiplicities realizing an ethic of inclusion, plenishment in the earth.

I must begin right away—I hope it is not too late, I suspect it is always too late—to say who and what I am, to name my kind. I am a heterosexual man. How important is that fact for undertaking the question of sexual difference? If I am a man, can I take up the question of sexual difference, or am I prohibited, silenced? Can I? May I? May what I have to say about sexual difference be included in an ethics of sexual difference, or do only women know that ethics? How can we ethically say "only"? How can we inclusively avoid "we"? I am a Western, heterosexual man of Jewish genealogy living and writing in the United States at the close of the twentieth century. Are these kinds relevant to my project here, to you, to me? Are other kinds to which I belong, or do not belong, also relevant?

I cannot undertake an ethic of inclusion without speaking of "us" and "we." Yet whenever I speak of "we" (or "w|e"), I mean to speak hesitantly of us, of you and me, reader and writer, together in this textual place, and some others, uncertain of different collective possibilities of place, remembering that collectives have traditionally formed themselves by acts of domination and subordination. My undertaking here is to sound the resonances and reverberations of an ethic of inclusion, to sing the song of the earth. I include in this task the endless heterogeneities opened up in the spaces of the "I" and "we." Every "I" that writes or speaks seeks a "we," yearns for others. Every "we" represents a kind that cannot be every kind and cannot cut itself off from other kinds. Such an understanding, with its endless responsibilities, gives us our ethic of inclusion, marked by the slits and gashes in "u|s" and "w|e." The voice in which I speak is mine. I hope it may be yours. I am confident it is not everyone's. To write, to speak, to read, to listen, is to participate in an ethical, inclusive relation struggling to know itself as "we," always hesitantly to know itself as "w|e," as you and I, and more. The difficult thought of this book, echoing in the repeated voices of a "we," is what kinds compose our collective relations as readers and writers, compose any human work. Such a question evokes the thought of ethical inclusion as unending proximity to heterogeneity.

I find an ethic of inclusion dispersed throughout the history of Western philosophy, surrounded by exclusions. The ethic of inclusion presented here emerges from readings of Plato, Aristotle, Spinoza, and Leibniz; others might find that ethic in Kant and Hegel. An ethic of inclusion also emerges in more recent Western writers: Whitehead, Dewey, and Heidegger as well as contemporary ethical and political writers such as Foucault, Derrida, Lyotard, and Levinas. But the inspiration behind the thought of ethical inclusion emanates from feminist interpretations of ethics and culture, represented here by an extended reading of Irigaray's *An Ethics of Sexual Difference,* and from interpretations of culture in other contemporary writers, Western and non-Western.

My reading of Irigaray is divided in two parts, the one a traversal of the history of Western philosophy from the standpoint of sexual difference, inspired by her reading of Plato's *Hystera* (Irigaray, *SOW*), otherwise known as the Cave, where she finds the good haunted by gender, the other following developments in contemporary continental, feminist, and multicultural thought from sexual difference to heterogeneity, leading to an ethic of inclusion, including every thing and kind in nature, excluding none from the good. Two avenues open here into ethical difference: one from the question of sexual difference back to "first philosophy," in chapters 3 through 6; the second from animals and other natural things to ecological feminism, in chapters 7 and 8. Chapter 9 enters heterogeneity through intimacy, face to face, and through sexual violence and gender inequality. Chapters 11 and 12 join sexual difference with other heterogeneities of sexuality, race, and culture, passing to the natural world. Different readers may desire different entry points: some into an engendered Western philosophy, in chapter 3; others into environmental feminism, in chapter 7. My goal is to show that these undertakings are linked. I hope that whatever entry point you may choose, you will be led to others.

If the question of sexual difference is the question of our age, it cannot be divorced from other questions of the age. To undertake that question is to read the works taken to define our age historically in gendered terms, to reconstruct our histories as sexed and gendered narratives. It is to understand the impossibility of carrying out an engaged philosophical thought, including traditional texts and authors, that does not concern itself from within with feminist, ecological, and multicultural issues. It is to take feminist and multicultural writings as seriously as possible, inseparable from other writings.

I invite you to join me on an ethical and political journey from the question of sexual difference through profusions of sexual and other identities to nature's plenitude, responding to the call of the good. Our journey will proceed through six musical movements, each separated from the others by a hesitation, an interlude or rest. In this "Prelude" and "Rest," I hope to anticipate the themes of this work, foreshadowing their development. I will begin to work ("Lullaby" and "Rest") with the question of sexual difference, perhaps of gender, which Irigaray suggests may be the question of our age. What can it mean for this or any question to be the question of our age, and who are "we" who may compose an age? I will closely follow Irigaray's train of thought from this question in relation, first, to Heidegger, who asks a similar question of *technē* and technology, then to other works of the Western tradition that bear upon our understanding of ourselves and our age, Plato and Aristotle, for example, and Spinoza, who according to

Kristeva excludes women from his ethics.[4] Such works echo different voices reverberating within questions of gender, sexuality, and culture, all questions of heterogeneity. These reverberations destabilize any thought of tradition and culture. We will move from thoughts of men and women, masters and slaves, the different places and kinds of nature and humanity, to listen to the *Stabat Mater*. The mother, the woman, stands sadly in her place. We will return thereafter ("Canon" and "Rest") to the thought of gender, to the dyad, the pair, man and woman, counting the pair as two, struggling with the scale, the canonicity, of measure. I will hesitantly regard[5] gender, first as two and, then, as a profusion of identities and kinds. Plato suggests in *Philebus* that we are to take up the intermediate numbers and then let them pass away into unlimit. I will retrace a thought of the indefinite dyad back to Plato in the thought of gender. Such a thought will lead to thoughts of economy and measure. I hope to resist the idea that gender belongs to a single restricted economy containing a single measure. Instead, it belongs to general economy, exceeding any measure, any mastery.[6] I hope to resist the idea of mastery. We will find that our discussion of the economy of gender returns us repeatedly to animals and other creatures, to nature's heterogeneity.

Our journey will lead from gender to nature, from the subordination of women to the domination of animals and other creatures and natural kinds, tracing a movement from an ungendered ethics toward animals and their "liberation" to ecological feminism ("Carnaval" and "Rest"). The movement from sexual difference to kindred difference expresses the heart of the movement in this book from ethical exclusion to inclusion, a movement toward heterogeneity.

The movement to natural kinds will take us away from intimacy, face-to-face proximity, and we will return to think of gender erotically, sexually, sensually, struggling with the idea of other genders and other embodiments with their *jouissances* ("Tango" and "Rest"). Throughout this itinerary, from "Canon" to "Tango," I will seek to understand ethical responsibility as a face-to-face relation with alterity. Each chapter in this path, with its rest, opens another movement in heterogeneity, beginning with the question of sexual difference, in chapter 3, leading through the history of Western philosophy viewed as a situating and re-situating of heterogeneity, concluding with the *Stabat Mater*, the mother in relation to the son. Each of the following chapters, together with its respective rest, opens a different perspective on heterogeneity, repeatedly beginning with Irigaray's critique of Levinas, that in the face to face he does not know something of radical alterity, marked by sexual difference.[7] Chapter 5 pursues the binariness of gender into the possibility of a measure, scale, or economy of heterogeneity, read throughout the history of Western philosophy. Chapter 7 moves from the heterogeneity of gender to nature's heterogeneity, to animals and other kinds, no longer reflecting Western philosophy's history. Chapter 9 returns to sexual difference erotically, understanding heterogeneity to bear a face-to-face relation to intimacy. In this chapter, I will follow Irigaray's suggestion that heterogeneity is sexual, erotic. I will move from the erotic dyad of men and women to other erotic proximities, heterogeneously. I will wonder with MacKinnon if relations between men and women can be intimate under conditions of gender inequality and sexual violence. I will pursue the thought that *erōs* destabilizes gender in face-to-face relations, find that ethical responsibility proliferates heterogeneities face to face.

With this thought of sexual and gender displacement, we will turn back to nature's heterogeneity with figures of disturbance and impurity, witches, lesbians, and others who disturb the regulations of the social contract and language ("Walpurgisnacht" and "Rest"). Our journey's displacements will bring us to colored figures on a rainbow sky, members of different human kinds and cultures, Western and non-Western, figures of fascination. With this arrival, we will find ourselves (in the concluding "Rhapsody") on the threshold of an ethic responsive to the heterogeneities of natural and human kinds, of cultural differences and identities. We end our journey with an ethic of inclusion, plenishment in the earth, an inexhaustible responsibility for and toward the heterogeneous things and kinds of the earth.

CHAPTER 2

Rest

Irigaray wonders if the question of sexual difference may be the question of our time, giving birth to an ethic of sexual difference promising to transform relations between men and women. Some readers—perhaps you and I—may be concerned that such an ethic might institute another subjection, privileging a dyadic sexual heterogeneity over multiply profuse heterogeneities. Yet do we know what an ethic of sexual difference might unearth? Can we separate sexual difference as gender from sex, gender and sex from culture? Or might an ethic of sexual difference give rise to a profusion of heterogeneities? I hope to pursue an ethic of heterogeneity pervading the earth. Such an ethic is an ethic of inclusion rather than exclusion, includes women and others, other human beings and other kinds, belongs to nature everywhere. In such an ethic, the good circulates from men and women to animals and other natural kinds, through all places of the earth, echoing nature's heterogeneous plenitude everywhere within the inexhaustible call of the good. This call imposes on whoever may hear it countless responsibilities, toward oneself and other creatures and things, to join in plenishing the earth. Such an ethic soundlessly echoes the rests of the earth, the silent remains of the good everywhere upon and in the earth.[1] Such an ethic echoes the movement of heterogeneity everywhere, in every place.

You and I know that the good has been heard to call human beings of every kind, everywhere we find humanity, to institute practices that exclude, especially women, other races, animals, and inanimate things, that exclude them from the highest good. Humanity lives within a recurrent movement of exclusion that institutes itself by rule. Kristeva reminds us repeatedly (Kristeva, *SM*, p. 185; *WT*, p. 211) that Spinoza excludes women from his ethics in the name of authority. "[P]erhaps, someone will ask, whether women are under men's authority by nature or institution?" (Spinoza, *PT*, p. 386). He answers, "women have not by nature equal right with men: but that they necessarily give way to men, and that thus it cannot happen, that both sexes should rule alike, much less that men should be ruled by women" (Spinoza, *PT*, p. 387). This movement of exclusion appears prominently in Aristotle, who under an image of perfection subordinates women, slaves, and animals, and excludes them from any possibility of bearing responsibility for the good.[2]

At the end of the twentieth century, millennial perhaps, in inspiration, the dream, the hope, of another ethics, or ethics|politics, has arisen on our planet.[3] This dream and hope, this possibility of a different thought of the good, at least a hesitant thought of a different relation between ethics and politics, unfolds moved by one event after another closing our century, memories of unthinkable violences, the Holocaust and other exterminations, countless memories of violence driven by blood fears, justifying the shedding of others' blood. Blood terror surrounds us as the threat of nuclear annihilation fades, a terror repeatedly visited upon women, for women have always borne an exceptional relation to blood. The stirring of blood sheds and cuts, annihilates and controls, along lines of gender. The taint of blood passes from men to women to men to women along lines of race and gender. It has been tainted at the end of the century by contaminants invading every human and natural space, everywhere that there is life and blood. Our world, our planet, the earth we share, has become more precious as we have diminished its plenitude, have darkened its rainbow hues.[4]

The possibility of another ethics|politics emerges from two directions, one from the sense that the old ethics|politics, Western or Enlightenment, Judeo–Greek–Christian or modern, have failed to provide us with the good and have produced a double failure: they have failed to bring to us what we know or believe to be good and have failed to give us knowledge of and responsibility toward the good. The other lies in the hope that within new movements of liberation—among women and members of different cultures, among different human identities and kinds—other, multiply heterogeneous goods may show themselves.

The need for an ethics|politics responsive to the disasters and oppressions as well as to the possibilities of liberation and betterment that pervade our planet at the close of this century emerges from every quarter and is directed everywhere. This book addresses the thought and possibility of other ethics|politics emerging from issues in feminist writings, deeply reflected in Irigaray's suggestion that the question of our age is the question of sexual difference. If we begin with this implausible claim that the question of sexual difference marks the beginning of the next millennium, to what kinds of ethics|politics may we be led? And to what different understanding of "our" tradition's ethics|politics? I believe that the "question of sexual difference" remains enigmatic, that we know neither what it means nor how it is related to other questions of our time, that it opens upon dark and striking places and desires. Pursuing the thought of sexual difference in relation to gender and women, also to culture, race, technology, and natural kinds, is to undertake ethical responsibility for Irigaray's question.

Contemporary ecological feminism[5] shares the inspiration that there is an intimate relation between concerns that involve women and concerns that involve the natural world, that the domination and oppression of women (and men by other men, but especially the oppression of women) cannot be separated from the domination of nature. From this point of view, my undertaking here is a work of ecological feminism, tracing a movement from an ethics|politics of sexual difference to an ethics|politics that includes animals and other natural kinds, a movement I call "ethical difference," an ethics|politics of inclusion rather than exclusion, profoundly concerned with heterogeneity.

I call your attention to two ingredients of my understanding of inclusion. One is that, like Irigaray, I take an ethic of sexual difference to make a profound difference in how w|e may understand ourselves, the world, and our memories, transforming the history of thought, of philosophy, and of how we read and relate to those histories. An ethic of inclusion may change men's as well as women's relations to each other and to the earth, may change them in common and in different ways. The second ingredient is that I seek to trace the force of an inclusive thought of gender and nature back to the beginnings of philosophy, less to retrieve that insight there than to mark the transformation of that tradition from the beginning under the thought of inclusion. In other words, I understand ethical inclusion to introduce so memorable a perspective on humanity and the world as to call upon us to trace its transformations throughout our histories in an inclusive way. We must do so without blunting the power of our critique or our ethical sensibilities. We must do so in a spirit of inclusion as we resist our histories' injustices.

I think of this historical movement as the haunting, the store of remembrances and forgettings, that make us who we are, same or different, Western or non-Western, men or women. I think of ethical inclusion as composed of these hauntings and hesitations, memories and forgettings, among endless others. I believe that we may find the Western tradition more divided than it has claimed itself to be, in some ways more heinous, more destructive to women, but also more inclusive, containing forking pathways foreshadowing feminist views of women and nature, some written by women, some by men.

I am speaking of an ethic of writing and reading closely related to ethical difference, an ethics of inclusion filled with excesses and remainders. You may ask why I read and reread Plato and Spinoza, why I read Irigaray so closely. I mean to read *An Ethics of Sexual Difference* intimately, lovingly, not as if I think of Irigaray as another master, nor to make her mistress under the sign of sexual difference, but to cherish representations and works as we might cherish other things of the earth. Works open up inexhaustible worlds for us to inhabit, worlds that open upon and illuminate other worlds, worlds of plenishment. Works open such worlds, sometimes in unexpected ways. An ethic of inclusion seeks to remain open to the unexpected possibilities in representational works, in human and natural works. To plenish the earth is to plenish human works, among other things. To plenish human works is on the way to plenishment in the earth.

I hope such a thought is truly feminist and truly ecological. But it is something else as well. Something ethically different. The thought around which our ethic of inclusion coalesces is a thought of natural kinds. An ethic of inclusion includes the plenitude of nature's heterogeneous kinds, asks us to undertake from the beginning another thought of and another relation to natural kinds.

Its heart and soul lie in unending restitution for what Anaximander calls the injustice, *adikia,* in things.[6] From this immemorial injustice, suffered throughout human history, but especially borne by women and by animals and other natural things and kinds, we draw the places of the good, close to, in intimate proximity with, resting in the earth. From this immemorial injustice we bear an endless responsibility everywhere in the earth, always in the shadow of our own injustices.

I begin my work echoing several notes of departure inspired by Irigaray. One is in the title of her book, *Éthique de la Différence sexuelle* (*Ethic of Sexual Difference.*) I undertake two modulations. One is from *The Ethic of Sexual Difference* to *The Sex of Ethical Difference,* understanding this "Sex" in relation to place, to *lieu* and *place.*[7] I echo the intervals and betweens that join bodies and places with *entre|antre,* with *intervalle, enveloppe,* and *reste* (Irigaray, *ÉSD,* pp. 15–20). I understand gender to disturb every thought of bodies and places, human and otherwise, every thought of rest. The second modulation takes place in the sound of the very first words, at the very beginning, of *Éthique de la Différence sexuelle,* the crux of our entire orchestration. "La différence sexuelle représente une des questions ou la question qui est à pense à notre époque" (Irigaray, *ÉDS,* p. 13).[8] *The question!* Perhaps the question of our age, the question perhaps of any age, is the question of sexual difference. If so, then ethics and ethical difference and the question of our age must all be sexed.[9] And indeed, Irigaray describes a sexed or gendered ethics. I hope to tell the sex of the good; I hope to remember the vulnerability of men's and women's pain and joy. For the moment, I leave ethical difference aside, to speak of sexual difference. W|e seek, men and women, to care about the *jouissance* and the *souffrance,* the suffering and violence, in sexual difference. We seek our joy in the sadness of the good.

For the third note we find in Irigaray, in her writing elsewhere,[10] echoes that culture is an economy based upon the exchange of women (Irigaray, *WM*). I hesitate at joining the exchange, at the thought of an exchange economy. I hope to shift from restricted to general economy.[11] I mean to record the circulation of women, of women and other goods, the circulation of men and their work under capitalism, to record an economy as the circulation of goods, everywhere, elsewhere, circulating excessively. I hope to echo the work of such an economy as the circulation of judgments and further judgments, together with whatever might become goods and judgments, all seeking, organizing, circulating goods, men, women, animals, and inanimate things, a general economy as ethical difference, as the work of heterogeneity. I add, from Bataille, that the circulation of goods may be orderly, ruled, may compose a restricted economy, a *régime;* or it may exceed, disturb, fragment every *régime,* composing a general economy, filled with lawless monsters. I add the monstrosities and distortions that inhabit capitalist and heterosexual economies, marked by the order of their rule, the suffering of subject bodies.[12] I sing of such lawful, excessive economies.[13] I listen to goods and judgments circulating excessively, hear this circulation as a musical *jouissance,* knowing that there cannot be just one *jouissance,* not just one ethical difference, not one general economy, not one song or rest. Nor one *souffrance, tristesse,* or *douleur.*

If I speak of multiple economies of ethical difference, will you ask me, exactly how many economies, how many goods, how many kinds of judgments and representations, circulate in how many different economies, how many questions make up the question of sexual difference or any difference? Can I measure the earth's inclusion? Will you require that I measure the difference between different economies, or does the inexplicable heterogeneity of the good disrupt any number? Does the good throw us up beyond any limit, out of number's measure? Does general economy, economy's music, give up any measure? I want to know the music's measure, to count the beats of every song. I hesitantly pursue the possibility of a good, ethical difference, otherwise than any being, exceeding any limit, even as Being itself is otherwise than any being, including its measure. I pursue the good echoing Levinas and otherwise than Levinas.[14] For Levinas speaks of an unlimited responsibility for the other that cannot belong to Being, to nature, speaks of "*otherwise than being*" (Levinas, *OB,* p. 3). And he speaks of that responsibility as proximity, face to face with an other. These two themes lie at the heart of ethical difference. Yet ethical difference displaces the places of limit and unlimit, even, perhaps against Levinas, the places of subjectivity. For subjects face to face may not represent irreducible heterogeneity. Irigaray asks, where in Levinas do we find the inescapable alterity of sexual difference, "the other sex as an alterity irreducible to myself" (Irigaray, *OEL,* p. 180)? Where in Levinas do we find other creatures as multiple alterities irreducible to ourselves? Where do we find animals in the ethical places of the earth? Ethical difference calls us to the limits of the earth in the face of heterogeneity.

The unmeasurable relation of the measure of limit to unlimit was narrated long ago by Plato, in a deeply enigmatic passage, told to Socrates by "the men of old" who passed on "a gift of the gods" "in the form of a saying":

> All things, so it ran, that are ever said to be consist of a one and a many, and have in their nature a conjunction of limit and unlimitedness. This then being the ordering of things we ought, they [the men of old] said, whatever it be that we are dealing with, to assume a single form and search for it, for we shall find it there contained; then, if we have laid hold of that, we must go on from one form to look for two, if the case admits of there being two, otherwise for three or some other number of forms. . . . But we are not to apply the character of unlimitedness to our plurality until we have discerned the total number of forms the thing in question has intermediate between its one and its unlimited number. It is only then, when we have done that, that we may let each one of all these intermediate forms pass away into the unlimited and cease bothering about them. (Plato, *Philebus,* 16cde)

What I find enigmatic is not the movement from limit to unlimit, but that, after we have discerned the total number of intermediate forms pertaining to our multiplicity, we are to let each one of these intermediate forms pass away into the unlimited and cease bothering about them. It is more congenial to a modern ear to seek the intermediate and forgo the unlimited, to look for measure rather than unmeasure, to order with the standard of measure. If there are many economies of ethical difference, many circulations of goods, how many are there? If we follow Plato, we must seek an answer to this question but must not rest content with that answer, must turn from it to the unlimit (leaving aside for the moment what it might mean to let the intermediate number "pass away," to know what death is marked). We may wonder how measure can haunt the excesses of unmeasure. We may wonder how the ethical rule can haunt the heterogeneities of the good. We may find the good in the spaces between the intermediate and unlimit.

If you and I follow the track of sexual difference, we may find striking analogies. For we think we know, we want to know, how many sexes or genders there are. We will not be able to escape the number two. Yet we cannot remain content with that answer, must not, not least because that number, gender's two, defines women's historical subordination;[15] because of the tremendous and recurrent pain that has been caused to many people who do not fit standard sexual and gender classifications; but especially, perhaps, because we do not know how many economies of sexual difference there are or might be. I hear the question of sexual difference as forcing us to remember, never to forget, never to turn away from, the number two, remembering that that number, the dyad of gender, is more than a classification, does not measure, but commits violence, oppresses as it expresses love, proximity, and intimacy. Limit, unlimit, and two circle endlessly around each other in an orbit of oppression and violence, ethical and political. The musical economy of sexual difference is always ethical|political.

I add that we are not sure of the parameters of the circulation of gender, not sure where gender begins and leaves off, more sure, perhaps, that the lines of gender subject and subjugate.[16] The question of gender becomes multiple questions of the circulation of goods, divided by sexual difference, by other differences and desires. For goods may circulate differently between men and women; moreover, men and women circulate as goods. And goods may circulate differently between men and women and others, those who are not men and women and those who are neither men nor women but for whom there is sexual difference—animals and other living creatures. Goods may also circulate differently for those for whom there is sexual difference but not different sexes, unicellular organisms perhaps, and for and among those we imagine do not know sexual difference.[17] Sexual difference breaks the boundaries of the hold of identity and being in multiply heterogeneous ways. It breaks the hold of one rationality and one truth for all into two, then into many. For if there may be different truths and rationalities for men and women, the hold of universality on reason and truth breaks apart. Here is one understanding of how the number two may pass away into unlimit. Sexual difference breaks the hold of two by proliferation, yet it resists the hold of multiplicity by insisting on the number two: men and women. The number two rests in its places of difference. And we must not forget *souffrance*, must not forget those who suffer violence. We must remember without another exclusion, against our own injustices. That is our hesitation.

For the moment, I hope to suspend these considerations by holding onto a single thought: the heterogeneity brought forth by sexual difference haunts every sense of limit and abyss with the number two, haunts every one with two, yet resists the hold of the number two with another abyss, another heterogeneity, proliferating into other kinds. The differences between men and women proliferate into differences among heterogeneous natural kinds, resisting superiority and domination. To the idea of one general and unrestricted economy of ethical difference, I respond with two. To the idea of two restricted economies of sexual difference, I respond with one general economy and with endless restricted economies, endless kinds and kinds of kinds, mixtures of kinds. To the idea of an endless succession of economies I respond with the ethical difference of heterogeneity. Heterogeneity contains within itself a restlessness, an inexhaustibility, understood in the guise of resistance. In the name of sexual and ethical difference, I hope to resist the hold of any particular difference and any particular circulation. And yet I hope to resist the hold of the One, unlimit, proliferation, inexhaustibility, as another collapse of difference into any and every difference. Sexual difference is not every other difference. That recognition strikes the heart of the question of sexual difference, expresses the irreducible alterity of gender. This alterity, irreducible among other irreducible alterities, is required in the name of resistance to the neutralization of the question of this or any other difference. The neutralization of heterogeneity is something I hope to resist, again and again, as you and I know that we will neutralize heterogeneity again and again, however much we hope to resist.

And so, if one of the (defining) questions of our age is the question of sexual difference, into what ethical economies does this question unfold, and does it compose or exceed any *régime?*

These three points define a triangle in whose ring we may seek our thought. What can it mean to say that the question of our age—louder! **THE QUESTION OF OUR AGE**—is the question of sexual difference? This work may be read as an extended meditation on that question, on the question of our age as the question of woman, when we know of endless other differences, other oppressions, and do not know how to measure sexual difference. I wonder if this thought of other differences in the vibrations of sexual difference marks the advent of ethical difference in our age. I wonder if every ethical thought of our age must include a thought of the question of sexual difference, of gender and of women, of heterogeneity.

Could the question of the age be the question of the earth? Could we return to the earth, to the Greek and Other Earth? Could we hope to sing the song, the many songs, of the earth, in many modulations? Earth, nature, *physis*, . . . et cetera et cetera. Including the good . . . et cetera et cetera. I undertake to sing with you the songs of the earth as the general economies of ethical difference.

I hope that you will always remember, if you continue to read here, that every *I* reverberates as a *w*|*e* (but not a *WE*): you and I, and some others. No *WE* can appropriate the other *w*|*e*s. I hope that my discourse does not appropriate women's writing as it learns from them; the dominant discourse does not own feminist writing; deep ecology does not possess the truth of ecofeminism. In speaking of the question of sexual difference, and of the inescapability of the dyad of gender, I mean to speak hesitantly of the irreducibility of the question of a feminist truth, a gendered truth. For we cannot escape the number two, and possibly other definite dyads, as they proliferate and disperse into silence, when we belong to an economy of ethical difference. Difference reminds us of two—or more. No *WE* can be universal, certainly not *UNIVERSAL*. With this and other reminders, I will cease to remind you incessantly of the kind of person who writes and reads. "We" (and "w|e") are you and I, and others.

CHAPTER 3

Lullaby

> La différence sexuelle représente une des questions ou la question qui est à pense à notre époque. Chaque époque—selon Heidegger—a une chose à penser. Une seulement. La différence sexuelle est probablement celle de notre temps. La chose de notre temps qui, pensée, nous apporterait le «salut»?
>
> —Irigaray, *Éthique de la Différence sexuelle*
>
> [Sexual difference represents one of the questions or the question that is to be thought in our age. According to Heidegger, each age has one thought to think. One only. Sexual difference is probably the thought of our time. The thing of our time that, thought, will bring us "salvation"? (my translation)[1]]

With these words, I undertake in this chapter and the next a reading of *An Ethics of Sexual Difference,* echoing some of the themes and movements Irigaray orchestrates under the question of sexual difference from the beginnings of Western philosophy to our time, through Nietzsche to Heidegger. All sexed. With a difference. Heterogeneously. The question of sexual difference, if the question of our age, deeply transfigures the thought of philosophy, from the beginning to the end, and beyond. I will turn to the dyad of gender, the measure of heterogeneity, in chapter 5. I will open another access to the question of sexual difference in chapter 7, relating heterogeneity to animals, to differences in kinds. For the moment, I listen to the question of sexual difference, with its wealth of intermediary figures, as defining the economy of our age.

Irigaray mentions Heidegger; she quotes him, with a question mark, the Heidegger for whom the question of the age is the forgetting of Being, the age of technology, for whom the question concerns technology's frame, the *Ge-stell.*

> Thus where enframing reigns, there is *danger* in the highest sense.
>
> But where danger is, grows
> The saving power also.
>
> (Heidegger, *QT,* pp. 309–10; excerpt of poem quoted from Hölderlin, "Patmos")

Sexual difference will bring "us," within the danger, "the saving power." Perhaps *(«?»)*. Irigaray's question mark reminds us of Heidegger as it displaces him. The question concerning technology will bring us "the saving power." Question mark![2] The question of the question . . . mark. Perhaps the question of the sex, the gender, of technology, perhaps the question of the technology of gender. If the question of gender or the question of technology is the question of our age, then perhaps each question turns toward the other. Questions of nature, technology, and gender may link every burning question of our time.

For a moment, let us think "*selon Heidegger,*" who dwells on the saving power that resides within the danger, inhabits technology, while technology frames the danger: "precisely the essence of technology must harbor in itself the growth of the saving power" (Heidegger, *QT,* p. 310). He adds two further thoughts, one the bringing forth, the *poiēsis,* in *technē,* the other the destiny *(Geschick)* of bringing forth. Modern technology, as the *Ge-stell,* represents a destining of revealing, a *Geschick* of *poiēsis,* something thrown forward from the beginnings of philosophy, from *technē* to modern technology, framing our age.

> The revealing that challenges has its origin as a destining in bringing-forth. But at the same time enframing, in a way characteristic of a destining, blocks *poiēsis.*
>
> Thus enframing, as a destining of revealing, is indeed the essence of technology . . . (Heidegger, *QT,* p. 311)

One thought here leads the question of technology to its essence, enframing, as a destining of revealing, leads back to first philosophy, to *poiēsis* as the bringing-forth of an enframing that blocks itself. From the beginning of Western thought, with the Greeks, the essence of technology has emerged within its destiny in the regions between *poiēsis* and *technē.* And so, still within the destining of *poiēsis,* we find a second thought, concerning what the saving power might bring forth, still a destining. What might be our "salvation"? And a third, how the thought of the question of the age, as thought, might save us, might save the earth. The bringing-forth in technology, thought in Greek, expresses the *poiēsis* in *technē,* the saving art in technology, returns us to the earth. "Could it be that revealing lays claim to the arts most primarily, so that they for their part may expressly foster the growth of the saving power, may awaken and found anew our vision of that which grants and our trust in it?" (Heidegger, *QT,* p. 316). We wonder if the saving power of art might found a new age of the world from within its technological destiny; if the arts might foster our salvation because they dwell closer to the earth than science or philosophy; if, returning to Irigaray, "our salvation" might "constitute the horizon of worlds more fecund than any known to date—at least in the West," that "would be a fecundity of birth and regeneration, but also the production of a new age of thought, art, poetry and language: the creation of a new *poetics*" (Irigaray, *ESD,* p. 5). We await a new ethics, brought forth from the fecundity of a new poetics, ringing in the silence of the earth. What but an art, a poetics, that recapitulates in a different voice the history of Western philosophy, that joins sexual difference with technology? What but an art of *poiēsis?*

You and I may hesitate at this recurrent thought of the new, however salvatory, however poetic; we may wonder if it might be a repetition of Western rationality, another exclusion. We may wonder, from our beginning with question(s) of sexual difference, whether the thought of a new age might still belong to men, to modern Western men, excluding others, women or non-Western men, wonder why the new must exclude the old, wonder why Irigaray gestures toward Heidegger on the question of sexual difference. If we think the question of the age as a question of sexual difference, we may hesitate before the "new," hesitate before the destiny, the possibility of the new . . . Germans, humans, technologists, philosophers . . . men. Perhaps every thought of the new, however poetic, excludes, as every new thought in the history of Western philosophy has excluded women, non-Westerners, and animals. Perhaps novelty excludes, destroys, as new. How new would it be to include the old?

A new thought of sexual and ethical difference may join two thoughts impossible to think together as new: one very old, that ethical and sexual difference take us back to something immemorial, archaic, to witches and goddesses,[3] and to Greece, to the birth of Western philosophy where ethics lost its way; the other the contamination of any thought of new or old, brought by questions of ethical and sexual difference. Our thought of sexual difference leads to an inclusive ethic that refuses to exclude the old in the light of the new because we insist on remembering witches, refuse to exclude women. And others.

Witches disturb the equilibrium of the new, join new and old, West and non-West. The new witches remind us of the old, of the murder of thousands of European women as witches, many more women than men, disturb the new with the old, as if there might still be witches.[4] We may hope that the end of women's oppression would be new, a liberation, in memory of murdered witches. We may wonder if the end of women's oppression, bubbling in the witches' cauldron, could be the end of the rule of the new, mourning endlessly for suffering women. The end of salvation. Or rather, the salvation (*«salut»*) of the end of salvation, something like the salvation of the death of God. We wonder if questions of ethical and sexual difference might bring us to an event in which a "new" thought of the "event" of salvation might arise in the West, abolishing the exclusion of the new, including memories of the old, of others, of heterogeneity. We might think of such an event as gendered, sexed, the arrival of sexual heterogeneity. What liberating thought arrives with thinking of the arrival of sexual difference, of the earth as sexed, an ethical questioning of the sovereignty of the new?

One question, you may say, that is both two and too many questions, the burning question of our time: a thought of salvation from within the destining of technology, emerging from sexual difference; and the new age to which such a thought may give rise, a new age with a new ethic of sexual difference that does not understand the new to exclude the old. For Heidegger, the question of technology leads to "the gift" of language, to the essence of "the human."[5] The disclosure of nature belongs to Us, not to insects, animals, or space and time. It belongs to us through the gift of language. Spirit is Ours, not theirs. Yet what if We, men and women, or you and I, spoke different languages as we thought we spoke the same, inhabited different spirits, knew different souls? And what if They, apes and cats, spoke ours or other languages? And what if they did not? What of their souls? Do we know, with certainty enough to justify destroying them with impunity, that animals neither speak nor have souls nor participate in the good? Does language mark the limits of the good? Do we possess the limits of souls? What if *psychē* roamed the earth?[6] (Or is it that We ravage the earth?) *Angels* with souls move between (*entre|antre*) heaven and earth, moving heaven and earth, intermediary figures. "These swift angelic messengers, who transgress all enclosures in their speed, tell of the passage between the envelope of God and that of the world as micro- or macrocosm. They proclaim that such a journey can be made by the body of man, and above all the body of woman" (Irigaray, *ESD,* p. 16). Angels, animals, and witches roam the earth. In the name of sexual difference, Irigaray calls our attention repeatedly to intermediary figures, circulating on their ethical journeys.

Reminding us of Plato, with a difference. For Diotima speaks of spirits as "the envoys and interpreters that ply between heaven and earth" (Plato, *Symposium,* 202e).[7] The difference is sexual, for Irigaray's angels and our animals and witches are sexed in their bodies. Yet Plato does not neglect bodily movements. "Love is not exactly a longing for the beautiful" but "for the conception and generation that the beautiful effects" (Plato, *Symposium,* 206e).

Two thoughts, resounding at this point and again. First, the new age, the salvation, echoes endless questions reverberating within the questions of ethical and sexual difference. One may recapitulate Western modernity: we hope to undertake a thought whose very thinking will save us from the injustices of the old. Yet at this time in late or "post" modernity, we may hesitate in the face of such a thought as recapitulating the hold from which we hope to be saved. Every thought of the new suggests a thought of the good under whose sway some will be excluded. A second thought, close to the first, is that if we are oppressed, subjected, we must seek to be saved, must pursue liberation. If we are women, non-Western, animals, even men, we must struggle to be saved from suffering and oppression. We must keep our oppression in view, must not let our suffering pass into another repetition of oppression, must not use our oppression to justify injustice. These two thoughts, among countless others, meet in thoughts of sexual difference.

The question, still taking Irigaray as seriously as possible, remains what it might mean (in our age, perhaps) to think questions of sexual difference as far as possible (in our age) as ethical. I mention Heidegger and the question concerning technology to mark his insistence that to think the *Ge-stell* is to think as deeply as possible of our age, of and in the *Ge-stell,* therefore of what came before and what will come after, and of their relation, all framed by modern technolog And we think in the mode of undertaking, bearing ethical responsibilities. We think, as Irigaray reminds us again and again, in the mode of ethics|politics, surrounded by injustices. The thought of the essence of technology is an ethical thought. Even as Heidegger denied it, everyone who reads him knows that the thought of technology, of the modern age, is ethical|political. This more than anything else is the scandal of his Rectorship and his continuing refusal to accept ethical|political responsibilities. Everything is ethical|political, we say and know because of Nietzsche, but especially, because of Heidegger, the thought of the age.[8] This truth, Lyotard reminds us, seems to have been unknown, forgotten, by Heidegger himself, scandalously, offensively, unethically. I am speaking of the extermination of Jews.[9]

Irigaray reminds Lyotard and us that ever since the beginning w|e have forgotten, to the point of exterminating, women as women, except that we (men and women) cannot endure without them. You and I, men and women, live in proximity with women, in proximity to the bodies of women, in the love of women. The scandal of the love of women is an endless extermination. Every thought of sexual difference is a profoundly ethical thought.

It is also, Irigaray tells us, again in a certain, hysterical mirroring of Heidegger, an ethical thought of "first philosophy" (Irigaray, *ESD,* p. 6).[10] The question of technology is for Heidegger a thought of the beginning of thought. Questions of sexual difference for Irigaray include thoughts of the beginning. Thoughts of sexual difference (and technology) make a profound difference in how to think of and relate to nature and the earth, a difference going back to the beginning of Western philosophy, and elsewhere. Such thoughts make a profound ethical difference in our thought of ourselves and our surroundings and the ideas around which we think ourselves in the earth. Questions of sexual or ethical difference, here, are questions of first philosophy, of something to be heard before philosophy, permeating Western philosophy.

We have arrived at one answer—among countless others—to questions of the question of the age. The idea of a question of an age is historical (and hysterical) in a far-reaching sense. One sense is that we, in our age, belong to history, with new questions coming on the scene among the old. A second is that such a question of our age, in characterizing us, characterizes our history, our temporality, our relation to our past and future, our genders, bodies, desires. This characterization is encompassing, enveloping. Questions of the age are questions of first philosophy. Questions of first philosophy ask how in philosophy we belong to the earth. Irigaray answers in intermediary figures.

Questions of our age are questions of first philosophy. But they are more. For they re-direct philosophy (back) toward ethics, from which it emerged. And they do so in echoes of difference. The movement back to where, in Plato, the truth of nature and being is a truth of the good, is a hesitation, a repetition with a difference, because the hold of reason on this truth of nature and the good is thought differently today, and will be understood to have been thought differently yesterday (and before). That difference is the way in which questions of sexual and ethical difference come on the scene as questions of the place of our age, turning everything upside down, displacing every place. I am speaking of Nietzsche's revaluation and transvaluation of all values in the name of truth, of Heidegger's questioning of the essence of *technē,* of the possibility that reason and its truth emerged within and belong to Western philosophy, and now of Irigaray's questioning of first philosophy as a thought of sexual difference. The history of Western philosophy undergoes a transformation from the beginning within the thought of sexual difference.

One repeated thought of first philosophy is a thought of *technē.* A repetition sounds in Aristotle, for whom even as *physis* is thought as moving from within itself rather than from without, it is thought as *technē,* an art of classification, dividing the world into kinds (Aristotle, *Physics* 2, 192b8–193a10).[11] A second again echoes in Aristotle, now in the relation between *technē* and *poiēsis.* For first philosophy, as a thought of eternity (if it has ever been such a thought), must include a thought of coming to be, of bringing-forth, of *poiēsis,* that is, of and in time. The question of technology, then, as a thought of *technē* and *poiēsis,* is a thought of time and history, thereby a thought of first philosophy. We may also, following Irigaray, think of first philosophy in a third way, and in other ways, in terms of Aristotle. For in the same *Physics* in which he speaks of nature moving from within while *technē* moves from without, of *tychē* [chance] as cause in nature among other causes (Aristotle, *Physics,* 195b30–198a13), Aristotle also speaks of occupying a place [*topos*] (Aristotle, *Physics* 4, esp. 208a25–213a12). Sexual and ethical difference turn space and time and place into and around the interval (*intervalle*), the place between (*entre*). Sexual and ethical difference give rise, in the thought of place, of the interval between or within the place of place.[12] This place, which gives rise to space, does not belong to woman, who has no place (of her own?). But we are ahead of ourself, as we will be throughout. Questions of sexual and ethical difference are always ahead of themselves. And behind.

I am closely following Irigaray, thinking of first philosophy as I think of ethics. Questions of sexual difference, as they shake the foundations of our time, do so in an ethical voice. Here we may depart from Heidegger just a bit, as we acknowledge his proximity. For I wish to take his conflicted relation to ethics seriously, do not wish to ignore his refusal of ethics as humanistic, as I wonder, together with Irigaray, if that very refusal is ethical.[13]

I wonder in what ways, if not all ways, sexual difference might lead to first philosophy and back, where first philosophy might represent a point of resistance against itself. We may think of three. Questions of sexual difference might lead us to, as Irigaray suggests, or give rise to an event: (1) in which first philosophy, as the Western Judeo–Greek–Christian tradition has it, would be given up; (2) in which first philosophy, as the Western Judeo–Greek–Christian tradition has it, would not be first, not the first event in the unfolding of Western philosophy;[14] (3) in which first philosophy would undergo an event in which it would be thought in a different way, in which all philosophical thinking would be thought in a different way, as gendered, sexed. Questions of sexual difference here present a complex and difficult event, somewhere between (*entre*) the beginning of a new thought that was never thought before—whose possibility is demanded by the thought of an event, by a thought of history after Nietzsche—and the thinking of a thought that was so inescapable that we could not avoid thinking it, always.[15]

Surely sexual (and perhaps ethical) difference is a thought that, in its absence, has always been thought, has been thought too much, is something with which human beings have always struggled. Two examples may suffice, if only to begin this thought, to initiate the contemporary event in which we come to say differently what we have always said, however strange it may be to say it. One may be heard in Irigaray herself, who writes of the work that has seemed to many to be, if not the very first philosophical work, to be the first work of Western philosophy—or rather, Irigaray does not write *of* that work, but re-writes it:

> As the story goes, then, men—with no specification of sex—are living in one, same, place. A place shaped like a cave (*antre*) or a womb (*ventre*). [*entre* again!] (Irigaray, *SOW,* p. 245)

> So men have lived in this cave since their childhood. Since time began. They have never left this space, or place, or topography, or topology, of the cave. The swing around the axes of symmetry necessarily determines how they live, but they are unaware of this. Chained by the neck and thighs, they are fixed with their heads and genitals facing *front, opposite*—which in Socrates' tale, is the direction toward the back of the cave. (Irigaray, *SOW,* p. 245)

Did you remember that these hominids, in the cave, had genitals, and that their genitals faced in a certain direction, if they were men? Women's genitals are not situated in the same plane of orientation to their bodies. And these hominids, with their genitals, inhabit a womb, between heaven and earth, ready to be born into the light of the sun. "Picture men dwelling in a sort of subterranean cavern with a long entrance open to the light on its entire width. Conceive them as having their legs and necks fettered from childhood, so that they remain in the same spot, able to look forward only, and prevented by the fetters from turning their heads" (Plato, *Republic,* 514ab).

Irigaray makes it plain, plainly shows as you and I might have forgotten, that if these are human beings, the fettering of their legs and necks also fetters their sexualities. For they are *anthrōpoi,* and we do not know, we can only surmise, that they are men and not women. We may wonder whether the story would be the same if they were women rather than men, or whether that might be the question of sexual difference. We note that the narrative of the cave|womb|hystera is a repetition of place. "Men" are in their place, fettered in place, chained in their sexual place in the womb, while the call of the good—of ethical and sexual difference—displaces them, moves them, from the womb to birth, from the sexual place to . . . what? Perhaps the narrative of the cave is a narrative of the security of the sexual place of men. Perhaps the question of ethical and sexual difference might displace place, security, and sexuality, all with a double blow (as Derrida says of *Geschlecht,* of gender, in Heidegger).

> What comes to *Geschlecht* as its decomposition (*Verwesung*), its corruption, is a *second blow* that comes to strike the sexual difference and to transform it into dissension, war, savage opposition.[16] The primordial sexual difference is tender, gentle, peaceful; when that difference is struck down by a "curse" . . . the duality or the duplicity of the two becomes unleashed, indeed bestial, opposition. (Derrida, *G2,* p. 193)[17]

For Derrida also, in the context of the truth that "[o]f sex, one can readily remark, yes, Heidegger speaks as little as possible, perhaps he has never spoken of it" (Derrida, *G1,* p. 65), tells us that bearing no sexual mark is, for Heidegger, a sexual mark, as it must be, perhaps, for us. "Being-there, being *there,* the *there* of being as such, bears no sexual mark" (Derrida, *G1,* p. 67). Yet in bearing no sexual mark, *Dasein* bears a sexual mark. For Derrida suggests that in this denial lies a suspicion. "What if 'sexuality' already marked the most originary *Selbstheit?* If it were an ontological structure of ipseity? If the *Da* of *Dasein* were already 'sexual'?" (Derrida, *G1,* p. 74). Perhaps when Spirit bears no animal body, it bears an animal soul.[18]

This is an extreme reading of Irigaray's remark, in her italics, of "*the sexual indifference that underlies the truth of any science, the logic of every discourse*" (Irigaray, *PDSF,* p. 69).[19] This indifference is a mark of sexual difference. Sexual difference, as neutrality, objectivity, sexual indifference, still, as Derrida and Irigaray suggest, reverberates everywhere in Western philosophy, from the beginning to the end and always. The absence of sexual difference is sexual difference. The absence of ethical difference (in science's objectivity) is ethical difference. Everything in nature, from the beginning and always, is ethical, in silence, in nature's rests. Everything in nature is ethical difference, the plenitude of the earth. The earth includes everything in the good.

Surely Spinoza and Leibniz have already said this, or something similar, not to mention Whitehead and Dewey. Yet questions of sexual difference evoke another reading of their writings, for after all, they were men. And they do not speak openly of gender when they speak of nature, or speak neutrally of women when they speak of gender. The neutrality with which they speak may be a mark of (their) gender. We will come to them, in their ethical difference|sexual indifference. But first, first philosophy.

For Irigaray echoes many thoughts of first philosophy as she develops her understanding of the question of sexual difference: thoughts of salvation, space and time, of God and immortality, angels, bodies, and places, intermediary figures. Aristotle resounds more than Heidegger in her thoughts of sexual difference. "A revolution in thought and ethics is needed if the work of sexual difference is to take place" (Irigaray, *ESD,* p. 6). I understand this revolution to reach to the edges of the earth. "We need to reinterpret everything concerning the relations between the subject and discourse, the subject and the world, the subject and the cosmic, the microcosmic and the macrocosmic" (Irigaray, *ESD,* p. 6). Perhaps the relation between microcosm and macrocosm, as we reinterpret it, will displace the subject from the center of Irigaray's discourse, beyond its displacement from the man who "has been the subject of discourse" (Irigaray, *ESD,* p. 6) to beyond-man, beyond-the-human, beyond-nature-in-nature.

As she says, "[i]n order to make it possible to think through, and live, this difference, we must reconsider the whole problematic of *space* and *time*" (Irigaray, *ESD,* p. 7). And place, for she suggests (preceded by an "if") that "traditionally, and as a mother, woman represents *place* for man" (Irigaray, *ESD,* p. 10). Man, here, owes his allegiance to time. "The subject, the master of time [in Kant], becomes the axis of the world's ordering" (Irigaray, *ESD,* p. 7), while "in the beginning there was space and the creation of space" (Irigaray, *ESD,* p. 7).

What inverts itself in sexual difference?[20] What in space and time? "The transition to a new age requires a change in our perception and conception of *space–time,* the *inhabiting of places,* and of *containers,* or *envelopes of identity*" (Irigaray, *ESD,* p. 7). Not to mention the angels, and God, but not God-the-King. For the moment, we remain with place as the meaning of space. In place, we find space in the interval, between (*entre*), as we enter, go between, space and time. And what of place? "Zeno's difficulty demands an explanation: for if everything that exists has a place, place too will have a place, and so on *ad infinitum*" (Aristotle, *Physics,* 209a24–28; Irigaray, *ÉDS,* p. 41). What in philosophy could be more first, at the beginning, than the question of the place of place? You may wonder what this has to do with ethical difference, with beasts and monsters.

Irigaray tells an originary narrative, reminding us of "the island of Atlantis" and the cave, as well as of "the men of old."

> In the beginning there was space and the creation of space, as is said in all theogonies. The gods, God, first create *space*. And time is there, more or less in the service of space. . . .
>
> Philosophy then confirms this genealogy of the task of the gods or God. Time becomes the *interiority* of the subject itself, and space its *exteriority* (this problematic is developed by Kant in the *Critique of Pure Reason*). (Irigaray, *ESD*, p. 7)

We hear two supplements:

> In the beginning God created the heaven and the earth.
>
> 2 And the earth was without form, and void; and darkness was upon the face of the deep. And the Spirit of God moved upon the face of the waters.
>
> 3 And God said, Let there be light; and there was light. (Gen. 1:1–3)

> In the beginning was the Word. (John 1:1)

> Knowledge is aware not only of itself, but also of the negative of itself, or its limit. Knowing its limit means knowing how to sacrifice itself. This sacrifice is the self-abandonment, in which Spirit sets forth, in the form of free fortuitous happening, its process of becoming Spirit, intuitively apprehending outside it its pure self as Time, and likewise its existence as Space. (Hegel, *PM*, pp. 806–7)

Hegel continues the thought of Absolute Spirit and Absolute Knowledge into nature: "[t]his last form into which Spirit passes, *Nature,* is its living immediate process of development. Nature—Spirit divested of self (externalized)—is, in its actual existence, nothing but this eternal process of abandoning its (Nature's) own independent subsistence, and the movement which reinstates Subject" (Hegel, *PM,* p. 807). Yet Hegel does not stop with nature as the subject's externalization in space and time. "The other aspect, however, in which Spirit comes into being, *History,* is the process of becoming in terms of knowledge, a conscious self-mediating process—Spirit externalized and emptied into Time" (Hegel, *PM,* p. 807).

Emptying, abandoning, externalizing, sacrificing. Could these be more masculine than time itself?

For God created heaven and earth, spirit and matter, *in the beginning,* as if in time, as if God might control space and time and matter, in time. God seems to know time as the creator of history. And Spirit throws space and time outside itself into nature and history, the forms of its empty relation to itself. No doubt this is a relation of mastery: Hegel says it is. But it is also a relation of sacrifice. Irigaray, in a sentence or two that we might have taken as our beginning, rather than the question of our age, that might also bring us "*le «salut»,*" speaks of sacrifice: "[h]e risks who risks life itself. In excess of it, scarcely, by a breath; a breath which, if it is held, saves through song" (Irigaray, *HR,* p. 213).[21]

Could the question of sexual difference, which might be our salvation, save through the resting, silent breath of song? We sing the song of sexual difference, the lullaby of ethical difference, for the moment, in space and time. Risk and sacrifice remain to be sung.

Irigaray suggests that space belongs to woman (for her? for man?) while man is the subject–master of time. Yet we do not know for whom. More important is the sound of the interval. "The subject . . . : God. He effects the passage between time and space" (Irigaray, *ESD,* 7). God the subject works between time and space, in the interval, the *entre.* For "[e]ach age inscribes a limit to this trinitary configuration: *matter, form, interval,* or *power, act, intermediary–interval*" (Irigaray, *ESD,* p. 8). God works in the *entre,* together with desire, which "occupies or designates [*désigne*] the place of the *interval*" (Irigaray, *ESD,* p. 8).

What inverts itself in the interval of sexual difference? What or who? Why does gender invert the order of time and space? In what economy? What difference does sexual difference make to Western philosophy? These questions call for a return. First a digression.[22]

In an essay written somewhat before *Éthique de la Différence sexuelle,* Kristeva speaks of the multiplicity of "Women's Time" (Kristeva, *WT*).[23] But first, she speaks of space and time in engendered terms. "[W]hen evoking the name and destiny of women, one thinks more of the *space* generating and forming the human species than of *time,* becoming or history" (Kristeva, *WT,* p. 190). And more, speaking of "the problematic of space, which innumerable religions of matriarchal (re)appearance attribute to 'woman,' and which Plato, recapitulating in his own system the atomists of antiquity, designated by the aporia of the *chora,* matrix space, nourishing, unnameable, anterior to the One, to God and, consequently, defying metaphysics" (Kristeva, *WT*, p. 191).[24] Could this duality of space and time, said to be overcome by Einstein, replay itself endlessly in our time as Western space–time, mirroring Western feminine–masculine? Or might it, as Irigaray and Kristeva suggest, echo sexual difference everywhere, in masculine economies everywhere, calling for inversion? And there is Kant, unlike Hegel, for whom time's primordiality expresses the inner (and masculine) subject. And over or under all is aporia. I wonder if the figure of aporia marks the *entre|antre* (or *aentre*), the intermediary–interval.

Kristeva takes responsibility to redefine the time of women as many times.

> As for time, female subjectivity [*le féminin*] would seem to provide a specific measure that essentially retains *repetition* and *eternity* from among the multiple modalities of time known through the history of civilizations. On the one hand, there are cycles, gestation, the eternal recurrence of a biological rhythm which conforms to that of nature and imposes a temporality whose stereotyping may shock, but whose regularity and unison with what is experienced as extrasubjective time, cosmic time, occasion vertiginous visions and unnameable *jouissance*. On the other hand, and perhaps as a consequence, there is the massive presence of a monumental temporality, without cleavage or escape . . . (Kristeva, *WT*, p. 191)[25]

The woman's movement, the struggle for liberation, "aspired to gain a place in linear time as the time of project and history" (Kristeva, *WT*, p. 193). Kristeva understands this idea of place to possess two forms: "*insertion* into history and the radical *refusal* of the subjective limitations imposed by this history's time . . . " (Kristeva, *WT*, p. 195). We may pause before the duality of her interpretive strategy, as if repeating the bipolarity we hope to question. But the pair of which she speaks reminds us of many women's times, many times for and of women, and many other places, identities, and differences. She also speaks of three "signifying spaces" existing in parallel in the same historical time, in which:

> the very dichotomy man/woman as an opposition between two rival entities may be understood as belonging to *metaphysics*. What I mean is, first of all, the demassification of the problematic of *difference,* which would imply, in the first phase, an apparent de-dramatization of the "fight to the death" between rival groups and thus between the sexes . . . in order that the struggle, the

> implacable difference, the violence be conceived in the very place where it operates with the maximum intransigence, in other words, in personal and sexual identity itself, so as to make it disintegrate in its very nucleus. (Kristeva, *WT,* p. 209)

She speaks of multiple times, multiple spaces, multiple identities, all the violent disintegration of personal and sexual identity, all the lightening of the problematic of difference. We may wonder if this lighter difference, this difference without the weight of rivalry, to the death (and without risk?), could be our thought of ethical difference. Even so, we may wonder what in this violence, this *polemos* of sexual identity, reminds us of pain.

I pause to collect the idea of the disintegration of space and time as belonging to the core (*chōra*) of sexual difference, except that Kristeva exposes us in this violent place of disintegration to an extreme thought of ethical difference, asking us again to think that women have never been subject to ethics (according to Spinoza). "Spinoza's question can be taken up again here: Are women subject to ethics?" (Kristeva, *WT,* p. 211). For her, as for Irigaray, such a thought raises questions of another ethic, less perhaps because of women than because of men who, like Spinoza, understand ethics in relation to women in an unethical way. For Kristeva answers, "[t]he answer to Spinoza's question can be affirmative only at the cost of considering feminism as but a *moment* in the thought of that anthropomorphic identity which currently blocks the horizon of the discursive and scientific adventure of our species" (Kristeva, *WT,* p. 211). "Feminism" (but not *le féminin*) is a moment in the hold of an anthropomorphic and humanistic identity, The Human, which an ethic that includes women must set aside. This appears to sound a violent note against the question of sexual difference. Yet Wittig says something similar in a different way.[26]

> the category "woman" as well as the category "man" are political and economic categories not eternal ones. (Wittig, *OBW,* p. 15)

> for us there is no such thing as being–woman or being–man. "Man" and "woman" are political concepts of opposition, and the copula which dialectically unites them is, at the same time, the one which abolishes them. (Wittig, *SM,* p. 29)[27]

This thought, that an ethic of sexual difference (perhaps an ethic of difference or ethical difference) abolishes the categories of gender, man and woman, overturns their dialectical relation, is a thought shared in one way or another by Irigaray, Kristeva, and Wittig, each in a different way. Perhaps this difference will tell us something of ethical and sexual difference. Perhaps we readers and writers must struggle with the idea of abolition, though if we remember slavery, how can we not be abolitionist?

I postpone these difficult questions in turning to another place where Kristeva describes Spinoza's view of women and ethics.

> Nothing, however, suggests that a feminine ethics is possible, and Spinoza excluded women from his (along with children and the insane). Now, if a contemporary ethics is no longer seen as being the same as morality; if ethics amounts to not avoiding the embarrassing and inevitable problematics of the law but giving it flesh, language and *jouissance*—in that case its reformulation demands the contribution of women. . . . For an heretical ethics separated from morality, an *herethics* [*héréthique*], is perhaps no more than that which in life makes bonds, thoughts, and therefore the thought of death, bearable: herethics is undeath [*a-mort*], love . . . *Eia Mater, fons amoris* . . . So let us again listen to the *Stabat Mater,* and the music, all the music . . . it swallows up the goddesses and removes their necessity. (Kristeva, *SM,* p. 185)

Spinoza himself said something close, and yet a little different: "perhaps, someone will ask, whether women are under men's authority by nature or institution?" (Spinoza, *PT,* p. 386). He answers, "that women have not by nature equal right with men: but that they necessarily give way to men, and that thus it cannot happen, that both sexes should rule alike, much less that men should be ruled by women" (Spinoza, *PT,* p. 387). The account he gives of the "ethics" from which women are excluded is of a democratic state:

> it is manifest that we can conceive of various kinds of democracy. But my intention is not to treat of every kind, but of that only, "wherein all, without exception, who owe allegiance to the laws of the country only, and are further independent and of respectable life, have the right of voting in the supreme council and of filling the offices of the dominion." I say expressly, "who owe allegiance to the laws of the country only," to exclude foreigners. . . . I added, besides, "who are independent," except in so far as they are under allegiance to the laws of the dominion, to exclude women and slaves, who are under the authority of men and masters, and also children and wards, as long as they are

> under the authority of parents and guardians. (Spinoza, *PT,* p. 386)

It may be important that the "ethics" from which women are excluded, along with children and slaves, is a polity of authority and rule, some ruling over others, some excluded from authority. Women fall under the authority of men, naturally, as slaves fall under the rule of masters, naturally, in Aristotle.[28] Perhaps another ethic, an ethic that includes women (but not "women"), an ethic that includes women, children, and insane people, an ethic that includes animals, insects, and plants, rocks and stones, an ethic of inclusion, of the earth, may disintegrate, tear down, de-massify, differentiate, the law of authority.[29]

But another thought echoes in herethics, besides or beyond disintegration. "So let us again listen to the . . . music," the songs we hope to sing of the earth. We heard the music in the breath of song. We hope to sing the song of the earth as the call of the good, to listen to the *Stabat Mater.* Later.

I first ask Spinoza his question in reverse. He concludes his *Ethics* with a Note on the "wise man":

> the ignorant man is not only agitated by external causes in many ways, and never enjoys true peace of soul, but lives also ignorant, as it were, both of God and of things, and as soon as he ceases to suffer ceases also to be. On the other hand, the wise man, in so far as he is considered as such, is scarcely ever moved in his mind, but, being conscious by a certain eternal necessity of himself, of God, and of things, never ceases to be, and always enjoys true peace of soul. (Spinoza, *E,* p. 280)

The question I ask, reversing what Spinoza says about excluding women, is, how could the Spinoza for whom the good life for a human being is "being conscious by a certain eternal necessity of himself, of God, and of things," deny this possibility to women? And further, what, in this consciousness of eternity and necessity, could give rise to authority and rule, even over oneself?

For the justification of rule and authority over others, Spinoza turns away from eternity. "From this it follows that men who are governed by reason, that is to say, men who, under the guidance of reason, seek their own profit, desire nothing for themselves which they do not desire for other men, and that, therefore, they are just, faithful, and honorable" (Spinoza, *E,* Part 4, Prop. 18, Note). He emphasizes reason and reason's profit, and the likeness of men toward each other (possibly, as we have seen, excluding women). He links the good for oneself to the good for other men, because their nature is like our own, based on knowledge of God.[30] He takes this thought of a like nature to an abysmal conclusion, however familiar, a conclusion I refuse to accept without challenge within the thought of ethical difference. It is a thought of animals, who cannot be thought of without a corresponding thought of women:

> we see that the law against killing animals is based upon an empty superstition and womanish tenderness rather than upon sound reason. A proper regard, indeed, to one's own profit teaches us to unite in friendship with men, and not with brutes, nor with things whose nature is different from human nature. . . . I by no means deny that brutes feel, but I do deny that, on this account, it is unlawful for us to consult our own profit by using them for our own pleasure and treating them as is most convenient for us, inasmuch as they do not agree in nature with us, and their feelings are different from our emotions. (Spinoza, *E,* Part 4, Prop. 37, Note)[31]

Animals feel but they differ from us, too much for their own good. Perhaps black and yellow human beings differ from "us" so much that we may use them to our profit. And women. Yet women, at least here, seem to share the world and rational liberty with men.

> With regard to marriage, it is plain that it is in accordance with reason if the desire of connection is engendered not merely by external form, but by a love of begetting children and wisely educating them; and if, in addition, the love both of the husband and wife has for its cause not external form merely, but chiefly liberty of mind. (Spinoza, *E,* Part 4, Appendix, 20)

Men and women, at least in marriage, can be caused to act by liberty of mind. Might we imagine that women nevertheless fail to "understand things by the third kind of knowledge"?[32] That they fail to share an intellectual love of God?[33] That they do not conceive "the essence of the body under the form of eternity"?[34] Perhaps that they do not possess "a body fit for many things," but fit only for reproduction?[35]

All these things, and many similar, have been said of women in general, sometimes with exceptions among women, sometimes with exceptions among men, who in general may not possess or seek the third kind of knowledge. What Socrates says in Plato's *Republic* on this issue would seem to lay the entire subject to rest, though it has frequently been read upside down. For if some deserve to rule, and some deserve to be ruled, to be slaves (as Aristotle says), men and women do not compose such classes, nor do any distinctions by gender, race, or blood. For Socrates moves from the claim that "the women and the men, then, have the same nature in respect to the guardianship of the stage, save in so far as the one is weaker, the other stronger" (Plato, *Republic,* 456), to conclude that

> if it appears that the male and the female sex have distinct qualifications for any arts or pursuits, we shall affirm that they ought to be assigned respectively to each. But if it appears that they differ only in just this respect that the female bears and the male begets, we shall say that no proof has yet been produced that the woman differs from the man for our purposes, but we shall continue to think that our guardians and their wives ought to follow the same pursuits. (Plato, *Republic,* 454e)

We may emphasize that he continues to call women weaker than men "as a class" (Plato, *Republic,* 457b). But the principle he follows belies every normative gender or class distinction. Some women are superior to some men, and consequently, should not be ruled by men in the interest of the good, and certainly not justifiably in the interest of the men. We may be ruled by a philosopher–queen.

Yet Spinoza gives none of the arguments I have suggested above concerning the respective relations between women and men and excellence. To the contrary, the argument he considers decisive is that if men and women were equal, sometimes women would rule the men. "And since this is nowhere the case, one may assert with perfect propriety, that women have not by nature equal right with men; but that they necessarily give way to men, and that thus it cannot happen, that both sexes should rule alike, much less that men should be ruled by women" (Spinoza, *PT,* p. 387). May we wonder how the Spinoza who demanded geometrical necessity could accept such a demonstration, unless we hear the entire force of the argument fall on "it cannot happen, that both sexes should rule alike"?

If we do the latter, then we may remember that this is the very last paragraph of Spinoza's account of democratic politics:

> But if we further reflect upon human passions, how men, in fact, generally love women merely from the passion of lust, and esteem their cleverness and wisdom in proportion to the excellence of their beauty, and also how very ill-disposed men are to suffer the women they love to show any sort of favour to others, and other facts of this kind, we shall easily see that men and women cannot rule alike without great hurt to peace. (Spinoza, *PT,* p. 387)

None of this argument, and none of the preceding, addresses the nature of women, as do Spinoza's arguments concerning the nature of "brutes." Could it be that "men and women cannot rule alike" because of men, and because of sovereignty? Could it be that men have always ruled women because of the quarrelsomeness of men, who do not act from reason very well? Could it be that because men are irrational, in the ways they are, that they insist on ruling women? For we are reflecting upon human passions.

Perhaps this conclusion tells us of the arbitrariness of the course of human history, as rule and law. As Spinoza says immediately following, "[b]ut of this enough" (Spinoza, *PT,* p. 387). Nothing, in Spinoza or elsewhere, can be said enough of women, and perhaps of animals, that justifies enslaving, murdering, destroying them in general, as a kind. Ethics tells us, under the aegis of ethical and sexual difference, that it is evil to argue, concerning those who are different from ourselves, that we may mistreat them in general, as a class, a kind. All kinds belong in the West to categories of domination: women, animals, brutes, insects, things; all "mere" rather than "highest." From the standpoint of ethical difference, nothing is "mere." All is inexhaustible. This understanding does not express the importance of the individual vis-à-vis the kind, but the alienness of classes, kinds, laws, rules, and principles to ethics and politics, to the good, with the proviso that we cannot get along without them.

We re-traverse our double parentheses—from Irigaray to Kristeva, and from Kristeva to Spinoza—back along the lines of demarcation, from animals and other monstrous creatures to multiple times to multiple places. We have traversed the question of ethical difference as a multiple traversal of heterogeneity.[36] Our note echoes in Irigaray and Kristeva: the breath of song, songs of the earth. Kristeva asks us in the name of another ethic, herethic, to "again listen to . . . all the music . . . " The *Stabat Mater.* The different times and places, could they be music? Could they be sung? And why?

We re-traverse our double parentheses back to first philosophy, if we ever left it, back to space and time from . . . space and time and music and the good, from which women are excluded, and under whose sign animals are used up for profit. If philosophy inhabits the place of sexual difference, then the subordination and displacement of women and animals, the subjection of some kinds of creatures to others, inhabits the ethical, inhabits it within its denial, as unethical. And if so, then the question of an ethic of animals and women may be at the heart of Western philosophy. I call this ethic, "ethical difference," an ethic of inclusion. Kristeva calls it "*hérethique,*" emphasizing its heresies and sexualities, but leaving animals aside. I also call it "heteroethics," or "hetaera-ethics": an ethic of heterogeneity, ethical difference.

We re-traverse our double parentheses back to our reading of Irigaray's tracing of the link between (*aentre*) first philosophy and sexual difference. If you wish to forgo the rest of this encounter with first philosophy, if you have heard enough of first philosophy, we will resume our general themes of ethical difference in chapter 5, after the *Stabat Mater.* Or you may wish to listen to the anticipatory notes echoing in chapter 4, leading to the *Stabat Mater.* If you choose to forgo the rest of this encounter with Irigaray's reading of first philosophy, I hope you will remember the ethic of writing and reading of which I spoke some time ago and will speak again.[37]

Do you remember, it seems long ago, when we found ourselves sounding the interval, a few pages ago, when we departed from "the question of *space* and *time*" to multiple space and times? We read through questions of ethical and sexual difference from the beginning of the world as space, in the feminine, along with the overcoming of time, in the masculine, to a possible inversion. We could not tell, from our reading, what or who might be inverted by sexual difference, but we read the beginning as a (feminine) space, in the depths of night, while masculinity belonged to time.[38] The transition to a new age required "a change in our perception and conception of *space–time,* the *inhabiting of places,* and of *containers,* or *envelopes of identity*" (Irigaray, *ESD,* p. 7). We found ourselves thrown into, echoing within, the interval, the *aentre,* in which we recapitulated God and first philosophy.

Our detour into first philosophy, after Irigaray, rings the interval in triangles of "*matter, form, interval,* or *power, act, intermediary–interval.*" We have passed by place, even as everything we have said reverberates in place. And we have come to, but not passed over, desire and love.

> A new age signifies a different relation between (*entre*):
>
> — man and god(s),
> — man and man,
> — man and world,
> — man and woman. (Irigaray, *ESD,* p. 8)

Entre again, and *homme,* always *homme,* who rests, remains, in sexual difference in a certain between, interval, together with one or many gods, who inhabit the anteroom, with the angels and the world and women. "*Homme*" is an intermediary–interval here, marked by sexual difference, but also by a "We." You and I may wonder at humanity and god, humanity and world, man and woman, and add (how drastic is their omission?) woman–woman, woman–world, human–animal, add other kinds in profusion. Everything here circles around *homme,* the interval of man, calling for inversion.

We remind ourselves, for just a moment, that these intervals, these intermediaries, belong to an economy of desire, an economy defined for us (in our age) by two movements, echoing repeatedly: of desire from death to slavery to reciprocity, in Hegel; of desire from Mother to Other, in Freud, expressed with a certain finality by Lacan, who speaks of the (M)Other in terms of the One, and of my|our relation to the Other|One, a "subject supposed to know," as love:[39]

> *There is something of One* is to be taken with the stress that there is One alone. Only thus can we grasp the nerve of the thing called love . . . : *the subject supposed to know.*
>
> . . . He whom I suppose to know, I love. (Lacan, *GJW,* p.139)

The Woman, written under erasure (by us, by we men), "she is not all" (Lacan, *GJW,* 144), giving rise to "a supplementary *jouissance*" (*GJW,* p. 144), "a *jouissance* beyond the phallus" (*GJW,* p. 145). The finality, for us here, is that the interval is inhabited by the not-all, the not-sayable as all, in the twin forms of "my" love and "her" *jouissance,* which I and even "she" are "supposed to know" even when I|we|she do not know it or her. Desire, here, inhabits the *entre* (which may be indistinguishable, so far as we may know, from the *antre* or *ventre*). We think of the opening words of Aristotle's metaphysics, that all human beings by nature desire to know, desire to know and love that which is most obscure, love to know the essences of heterogeneous things, what they are by nature.

The new age of ethical difference inverts the economy of desire in the *aentre*. Yet desire has always inhabited the between, in *Republic* between the cave and the sun, in *Phaedrus* between mortal and immortal, in Hegel, with whatever abomination, between master and slave. No one said the between was safe. No one has dreamed that desire was safe. We do not think of ethical difference, in the *entre|antre|ventre* (*vaentre*), without risk. Even so, as we acknowledge danger, you and I may wonder if we must demand control, mastery and rule, as if we could expel danger, control desire, overcome destructive passions. We wonder why anyone continues to demand mastery and rule at the expense of different kinds of human beings and creatures.

We are ready to speak of the interval differently, after its inversion.

> Our age will have failed to realize the full dynamic reserve signified by desire if it is referred back to the economy of the *interval,* if it is situated in the attractions, tensions, and actions occurring between *form* and *matter,* but also in the *remainder* [*reste*] that subsists after each creation or work, *between* what has already been identified and what still has to be identified, and so on. (Irigaray, *ESD,* p. 8)

With the "*reste,*" with the silent traces, remains, we return to the place of place, inhabiting the intermediary intervals between work and place and restoration, echoing property and restitution. The "*reste*" of work places and displaces work, places and displaces the work of first philosophy, in the interval. The place of place echoes in the intervals of *reste.* And the economy of the interval inhabits the places of *reste,* sexual|ethical difference.

We may begin to understand the place of place, of *topos*'s place, in Zeno and Aristotle, as a silent and ethical echo of the firstness of first philosophy, the Westernness of Western philosophy, the intermediariness of all philosophy, in the interval of *reste,* as supplementarity, excess. The place of place is the place of displacement, excess. The place of place is the dis- and re- of place. The place of place is excess, displacement, woman's no-place.

Also, the matter of (or with) matter, the time of time, place of place, engendered remains of bodies. And the music of music. These all ring in the French of "*reste,*" as they do in the rest of the passage, marked by Irigaray as first philosophy. For in the passage we find a number of italicized words, some in first philosophy, traditionally, others marking sexual difference. *Form* and *matter* are words of first philosophy, together with "*interval, remainder, between,*" all italicized, not to mention "work, economy, identified" unitalicized. "*Reste*" is translated as "remainder," but together with first philosophy, with space and time and matter and form, *reste* echoes in and of *intervalle* and *vaentre,* pertaining to them all. For in space and time, we find endless intervals, come to inhabit intervals, spaces, divisions, between spaces, empty spaces. *Intervalle, entre, reste* all together, and each separately (in their intervals, rests, betweens), echo space and time, matter and form. *Intervalle, entre, reste* are space and time words, but also matter and form words, place words and words of the absence as well as proliferation of place, all in tones of sexual difference. "*Reste*" speaks of time and place as the interval, but of matter and form as the remains, brings us face to face with bodies, as intervals–between, divided by gender, and by different genera, kinds, identities and identifications. The triangle of *intervalle, entre, reste* places, re-places, and dis-places (inverts) time and space, form and matter. That is why I have spoken of the place of place, another *intervalle, entre, reste* in the "of," another intermediary figure. But perhaps more important for the sound of the triangle is the ring of music. First philosophy begins again for us in the question of ethical and sexual difference, echoing in the *intervalle, entre, reste,* as music; song as restitution.

I hope to sing of woman and man, of sexual difference, also of woman and woman and man and man, of heterogeneous human beings, and of animals, humans and animals, animals and natural things. I hope to listen to the music of the rests of the earth.

This thought of music is a Nietzschean thought, though we have heard its sound in Kristeva. We have also heard its song in Irigaray and have understood, from the beginning, the possibility that the thought of our age, what I have called "the question of ethical and sexual difference," the transformation of the movement of thought from the *logos* of *protē philosophia* to something else, the gathering of language, *legein,* might be a musical gathering, the restful songs of the earth. Questions of ethical difference echo in the endless dispersions and proliferations of sexual difference—in the *intervalle, entre, reste,* in French; in the *r*est–*i*nterval–*b*etween (*r–i–b*), in English. We re-situate, as the very moment of the beginning of philosophy, sexual difference as Adam's r–i–b, laughing, crying, with *jouissance et souffrance,* joy and pain, remembering to sing while we do not mistake our women for an instrument.[40]

With sexual difference, Adam's rib, we remember sexual difference in ethical difference. We might have forgotten it. We remember that gender haunts the thought of ethics as something it has repeatedly forgotten, even as women were excluded. And so perhaps I should remind you, as I must perhaps do repeatedly, that in the silence of the sexual in ethical difference, we have not replaced sexual difference as the question of our age with that of ethical difference. To the contrary, I am exploring what it could mean that questions of sexual difference might compose the ethical question of our age, understanding that if we remember our age as a history, the question of our or any age re-traces the movements of our history in a different voice, a voice of ethical difference. We have followed this voice, a voice of sexual difference, in several directions, one to its music, listening to its song; a second to first philosophy, where space and time and matter and form all compose themselves in a relation;[41] a third into the interval (*aentre*) or *reste* of space and time and matter and form; a fourth into ethical difference, including sexual difference, to questions of what kind of ethic sexual difference might call forth, an ethic belonging to the earth's plenitude; fifth, then, we considered the possibility that sexual difference emerges as another difference, comes forth as heterogeneous differences of kind, somewhere between, resting in the interval between (*aentre*), sexual difference and animal, natural, inorganic difference, between sexual difference and heterogeneous ethical difference, everywhere.

The question of the age is the question of sexual difference.
The question of the age is the question of technology.
The question of the age is the question of ethical difference.
The question of the age is the question of animal difference.
The question of the age is the question of differences in kind.

Could these be one question? Could the one question of them all be each of them, separately and together, their univocity and heterogeneity, within their *vaentre?* Consider the following response:

If we ask, where do we find sexual difference, the answer must be, if it echoes as the question of our age: *everywhere.* If we ask, where do we find ethical difference, as we have understood it, the answer must again be: *everywhere.* These two *everywheres* are different, giving rise to an interval between, *vaentre,* as we turn back to first philosophy, to space and time and matter and form, from within each. This remainder or interval or intermediary between one everywhere and the other, in first philosophy, in the earth, between countless everywheres circulating excessively, is what we may hear as ethical and sexual difference, displacing the place of place in the movement of Western philosophy.[42]

Where do we go to listen to first philosophy? There is nowhere—no other place—to go but Greece and Aristotle, where we found matter and form and space and time. And among (*aentre*) them all, we found a certain heterogeneous sense of among, a certain sense of *reste.* We have understood this *entre* and *reste* to sound in the interval of place, the place of place, the dis- and re- of place.

This returns us to sexual difference, to the possibility that woman (*la femme*) is the *vaentre,* belongs in the remainder–interval–between, even as she is deposited in history by men. "Woman ought to be able to find herself, through the images of herself already deposited in history and the conditions of production of the work of man, and not on the basis of his work, his genealogy" (Irigaray, *ESD,* p. 10). Returning us to a powerful and irresistible place of sexual difference, with an "if."

> If, traditionally, and as a mother, woman represents *place* for man, such a limit means that she becomes a *thing,* with some possibility of change from one historical period to another. She finds herself delineated[43] as a thing. Moreover, the maternal–feminine also serves as an *envelope,* a *container,* the starting point from which man limits his things. The *relationship between envelope and things* constitutes one of the aporias, or the aporia, of Aristotelianism and of the philosophical systems derived from it. (Irigaray, *ESD,* p. 10)

First philosophy and Aristotle again. The relation between the envelope and the things (from the place of limit given by woman|women), as *mère* and as *maternel–féminin.* Sexual difference appears here at the very point (or *bordée*) at which things receive their limits. We (men) take things up at the edges of their limits in the place of woman. Or in the envelope of woman as place. In all of this, women ought to rediscover themselves without knowing if that means woman. But certainly it does not mean by men.

There remains, so far at rest, the word "envelope" [*enveloppe*], another intermediary limit–place–border word, the place at which things receive or have their identities. Things are identified in the interval within their envelope, a limit–place–border–matter–form word. "Envelope" in English, and certainly in French with a much stronger emphasis upon the verb *envelopper,* wraps material things in form so that we (men) may discern their limits, their kinds, derived from the place(s) in which they lie. But *enveloppe* also gives us (in French) a place of safety, possibly unheard in English, taking us back to some of the meanings of "*le «salut»,*" but also to deception, appearance, a certain interesting word for "presence."

What if the presence of things, in the Opening|Clearing of Being, were (in) their intermediary envelopes, re-tracing place, as woman, and the place of place as sexual|ethical difference? What if we were to invert the thought of presence from within the question of sexual difference? Would the earth move? Would it come to *reste?*

Questions of ethical and sexual difference become, in relation to the envelope, questions of the relation between envelope and things, of intermediary kinds of things, recurrent questions of Western philosophy. We rethink the history of Western philosophy from the place of its aporia between the envelope as maternal–feminine, as sexual difference, and enveloped things. The maternal–feminine is situated between (*vaentre*) Being and beings, intermediarily, with the understanding that Heidegger explicitly denies that ontological difference is a figure of sexual difference, thereby obliquely instituting a figure of sexual difference. Irigaray inhabits the question of sexual difference as Heidegger inhabits the question of ontological difference, with the difference that Heidegger denies sexual difference in the very emergence of Being: matter, form, space, time, limit, unlimit. The envelope wraps things in their matter, form, space, time, limit, unlimit, defines them by wrapping them materially with gender, impregnates them (Irigaray, *ESD,* p. 10).

They are impregnated by men "with a psychologism" (Irigaray, *ESD,* p. 10) in which the

> woman–mother is *castrating*. Which means that, since her status as envelope and as thing(s) has not been interpreted, she remains inseparable from the work or act of man. . . . If after all this, she is still alive, she continually undoes his work—distinguishing herself from both the envelope and the thing, ceaselessly creating there some interval, play, something in motion and un-limited which disturbs [*dérange*] his perspective, his world, and his/its limits. (Irigaray, *ESD,* p. 10)

So mother–woman, so that she may continue to exist, a little, disturbs the safety of the envelope in which man wraps the order of his things. In the space, the *entre* (and *antre,* disturbing the safety of the envelope of sexual difference) of her non-being, non-interpretation, neither thing nor god, woman continues to *dérange* the world.[44] The question of sexual difference echoes in an event of derangement, madness and disruption, or monstrosity.[45] Aristotle calls it *tychē,* the good bestowed by the gods. Fortune has always been a woman. Put another way, Man is "[t]he slave, ultimately, of a God on whom he bestows the characteristics of an absolute master. Secretly or obscurely, a slave to the power of the maternal–feminine which he diminishes or destroys" (Irigaray, *ESD,* p. 10). Yet in this abolition of the woman, she continues, if a little madly, to disturb and displace.

She, Woman, continues to disturb and displace Man [*l'homme*] and his work even as she continues to remain displaced, by place and gender. Even as mother–woman, she falls under masculine gender.[46] We find the place of place as a figure of *reste,* doubly a figure of *reste,* where we may follow Aristotle's Zeno to imagine that in place, a figure is at rest, to see that in place, its "proper" place (Irigaray, *ESD,* p. 11), the masculine hopes to find itself at rest in virtue of a displacement of gender, organized around the maternal–feminine, in which place for man is displaced and thereby displaces the place for men. Sexual difference marks—the mark of gender—that *reste* occupies the place of place. The place of place is un-place. It exists in the form of the other, the else (where), the lack. The maternal–feminine lacks a proper place,[47] "threatening because of what she lacks" (Irigaray, *ESD,* p. 11). She threatens herself, threatens *him,* threatens the social order, the law. Sexual difference threatens the possibility of ethics.

But to give her a place, for her (or her mother) to give herself a place, "[s]he would have to re-envelop herself with herself, and do so at least twice: as a woman and as a mother" (Irigaray, *ESD,* p. 10). This would presuppose a change in the whole economy of space–time. To wrap oneself in an identity is to enter (perhaps *aentre*) the entire fabric, economy, of space–time, to occupy the "–," the intermediary–interval. And this is an "ethical question," played out for the moment in the realms of "*nudity* and *perversity*" (Irigaray, *ESD,* p. 10). For in place of being situated in her place, woman will be nude, stripped bare (by the men, even), unclothed, unenveloped by her proper place (Irigaray, *ESD,* p. 11). The place of place, in "our" time and place given as space–time, is a place in which women are bare, without their place, circulate in many different places. Envelopment surrounds and enters the place of place where women have no place, except by clothing themselves in a disturbingly bare and disconcerting movement of ornamentation (*parergon*)[48] and investment [*vêtement*]. All *en attendant,* meanwhile, waiting for her proper place (if the "proper" does not repel her from any place).

First philosophy, the thought of nature and being, under the guise of space and time (now, space–time), matter and form, of proper place, and kind, envelopes itself in a garb of gender in which woman is place for man while she (even as "*le*" maternel–féminin) has no place, envelopes herself in no proper place, wraps her body in ornaments that display her in an improper place, her nudity wrapped in clothing and jewels. Men wear clothing, but do not envelope their lack of identity in clothing. At least, that is what Irigaray seems to say. We men may wonder if our proper identity is so well placed.[49]

Identity comes to us, here, in its heterogeneous envelopes, wrapping the body in its space and time, but not simply finding bodies—whose, which, how many?—in "their" proper places in space and time. The proper place of the body, in its place, depends upon an envelopment. The place of place, in the (male) Western tradition, seems to occupy (or be occupied by) a "proper," to be enveloped, at the limits, borders, of the work that takes place in place, by a propriety of identity placed and displaced by sexual difference. All this is ethical. The (traditional) ethic of sexual difference materializes in the envelopes of flesh, deep in the earth, filled with bodies.

> From the depths of the earth to the highest skies? Again and again, taking from the feminine the tissue or texture of spatiality. . . . he buys her a house, even shuts her up in it. . . . He contains or envelops her with walls while enveloping himself and his things with her flesh. The nature of these envelopes is not the same . . . (Irigaray, *ESD,* p. 11)

The last line gives us our place, the nature of the different envelopes is the place of place.

"We need to change the relations between [*entre*] form, matter, interval, and limit" (Irigaray, *ESD,* p. 12) in relation to place, giving us another ethic of the passions, allowing "a relationship between two loving subjects of different sexes" (Irigaray, *ESD,* p. 12).[50] The figure of this ethic is the envelope and enveloping, the place of place. The economy of sexual difference leads to the place of place shimmering with different envelopes. Even between the same sexes and genders there is sexual difference. And other kinds.

An ethic of gender is an ethic of love. In what *aentres?* Between men and women, and women and men, but also men and men and women and women, and . . . The others . . . And more . . . This *aentre* has been clothed repeatedly in one envelope after another: space–time, matter–form, identity, angels, *erōs*. Today we wear the clothes of the frame, the *Ge-stell.* We wear them in the *antre* of *physis* and *technē,* with the qualification that in this (animal) place, we give up the clothing of fur and skin, give them up doubly and triply, not only for *technē*'s metal and plastics, but in Our Human *physis,* which does not belong to animals. Let us reconstitute ethical difference in a return to the beast's *antre,* doubled and tripled and . . . more. Could the economy of ethical difference circulate in an endless, heterogeneous more, that we do not know|suppose to know|always cherish? That is, an endless, heterogeneous, incomprehensible, loving truth of incomprehension. All circulating in place and out, judgments circulating here and there.

To this place, in which we come with the greatest danger, where the ethic of sexual difference is transported from a place it never had into a general economy of ethical difference, we arrive unable to know if the ethic of sexual difference belongs to or is violated by the economy of ethical difference. If I rephrase this unknown|unknowable in the voice of my playful introduction, I ask if ethical difference is sexed, always sexed, always gendered. And here we may, without diminishing the danger, enter the *aentre* of the beast, the lair of the monster, beard the monster—who is u|s—with the following possibility: that wherever sexual difference gives rise to an ethic, it is an ethic in which the question of ethical difference disturbs the gender|sex|identity|kind that gave rise to it, disturbs it in an intermediary movement from man–woman to man–man|woman–woman, to homo- and lesbian and other sexualities, then to human–animal, and human–others, other kinds, all sexed, gendered, all cherished, engendered, sexed, monstrous, impure. The machines know gender. At least, in French and German (and other languages), if not in English.

Could the natural world be gendered, sexed? Could the world be unsexed?

May these two questions give birth to an ethic of sexual difference? May they give birth to an economy of ethical difference? May they engender, if we refuse to let go of the question of sex–sexuality–gender, a remainder, a more, a *reste?* "One sex is not entirely consumable by the other. There is always a *remainder* [*reste*]" (Irigaray, *ESD,* p. 14). In this place of *reste* is always a more that cannot be consummated or consumed, cannot be abolished, and cannot be known while it is supposed to know and we must grant it its truth, if only in disturbance and death, all the while cherishing its truth, its knowledge, and its disturbance. All this, in the *intervalle* of *reste,* the double, triple, inexhaustible *vaentres* of sexual|animal|natural difference, insists on the excess–remainder–surplus of sexual|ethical difference. We may hope to save ourselves from danger by understanding, with Irigaray, the *reste* of sexual difference, and then understanding the *reste* of that *reste* as ethical difference, given to us as the place and unplace of place, as transportation between. As love. As the good, heard everywhere.

With this note we come (back) to the angels singing the *Stabat Mater.* Kristeva asks us, herethically, to "again listen to the *Stabat Mater,* and the music, all the music . . . it swallows up the goddesses and removes their necessity" (Kristeva, *SM,* p. 185). Irigaray asks us to sing of the angels, a beautiful example of sexual *vaentre,* still in relation to space and time, "who never remain enclosed in a place, who are also never immobile" (Irigaray, *ESD,* p. 15). "Between God, as the perfectly immobile act, man, who is surrounded and enclosed by the world of his work, and woman, whose task would be to take care of nature and procreation, *angels* would circulate as mediators of that which has not happened, of what is still going to happen, of what is on the horizon" (Irigaray, *ESD,* p. 15).

These intermediations, traversals, inhabit the *vaentre,* which we may take to give us the place of an ethic of sexual difference, give us that place in the disturbance of place. For "[t]he angel is that which unceasingly *passes through the envelope(s)* or container(s), goes from one side to the other, reworking every deadline, changing every decision, thwarting all repetition. Angels destroy the monstrous, that which hampers the possibility of a new age; they come to herald a new birth, a new morning" (Irigaray, *ESD,* p. 15). Angels inhabit the *entre,* the *intervalle,* the *reste,* undoing every repetition, giving rise to a new world. Yet they do so by destroying monsters who live in the same places, lairs, *aentres.*

Two additional ethical thoughts. One is that the monsters, the beasts, that offend nature, live together with the angels. The *entre* of the angels is the *antre* of the beast, the monster—for what are monsters but animals, what have they ever been but animals, except when they have been fusions of women and animals: harpies, gorgons? How can we destroy monsters, hope that the angels, or reason, or work can destroy monsters without destroying ourselves, destroying the *intervalle* and *reste?* If the angels give us *reste* in virtue of their sexual difference, we know in our hearts that animals are closer to our *reste,* especially since we eat their *reste,* live in their *reste,* sacrifice them, their fleshy envelope, for our humanity? In *reste.* To every animal, may you *reste,* in piece.

The other ethical thought is that Irigaray, in the thought of sexual difference, cannot release the thought of monstrous animals. The intermediary *entre|antre|intervalle|enveloppe|reste* belongs to angels, women, and animals in a moment of exclusion. Monstrosity plays itself out in the monstrosity of women and in hatred toward animals, all gendered. This means that the place of sexual difference repeats the question of the place of place, in the roars and moans and screams and whiffles and grunts of animal monsters.

An ethic of the exposure of another difference. An ethic of heterogeneity, the endless injustice of heterogeneity. Other kind after other kind after other kind.

Yet the angels, in their lightness, do not take us away from the body, nor from monsters, but bring them into another *entre,* the body's (and animals') *parousia* [presence]. But this is beyond, the *parousia* of, sexual difference. When we attempt to return from this *parousia* to the body's *reste,* we hope to bring angels and bodies (and monsters) together.

> A sexual or carnal ethics would require that both angel and body be found together. This is a world that must be constructed or reconstructed. A genesis of love between the sexes has yet to come about in all dimensions, from the smallest to the greatest, from the most intimate to the most political. A world that must be created or re-created so that man and woman may once again or at last live together, and sometimes inhabit the same place. (Irigaray, *ESD,* p. 17)

I respond with two additional movements, wishing they were in *reste,* in the music of sexual difference. One is to wonder if when angel and body are found together, they do not have a dog or cat at their side, mites in their hair, and bacteria in their minds. And in the same thought, to wonder if humans and animals have not always been together, side by side, in love, or hate, or something else, however monstrously, in *reste?* The second movement is to wonder again, in *reste,* of a carnal, embodied ethic. A version of such an ethic:

Ethical difference, an embodied, fleshy ethic, would demand that both monsters and bodies remain together. This is a world that must be constructed or reconstructed, even as it has always surrounded us, where animals and humanity live in proximity. A genesis of love between the species, between the sexes, between the heterogeneous, has yet to come about, even as it has always been coming about, from the smallest to the greatest, from the most intimate to the most public. Yet it has always been present at the gates, hidden in the crevices, intermediarily. It is a world to be created or re-created so that man and woman and beast and thing may once more or may finally live together (as they have always lived together), may meet, and sometimes inhabit the same places (as they have done, always), in their different kinds, pure and impure.

Monster and beast inhabit the same spaces, envelopes and intervals, as woman, even as she seems in greater proximity to Man-the-essence-of-The-Human. For The Human resists Woman as the interval within, the *reste,* and resists Animal as the *reste* without. The Envelope of The Human divides by gender into two, by sexuality into an unknown number, perhaps two, by race into an unknown number greater than one, constantly diminishing, by kinds and species into a plenitude greater than anything, increasing and diminishing, mixing and coalescing. In this scaling of heterogeneity, sexual difference presents the number two in its force, while kindred difference presents the unknown number, unlimit, as another force. The force of the number two plays out in the dyads and bipolarities of the *logos,* from proximity, face to face, to *polemos,* opposition and strife. The force of the unknown number plays out in monstrosity, demonstrates the human in the jungle of monstrosity, collapsing somehow into bipolarity, opposition and proximity. In this way, an ethic of animal difference is in closest proximity to an ethic of sexual difference, and conversely.

But these are proximities that await consideration. We are still in the place of place. What ethic is possible in the place of place, understood as the displacement of work? I wish to question, from the very beginning, Irigaray's understanding of man's place. The beginning here is Greek. We remember that what Irigaray says, echoing Aristotle's Zeno, is that "man . . . is surrounded and enclosed by the world of his work"[51] (Irigaray, *ESD*, p. 15). Man's work is put in place, a place in which he hopes to remain. But, Irigaray says in French, as the English does not, man *surrounds, encloses, encompasses|is surrounded, enclosed, encompassed* in his world of work. The place of man is somewhere between (*aentre*) something he finds himself within (*vaentre, enveloppé*) and where he chooses to remain. Human work works within the horizon of enclosure at the very time and in the very place in which work works between, in *reste.* Man rests in place, where that place displaces itself.

Irigaray speaks of this discovery of a place of *reste* as celebrative. "As Heidegger, among others, has written, it must forge an alliance between the divine and the mortal, such that a sexual encounter would be a festive celebration and not a disguised or polemical form of the master–slave relationship" (Irigaray, *ESD,* p. 17). You and I must wonder that the Heidegger who spoke of nothing less than sexual difference (and of whom Derrida suggests, may therefore have spoken of nothing more), the Heidegger who repudiated ethics as belonging to modern technology (intimating that we might yet begin to think of the essence of action, however far we might still be) (Heidegger, *LH,* p. 193) should be given voice by a French feminist woman on the "proper" form of a sexual encounter, a celebration between gods and mortals.

This form, proper or not, a movement of places without a fixed and lawful place, echoes the angels, linking heaven and earth, away from the murderous light of God-the-Father. This sexual encounter is "not a meeting in the shadow or orbit of a Father–God who alone lays down the law, who is the immutable spokesman of a single sex" (Irigaray, *ESD,* p. 17). The celebration between the sexes from which or according to which an ethic of sexual difference is born gives up both the law (of sex) and its universality (or both together, the universality of the law of sex).[52]

Irigaray understands this celebration as material, embodied, replaying the envelopes of form and matter into another understanding of space, another place of space, another time.

> To do this requires time, both space and time. Perhaps we are passing through an era when *time must re-deploy space.* A new morning of and for the world? A remaking of immanence and transcendence, notably through this *threshold* which has never been examined as such: the female sex. The threshold that gives access to the *mucous.* Beyond classical oppositions of love and hate, liquid and ice—a threshold that is always *half-open.* The threshold of the *lips,* which are strangers to dichotomy and oppositions. (Irigaray, *ESD,* p. 18)[53]

We remember our list of musical rests: space–time, matter–form, *aentre, intervalle, enveloppe, reste.* We add, here, an unmistakably engendered, sexual figure, a place of woman, add to the redeployment of space, threshold, mucosity, lips, all (perhaps?) vaginal. To the still somehow sexless intervals, envelopes, and remains, we add an undeniably material and sexual figure. Even here, threshold links without sexuality, links sky and earth, mortals and divinities, under the call of language, without sexual difference. I am speaking of Heidegger's reading of Trakl's poem, *A Winter Evening,* containing the extraordinary line: "[p]ain has turned the threshold to stone" (Heidegger, *L,* p. 203).

Threshold links (*aentre*) the fourfold, coming right up to the number two, sexual difference, and recoils.

> The speaking of the first two stanzas speaks by bidding things to come to world, and world to things. The two modes of bidding are different but not separated. . . . The intimacy of

> world and thing is not a fusion. Intimacy obtains only where the intimate—world and thing—divides itself cleanly and remains separated. In the midst of the two, in the between of world and thing, in their *inter,* division prevails: a *dif-ference.* (Heidegger, *L,* p. 202)

World and thing inhabit a fourfold ruled by the number two, linking, mediating, dividing: dif-ference. Why not sexual difference, gender? Why resist sexual difference, animal difference? Why exclude any of the earth's heterogeneities? And why, within the intimacy of dif-ference, why emphasize the number two? Does the number two repeat the *polemos,* the strife, against which difference prevails?

Heidegger continues:

> The intimacy of world and thing is present in the separation of the between; it is present in the dif-ference. The word difference is now removed from its usual and customary usage. What it now names is not a generic concept for various kinds of differences. It exists only as this single difference. It is unique. Of itself, it holds apart the middle in and through which world and things are at one with each other. (Heidegger, *L,* p. 202)

Do we hear Irigaray telling us what Heidegger seems to have forgotten, that this unique and single difference is sexual difference? And do we give our response to her call to sexual difference, our response in terms of ethical difference, not as a removal back to the in-difference of dif-ference, back to Heidegger, but as a movement that circulates in both Irigaray and Heidegger?

I am concerned with the unique difference in which the fourfold celebrates, listening to the *Stabat Mater,* heretically, herethically. In his early writings, Foucault speaks of this univocity.

> The univocity of being, its singleness of expression, is paradoxically the principal condition which permits difference to escape the domination of identity, which frees it from the law of the Same as a single opposition within conceptual elements . . . Being is that which is always said of difference; it is the *Recurrence* of difference. (Foucault, *TP,* p. 192)[54]

I hear this univocity in the song of the earth, the ring of music. I understand instrumentality, with technology, as musical, mattering, making a difference, more than as instrument forming matter. I hear the rests of the earth in orchestration.

But these are other intermediary figures, along with monsters and witches. I am for the moment concerned with the figures of threshold, mucosity, and lips. For Heidegger takes the univocity of dif-ference to another univocity, of language.

> Language speaks. Its speaking bids the dif-ference to come which expropriates world and things into the simple onefold of their intimacy.
>
> Language speaks.
>
> Man speaks in that he responds to language. This responding is a hearing. It hears because it listens to the command of stillness. (Heidegger, *L*, p. 210)

The crucial word for us here is "onefold": the fourfold become one, as language. And what if men and women spoke different languages?[55] What if they spoke different languages because they crossed and re-crossed different thresholds, different mucosities? What Heidegger says of the pain at the threshold touches our hearts. "Pain is the joining agent in the rending that divides and gathers. Pain is the joining of the rift. The joining is the threshold. It settles the between, the middle of the two that are separated in it. Pain joins the rift of the dif-ference. Pain is the dif-ference itself" (Heidegger, *L*, p. 204).

Even so, whose pain? What of *jouissance?* And is pain the same for men and women, humans and animals? Spinoza seems to deny it, in a passage I have quoted in a profoundly contaminated context, a context that allows animals to be destroyed for human profit and excludes women from democracy.

Heidegger tells us that pain is difference itself in the speaking of Language. Irigaray responds with another threshold, where women's lips touch and the interval is filled with mucus. This is a threshold filled with materiality and embodiment. We have listened to its music, the theme of mucus, of women's bodies.

Yet men's and animal's bodies have lips that half-touch, bodies filled with mucus, bodies singing their angelic music in the *aentre* of the fourfold, this time including women along with men (but not always alongside men), and including animals along with human beings (but again not always alongside human beings). Men have many lips, if not women's or animal's lips. Men and animals live in their bodies, mucously. What of women's, witch's lips? Do we take for granted something of sexual difference, something we do not want to take for granted, when we speak of half-open lips, mucous lips, as especially maternal–feminine? Or do we wish to bring this taken-for-granted to men as they seem to have ignored it, ignore the mucous, fleshy body?

These questions, of witchcraft, mucus, flesh, ring throughout *An Ethics of Sexual Difference.* I will postpone them for a while, procrastinate the movement from the sky to flesh, with the angels, and with a certain "God" and love that

> forms the supple grounding of life and language.
>
> For this, "God" is necessary, or a love so attentive that it is divine. Which has never taken place? Love always postpones its transcendence beyond the here and now, except in certain experiences of God. (Irigaray, *ESD,* p. 19)

A love that has never had a place. We have not entered far enough into the place of place. For we enter the half-open, mucous lips through the limit:

> Unhappiness is sometimes all the more inescapable when it lacks the horizon of the divine, of the gods, of an opening onto a beyond, but also a *limit* that the other may or may not penetrate.
>
> How can we mark this limit of a place, of place in general, if not through sexual difference? (Irigaray, *ESD,* p. 17)

What is the place of sexual difference, the witches, angels, monsters, gods of sexual difference?

As we come to rest, I remind you that we are sounding the themes of Irigaray's *Ethic of Sexual Difference* to note their inclusion. We have heard that they include the enigma of sexual difference, proliferating into genders and other human kinds. We have heard that they echo Nietzsche's revaluation of all values, from the beginning of Western experience, and the forgetting of Being. Sexual difference has repeatedly been forgotten, together with the will to power and the ontological difference. We have traced the theme of sexual difference from the first to perhaps the last, from Anaximander to Irigaray and beyond, finding that it leads through intermediary figures to every place in philosophy, especially the thought of natural kinds, of genders, genres, genera, species, and kinds, to every distinction that thought requires, while every such distinction reenacts injustice. If we cannot live without distinctions, we cannot live without injustice. This is the terrible thought of ethical difference. The witches, angels, monsters, and gods of ethical difference call upon us repeatedly to remember the good.

CHAPTER 4

Rest

For the moment, in this place, let us refuse to be distracted in our reading of *Ethics of Sexual Difference* by Diotima, the witch, by "Sorcerer Love" (Irigaray, *ESD*, chap. 2). I leap over the sorcerer/witch into the interval, the place, where Aristotle speaks of Zeno's aporia of place, a place I understand to resonate with sexual difference, the *manque* of place that echoes women's no place. I approach Zeno's question of place as the place of place, under the signs of *aentre, intervalle, enveloppe, limite,* and *reste.* Especially I think of the place of place as the place of *reste,* the interval in "our" resting-place, where we hesitate.

What, then, is the *lieu du lieu* [place of place] (Irigaray, *ÉDS,* p. 41)? *kai ton topon topos* (Aristotle, *Physics,* 209a)? We have heard Irigaray's answer, as it rests in question, the body (matter–form, in space–time), in its mucous envelope, from mucosity to God. "I go on a quest through an indefinite number of bodies, through nature, through God, for the body that once served as place for me, where I (male/female) was able to stay contained, enveloped"[1] (Irigaray, *ESD,* p. 34). Body, in its fleshy materiality, finds itself in intermediary place.

"As for woman, she is place [for man]" (Irigaray, *ESD,* p. 35). "Passage from one place to another, for her, remains the problem of place as such, always within the context of the mobility of her constitution" (Irigaray, *ESD,* p. 35). The movement from one place to another, the limits and enclosure of space, remain, rest in, the problem of space as such, for her, in the mobility of *her* constitution.

I pursue the following line of thought:

Place is woman.
Woman's place is no place.
The place of place is no place.

Yet I pursue it with a difference, because the final line, if it pertains to woman, if it falls under sexual difference (insofar as it falls under, falls abjectly), opens the place of place in a troubling way, brings the place of place to *reste*. But that is our task, to listen to the fall of sexual difference onto the bodies of women, their non-place, at *reste,* as we sing the music of the places in which they disturb their and our *reste*.

This disturbance, *reste,* this group of disturbances of which Irigaray speaks, yet withholds from men, I cannot hear it as she hears it, cannot hear its restitution. Within the echoes of the lairs of the beast, men the beasts, women the animals—I speak again of *aentre, intervalle, enveloppe, reste, limite*—I add to the above the following, in restitution:

> Ethical difference denies that bodies have a (proper) place.[2]
> Place is an intermediary figure.
> The place of place is rest.[3]

Sexual difference takes us to ethical difference along a "proper" path, moves from one place to another, excoriating the proprieties of place, the proper place of place.

I continue to circulate with Irigaray, as I hesitantly displace her, to place the place of place under the following headings (within the subsequent chapters), heterogeneously, each spoken within its rest:

1. economy and the dyad of gender (chap. 5)
2. human, animal, property|propriety (chap. 7)
3. sexuality, intimacy, gender, heterogeneity (chap. 9)
4. witches, magic, kinds, social worlds (chap. 11)
5. music, rest, the earth (chap. 13)

1. The place of place is woman's no place, in the place of woman-as-receptacle, without a place. But in addition, women, places, things circulate, everywhere. The place of place circulates within the general circulation of women and things and judgments. And angels, who circulate "nowhere," "everywhere," and in between, in the intermediary interval.

> The physicist must have a knowledge of Place, too, as well as of the infinite—namely, whether there is such a thing or not, and the manner of its existence and what it is—both because all suppose that things which exist are *somewhere* (the non-existent is nowhere—where is the goat-stag or the sphinx?), and because

> "motion" in its most general and primary sense is change of place, which we call "locomotion." (Aristotle, *Physics,* 208a)

Place echoes together with the infinite and with movement. With respect to the former, I dream of the infinite in relation to place, that is, in a heterogeneous place of rest. With respect to the latter, Aristotle speaks of moving, being carried, and growing in place, without intermediary movements. The difficulties for place relate to these movements in place, as if place cannot be in itself except at rest elsewhere. Something rests in place like an angel|demon, the demon|angel of desire. Something rests in place, circulating, exchanging, marketing bodies.

Women circulate, move and grow, from place to place; their bodies provide the flesh of judgment.

> The society we know, our own culture, is based upon the exchange of women. Without the exchange of women, we are told, we would fall back into the anarchy (?) of the natural world, the randomness (?) of the animal kingdom. (Irigaray, *WM,* p. 170)

> *Women-as-commodities are thus subject to a schism* that divides them into the categories of usefulness and exchange value; into matter–body and an envelope that is precious but impenetrable, ungraspable, and not susceptible to appropriation by women themselves; into private use and social use. (Irigaray, *WM,* p. 176)

The circulation and exchange of women composes an economy, the place in which the law of ethics composes itself, in rest, in circulation, in exchange and use, the production of goods and representations, doing good work, instituting the canon. All this is organized around women's bodies, not women's bodies as such, but in usefulness and exchange value, into a certain envelope of matter–body.[4]

This matter–body in this economy (but not economy itself, not every circulation, not the general economy of motion and rest) divides men's and women's bodies in two. The number two invades the economy of sexual–ethical difference, divides and displaces the places of difference. The dyad of gender endlessly succeeds itself with one hesitation after another.

2. Irigaray speaks of woman as (man's) place, even as woman has no place (with an "if," she questions as she repeats Freud's "riddle of the nature of femininity") (Irigaray, *SOW,* p. 13), and as

she repudiates it. "If traditionally, and as a mother, woman represents *place* for man, . . . " (Irigaray, *ESD,* p. 10). "As for woman, she is place" (Irigaray, *ESD,* p. 35). This no place is where the hu|man finds a place. The place of place, then, is woman first, then woman's no place, giving birth to man.[5] Yet which of these two places is properly human? The idea of propriety is called in question by sexual and ethical difference. And, with them, we remember Spinoza's scandalous subjection of women and profitable use of animals. Women serve men, half in place, placed to serve. Animals have only a human place. The place of place, here, is man's, defined by Spinoza in terms of profit.[6] If man owns the place of place, does he impose his rule on women in the same way he imposes his mastery on animals? Does Spinoza dissolve man's mastery in the love of God?

3. Woman is man's receptacle, place. We struggle with the place of a woman that cannot have a place. Irigaray says, repeating Aristotle's circulation into the place of place, "if everything that exists has a place, place too will have a place, and so on *ad infinitum*" (Irigaray, *ESD,* p. 34; Aristotle, *Physics,* 209a), where we are reminded of everything, the infinite, and all the things and bodies, in place: "[i]f the matrix [*matrice*] is extendable, it can figure as *the place of place*" (Irigaray, *ESD,* p. 34). *La matrice,* the extensive matrix of which Irigaray speaks, the receptacle, is the womb. In the very heart of the question of place of place (in French), we find the womb, while in Greek we find the *chōra,* the receptacle. Woman represents the place of place without any place of her own. (We cannot escape this "own," this *propre.*)

> it is the receptacle [chōra], and in a manner the nurse, of all generation (Plato, *Timaeus,* 49b)

> the universal nature which receives all bodies—that must be always called the same, for, inasmuch as she always receives all things, she never departs at all from her own nature and never, in any way or at any time, assumes a form like that of any of the things which enter into her . . . (Plato, *Timaeus,* 50c)

The receptacle has a proper nature, here, if never in motion, but a nature altogether at rest. And she, the universal nature|receptacle, is unmistakably a woman. You and I may hesitate at this repetition of propriety.

More to the point, perhaps, we are unable to think of place, and bodies, and the place of place, containing bodies, except in terms of containers, envelopes, vessels.

> Since the vessel (*vase*) is no part of what is in it (what contains in the *strict* sense is different from what is contained), place could not be either the matter or the form of the thing contained, but must be different . . . (Irigaray, *ESD,* p. 43; Aristotle, *Physics,* 210b)

> Place is what contains (*l'enveloppe*) that of which it is the place. Place is no part of the thing. (Irigaray, *ESD,* p. 49; Aristotle, *Physics,* 211a)

Irigaray asks us to think of containers, vessels, envelopes, receptacles, *matrices* under the sign of sexual difference, where they have always|never been located. Space–time–matter–form are the mother–nurse–womb of being.

If not, what is the womb of generation? And how engender being without a womb, under God, filled with love?

4. As Diotima, the witch, says of love, the sorcerer, "[h]e is neither mortal nor immortal. He is between the one and the other, in a state that can be qualified as daimonic: love is a *daimon [Démon*]" (Irigaray, *ESD,* pp. 22–23).[7] I am reminded of the angels, of Socrates as *pharmakeus|pharmakos,* the *pharmakon,*[8] and of women, who having no place but always being place, have their place of place in mobility. The place of place, for angels, witches, spirits, demons, and women, for Socrates and men, is rest.

In this intermediary figure of rest, desire, love, *erōs, philia,* all are *sorcier.* Desire is witchcraft, obscure, somewhere *aentre,* in the interval and envelope, along with the angels and demons, between God and humanity, humanity and animals. The place of all of these, love and desire, is *aentre,* the interval|envelope, space–time, rest, always halfway, intermediary. The place of place is halfway, where we do not know the measure of the half. And half is one divided by two.

I have spoken repeatedly of measure's economy and the measure two of gender. The question for us, Plato's question, is whether we can think of one and two, with their difference, together with somewhere and everywhere and nowhere, limit and unlimit, all at once, together. What is the *reste* of two, of gender? What is gender's demon?

5. This heading, perhaps unlike the others, does not echo

quite so audibly in *ESD,* though we have heard it in "He risks who risks life itself." We have heard the music of the *Stabat Mater.* Something like it, still perhaps inaudible, appears in what Irigaray says of Spinoza. For as she takes woman (in whose name? we must begin to ask) to be place for man, no place herself, Irigaray takes man to know his place. Yet as she says this, she knows that if woman is man's place, and woman is no place, a thing silently at rest, then man does not "know" his place, but remembers his place always in a forgetting. The forgetting of Being is the forgetting of sexual difference. Remembering this forgetting, and others, is ethical difference. Remembering the earth.

In the extreme, where sexual difference and place meet the earth and God, we find Irigaray's understanding of the limits, the place, of place. In the extreme of Spinoza. Here, on her (French) reading, we find God enveloped in place. "By cause of itself I understand that whose essence involves [*enveloppe*] existence, or that whose nature cannot be conceived without existing" (Spinoza, *E,* Part 1, Def. 1). The French, as the English refuses to do, continues to find God's existence enfolded in the *enveloppe* of his essence. Could we say, in English, that God's essence envelopes, enfolds, embraces, his existence? Can we understand, in English, French, or Latin, the relation between God's existence and essence in such a fleshy way?

From this material opacity of a relation around which the entire *Ethics* turns, including the subjection of women and the use and destruction of animals, Irigaray finds God's place. "This definition of God could be translated as: *that which is its own place for itself,* that which turns itself inside out[9] and thus constitutes a dwelling (for) itself [*son propre habiter*]" (Irigaray, *ESD,* 83). What, I ask, is God's (proper) place? God (Substance) is "that which is in itself and is conceived through itself" (Spinoza, *E,* Part 1, Def. 3). To be "in" itself is to be "in its own proper place." But what is this place, or where? God turns back to itself from inside and outside, composes its own dwelling-place. In this way, Irigaray asks us to think of Spinoza's God as a self-defined limit, wholly in place, except that this place is everywhere, a general economy of all things in all places, exceeding every place. *Natura naturans* is God conceived through itself, in place. But *natura naturata* is *everything* "in God."[10] God's place is a somewhere that is everywhere, a place I call rest, the rests of the earth; a general economy that envelopes the earth.[11]

Everywhere is not totality, not a total place. If, together with Irigaray's reading of God's place, we take it to be Nature's Total Place, we understand it as rest. I read it as being's, nature's, creativity's otherwise, as the somewhere else in every somewhere, the other places in every place. The otherwise than being belongs to being, resounds in being, rests in being, as plenishment in the earth.

I read Heidegger's reading of Aristotle's reading of *physis,* after Whitehead and Spinoza, as a displacement of place. "*[N]ature [physis] is a source or cause of being moved and of being at rest in that to which it belongs primarily,* in virtue of itself and not in virtue of a concomitant attribute" (Aristotle, *Physics,* 192b; Heidegger, *OBCP*). I understand "being moved" and "being at rest" as intermediary figures, *topon topos,* echoing Zeno's account of "rest," as always something more, remaining at rest in place and elsewhere. Nature, in Spinoza and Whitehead, is a principle of plenitude, movement, succession, always moving from one place to another, always (even in God), a principle of unrest. Rest is unrest, or Creativity, or *natura naturata:*

> An individual thing, or a thing which is finite and which has a determinate existence, cannot exist nor be determined to action unless it be determined to existence and action by another cause which is also finite and has a determinate existence; and again, this cause cannot exist nor be determined to action unless by another cause which is also finite and determined to existence and action, and so on *ad infinitum.* (Spinoza, *E,* Part 1, Prop. 28)

This *infinitum* pertains to (envelopes) *natura naturata,* thereby *natura naturans.* Substance, or God, or *natura naturans,* contains (envelopes) the infinite repeatedly, here an endless succession of finite things, each with its own essence, able to act and to pursue and to persevere in virtue of its essence (Spinoza, *E,* Part 3, Props. 6–8). In addition, God, or Substance, envelopes two additional infinites, everywheres and elsewheres, that all who read Spinoza have found enigmatic.

> From the necessity of the divine nature infinite numbers of things in infinite ways (that is to say, all things which can be conceived by the infinite intellect) must follow. (Spinoza, *E,* Part 1, Prop. 16)

> God or substance consisting of infinite attributes, each one of which expresses eternal and infinite essence, necessarily exists. (Spinoza, *E,* Part 1, Prop. 11)

Whatever place Substance may find itself, in its own place, in itself, it includes, envelopes, infinite numbers of things in infinite numbers of ways, each of which, expressing eternal and infinite essence, pertains to, envelopes, or expresses Substance. How can such an infinite of infinites, enveloping an infinite succession of different things and different kinds, be at rest except restlessly, a restlessness that plenishes the world? We are led to think of God's place as a place of rest, understanding the infinite succession of temporality and the infinite kinds, each of which is infinite, each expressing Substance Itself, as restlessness. This is the point of rest, that it includes restlessness within itself, everywhere.[12]

As for woman, she is place but has no place, still everywhere. In this role, she is dangerous, restless. Give her, help her find, demand her place! Not a place enveloped by her identity, but a place of rest, a place remaining in the abyss.

> She must lack
> —neither body,
> —nor extension within,
> —nor extension without,
> or she will plummet down (*s'abîme*) and take the other with her. (Irigaray, *ESD,* p. 35)

All this abysmal resting in place, displacement, works around the body, under the seal of sexual difference. "Again, just as every body is in place, so, too, every place has a body in it. What then shall we say about *growing* things?" (Irigaray, *ESD,* p. 36; Aristotle, *Physics,* 209a).

That they are at rest, like *la matrice,* and woman, and the *Stabat Mater,* Mother standing at rest, in sorrow, *douleureuse.* All in the relation of sexual difference (Irigaray, *ESD,* p. 36). If every place has a body in it, and if not, if places contain bodies or if they do not, but could, then questions of sexual and ethical difference ask us what difference to place(s) is made by different (sexual, engendered) bodies. This returns us to the (sexed) question of the (sexed) place of place.

"If the place is in the thing (it must be if it is either shape or matter) place will have a place: . . . Hence the place will have a place" (Aristotle, *Physics,* 210a). If the place is in the thing (the woman-as-thing), then the thing is in its place, and the place is in its place. "The place is in the thing, and the thing is in the place. *Place is within and without and accompanies movement . . .* " (Irigaray, *ESD,* p. 40). Place is inside and outside the thing, remains inside, and goes outside, in a disturbing rest, intermediary between war and peace. As for woman . . . "[i]f woman could be inside herself, she would have at least two things in her: herself and that for which she is a container—man and at times the child" (Irigaray, *ESD,* p. 41). Woman, as place, finds that her place is a divided place of rest, between [*aentre*]

> —the container for the child,
> —the container for the man,
> —the container for herself. (Irigaray, *ESD,* p. 41)

If we understand ethical|sexual difference to take place at the place of place, as we have understood it, we have heard this as a place between (*aentre*), in rest, where rest echoes, resounds, reverberates throughout time and space and matter and form, echoes their residue, in the place of place. Man's place is woman, a place (*antre*) of rest. Woman's place is *entre,* a place of rest, envelope, vessel, container, *matrice.* "The female sex (organ) is neither matter nor form but *vessel*" (Irigaray, *ESD,* p. 43). The vessel is the place where form and matter have their place. The vessel is place, and the place of place is rest.

Aristotle concludes that:

> (1) Place is what contains that of which it is the place.
> (2) Place is no part of the thing.
> (3) The immediate place of a thing is neither less nor greater than the thing.
> (4) Place can be left behind by the thing and is separable. (Aristotle, *Physics,* 211a)

I understand Irigaray to say that place contains the thing without being "the thing." Woman, the receptacle, contains without identity. I understand this "without identity," not as lack, but as rest, as the remains of place, as what is "left behind." Place as rest is left behind, not in the sense of being discarded (if that is how one reads "separable"), but remains, surplus, supplement, circulation, plenishment. The place of place is rest, in the relation of sexual difference. The catastrophe for woman is that she is man's dangerous excess, gives him no rest.

For Aristotle says that "the place of a thing is the innermost motionless boundary of what contains it" (Aristotle, *Physics,* 212a; Irigaray, *ESD,* p. 51). I understand this "motionless boundary" as rest, where place exceeds its place. I understand this place of excess as both *entre,* between one sex and another, where the *enveloppe* separates and destroys sexual difference in its place, and *antre,* the lair of the beast, where the monstrosity of animals gives them no place in the human envelope. Yet every human place teems with animals. Irigaray concludes her discussion of Aristotle with Lacan's question of the woman without speaking of its monstrosity. "Does man become place in order to receive and because he has received female *jouissance?* How? Does woman become place because she has received male *jouissance?* How? How does one make the transition here from physics to metaphysics?" (Irigaray, *ESD,* p. 55). This reminds us, in a different voice, of the different places of men and women, the displacements of sexual difference, which we have heard as their rest:

> Thus man and woman, woman and man are therefore always meeting as though for the first time because they cannot be substituted one for the other. I will never be in a man's place, never will a man be in mine. Whatever identifications are possible, one will never exactly occupy the place of the other—they are irreducible to the other. . . .
>
> Who or what the other is, I never know. But the other who is forever unknowable is the one who differs from me sexually. (Irigaray, *ESD,* p. 13)

Irigaray asks us to think that the different places of men and women, unknown others to each other, sexually different, are places of *jouissance et souffrance.* If we pass from the *entre* of gender to the *antre* of animal monsters, we pass from their suffering to their joy, the *jouissance* of the other–animal–monster–beast, with whom we share the earth, the places of nature, but never, even in the same abodes, share *antre* or *jouissance.* Woman's *jouissance* represents what man cannot know but must suppose to know; animal *jouissance* represents what men and women cannot know but must suppose to know. The animal–other's *jouissance* does its work in the animal soul.

What if, as Leibniz says, the world, every particle of the earth, were filled with souls? "(T)here is a world of creatures, of living beings, of animals, of entelechies, of souls, in the smallest particle of matter?" (Leibniz, *M*, p. 547). What kind of ethic is possible if we think of every animal, every thing, as souled? Can we imagine such an ethic without collapsing into despair? Physicians treat ill children, knowing that many will not survive; veterinarians treat animals, knowing that their owners do not want to pay for their survival. We know what it is to live ethically even when we cannot institute the good. We reach, in an impossible movement, toward every soul.

Do we think strongly enough of heterogeneity, think at and in rest, if we remain within the dyad of sexual difference? Or do we find that remaining at rest in sexual difference promotes a remainder, a rest, of difference, leading to race and blood, to animals and beyond, to the plenitudinous kinds of the earth?

"But what if the 'object' started to speak?" (Irigaray, *SOW*, p. 135). And what if the 'object' included other heterogeneities, even those who, as Lyotard claims, are victims because they cannot speak, but feel, feel joy, know their *jouissance?* And suffer.[13] Could it be that joy measures life as much as suffering? What if the creatures, the objects and things, started to feel, to know, to know joy? What if they already did, have always known joy? And what of sadness?

Ethical difference is the relation we bear to others when we know that they experience joy, know joy, even as we can neither experience nor know their joy, can never experience their experience. That is the measure of *jouissance.* It places us at risk, at rest, exceeding our joy in the others, bears a certain joy and sadness. Enveloping our *jouissance.* And women's. We have not thought, have not listened to the monstrosity of men and women and animals, rested in nature's monstrosity, where monsters show, demonstrate, their joys. We find the monsters in nature. We find the witches, women as witches, at rest, remaining, with the monsters.

> The sorceress, who in the end is able to dream Nature and therefore conceive it, incarnates the reinscription of the traces of paganism that triumphant Christianity repressed. The hysteric, whose body is transformed into a theater for forgotten scenes, relives the past, bearing witness to a lost childhood that survives in suffering.

> This feminine role, the role of sorceress, of hysteric, is ambiguous, antiestablishment, and conservative at the same time . . . *conservative* because every sorceress ends up being destroyed, and nothing is registered of her but mythical traces. (Clément, *GO*, p. 5)[14]

We understand, we listen to, the silence of rest as the song of the witches, the music of the earth. The earth in its place is always displaced, somewhere and elsewhere. Nature is a somewhere–elsewhere. We understand this as plenishment in the earth. We listen to the *Stabat Mater*, in several languages and tones:

Stabat Mater dolorosa Juxta crucem lactimosa, Dum pendebat Filius	A weeping mother was standing full of sorrow beside the cross, while her Son was hanging on it.
Cuius animam gementem, Constristatam et dolentem Pertransivit gladius.	Her grieving heart, anguished and lamenting, was pierced by a sword.
O quam tristis et afflicta Fuit illa benedicta Mater unigeniti! Quae Moerebat et dolebat, Pia Mater dum videbat Nati poenas inclyti.	Oh, how sad and afflicted was that blessed mother of an only Son! She mourned and grieved, the loving mother, as she saw the suffering of her glorious Son.
Quis est homo qui non fleret, Matrem Christi si videret In tanto supplicio?	What man would not weep seeing the mother of Christ in such torment?
Quis non posset contristari, Christi matrem contemplari Dolentem cum Filio?	Who would not feel compassion watching the mother of Christ in sorrow with her son?
Pro peccatis suae gentis Vidit Jesum in tormentis Et flagellis subditum. Vidit suum dulcem natum Moriendo desolatum, Dum emisit spiritum.	She saw Jesus in torments and subjected to scourging for the sins of His people. She saw her dear Son dying forsaken as He yielded up His spirit.
Eia mater, fons amoris, Me sentire vim doloris Fac, ut tecum lugeam.	Oh mother, fount of love, make me feel the strength of thy grief so that I may mourn with thee.

Fac ut ardeat cor meum In amando Christum Deum, Ut sibi complaceam.	Make my heart burn with love for Christ, my God, so that I may please Him.
Amen.	Amen.[15]

Always amen! We sing the amen of sexual and ethical difference. Or rather, we hesitate before sexual and ethical difference as our amen to the *Stabat Mater.* In four Western languages. Does the *Stabat Mater* exist in other languages, in un-Christianized languages? Does Christ's mother sadly stand at rest elsewhere, outside the gates?

Mother, the woman, stands in place, serving her Son (and son), her Master. Is that where woman always stand, in God's (Man's) place, in servitude? Amen?

We pursue an ethic of love without a master, an ethic of responsibility toward a world teeming with souls, teeming with love, but where we cannot save them all, an ethic of responsibility toward ourselves and our kinds that does not make us masters. Ethics, with its infinite responsibilities, places us in service without a Master or Law or Slave, but gives responsibilities beyond everything, at rest, in place, elsewhere, everywhere, teeming in profusion, responsibilities to everything, not just *L'Autre* or *Autrui.*[16]

Stabat Mater, resting in your *jouissance et douleur.* An ethic of rest, of pain and suffering and obsession, and *jouissance.* An ethic of inclusion, of what plenishes the earth.

The mother of God stands at rest, in sorrow; her son hangs at rest, in torment. The mother remains standing, *stabat;* her son remains, his remains rest with us. For ever. Women stand in sorrow, in service, stand at rest, at the edges of men's works. And what of women's work? What of the work of ethics, plenishment in the earth, except *doloroso, dolorosa?* We hear that work in the sound of the *Stabat Mater,* in the music, and rest, and in the rest of the music. The mother's music, musical work, at rest; the mother remains at rest, the remains, her work remains, flowing with her *jouissance,* her sorrow, her milk, and her blood.

Hush, my little one, rest in peace. My son, my son: where can you find your rest?

I ask, as you and I must ask repeatedly, where the work of sexual difference is to take place, in what place(s); and who is to undertake it, men or women, in public (still controlled by men) or among those upon whom the violence of sexual difference falls?

Irigaray suspends the question of what sexual difference might mean to men, for men: "I am constantly being asked what that 'other' man will be. Why should I appropriate for myself what that 'other' man would have to say? What I want and what I'm wanting to see is what men will do and say if their sexuality releases its hold on the empire of phallocratism. But this is not for a woman to anticipate, or foresee, or prescribe . . . " (Irigaray, *Q*, p. 136). She does not address the "we's" that reemerge in "what men will do and say." Perhaps, only perhaps, the question of sexual difference will dissolve the identities of men and women at the same time that it dissolves the identity of Man into multiple and heterogeneous envelopes, will dissolve an ethic of sexual difference into an ethical difference in which sexual difference does not rest.

In the *hystera* of sexual difference, the earth will move. In the *jouissance* of sexual difference, the earth moves. In the *hystera* of ethical difference, the earth, the sun, the stars, nature, and the world, all move, continue to move, in their place, in and out of their places, move heterogeneously, at rest. The work of nature, of women, of men, the endless succession of works sing the songs of the earth in their different places, remaining at rest, restlessly at rest, heterogeneously, in their places. The place of the good is plenishment in the earth.

CHAPTER 5

Canon

Irigaray asks Levinas, "is there otherness outside of sexual difference?" (Irigaray, *QEL,* p. 178). She answers:

> The function of the other sex as an alterity irreducible to myself eludes Levinas for at least two reasons:
>
> He knows nothing of communion in pleasure. . . .
>
> . . . he substitutes the son for the feminine. (Irigaray, *QEL,* pp. 180–81)

Yet an "alterity irreducible to myself" pervades Levinas's writing, pervades ethical responsibility, while Irigaray finds it lacking. Proximity with the other knows an infinite responsibility face to face with radical alterity. *Heteros,* with its Latin *alter,* gives us the dyad, two, one and the other. Yet Irigaray finds woman absent, *manquée,* even in the maternal.[1] Heterogeneity is lacking. The heterogeneity of the woman is missing within the alterity of the number two. Levinas's ethics is dyadic, face to face, yet seems to know nothing of what a woman might know of sexual difference. We find ourselves in the place of the number two, the dyad of gender, as irreducible alterity. Yet that place is displaced, at rest elsewhere, without the mother, and lacks sexual difference, its life and blood.

I have explored the possibility that the face to face bursts into nature everywhere, sung as plenishment in the earth, nature's inexhaustible cacophony. That shattering percussion of the earth gives us the resting places of ethical difference. Yet something in sexual difference works against nature's plenitude, resists profusion. Heterogeneity may vanish silently into dispersion so completely that only a lost echo remains. My name for this heterogeneity, the song of the earth, is rest, plenishment and rest. My concern in this chapter is with the dyads that have, from time immemorial, sounded the music of rest, sonorous and discordant, especially with the dyad of gender, men and women, with sexual difference face to face. My concern is with the number two, resisting its dispersion. How can we ensure that sexual difference remains within ethical difference, except in virtue of the dyad of gender, men and women in proximity? Here I do not mean heterosexuality, sex between men and women, though that dyad remains.[2] I hope for different sexualities, profuse sexualities, diverse sexual envelopes and plenishments. We may wish to know them and to nurture them. But there are men and there are women, among others. Irigaray suggests that men and women represent alterities irreducible to each other, in the language of place.

> Thus man and woman, woman and man are therefore always meeting as though for the first time because they cannot be substituted one for the other. I will never be in a man's place, never will a man be in mine. Whatever identifications are possible, one will never exactly occupy the place of the other—they are irreducible to the other. . . .
>
> Who or what the other is, I never know. But the other who is forever unknowable is the one who differs from me sexually. (Irigaray, *ESD*, p. 13)

"Man and woman," "woman and man": two dyads organized around sexual difference into two. One will never occupy the place of the other. One and the other equals two. The place of rest is an indefinite dyad. The mark of gender.

Who or what the other is, I never know. Every other; nature's heterogeneity. I do not know (the irreducible alterity of the other), that which I suppose to know; and love. Yet the predominant form of the dyad, face to face, is master–slave, in Wittig for example. Man and woman are categories of domination and subjection.

> "Man" and "woman" are political concepts of opposition, and the copula which dialectically unites them is, at the same time, the one which abolishes them. It is the class struggle between women and men which will abolish men and women. The concept of difference has nothing ontological about it. It is only the way that the masters interpret a historical situation of domination. (Wittig, *SM*, p. 29)

"Man" and "woman" echo "master" and "slave," and the "and" that unites them abolishes them. There can be no reciprocal, equal pair, no couple, where one is dominated by the other. As a consequence, women among women, breaking off copulation with men, are not "women." "Lesbians are not women" (Wittig, *SM*, p. 32). Lesbians disperse the dyad.[3]

Even so, the number two continues to circulate, in *The Lesbian Body,* for example, in the predominance of I with you (*j/e* with *toi*), within the subject's slit (*j/e*), among the multiplicity of corporeal profusions.[4] The ethical, amorous, caring gather around the number two, even as it is, in its dialectical forms, the most contaminated number in Western civilization, the number in *polemos,* opposition, strife, and gender. The number two presents us with two in love, two who care, mother and child, with intimacy and proximity; with binariness, bipolarity, the law of the *logos;* with domination and subordination.[5] Shall we go so far as to say that wherever there are two in proximity, one must rule? That is what Spinoza says. One must rule, and men are ill-disposed to allow themselves to be ruled by women, intolerant of being ruled by others. And so some rule and others are slaves.

One question, perhaps the darkest question of ethics, is whether the number two must issue in domination and subordination, if not death. This is Hegel's question, and perhaps we should not repeat it. His answer, instituted by that beginning, is that two may become ethical only in a reciprocity that the two cannot of themselves sustain. An ethic of two demands a *polis* built on All, on universal reason. Ethical responsibility for sustaining a dyad in reciprocity, man and woman, man and man, belongs to the force of law and the authority of the state, all in a universal, dialectical movement. In Hegel, two becomes three in the shadow of universality.

Can we give up this Hegelian line of thought, from the one to two to the state under the law of three, as the mark of the ethical, except by giving up the number two? Can we give up the binariness of *polemos* without destroying heterogeneity? I am exploring the possibility that the good inhabits the earth without number, without measure, without the measures and numbers of dyads, face to face. I am exploring the possibility that the man–woman dyad might give birth to another understanding of gender, of sexuality.

I emphasize the number two, but my concern is with any definite number, with number and measure in general perhaps. I hesitantly recapitulate the movement of Greek philosophy, if only to examine the hold of number upon our relation to the good, nature's measure as the good—in *Philebus,* for example, where that measure rests within the indefinite dyad. What we find at the beginning of Western philosophy is that justice (*dikē*) is strife (*polemos*), the ordinance of time is restitution for the injustice (*adikia*) in things. Justice and injustice, another dyad, belong to all things, everywhere, permeate the earth; and things, in their injustices toward one another, spend all of time, under law and truth, making, paying, restitution. The dyad justice–injustice collapses into an inexhaustible profusion of restitutions for an injustice that bears no measure.[6] Put another way, justice is endless restitution in the call of an immemorial injustice that knows nothing of measure, of justice's measure. There the number two gives way, to rest.

How far, we ask, can the number two, the oppositions of our lives, give way, either before the cut of truth from untruth, good from bad, justice from injustice, or before the irreducibility of the other? How far can the dyad give way, from peace to war, from love to slavery? And why must the two give way, if that means vanishing into silence? I would rather understand the number two, here sexual difference and gender, elsewhere other differences, to lead the way to rest. For plenishment in the earth, inexhaustible profusion, does not abolish the number two, but loosens the hold of exclusion upon it. Ethical difference does not abolish sexual or any other difference with a multiplicity of alterities and subjections. Ethical inclusion does not destroy what it includes, does not even destroy exclusion. Rather, the rests of the earth recall the remainders of irreducible alterities enveloped in sexual difference.

When Levinas speaks of what is "otherwise than being," he resists a being of rational peace under the signs of "calculation, mediation and politics," where "the struggle of each against all becomes exchange and commerce" (Levinas, *OB*, p. 4). In this way, he resists the Hegelian movement from the two through reciprocity to the all. The face to face is no number, participates in no calculation, mediation, exchange, or commerce, knows no reciprocity. Law belongs to the number three, but the dyad of alterity knows no measure. We have seen this resistance to calculation and exchange elsewhere, in Heidegger and others, spoken of against *technē*'s measures. It appears there and is resisted in relation to the number two, resisting its hold, in the entwining of nearness and farness, concealment and unconcealment, an entwining that is not a dyad, certainly not a strife, but a belonging-together, all intermediary figures. And it is resisted in relation to Being. For it may be possible to say that Being *is* the otherwise for Heidegger, that the otherwise is the ontological difference.[7] I have read Foucault as saying something similar, speaking of heterogeneity as "the univocity of being."[8] I understand this univocity of being in terms of two ideas—always a count of two (?)—one of general economy, freeing us from the domination of restricted economies, the other a musical voice, the songs and rests of the earth. Even so, general economy plus restricted economy makes two. Economy, general or restricted, plus song makes two, where two echoes in silence's rest. Two returns again and again, without opposition, returns in supplementation.

I have spoken of this notion of general economy, echoing in Bataille.[9] I add sexual difference, from Irigaray's understanding of the circulation of women, but I understand, with her, that this circulation echoes ethical difference. Sexual and ethical difference circulate in general economy, exceeding any work, together with an authority circulating beyond any work. I add the sound of music echoing our general circulation. Yet these general circulations deposit themselves in restricted economies, hierarchical, measured. The dyad of gender represents a restricted, exchange economy, the exchange of women, while women and gender circulate wildly in general economy.

For the moment, let us set aside the relation of general economy to political economy, and more important, the relation of general economy to sovereignty.[10] Authority precedes every authorization, enters every authorization, as general economy. I echo Bataille, who says that authority is an excessive energy that can only be lost, without any meaning. This useless, senseless loss *is* sovereignty. In this way, we may emphasize the arbitrariness and unworking of authority. Yet we may say instead—still hoping to express the arbitrariness and unworking of sovereignty and rule, but overwhelmed by too much authority—that authority and sovereignty do too much work, are at work excessively wherever there is work (and even when not). Authority and sovereignty are two pervasive forms of work's and truth's and law's excesses.

The heterogeneous excesses of works in circulation compose general economy. Authority does not dissolve meaning and truth, but exceeds them, enters them and circulates them in excess of themselves. Meaning exceeds any authority even as authority represents that excess. General economy, here, both installs and dissolves authority and sovereignty, rule and law, in the same circulatory movement of excess.

The thought of ethical difference follows Anaximander, tracing the movement of justice as the work, in the ordinance of time, of unending restitution for immemorial injustice. This unending movement is general economy. Immemorial injustice is the excess that reverberates in nature's plenitude, under all human work, giving voice to ethical difference.[11]

I hope to understand the dyad of gender after Plato's indefinite dyad, perhaps in a different way. The dyad appears in *Philebus* in an enigmatic way, emerging from the very voice that tells it: "[t]here is a gift of the gods—so at least it seems evident to me—which they let fall from their abode, and it was through Prometheus, or one like him, that it reached mankind, together with a fire exceeding bright. The men of old, who were better than ourselves and dwelt nearer the gods, passed on this gift in the form of a saying" (Plato, *Philebus,* 16c). Plato retraces our concern with place, telling us of a gift of the gods that comes from their place to us, through an intermediary like Prometheus, together with fire, with the sun, with the figure that marks the earth at rest, otherwise. Whatever else we may wish to say of Plato, the sun, the fire, represent ecstasy.[12] Nietzsche tells us repeatedly that Apollo's light is ecstasy, returns us to the number two, Apollo and Dionysus, ecstatically. We might say, taking Nietzsche seriously, that the idea of the number one (The Sun, The Good) is an ecstatic idea of the number two. In a certain way, this is the advent of the *logos,* the way into the principle of noncontradiction. Contradiction and noncontradiction are two together and two in each. In *Philebus,* something different happens.

For what we are to do with the number two, or any other number, Socrates tells us, is to let it pass away.

> But we are not to apply the character of unlimitedness to our plurality until we have discerned the total number of forms the thing in question has intermediate between its one and its unlimited number. It is only then, when we have done that, that we may let each one of all these intermediate forms pass away into the unlimited and cease bothering about them. (Plato, *Philebus,* 16de)

Many have read Plato under the sign of measure to imagine that philosophy is fulfilled in the intermediate number. Yet this story tells of the indefinite dyad, which has haunted philosophy from its beginnings, and which we find ourselves retracing in the name of sexual and ethical difference. I am imagining that an ethics of sexual difference takes place in the indefiniteness of the dyad, in the two of man and woman, in the general economy of the circulation of dyads.

I am considering the possibility that Socrates' enigmatic account of the gift of the gods[13] tells us of the number two, indefinitely, giving us a way to hear the number two in difference, including sexual and ethical difference, destroying sexual and ethical indifference. I suggest that the question of ethical and sexual difference is a question of the indefinite dyad, including man and woman, and other dyads, understanding the dyad to echo inexhaustibly from the beginning of the world to the end, across every limit.

Socrates says that we are not to give way to unlimit without an intermediate number, but when we have gained that intermediate number, the "total number of forms intermediate," we are to let each of these forms "pass away into the unlimited." Limit and unlimit, without their intermediate number, lack something. This lack is fulfilled by the intermediate number. Ethical difference as such, without number, without the number two, lacks alterity, the difference between the one and the other, one kind and the other, the difference between men and women, given by the limit that divides them within their different envelopes. I am speaking of the two within the *entre,* and the unlimit within the *antre*. Sexual difference "as such," as two, men and women, knows much too little of its own unlimit, gives itself over (even in Irigaray and Wittig) to its intermediate number, lacking heterogeneity, knowing no rest in kind. Ethical difference "as such," as indefinitely and profusely many, knows too little of the number two, of divisions, oppositions, of strife and *polemos,* as it would relinquish their hold upon us. Reciprocity sneaks in upon us from difference as such, without the number two, and from irreducible alterity, within the number two.

We are to think the number two to the very end, think the intermediate to the very end, then let it pass away into unlimit and forget it. What could it mean to forget the number two, for example the dyad of gender, men and women, or to remember it? What could it mean to cease bothering about two sexes, two genders, among homosexual men and lesbian women? Animals who reproduce sexually divide mostly (but not completely) into two sexes. Shall we divide them and their *jouissances* from others, from the ones that are not two (but still divide into two, and more), from the ones that do not reproduce sexually? What of animals who seem to choose how they will reproduce, two or less, as we humans cannot choose? And the others, neither human nor animal nor plant, but . . . ? Do we cease bothering about two to pass to these others? All in the name of death.

The idea of two, as measure, on this reading is both irresistible and wanting. I seek an ethical reading of passing "away into the unlimited and cease bothering about" the number two, every intermediate measure. The most difficult part is to understand what it might be to "cease bothering" in a time in which the question of difference seems to be the one thing worth bothering with, in the form for us here of sexual and ethical difference. For the moment, let us pass from the number two to the unlimited. I will return later to bother with what we might cease to bother about.

We have understood unlimit in several ways related to sexual difference. Irigaray and Wittig are struck by the claim that society as we know it is based on the exchange of women—the "social contract."[14] "[T]he society we know, our own culture, is based upon the exchange of women. Without the exchange of women, we are told, we would fall back into the anarchy (?) of the natural world, the randomness (?) of the animal kingdom" (Irigaray, *WM*, p. 170; her question marks).[15] The protection (male) human society needs against becoming animal again, monstrously natural again, is given by the circulation of women, from which every society derives its law. Civilization's mastery over nature depends on the exchange of women.

Wittig includes the theme of authority, which I include within the circulation of goods, of judgments and work; she also understands the exchange of women as domination. "But what does women being exchanged mean if not that they are dominated?" (Wittig, *SM*, pp. 31–32). "The category of sex is the product of a heterosexual society in which men appropriate for themselves the reproduction and production of women and also their physical persons by means of a contract called the marriage contract" (Wittig, *CS*, p. 6). The exchange of women, the economy of women, in heterosexual society, is domination and appropriation, works by authority. Irigaray suggests much the same: "[w]hich means that the possibility of our social life, of our culture, depends upon a ho(m)mo-sexual monopoly?" (Irigaray, *WM*, p. 171). Our culture depends on the joined property|propriety (*propre*) of women.

My concern for the moment is with the idea of economy, the circulation of goods and representations, including women (with animals and men), especially the idea of the general economy of work and judgment. The economy before us, the exchange and commodification of women, closely pairs with the number two, the scale of gender. An exchange economy is a restricted economy, in this context by men appropriating women under the sign of the number two. "*Women-as-commodities are thus subject to a schism* that divides them into the categories of usefulness and exchange value; into matter–body and an envelope that is precious but impenetrable, ungraspable, and not susceptible to appropriation by women themselves; into private use and social use" (Irigaray, *WM*, p. 176). Women-as-commodities begin in the toils of the number two, biologically, then are repeatedly subjected to one exclusion after another, man–woman, public–private, matter–spirit, human–nature, all in the dyadic measure of gender.

We may understand the circulation of goods and representations as an economy. We may understand the circulation and exchange of women, upon which the heterosexual social contract is based, as an economy of sexual difference, imposing the number two, measuring the worth of women as commodities. The subject, here, is masculine even when women are granted subjectivity (by men). We may understand the principle of exchange, of commodities, in a market economy, to be based on substitution and equivalence. That is why I have recoiled from Levinas's ethics of substitution, without reciprocity and equivalence. With regard to the obsession of responsibility for the other, "[w]hat can it be but a substitution of me for the others?" (Levinas, *OB*, p. 114). Levinas speaks of substitution as "the other in the same" (Levinas, *OB*, p. 114) "for which, I am summoned as someone irreplaceable" (Levinas, *OB*, p. 114). Same and irreplaceability war in substitution. I am thinking, if I can, of an economy without dominance by the same, in the irreplaceability of subject or soul.

The topic before us is how to think "otherwise" than through the cuts of exchange and equivalence. I am pursuing two ideas, that to be goods, to be effective, goods must circulate. Things circulate, women, men, and animals, among all the things that circulate in nature, in human society and life, in representation and judgment, doing their work. The circulation of goods is an economy. I am also pursuing Bataille's distinction between restricted economy—under measure, an economy of equivalence and exchange, of substitution under the same—and general economy—of excess, exceeding, otherwise than, any measure of equivalence, any work.

I now propose two hypotheses, based on the idea that ethical difference composes the circulation of general economy. One is that wherever there is restricted economy (wherever there are restricted economies, always plural), there circulates general economy. Restricted economies are general economies under rule, given measure, as if to bring excess under control, but always failing to do so. Things circulate in their places in restricted economy, but every place is elsewhere. Things do their work, in place, in restricted economy, but every work unworks, exceeds any work done by anything whatever.[16]

The second hypothesis is that the excess, immeasurability, of general economy is a function not of the singularity, individuality, irreplaceability, or subjectivity, the unique and irreplaceable identity, of things in circulation, but of circulation itself, the velocity and displacements of works and judgments in circulation. It is not my or the other's irreplaceability that guarantees my responsibility for the other, that makes me responsible. If I were not responsible for this other, I would be responsible for that. Responsibility is my way of being in circulation among other circulating goods, my way of plenishing the earth. This plenishment includes the others, individuals and kinds, that obsess me, who circulate in my obsession. Others may not be able to circulate in their own responsibility—stones and clouds, for example. My responsibility for their good does not presuppose that they may take responsibility for mine. My identity is caught up in my responsibility for the work of the good, circulating around me and you and others. This general circulation of work and goods is the inexhaustible plenishment of judgment, ethical difference. Inexhaustibility imposes responsibility toward the ideal, everywhere and in every thing. It is a responsibility that every thing knows, but one met by creatures that can respond, can judge, in certain ways. Even so, as Levinas emphasizes, the characteristic trait of ethical difference lies in my concern, my responsibility for and cherishment of the other in the other's heterogeneity, not in the measurable merits of the other. To measure the other to fit the demands of virtue is incompatible with ethical difference. Even so, we live in loss, cannot live without injustice.

Responsibility belongs to and exceeds every identity, every envelope, remains excessive, because every identity–envelope is excessively at rest, The rests of the earth, the songs of plenishment in the earth, resonate with the excessiveness of every economy, in or on the earth. Man (in the masculine) but also humanity (in the multiple–gendered–otherwise) has struggled since time immemorial with bringing the plenitude of the world under measure, in restricted economies, always failing. I want to say this again.[17] Society as we know it presupposes a (heterosexual) contract based on the exchange and circulation of women (among other things and material envelopes), a circulation in blood (of animals and women) that guarantees the production and reproduction of social law and order within the heterogeneous plenitude of things. It presupposes that women will bear men's children lawfully. It presupposes it, imposes it, and always fails somewhere at it, even when it succeeds in holding women and animals and things in thrall. For society as we know it circulates goods—women and children (among other goods)—in underground economies. The underground economy in every restricted economy is the earth's irruption, transporting the circulation of goods from one place, or system of places, to other places, or no place, displacing the replacement of goods, their circulation in kinds. In the midst of the greatest works is rest, under or on the ground.

The circulation of goods, under rule, composes the general economy of law, law of place and law of the same. But place is always at rest, displaced, transported, and the same, replaced, imposes difference, transports the same, again at rest. The circulation of goods, under rule, a restricted economy, always finds itself resting within general economy. Within everything Irigaray and Wittig say, and within a feminist critique of Western society, this truth echoes aloud. The ways in which women have no place, the places they provide (or are) for men, are dangerous, disruptive, displaced, resting places. Give women their identity or beware! Look out for witches! Mother is the eternal danger! Mother exceeds all law, all of Father's Law! Something does, and something always will, in the general economy of law. Why do you not see the unforgiving threat to culture of melancholy, depression, and abjection? Of hysteria, named as belonging only to women? Kristeva ascribes these to the abyssal theme of the Mother. I insist that they belong to, work within, the restricted economy of the exchange of women. Or rather, I insist that within this restricted economy, all of them circulate under and on the ground in our general economy, the earth's plenishment and replenishment.

The circulation of goods composes an economy. We may think of such an economy as belonging to the state, under the social contract. Or we may think of it as present in the state of nature, responding to the sense that goods circulate in the earth, throughout the world, wherever goods work, not just where humans work. Goods circulate wherever they are and work, in and out of place, doing the work of ethical difference. Goods circulate everywhere, all the time, excessively, in general economy, in their place, moving from one place to another, multiply, heterogeneously placed and displaced. I understand the flow, the plenitude, and the rests of the earth to compose general economy; to compose the univocity of being, of nature, dismantling the dominion of identity as responsibility for ethical difference.[18]

If we think of the circulation of goods within a state or society bounded by borders, terrain, and force as restricted economy, then we understand from one consideration after another that what restricts an economy are barriers of force and authority that remain permeable as they do their work. They work in place by the circulation of what displaces every place. Work in place displaces itself and place. Authority has no authority, in no way diminishing its force. We have seen this displacement in our thought of place in Aristotle. After Irigaray, I call this relation of place to itself "rest." But we may also understand that borders, terrain, and force all work, divide and rule, only insofar as they are crossed. Goods must circulate across the boundaries that direct their movement if they are to be controlled.[19]

I conclude that the circulation of women has always depended on the ability of some women, more or less, to refuse to be circulated in a heterosexual economy—spinsters and witches, for example. I conclude as well that every restricted economy belongs to general economy. It may follow—I am still exploring this possibility—that the excesses of general economy can be expressed as plenishment in being, nature, or the earth. It may also be possible to express the excesses of the good multiply, as being, nature, and the good, and more. It is possible that we may sing of the circulation of goods in general economy, exceeding all measure and rule, in the restless voices of the earth.

But before we return to the earth's general economy, before we pass away to the circulation of goods far beyond their irreplaceability, we must return to the number two and other intermediate numbers. For I approached the idea of restricted economy under the idea of measure, driven by the inescapability of the number two. I wondered if the number two might be a heterogeneity, an excess, beyond any substitution. What of the two of sexual difference, of gender? Could it exceed all excess?

Could the intermediate number two, the dyad of gender, man and woman, be an intermediary figure? Could it cross the threshold of heterogeneity? Is this what Socrates means by letting the intermediate numbers pass away, passing from the intermediate between one and many? With this thought of the intermediate as intermediary, that is, of numbers circulating together with angels, spirits, souls, envelopes, and betweens, *vaentres,* we hesitate at the close of mathematics upon the plenishment of nature, hesitate at the close of restricted economies on general circulation. Wherever there is measure, there is unmeasure, excess, and more. Every intermediate opens another excess, diverts and complicates the general economy. Every intermediate, including modern technology and sexual difference, is an intermediary. Measure is an intermediary figure.

Women are commodities, measured by dowry, family, and progeny, and are frequently destroyed where they do not measure up, or where another measure arises, or simply to punish men. In this circulation, as commodities, women die, are allowed to die, beyond biological necessity. One hundred million have died in the past few decades (Sen, *MMWM,* pp. 61–66). What are we to make of 100 million against the number two? Or of 100 million dead women against 3.5 million cattle, whose body weight exceeds all of humanity, certainly all women? Or of 2.5 million German women raped by Russian men? Or of 6 million Jews, murdered by Germans and others? What are we to make of the numbers of the earth, 2 or 3 or 2.5 million or 6 million or 100 million or more?

We may wish to distinguish between general and exchange economy in a different way. Foucault speaks of exchange economy in relation to classical representation, in the seventeenth and eighteenth centuries: "a general domain: a very coherent and very well-stratified layer that comprises and contains, like so many partial objects, the notions of value, price, trade, circulation, income, interest. This domain, the ground and object of 'economy' in the Classical age, is that of *wealth*" (Foucault, *OT,* p. 166). I understand economy in terms of circulation, around and through which the other terms disseminate. Value, price, income, and interest are measures of equivalence and substitution. Trade is the predominant visible avenue of circulation, by no means alone. Goods circulate with or without design, with or without planning, visibly and invisibly. Goods cross borders designed to intercept them, elude channels designed to guide them, dissipate and consolidate away from the powers and rules designed to manipulate and regulate them. Circulation breaks down even where channels of regulation exist and accomplish their work.

I present two examples from our time, the late twentieth century, where the circulation of goods defies the most solicitous regulations. One is famine. By now, in the second half of the twentieth century, after several famines in Africa and Asia, and many more shortages of food without famine, we may conclude one fact. Hunger to the point of mass extermination is not a function of shortage of food, has not been a function of shortage of food for centuries. All the major starvations of the last third of our century have been accompanied by more than enough food in the country involved to feed everyone, in some cases after exceptional harvests.[20] Rather, within relative plenty, large groups of people are unable to buy food at prevailing prices. Prices, measures of equivalence and substitution, sometimes impede the circulation of goods. Yet goods circulate by theft; people and things circulate secretly at night, across borders. The economic–political system, designed to facilitate the beneficial circulation of goods, establishes structures and regulations that impede circulation, which proceeds in any case, sometimes violently and disastrously.

I have alluded to the other example, the disappearance of women from countries whose level of affluence is high enough for women's biological life span to exceed that of men, but where the actual term of life for women is much lower than that of men. In such societies, female children and women are deprived of the medical care and nutrition that boys and men normally receive. Millions of females have died, in many countries, from such deprivation but not in similar neighboring countries.

I will speak for the moment of the circulation of food, care, and women together as the circulation of goods. I will return later to the circulation of women, the impetus of this discussion. We have two extreme examples of what we may think of as the collapse of circulation to the point of death. Yet these are not the end of the circulation of goods, for goods continue to circulate in these economies. Food circulates when stored in warehouses; women circulate among men even with shortened life expectancies, as they did when countless numbers died in childbirth in Western societies. Wholesale death and starvation, together with violence and destruction, are not the end of circulation but represent certain moments in restricted economies. Goods continue to circulate, sometimes together with violence and destruction. We may call these circulations underground economies if we wish to emphasize that they take place away from visible regulation, represent intermediary figures. We may rather think that they reveal the contaminated side of the resistance of any economy to let itself be regulated.

I understand the reverberations of general economy after Bataille. Echoes of general economy appear in other places, some seemingly far from the circulation of women. For example, Foucault's view of power echoes general economy.[21] He speaks repeatedly of general economy (and univocity), with and without the words. In particular, he speaks of power dispersed in its general economy.

> It seems to me that power must be understood in the first instance as the multiplicity of force relations immanent in the sphere in which they operate and which constitute their own organization; as the process which, through ceaseless struggles and confrontations, transforms, strengthens, or reverses them; as the support which these force relations find in one another, thus forming a chain or system, or on the contrary, the disjunctions and contradictions which isolate them from one another; and lastly, as the strategies in which they take effect, whose general design or institutional crystallization is embodied in the state apparatus, in the formulation of the law, in the various social hegemonies. (Foucault, *HS*, pp. 92–93)

This multiplicity of force relations, described as immanent, ceaseless, contradictory, issuing in strategies and institutional crystallizations, either fulfills itself in the state apparatus and law, as if it were a teleological structure, or exceeds itself in them. Foucault distinguishes power from Power in these terms, as if Power defines the hold of sovereignty in a restricted economy, however powerful, while power pervades, permeates, circulates everywhere, excessively. Power circulates everywhere, productively, whereas "Power" remains permanent and inert. "Power is everywhere; not because it embraces everything, but because it comes from everywhere. And 'Power,' insofar as it is permanent, repetitious, inert, and self-reproducing, is simply the over-all effect that emerges from all these mobilities, the concatenation that rests on each of them and seeks in turn to arrest their movement" (Foucault, *HS*, p. 93). This circulation of power everywhere is not another rule (or Rule), a Total Sovereignty, Fixed in Place, but a sovereignty and authority that in every way exceeds itself. The "everywhere" of power is both each and every place and no place. I have called it the "elsewhere" in every "somewhere." This inexhaustible excess of the other places in any place is the circulation of general economy, nature's plenitude, the rests of the earth. There remains—another "rest"—the question of why this circulation issues in power, takes the form of authority.[22]

We have seen that Foucault also speaks obliquely of restricted and general economy in relation to wealth. For he understands exchange economies to be intimately bound to classical representation, to the Classical *episteme* and

> the articulated system of a *mathesis*, a *taxinomia*, and a *genetic analysis*. The sciences always carry within themselves the project, however remote it may be, of an exhaustive ordering of the world; they are always directed, too, towards the discovery of simple elements and their progressive combination; and at their centre they form a table on which knowledge is displayed in a system contemporary with itself. (Foucault, *OT*, p. 74)

These three elements compose a system of signs based on assumptions moving inexorably toward tabular ordering. The world is exhaustively ordered in a circulation of signs displayed in tables and hierarchies, from simple elements to combinations. This classical scheme simultaneously presupposes endless circulation and exhaustive ordering.

Exchange economies mirror this ordering in the sphere of wealth. The system of classical representation came to a head with the ordering of wealth, the production of money, because exhaustiveness took on a new and special role, breaking the simultaneity of excess and order that composed the world of representation. I interpret this coexistence as the interplay, the *aentre,* of general and restricted economy. Money imposes a common measure upon a general economy, transforming it into a universal restricted economy.[23] "The two functions of money, as a common measure between commodities and as a substitute in the mechanism of exchange, are based upon its material reality. . . . money was a fair measure because it signified nothing more than its power to standardize wealth on the basis of its own material reality as wealth" (Foucault, *OT,* p. 169). The crucial idea is standardization, understood as repetition and equivalence. The equivalence in money was repeated again and again, rather like the standardization of words. "The standard of equivalences is itself involved in the system of exchanges, and the buying power of money signifies nothing but the marketable value of the metal" (Foucault, *OT,* p. 171). Standards, measures, equivalences, and exchanges define market value and market economy. In this sense, it is not that money "came on the scene" as that it fulfilled a promise in classical representation in relation to the idea of the orderly circulation of goods.

The thesis we may consider—though we may need to give ourselves over to it excessively—is that the exchange, substitutive, and equivalence value of money in a restricted economy is repeated mimetically throughout the thought of Western societies after the Enlightenment, especially in relation to value, to ethics. Utilitarianism is a substitution and equivalence theory based on the standardization of units of pleasure. The rights-based critique of utilitarianism is that within this standardization, some individuals and groups may be calculated to have less value than others, justifying their suffering and destruction for the greater good. Punishing an innocent person to make a society feel safer might be calculably the better alternative. In other words, within the circulation of goods that we call "ethical," we impose a measure that obstructs the circulation based on a calculation, restricts the circulation of goods by exclusion. A restricted economy must always halt the circulation of goods in a general economy of ethical difference at a point of injustice.

Yet a rights-based theory obstructs the circulation in a different way, by protecting individuals absolutely. For the absolute individual, with absolute and calculable rights, halts the circulation of goods at the borders of that individual's skin. The absolute agent offers either an absolute impediment to ethical difference or must be entirely disregarded. More precisely, in a world in which goods circulate in blood, what kind of ethics can provide for the value of embodied individuals?

What kind of ethic can allow goods to circulate excessively and immeasurably, uselessly in Bataille's words, doing no work, in general economy, even so making a difference? In what way, or sense, can ethics do no work? At this point I give up Bataille's language. Goods and representations circulate in general economy so excessively that they do too much work. Even so, we may return to our question to ask, what kind of ethic can allow goods to circulate excessively without impediments? Is it not the purpose of an economy and an ethic to channel, to work, to impose order on circulation, to select and exclude?[24] The analogy with money and the link with representation provide the Western Enlightenment answer. "For Classical thought in its formative phase, money is that which permits wealth to be represented. Without such signs, wealth would remain immobile, useless, and as it were silent; in this sense, gold and silver are the creators of all that man can covet" (Foucault, *OT,* p. 177). Classical representation is concerned with the representation of goods, here of wealth, with money that which transforms wealth into its representativity. Similarly, the good, immeasurable and excessive, incapable of representation and measure, passes into units of measure, providing for its circulation.[25] The circulation of goods composes general economy upon which representation, to represent those goods, to take them into rule and law, must render them countable.

I respond that judgment and representation provide channels for the measures of goods in circulation, but they also belong to general economy, to excessive circulation.[26] This excess in representation represents the work of general economy against the hold of any restricted economy. Judgment and representation, turning onto themselves, break the hold of any system of representation. They inhabit general economy as intermediary and disruptive figures.

The number of sexes and genders might be innumerable; sex and gender might circulate in a general economy of individuals and communities without number or measure. Yet we must make them two, must count them, to represent them, to reach for an ethic of sexual difference. We represent the unrepresentable as two.

That is how we pay our debt. Foucault says something similar in relation to goods and values. "The creation of value is therefore not a means of satisfying a greater number of needs; it is the sacrifice of a certain quantity of goods in order to exchange others. Values thus form the negative of goods" (Foucault, *OT,* p. 192). Goods in circulation circulate in a general economy of representation that surpasses any restricted representation. If these goods are women (and men), are sexed and gendered, subjects and objects of desire, then their value, the value of any goods, but especially of goods inhabited by excesses of desire and power, must sacrifice not just the excessiveness, the immeasurability, of these goods, but a "certain quantity" in order to exchange others. Without this sacrifice of goods circulating, women would have no value. And so with the circulation of animals. The value of animals is incalculable, both in the wild and in the larder. And in our memories and judgments. The value is incalculable, so we pay the butcher's price.

But "[w]hat is the origin of this excess that makes it possible for goods to be transformed into wealth without being effaced and finally disappearing altogether as a result of successive exchange and continual circulation?" (Foucault, *OT,* p. 192). Foucault gives two equivalent answers. "The whole system of exchanges, the whole costly creation of values, is referred back to the unbalanced, radical, and primitive exchange established between the advances made by the landowner and the generosity of nature" (Foucault, *OT,* p. 195). More sweepingly, taking us back to general economy, "[i]t would be untrue to say that nature spontaneously produces values; but it is the inexhaustible source of the goods that exchange transforms into values, though not without expenditure and consumption" (Foucault, *OT,* p. 195).

I understand nature here not as something remote from humanity, the source "out there" of goods that human exchanges transform into values. Rather, nature is the general economy, the circulation of goods and representations, excessively and spontaneously, whose sacrifice gives us values. Nature must be sacrificed, general economy must be restricted, for goods to circulate in systems of representation. But this sacrifice, even unknowingly, represents inexhaustible excess. The restricted economy depends on the general economy in whose name it carries on its sacrifices. It reaffirms excess every time it represents a good, holds a good as if without excess, gives a good as a gift.[27]

In the same way, money represents, measures, and circulates goods in the name of an underground economy, an economy of men and women on street corners, beggars and dealers, an economy deep in the earth. Goods circulate generally and excessively, immeasurably, from the earth's plenitude into society's measures. And among these goods are animals and women. We return to the number two: men and women; humans and animals. We return to the earth. And Plato.

For I am trying to understand the number two, in sexual difference, as an intermediate number, trying to understand the idea of letting all such numbers pass away, after we have discerned them, into the unlimit. What can it mean to let the number two, the dyad of gender, pass away into unlimit? Into death? I am reading the number two to belong to restricted economy, the circulation of goods under rule and measure, ordered by the number two, kept safe in life. In this way we understand both the exchange of women, as composing "our own culture," and the circulation of other goods divided between men and women—for that role too is important in all "our" cultures. Our Own Culture circulates and exchanges women, and also circulates and exchanges other goods dividing the work of exchange and circulation between men and women.[28] However excessively.

The number two, then, pervades the work of culture. Cixous and Clément speak of this work of culture as "mastery," both in the framing of "Exchange," closing *The Newly Born Woman,* and in their exchange a few pages later.[29]

> *Mastery ensures the transmission of knowledge.* (*NBW,* p. 138)

> H: That there could be a culture without culture or a world, a society without education is something I never thought.
> C: At the moment, it seems to me, you are making mastery absolutely coincide with knowledge, except in a few exceptional cases. (*NBW,* p. 144)

We are tracing a line of thought in which something precedes, gives rise, to the idea of mastery. Provisionally, I have identified it as the number two, though we may be inclined to think that mastery imposes the number two: master–slave, for example, the one subordinating the other. The line of thought that draws us follows Cixous's acknowledgment that she has supposed that the transmission of culture means mastery, so that feminist writing, an ethic of sexual difference, must be at war with culture and its law.[30] Clément's reply is to deny the equation between knowledge and mastery. This is equivalent in our account to denying the equation between knowledge and restricted economy.

This denial opens the question of "the canon," that traditional measure defining the restricted economy of Western knowledge. What of the rule under whose authority women have been silenced and excluded? Especially, feminist philosophy has been excluded, is still excluded from the canon.[31] Why then have feminists been motivated to reread the canon? "Why have we sought to return to the site of our own exile, and what do we hope to accomplish through that return?" (Singer, *DC*, p. 165). This canon echoes mastery.

Linda Singer discusses three kinds of rereadings: (1) seeking the conceptual forefathers of feminism (Singer, *DC*, p. 168); (2) critical combative readings challenging what the history of philosophy says about women (Singer, *DC*, p. 170); (3) deconstructive readings "against the grain" (Singer, *DC*, p. 171). The first kind of rereading restores "faith in the rational benevolence and gender neutrality of philosophical discourse" (Singer, *DC*, p. 168), but "misrepresents the development of phallocentric discourse and feminist as a historically specific discourse of resistance" (Singer, *DC*, p. 169). The second kind minimizes "the possibility that there is some place within traditional philosophical discourse to dwell or to hide" (Singer, *DC*, 170); yet such a strategy "tends to bog one down in the eternal return of the same, the same motifs, same logic" (Singer, *DC*, p. 171). The third kind of rereading "constitutes an intervention into the phallocentric dynamic of authoritative textual closure" (Singer, *DC*, p. 172); provides "some very insightful and unsettling scholarship"; but risks "severing feminism from its historically specific roots in women's self-initiated political struggles"; and "is still dependent, conceptually and epistemologically, on . . . the canon and its traditions of interpretation" (Singer, *DC*, p. 173).[32]

All are strategies of profit, usefulness, and advantage for feminists who need to develop liberating strategies of power in knowledge, writing, and reading. All are within restricted economies of masculine and feminine genders. The canon operates as a measure in restricted economies, excluding women. Feminist strategies to promote the liberation of women are vital for them and for men. Yet reading and writing circulate rapidly in general economy as intermediaries. "The canon" presupposes restricted if dominant authority—Power. Reading and writing presuppose dispersed power and authority—power everywhere—even when they serve entrenched authority. Mastery belongs to and works within restricted economy. Culture names something different, the general circulation of goods and representations.

The question of ethical|sexual difference opens the general economy of culture to a torrent of heterogeneous works and words, circulating wildly, dispersing power and authority, to the point where we cannot set limits on reading the canon, where we refuse limits defining the canon and demand that excluded writing be read in the circulation of general economy, in the same gesture reading included writing in the same economy.

If we are to include writings that have been excluded from the canon, silenced writings, is it because we will find them more profitable to us, feminists or others? Or is it our responsibility to include the silenced, to include the excluded? An ethic of inclusion must include the excluded and the included, separately and together, in multiple ways, opening the general economy of reading and writing. This general economy circulates culture everywhere even where culture exists by exclusion. The very possibility of exclusion within the excessive plenitude of representation represents that excess, imposes responsibility toward every representation, to bear the burden of its sacrifices. Reading and writing, among countless other kinds of representations, circulate this responsibility as a debt.

I propose a view of culture based less on mastery than on restricted economy, where mastery is one of the restrictions, sacrifices, limits, coercions society places on the circulation of goods, where knowledge, representation, truth, power, and desire, but also men, women, children, and animals, and much more, all organize and participate in the circulation of goods and circulate themselves, plenishing the earth. A mastery culture is a restricted exchange economy. But there are other exchange economies that divide in pairs, binaries, in which mastery may not be predominant, binaries that do not exclude, perhaps gift economies.[33] Even so, where knowledge and truth divide into true and false, scientific and unscientific, legitimate and illegitimate, mastery predominates by exclusion. Similarly, Western culture seems to understand ethics, politics, and culture as divided by one form of exclusion after another, by legitimate and illegitimate power, acceptable and unacceptable desires, by codes of conduct and by the possession and use of animals. In the extreme, a monstrous caricature, Enlightenment thought succeeds in all these divisions based on the power and authority of reason. This reason, moreover, gains its authority, as universal, for everyone, disregarding the particularities and differences that make ethics difficult if not impossible. In another monstrous extreme, Western thought succeeds in these divisions based on the rule of form over the heterogeneity of kinds, imposing a good on every kind, a good that excludes according to the cut of two.

Such an understanding repeats the number two incessantly, dyad after dyad, to the point where we must recoil from reasserting it in the name of ethical difference. Yet we can see it emerge in Cixous's and Clément's discussion of the hold of mastery on culture, since they replace mastery with exchange, one dyad by another.[34] The master–slave dialectic seems to be the repeated form in which two appears and reappears in Western thought, overcome repeatedly, but in the account we are struggling with, overcome by All on the one hand, universality or generality, or by another dyad.

This, we may say, is what Cixous hears herself caught within, according to Clément, understanding that culture itself, ethically, politically, existentially, cannot begin to imagine itself displaced from mastery, from exclusion. We are finding the hold of the number two even stronger, more irresistible, for we recall that the ethic of sexual difference, like the understanding in conversation, demands another dyad, perhaps a more heterogeneous, but not a proliferated, dispersed dyad. What Irigaray says, promoting the ways in which her critics have assailed her for overemphasizing a biological gender, is that an ethic of sexual difference must come to terms with the number two, men and women, because that dyad presents something of heterogeneity that profusion and dispersion cannot express. Only in this dyad of sexual difference may women institute their own identities.

We repeatedly find ourselves returning to the gift of the gods in *Philebus,* because in a bare and exposed form, in a form beyond every other representation, Plato presents the intermediate number in relation to unlimit, presents it as essential and inescapable, but even so, we are to let it pass away into the unlimit, to die (away). I have been struggling through a variety of ideas to understand this idea of passing away. I understand the history of the West to compose a restricted economy, turning around the number two, made visible in mirrors, substitutions, exchanges, I for you, he for she. In my reading, an exchange economy, with its transformation of women, children, and animals, perhaps including men, into commodities, transforming subjects into objects with prices and values, exchangeable for each other, is a response to the coerciveness of mastery, the twisting of the number two into masters and slaves.

Perhaps women will resist this understanding. And perhaps they should. Perhaps Irigaray would resist the idea that replacing mastery with exchange does anything for either women or an ethics of sexual difference. My point is somewhat different, for I do not mean to suggest that an exchange economy is better than a system of mastery, a system in which women are subjected. Like Foucault, I recognize one system of subjection to replace another, modernity presenting an even less accessible realm of liberating practices. I am more concerned with the idea of better, since it must belong to an ethic and an economy, must struggle with the worse. What can better be but a moment in a restricted economy, a measure, an exclusion, an escape from worse? As every two seems to pass into mastery, and every ethical relation seems to demand the number two—in partners, lovers, friends, and others—the dispersion of two into a restricted economy, under measures of substitution and equivalence, circulates goods in multiple channels, disperses them.

Foucault tells us that power is dispersed, everywhere, and that consequently, strategies of domination and subjection, crystallizations of oppression and control, offer fewer levers to us today (if any) whereby oppression and violence may be overcome. In the extreme, in his expression of Nietzsche's will to power,

> Humanity does not gradually progress from combat to combat until it arrives at universal reciprocity, where the rule of law finally replaces warfare; humanity installs each of its violences in a system of rules and thus proceeds from domination to domination.
>
> The nature of these rules allows violence to be inflicted on violence and the resurgence of new forces that are sufficiently strong to dominate those in power. (Foucault, *NGH*, p. 151)

We may think of violence and domination as repeating the endless play of mastery and subjection. Yet in its endless violences and resurgences, in the turning back of violence and mastery upon themselves, the repetition of two in different voices, we pass from master–slave through subjection to the number two as a moment first in a restricted economy, a system of rules, then in a general economy of unruling rules, of restricting the restrictions, that is sufficiently strong to dominate the dominators, sufficiently strong to disperse the dyad into unlimit. Violence and domination here are intermediary figures.

The dyad begins to eliminate itself, bringing its mastery under its authority. It does so, however, by taking the everywhere of violence, domination, and power—and, for us here, of sexual difference—so seriously that the ability of power to exclude is eroded by the exclusiveness of power. Similarly, as Irigaray says, the exchange of women, the subjection of women, brings with it an enormous price for men, and certainly for women, of remaining in fear and terror of being subordinated, thereby of subordinating subordination. Even so, this subordination repeats the dyad while it resists it.

The thought I am exploring is that the passing away of the intermediate number to unlimit is a movement from mastery's restricted economy to general economy, a musical movement, a plenishment, and it is accomplished not by abolition of all traces of the intermediate number, in this case the number two, but by its profusion to the point where it gives rise to unlimit out of itself: still two, turns itself into an intermediary, *vaentre*. In a tentative and weak formulation of my general hypothesis, mastery taken in itself, as a two, is a relation of domination and subordination. Taken as the all, mastery must turn back upon itself, following Foucault's understanding, to divide mastery itself into domination and subordination, true and false, undermining its authority. This is Socrates' technique, employed repeatedly with Thrasymachus, Euthyphro, and Gorgias. On my reading, Plato does not reassert the primacy of the true as such, which if we knew it would give us the good directly, but the impossibility of separating the good from the true, because the cut of the good is always accompanied at cross-purposes by the cut of the true. Is it true that the Good is the Sun, that it shines its light into the cave, where men and women are bound?

The number two defines a restricted economy of sexual difference and the good in which goods circulate away from bads, in which we cut channels to divide goods from bads, rights from wrongs, justice from injustice, truth from falsity, men from women, reason from unreason, humans from animals, and more. Even so, in such an economy, goods and judgments circulate rapidly, excessively, escape from the channels we cut to contain them.[35] The circulation is uncontainable, containing multiple envelopes. The places in which we hope to contain, to envelope, the good are always places elsewhere as well as here, where the good slips away. I have understood this displacement of place to give rise, endlessly, to a general economy of goods, desires, and powers, to an endlessly proliferating circulation of goods, endlessly repeating the number two. For we have not forgotten it and cannot escape it. But we understand it to repeat exclusion and to inhabit intermediary regions. An ethic of inclusion cannot put exclusion away. A profusion of sexual differences cannot neglect the dyad of gender.

My reading of Cixous's wonder at the possibility of a culture without mastery is that culture may not require mastery even as it cannot turn its back on the number two, as its back and front repeat exclusion. Toward and away are two. Liberation and oppression are two. Liberation and oppression and something else are two and another two. Even as we pass from two to three, from one intermediate number to another, we repeat the hold of two, again and again, if we must choose, one or the other. Yet the "hold of two" expresses Foucault's understanding of violence upon violence and domination of domination, passing from restricted to general economy. My reading of the gift of the men of old is that the dyad belongs to both restricted and general economy, that mastery, slavery, power, desire, truth, and the good, et cetera et cetera, all inhabit restricted and general economy, inhabit multiple places, but the multiplicity, the inexhaustibility of the places also belongs to restricted and general economy.[36]

I now undertake another reading of Plato to explore the indefinite dyad as general economy. I will come to rest in chapter 6 to explore general economy elsewhere in the Western tradition, in Whitehead, Dewey, and Lyotard. All of this is to understand the Western tradition as a general economy of reading and writing, to understand tradition's canonical place as elsewhere. If you wish to forgo this textual excursion, you may come to rest again in chapter 7, in the general economy of animal life.

According to Socrates in *Philebus,* we are to give ourselves to the intermediate number that pertains to the thing in question between its one and its unlimited number. "It is only then, when we have done that, that we may let each one of all these intermediate forms pass away into the unlimited and cease bothering about them."[37] We should not overlook that *Philebus* is concerned more than anything with the good and with its relation to pleasure. Nor should we overlook that the examples Socrates gives in response to Protarchus's request for explanation follow the movements of language and music, circulate in representation.

> My meaning, Protarchus, is surely clear in the case of the alphabet; so take the letters of your school days as illustrating it. (Plato, *Philebus,* 17b)

> What makes a man "lettered" is knowing the number and the kinds of sounds. (Plato, *Philebus,* 17b)

> Then again, it is just the same sort of thing that makes a man musical. (Plato, *Philebus,* 17c)

Music works in *Republic* between pleasure and the good, works in the movement in which we are reading *Philebus.* Yet Socrates does not take the intermediate back to unlimit in either of the examples he gives. Perhaps he leaves it to us to do so. But in the case of knowing the numbers and kinds of letters, we know them only in relation to language's unlimit, its inexhaustibility, the possibility that we may say anything of anything beyond any limits. The limits of language exist so that language may speak unlimitedly.[38] Similarly, and perhaps more aptly for the discussion here, the notes and staffs, the inscriptions of music, all work under measure and control so that they may exceed any limits, even their own.

This understanding echoes the thought that the good of language and music belongs to them as the unlimit in which their intermediates do their work. And conversely, the work of intermediate numbers is not given by number, but by the unlimited good, unlimited work, that their measures make possible. For even as Socrates insists on the intermediate, we know the unlimit in language and music to be the work of the gods, especially that same god of writing who appears in *Phaedrus.* "The unlimited variety of sound was once discerned by some god, or perhaps some godlike man; you know the story that there was some such person in Egypt called Theuth" (Plato, *Philebus,* 18b). The unlimit and the one both belong to the gods, but they require the movement of their intermediate numbers. And when Socrates returns to the good, he emphasizes the return to unlimit. "Then what the foregoing discourse requires of us is just this, to show how each of them [intelligence or pleasure] is both one and many, and how—mind you, we are not to take the unlimited variety straightaway—each possesses a certain number before the unlimited variety is reached" (Plato, *Philebus,* 18e). We are not to take the unlimited variety straightaway, but we are to take it and reach toward it. For what Socrates calls "disputed terms" in *Phaedrus*—love, justice, the good [*erōs, dikē, agathon*] are terms of unlimit. That is why they are and remain disputed, because the intermediate number does not settle them. But neither can excess, unlimit, replace their number. Number and the good exceed each other in general circulation.

The originating question in *Philebus* concerns the numbers of pleasure. "Has it different kinds, or has it not, and if it has, how many are there and what are they like? And exactly the same question arises with regard to intelligence?" (Plato, *Philebus,* 19b). We may hear it as a repetition of the question of sexual difference. How many kinds of *jouissance* are there, and how many forms of knowledge (that we suppose to know)? What has knowledge to do with numbers of kinds, and what with heterogeneity?

Yet neither pleasure nor intelligence is the good, as Socrates remembers as if in a dream. "I remember a theory that I heard long ago—I may have dreamed it—about pleasure and intelligence, to the effect that neither of them is the good, but that it is something else, different from either and better than both" (Plato, *Philebus,* 20bc). This is the major theme of *Philebus:* the triangle of pleasure, knowledge, and the good. At the very end of the dialogue, Socrates returns obliquely to the theme of number.

> What I wanted to discover at present, my dear Protarchus, was not which art or which form of knowledge is superior to all others in respect of being the greatest or the best or the most serviceable, but which devotes its attention to precision, exactness, and the fullest truth, though it may be small and of small profit—that is what we are looking for at this moment. (Plato, *Philebus,* 58bc)

This precise and exact knowledge, of intermediate numbers and measure, is *technē,* described here on the way to unlimit as it is described in *Phaedrus* as lacking *erōs,* madness and life. I understand *technē* as representation, or rather, understand representation and judgment to fall between *poiēsis* and *technē*. Representation bears responsibility for order so that goods can circulate in restricted economies, doing good work. Representation bears the burden of sacrifice. But it can undertake this burden only within general economy, the excessive circulation of goods and representations, disturbing the places of every kind in the earth. There is no escaping measure, even standing on the spine of the world (Plato, *Phaedrus,* 247c). But just as the good far surpasses pleasure and intelligence, living truth far surpasses exact science. This is what Socrates says, repeatedly.[39]

For like *Phaedrus, Philebus* circulates in the presence of two gods, one Aphrodite (Plato, *Philebus,* 12bc), the other Theuth, again ascribed to Egypt, but the god from whom truth and writing flow (Plato, *Philebus,* 18b; *Phaedrus,* 274). The presence of such gods must make us cautious about giving way to measure, as if intermediate numbers cut off the circulation. And indeed, Socrates says, and I am pursuing his saying so, that we must pay attention to the intermediates and then let them pass away. Do they pass away in *Philebus?* Do they lead to the gods?

We read up to the point where Socrates gave us two examples of intermediates that we would classify with representation's unlimits: language and music. "What makes a man 'lettered' is knowing the number and the kinds of sounds." (Plato, *Philebus,* 17b) But being lettered has nothing to do with knowing truth and being able to tell it. "When you have grasped . . . the number and nature of the intervals . . . features that must, so we are told, be numerically determined and be called 'figures' and 'measures,' . . . only then, when you have grasped all this, have you gained real understanding" (Plato, *Philebus,* 17e). Yet you might know nothing whatever about composing or performing music. Ion's divine power and Socrates' divine Muses remain our exemplars.

Yet Socrates tells us explicitly how he understands the saying of the gods.

> When you have got your "one," you remember, whatever it may be, you must not immediately turn your eyes to the unlimited, but to a number; now the same applies when it is the unlimited that you are compelled to start with. You must not immediately turn your eyes to the one, but must discern this or that number embracing the multitude, whatever it may be; reaching the one must be the last step of all. (Plato, *Philebus,* 18b)

Reaching the one and the many, returning to limit and unlimit, must be the last step of all. The intermediate number, read as measure, is not the last step, must remain in circulation.

Socrates' immediately following example, alluding to Theuth, repeats this point obliquely. For it is because Theuth

> realized that none of us could ever get to know one of the collection all by itself, in isolation from all the rest, that he conceived of "letter" as a kind of bond of unity, uniting as it were all these sounds into one, and so he gave utterance to the expression "art of letters," implying that there was one art that dealt with the sounds. (Plato, *Philebus,* 18d)

Yet Theuth does not return to the many, to the unlimit. Perhaps for that reason, Philebus says, "I still feel the same dissatisfaction about what has been said as I did a while ago" (Plato, *Philebus,* 18d). And Socrates repeats the point of the return. "Then what the foregoing discourse requires of us is just this, to show how each of them [intelligence or pleasure, the two of them] is both one and many, and how—mind you, we are not to take the unlimited variety straightaway—each possesses a certain number before the unlimited variety is reached" (Plato, *Philebus,* 18e).

The method Socrates undertakes with Philebus and Protarchus is one of classification, the method described in *Sophist* and *Phaedrus,* associated by Foucault with classical representation. I am thinking of this as intermediate, and associate the intermediate number with *technē,* measured by the number two. Most of the dialogue concerns pure knowledge and pure pleasure, each alone, neither of which is good by itself, leading to their mixture, told in the language of *technē*. Socrates himself here and there speaks in a different voice. "I remember a theory that I heard long ago—I may have dreamed it—about pleasure and intelligence, to the effect that neither of them is the good, but that it is something else, different from either and better than both" (Plato, *Philebus,* 20bc). What if we took "better than both" in an extreme way? What if the good that is better than both remains unnamed in this dialogue, which has measure for its concern, the intermediate number? Socrates also speaks of "*my* reason," or *our* reason, compared with "the true, divine reason which . . . is in rather a different position" (Plato, *Philebus,* 22c). Could this divine reason and good belong to an unlimit far beyond any measure of ours in this dialogue?

For the good echoes an unlimit beyond measure while the only unlimit of which Socrates speaks is measured. "And in point of fact 'more' and 'less' are always, we may assert, found in 'hotter' and 'colder.' . . . Our argument then demonstrates that this pair is always without bounds, and being boundless means, I take it, that they must be absolutely unlimited" (Plato, *Philebus,* 24b). In what may be read as ironic reversal, he asks "whether we can accept what I shall say as a mark of the nature of the unlimited" (Plato, *Philebus,* 24e). We may consider once more that we should not accept it, that the movement to the divine, to the good, to *erōs* and *mania,* all displace *technē.* The more and less belong to measure. There is an infinite in measure. This infinite is neither the one nor the many. Multiple infinites haunt measure and representation.

It is essential that we pause here, at rest, to praise the number two, and three, to praise order, representation, and measure. That we should pass from intermediate numbers to the one and unlimit does not mean that we can set representation's measures aside. To the contrary, beauty and truth require representation, require its intermediation. "[I]t is here that we find the source of fair weather and all other beautiful things, namely in a mixture of the unlimited with that which has limit" (Plato, *Philebus,* 26b). But there remains the passing away, passing from beauty and truth and law and the good to . . . the good, to divine reason, to "the most perfect of all things" (Plato, *Philebus,* 20d). There remains the intermediary movement, between restricted and general economy.

Because the only unlimit *Philebus* explicitly acknowledges belongs to measure, we may imagine that the good as unlimit remains present only obliquely, in the gods and in what remains unspoken. I allude to Aphrodite and Theuth, to a certain incompleteness in each that makes it impossible for either to compose unlimit, any more than more and less, hot and cold. An infinite number is no more unlimit than two, or three, or very hot. But the good, and truth, and beauty, all disputed, in what can we find their measures? And concerning pleasure herself, Aphrodite's goddess, can we count the kinds and degrees of pleasure? "Has it different kinds, or has it not, and if it has, how many are there and what are they like?" (Plato, *Philebus,* 19b). Have order, representation, and measure different kinds, and if so, how many are there and what are they like?

Reminding ourselves where we are, we remember *jouissance.*

Does sexual difference lead us to think of *jouissance* beyond any limit, beyond counting, bringing us to Aphrodite's *jouissance?* May we ask how many kinds of *jouissance* there are and what they are like? And what of knowledge, including the other that I suppose to know. Can we imagine that knowledge, truth, and reason, in their divine forms, compose a more and less? Or do we find that Theuth's greatest gift, and transgression, his most misleading achievement, is to turn language's and sound's unlimit—representation's unlimit—into a more and less. For what we may say in language exceeds any more and always exceeds any less. And what we may echo in music exceeds any bounds but especially exceeds the numbers of notes.

What, in *Philebus,* is "the last step of all," where we return to the one and the multitude? If neither reason nor pleasure is the good, is the good the two together, mixed, except under measure? Or is the good something that takes us away from measure? Is the universe a "sum of things" under measure or, "governed by reason and a wondrous regulating intelligence" (Plato, *Philebus,* 28e), unlimitable by measure? If pain and pleasure admit of more and less and are in that sense limited (Plato, *Philebus,* 41d), are truth, reason, beauty, and the good also limited? All these questions suggest that truth, reason, beauty, and the good, the disputed terms, offer another unlimit, take us from measure's more and less to something unlimited in a different way, something more Dionysian, in the circulation of goods and representations. But it is by no means clear that *Philebus* gives us this unlimited.

Except obliquely. For Socrates describes one of his most important ideas in relation to measure.

> If anyone does not know himself, must it not be in one of three ways? . . .
>
> First, in respect of wealth, he may think himself richer than his property makes him. . . .
>
> But there are even more who think themselves taller and more handsome and physically finer in general than they really and truly are. . . .
>
> But far the greatest number are mistaken as regards the third class of things, namely possessions of the soul. They think themselves superior in virtue, when they are not. (Plato, *Philebus,* 48de)

Can we imagine that this list relates the good for which Socrates gave up his life? Wealth and physical appearance are measurable, possess magnitudes in their nature, a more and a less. Virtue seems different, yet repeatedly, Socrates' compatriots think that the good can be measured, is a possession. The three forms of self-knowledge (or its absence) here are all described under measure. That, perhaps, more than their absence, presents us with their deficiencies. Something similar appears in *Phaedrus* on good writing, which after having been shown to be dead under *technē* is subjected again to *technē*'s rules.

But Socrates virtually says this, in *Philebus,* speaking of being and becoming. "Now I hold that while it is with a view to something coming into being that anyone provides himself with medicine, or tools of any kind, or any sort of material, the becoming always takes place with a view to the being of this or that, so that becoming in general takes place with a view to being in general" (Plato, *Philebus,* 54c). Let us think of the becoming of tools and materials as circulation in time under *technē*'s measures. Goods circulate under measure, through representations, and that is the task of *Philebus:* to present measure's intermediate numbers by describing their circulation. We may hear this as restricted economy. But "becoming in general" may not be *technē,* may not repeat measure even as it demands it, may be closer to *poiēsis* and general economy than *technē.* Moreover, Socrates tells us that "becoming in general" (the circulation of goods, works, and representations) takes place only in relation to being in general, to general economy. The latter has no measure, affords no measure, knows no numbers, belongs to unlimit. And the one. And two.

For the number two returns in *Philebus* in a striking way.

> If, for instance, from any craft you subtract the element of numbering, measuring, and weighing, the remainder will be almost negligible. (Plato, *Philebus,* 55de)

> For after doing so, what you would have left would be guesswork and the exercise of your senses on a basis of experience and rule of thumb. . . . (Plato, *Philebus,* 56)

The examples are music—"not by measurement but by lucky shots of a practiced finger" (Plato, *Philebus,* 56a)—contrasted with building—by "considerable use of measures and instruments, and the remarkable exactness thus attained makes it more scientific than most sorts of knowledge" (Plato, *Philebus,* 56b). This distinction divides the arts of production into two, divides the circulation of works and representations into two. "Let us then divide the arts and crafts so called into two classes, those akin to music in their activities and those akin to carpentry, the two classes being marked by a lesser and a greater degree of exactness, respectively" (Plato, *Philebus,* 56c). We may read this as defining the fork in the road taken by our Western tradition a millennium later, giving all truth and art over to science, to exactness—though we may hesitate at praising carpentry. Or we may read it as distinguishing art by inspiration from art by measure, *poiēsis* from *technē,* all within the work of representation. We may ask ourselves, within this pair, which of the two we would choose.

Or should we conclude that the two gives way under the question of the good, resists exclusion, leading to an enigmatic union under the sign of Aphrodite, unlimited love? For we cannot separate *poiēsis* from *technē,* bringing being forth out of nonbeing from bringing forth according to measure. We cannot separate representation into its poles, order from disorder: it continues to circulate as excessive, intermediary. We bring forth being from nonbeing, limit into unlimit, by intermediate numbers, by intermediaries. But we do not remain, or *rest,* with the intermediate, but after we have disclosed the number, we remember *poiēsis.* On this reading, the number two works in two different ways, so closely related that we cannot divide them from each other. One two belongs to *technē,* measures and cuts, separates the one from the other, imposing the good as a standard against which the other fails. The other two belongs to unlimit, to *poiēsis,* cannot cut or measure, or divide, but restores the good as knowing no standard, redeeming the failures of every standard. These two inseparable twos, belonging together, express the work of representation.

How do we know that Socrates has such a dyad in mind when he speaks at such length of exactness and precision? He tells us, we have seen, by making another cut, this time against the primacy of exactness. The arts of exactness and precision may not be the good, may not be the best.[40] Nietzsche asks the question before us in extreme form. For here and in *Phaedrus,* Plato has Socrates pursue the properties of a scientific or rational art, under *technē,* while he wonders at, even denies, the possibility that such an art may be the good, the best of which we or the world are capable. *Technē,* we may say, may be the best when we are concerned with "what is coming into being, or will come, or has come" (Plato, *Philebus,* 59a). In time, caught up in becoming, we cannot avoid, do not wish to avoid, may have nothing better instrumentally than *technē*. But *technē*'s virtue is inseparable from something that exceeds it. I identify it with the good. The number two passes away into being, nature, the earth, passes into the rests of the earth to do the work of the good.

This gives us a different reading of the excessiveness of the good, which "differs from everything else in a certain respect. . . . A creature that possesses it permanently, completely, and absolutely, has never any need of anything else; its satisfaction is perfect" (Plato, *Philebus,* 60c). We may take the circulation of goods under limits to compose restricted economy. The good, however, exceeds the movements and disruptions of time, circulates in general economy through judgments and representations. Here the number two again divides into two, the one into the restricted economy of *technē,* the other into the general economy of the good. Sexual difference, gender, give us the number two circulating in both of these economies, give us ethical difference.

With this understanding that the general economy of the good circulates in *Philebus* at or beyond its limits, while the dialogue is written under *technē,* we may understand a figure toward the dialogue's close. For after all this talk about the best forms of knowledge and truth under *technē,* of representation, we are asked to resist remaining under divine knowledge, resting with the gods, and to let knowledge in its unlimited plenitude crash upon us.

> SOCRATES: Do you want me, may I ask, to give way like a porter jostled and knocked about by the crowd, to fling open the doors and allow every sort of knowledge to stream in, the inferior mingling with the pure?
> PROTARCHUS: I don't really see, Socrates, what harm one would suffer by taking all those other sorts of knowledge, providing one had the first sort.
> SOCRATES: Then I am to allow the whole company to stream in and be gathered together in a splendid Homeric mingling of the waters? (Plato, *Philebus,* 62de)

This is a magnificent expression of passing from the intermediate number of forms of knowledge and different arts into a panoply of knowledges and representations, without limit and restriction, entirely overcoming measure.

Toward pleasure, we find a different story.

> But to mix with reason the pleasures that always go with folly and all other manner of evil would surely be the most senseless act for one who desired to see a mixture and fusion as fair and peaceable as might be, so that he might try to learn from it what the good is, in man and in the universe, and what form he should divine it to possess. (Plato, *Philebus,* 64)

Here the number two still works, but in a way unknown to measure, because we are not told, and cannot be told, exactly and with precision which are the pleasures that always go with folly and which are the pleasures that come with the stream of different knowledges. "We now stand upon the threshold of the good" (Plato, *Philebus,* 64c) where the unlimit of knowledge, truth, beauty, and the good meet pleasure. We stand upon the threshold of mucosity and pain between one good and another, intermediate and intermediary.

Yet on this threshold, do we cross? Socrates turns back from what seems to be the answer of the dialogue: that we understand the intermediate numbers only to let them pass away into nature's and being's unlimited plenitude, all the arts and crafts and sciences, all knowledges, of any kind, joining with those pleasures suitable to them, but avoiding pleasures of folly and evil. Socrates turns back to other intermediate numbers. "[I]f we cannot hunt down the good under a single form, let us secure it by the conjunction of three, beauty, proportion, and truth . . . " (Plato, *Philebus,* 65). We retreat from the inexhaustible and uncountable plenitude of representations and goods to three, then from three to five and more:

> Pleasure is not the first of all possessions, nor yet the second; rather, the first has been secured for everlasting tenure somewhere in the region of measure . . .
>
> And the second lies in the region of what is proportioned and beautiful, and what is perfect and satisfying and so forth . . .
>
> And if you accept what I divine, and put reason and intelligence third, you won't be very wide of the truth. . . .
>
> Nor again, if beside these three you put as fourth what we recognized as belonging to the soul itself, sciences and arts and what we called right opinions, inasmuch as these are more akin than pleasure to the good. . . .
>
> And as fifth, the pleasures which we recognized and discriminated as painless . . . (Plato, *Philebus,* 66a–c)

We stop at five, though we could go on, to unlimit, to mucosity and *jouissance.* But we found ourselves at unlimit and came back to measure. This suggests that as we found two forms of production of being from nonbeing, two forms of art, analogous to music and carpentry, distinguished as *poiēsis* is from *technē,* we find two measures. One belongs to unlimit, to *poiēsis* and the earth, containing within itself all (or any) knowledge, truth, or reality, close to the gods. The other belongs to *technē,* provides us with intermediate numbers, circulates excessively in intermediary figures, judgments and representations. We cannot have the good in time, in becoming, without intermediate numbers, but these are not the good, which demands that we pass from these numbers back to unlimit and the one. The intermediate numbers, with all judgments, are intermediaries.

This reading gives us an understanding of how the number two bears upon our understanding of sexual and ethical difference, explains why we cannot let the two of sexual difference disappear into a profusion of sexual identities, or no identities. It also explains how we may understand the *jouissance* of the woman, and more, including the *jouissance* of the animal, and more—all different joys and sufferings, sexual and otherwise, of billions upon billions of animals and women, and more, of unknown kinds of creatures and things. There cannot be one *jouissance,* one joy, or good, amid countless sufferings. If we are to think of women and animals suffering, we must think of them as suffering differently, as deprived and as depriving us of countless, unlimited *jouissances.*

In this way we finally resist the look of that good old God upon the *jouissance* of the one and only woman. We must suppose to know, within the inexhaustible divinity of the good, inexhaustible *jouissances.* All within the number two. Mine and yours, and the others. The other always gives rise to the number two. Humans and animals. Heterogeneity and monstrosity.

For *Philebus* ends, not with humans but with animals and the gods.

> no, not even if all the oxen and horses and every other animal that exists tell us so by their pursuit of pleasure. It is the animals on which the multitude rely, just as diviners rely on birds, when they decide that pleasures are of the first importance to our living a good life, and suppose that animals' desires are authoritative evidence, rather than those desires that are known to reasoned

> argument, divining the truth of this and that by the power of the Muse of philosophy. (Plato, *Philebus,* 67b)

The Muse of philosophy tells us to disregard animals, certainly not, among the multitude, to rely on animals. Yet could this philosophy belong again to a *technē* that divides humans from animals, human good from animal pleasure, while the good cannot? With the division of humans from animals once more, do we conclude our technical account of the good, to let it pass away into general circulation?

We remind ourselves that Aristotle, upon a premise that I read as expressing the plenitude of nature, of natural things, which populate and plenish the earth, from an insight concerning nature's unlimit and profusion, imposes an oppressive *technē* without expressing its intermediateness, without letting it pass away. For the Aristotle who tells us that "*nature is a source or cause of being moved and of being at rest in that to which it belongs primarily,* in virtue of itself" (Aristotle, *Physics,* 192b), the *physis* that moves from within itself toward itself, as compared with *technē,* which moves from without, also tells us that every thing in nature "has a nature," embodied in its form, "for a thing is more properly said to be what it is when it has attained its fulfilment than when it exists potentially" (Aristotle, *Physics,* 193b). Every thing in nature moves from within itself toward itself, in a plenitude and profusion, things moving, flowing, toward fulfillment, each thing with an end pertaining to its kind, each end blocking general circulation.

Here the intermediate idea rules, in the extreme (but not infrequently), the rule of one kind over another, men over women, rulers over slaves, Greeks over barbarians. The nature whose profusion passes away into unlimit displaces every place, unlimits every limit, occupies a world of places of sovereignty and rule, defined by ends and kinds, by what things are in nature, as what they are, a what of rule. "[T]o know a thing's nature is to know the reason why it is"; "the nature of the thing and the reason of the fact are identical" (Aristotle, *Posterior Analytics,* 90a). In greater and more specific detail, reminiscent of one side of *Philebus:*

> We must start by observing a set of similar—i.e. specifically identical—individuals, and consider what element they have in common. We must then apply the same process to another set of individuals which belong to one species and are generically but not specifically identical with the former set. When we have

> established what the common element is in all members of this second species, and likewise in members of further species, we should again consider whether the results established possess any identity, and persevere until we reach a single formula, since this will be the definition of the thing. (Aristotle, *Posterior Analytics,* 97b)

We begin with plenitude and heterogeneity, a profusion of things and kinds, bringing them under the rule of *technē,* under a formula that gives us their definition by nature, a taxonomy of things by nature as if without excess, though Aristotle certainly knows excess by nature.[41] He presents us with nature's heterogeneity joined with its order under the rule of homogeneity, a repeated rule of the same in which the kind, the genus and species, orders the profusion of nature under representation's sovereignty.[42] The represented order of things by nature gives us slavery and subjection.

For "[n]ature belongs to the class of things which act for the sake of something" (Aristotle, *Physics,* 198b). Aristotle rejects the possibility that "nature [might] work, not for the sake of something, nor because it is better so, but just as the sky rains, not in order to make the corn grow, but of necessity" (Aristotle, *Physics,* 198b). Nature's work, the work of things by nature, things of certain kinds, genera and species, is better so. Nature's order defines the good, taxonomically, where we have understood the good to circulate in general economy exceeding any taxonomy, any number. "If then, it is agreed that things are either the result of coincidence or for an end, and these cannot be the result of coincidence or spontaneity, it follows that they must be for an end" (Aristotle, *Physics,* 199a), an end under the rule of the good. "[T]hose things are natural which, by a continuous movement originated from an internal principle, arrive at some completion" (Aristotle, *Physics,* 199b). Or as he puts it in his *Metaphysics:*

> The essence of each thing is what it is said to be *propter se*. For being you is not being musical, since you are not by your very nature musical. What, then, you are by your very nature is your essence. (Aristotle, *Metaphysics,* p. 1029b)
>
> Nothing, then, which is not a species of a genus will have an *essence*—only species will have it, for these are thought to imply not merely that the subject participates in the attribute and has it

> as an affection, or has it by accident. . . . (Aristotle, *Metaphysics*, 1030a)

What something is is given by its essence, the kind it is represented as being. This leaves us with a certain view of individuals by nature, where they exceed their kind.[43] My concern with heterogeneity takes me in a different direction, not toward individuals as if they were ultimate, but toward the plenitude and excess of a nature filled with kinds whose relations are mobile, disorderly, fluid, excessive. Heterogeneity pertains to kinds. In this way, ethical difference belongs to kinds, to genera and species, is kindred difference. Nature circulates in a general economy of goods and representations as heterogeneity, as the otherness, the otherwise, of kinds. That is what I understand from sexual difference.

And it is what I understand from *Philebus,* which imposes intermediate numbers, taxonomies and dyads, but lets them pass away as intermediaries into nature's unlimit, profusion, into an inexhaustible panoply of animals and creatures and kinds. These animals and creatures and natural kinds, all the individuals and kinds in nature, impose upon us an endless, inexhaustible task, of plenishment in the earth.

"There is only a little left to be done, Socrates. I am sure you won't give up sooner than we do; so I will remind you of the tasks that remain" (Plato, *Philebus,* 67b). The task that remains, upon which we rest, is to move again from the intermediate number, where we found ourselves face to face with animals, to unlimit. Here, then, we know that there are unlimited numbers of animals upon the earth, more or less, unlimited kindred differences.

CHAPTER 6

Rest

I return in this rest to different echoes of ethical difference in the Western tradition expressing nature's general economy. If you wish to bypass further discussions of this tradition, in Whitehead, Dewey, Lyotard, and others, I take up nature's general economy in relation to animals and ecological feminism in chapters 7 and 8.

I have devoted a chapter to the measure of the intermediate number, especially to the number two of gender and other binary oppositions, circulating beyond limit. I have interpreted this circulation as a general economy surpassing the restricted economy of the number two, so that it, with other intermediate numbers, passes away. One, two, . . . many; the dyad moves between limit and unlimit. On this understanding, thought and practice do not pass *from* the number two, or any other measure, *to* unlimit, as if there were another pair, the intermediate and unlimit, limit and unlimit. Rather, unlimit circulates within and belongs to limit, the indefiniteness of the dyad, the intermediariness of the movement. The number two, as an intermediate number, is beyond number, intermediary between restricted and general economy. The measure of gender, the representation of binariness and opposition, is unlimited, displaced, intermediary.

If we follow this understanding that limit and unlimit are not alternatives, represent a dyad circulating together and apart, place and displacement, somewhere and elsewhere, then we do not think of unlimit as general economy, excess, as such, but of limit and unlimit together as excess and circulation. This may explain a somewhat different possibility within authority's excesses. For if authority rules only at and beyond the limit, then it is impossible to see how it does work. Yet power works as Power; authority works at and disrupts every site; gender holds men and women in its grip within its excesses. The displacement of place, elsewhere, still occupies this and that place. We do not escape from work to unlimit, from Apollo to Dionysus, but find each circulating in the other. No matter what we impose in Apollo's name, Dionysus, disorder's frenzy, rests within, composes the margins. Measure exceeds unlimit as its unlimit. Ethical difference repeats sexual difference and exceeds it as its unlimit.

We ask ourselves again how we wish to think of the number two, an intermediate, as unlimit. I have noted several possibilities, and will now consider others. One is heard in Peirce, where the dyad becomes a triad, proliferating into chance and creativity, unlimit.[1] Another can be heard throughout, pervading our entire discussion, echoing in Whitehead's understanding of evil, everywhere, dyadic reflections of general economy. The world is the general circulation of events exceeding any work, of goods and evils linked together. "The nature of evil is that the characters of things are mutually obstructive. Thus the depths of life require a process of selection" (Whitehead, *PR*, p. 340). This evil is the circulation of goods and events beyond any work. In this sense of evil, and in the ideality of each event, Whitehead comes as close to plenishment as any Western philosopher has, still lacking the dyad of gender. "There is not just one ideal 'order' which all actual entities should attain and fail to attain. In each case there is an ideal peculiar to each particular actual entity . . . " (Whitehead, *PR*, p. 84). This sense of the ideal—Whitehead calls it "Platonic" (Whitehead, *PR*, p. 84)—is cherishment; its work is plenishment. With this understanding, Whitehead's entire work is ethical, with every event acting face to face with others in the call of the good.[2]

Whitehead speaks, at the end of *Process and Reality,* of eight antitheses, each in the form of a dyad, each a cancellation of an opposition—into what? The two are God and the World. He describes the "and" as a "contrast":

> In each antithesis there is a shift of meaning which converts the opposition into a contrast.
>
> It is as true to say that God is permanent and the World fluent, as that the World is permanent and God is fluent.
>
> It is as true to say that God is one and the World many, as that the World is one and God many. . . .
>
> It is as true to say that God transcends the World, as that the World transcends God.
>
> It is as true to say that God creates the World, as that the World creates God. (Whitehead, *PR*, p. 348)

I have not listed all eight "antitheses": four will do, and two might have done. We can always make do with two.[3] Whitehead retraces

Plato's movement in Socrates' voice from one to many to the intermediate number, perhaps two, circulating back to one and many. It is as true to say that God is one and the World many as that the World is one and God many. God and the World are each one and many; God and the World are two, but a pair that, spoken, vanishes into one and many, into unlimit. And in this unlimit, the two rest. God and the world compose nature's general economy.

Whitehead describes the dyad, God and the World, as "the contrasted opposites in terms of which Creativity achieves its supreme task of transforming disjoined multiplicity with its diversities in opposition, into concrescent unity, with its diversities in contrast" (Whitehead, *PR,* p. 348). Contrast follows the idea in Coleridge, drawn from Schelling, of a multiplicity, still a multiplicity, become one. Coleridge calls it "beauty."[4] Contrast takes dyadic relations between one and many, unity and multiplicity, and from the dyads produces another one and another multiplicity, multiplicity upon multiplicity, in other words, unlimit, circulating beyond measure, all in the circulation of judgment and representation.

Sexual difference, man and woman; differences in kind, human and animal; subject–object differences; human–machine differences; differences in purity and blood: all are indefinite dyads, binary differences whose measures give way to unlimit, indefinite and unlimited dyads, composing nature's general economy, the circulation of inexhaustible and multiple kinds. How do we count the number of ways that divide subject and object, except as Levinas suggests, otherwise? How do we count the number of ways that divide human and machine, except by bewaring of the order and measure of representation, even as we cannot live without it? How do we count the number of ways that divide man and woman, pure and impure, except otherwise, cautiously, gingerly, heterogeneously, on the heels of unlimit, dancing with Dionysus? And how do we count the animals, except as Noah did, preparing them for slaughter?

I speak of two obliquely, again and again, opening the dyads' orchestration. Let us listen again to two, resisting its rule:

> This is the world in which I move uninvited, profane on a sacred land, neither me nor mine, but me nonetheless. The story began long ago . . .
>
> The story never stops beginning or ending. It appears headless and bottomless for it is built on differences. Its (in)finitude

> subverts every notion of completeness and its frame remains a non-totalizable one. (Trinh, *WNO*, pp. 1–2)

Listen to the repeated pairs that move through a discourse that would disperse them: I and world, beginning and ending, headless and bottomless, finite and (in)finite. Let us take the last, the (in)finite that subverts every notion of completeness (producing incompleteness?), whose frame resists totality (by demanding locality?). I do not wish to make too much of these dyads, certainly not to criticize a writer who writes delicately of the jeopardy in which she finds herself, multiply, in pairs. "We are therefore triply jeopardized: as a writer, as a woman, and as a woman of color" (Trinh, *WNO*, p. 28). This triple is a triple of kinds, dyads of exclusion: writer, or not; woman, not a man; woman of color, not uncolored. She names her writing, "in the feminine. And on a colored sky." (Trinh, *WNO*, p. 28). In the feminine, not the masculine. On a colored rather than on a pale white sky.

I write, for the moment, of two as the representation of exclusion, the cut that truth demands, and of two as face to face with the other. The one intermediate number we need to speak, to write, to think, told by the law of noncontradiction, is the number two. The number two holds us in its logical grip, as it becomes three, or four, or more. And it is important to keep in mind that two is not All, that two and three are not (in)finite. Or, in the provocation I am taking seriously, the two of (sexual, racial, blood, colored, rainbow) difference is a figure of inexhaustible excess. The hold of a restricted economy of dyads fades, dissolves, before the plenitude, multitude, of twos.

There are too many pairs to be of use. That, at least, is how I think we should read Trinh's pairs, telling a story of the earth, of long ago, where the earth adds two to two to two and more . . . But we have not succeeded in avoiding two, except in silence. And that is where I returned to Plato. But I have not finished my digression, Trinh's digressions, reflecting on the dyads of the Western tradition. For she offers two additional dyads disappearing into infinity. "As long as words of discourse serve to legitimate a discourse instead of delaying its authority to infinity, they are, to borrow an image from Audre Lorde, 'noteworthy only as *decorations*'" (Trinh, *WNO*, p. 101). The twin figures of delaying authority rather than letting it impose itself upon us and of refusing legitimation rather than authorizing its authority when we write and speak echo general circulation, bringing us to pause before the work that defines restricted economy. Work works, we say, and Bataille says, in restricted economy, where goods circulate beyond any work in general economy. Yet delaying to infinity, here, comes up in a figure of work. I am exploring the possibility instead, evident in some remarkable way, that this movement Plato describes in *Philebus*, of the one and many and two (with other intermediate numbers, three or more, delaying each to infinity, but not denying them), expresses general economy. Two does not name closure, binary exclusion, under measure, but names a delay, an intermediary, a rest, in circulation. Two is a decoration, displacing work.

Let us listen to another striking figure from Trinh:

> What is at stake is not only the hegemony of Western cultures, but also their identities as unified cultures. Third World dwells on diversity; so does First World. This is our strength and our misery. The West is painfully made to realize the existence of a Third World in the First World, and vice versa. The Master is bound to recognize that His Culture is not as homogeneous, as monolithic as He believed it to be. He discovers, with much reluctance, He is just an other among others. (Trinh, *WNO*, pp. 98–99)

The diversity, heterogeneity, exists in the Third World,[5] and in the First World, and in the two (or three, or more) together, painfully. Why painfully? Perhaps because it belongs to the dyad that includes *jouissance*. Strength and misery. Master and Other. The Master and His Culture are not One, but an other. The presence or displacement of others, of being among others, always others, in the plural, recalls and dissolves the dyad of master–slave, homogeneity–heterogeneity. The two passes away into the unlimit, where it always rested. But unlimit cannot be unlimit without measure, without two, or three, or other intermediates. The unlimit of unlimit, crucial for delaying its own authority to infinity, to its inexhaustibility, is the intermediate number, the indefinite, unlimited dyad. The intermediate number is a decoration, an ornament,[6] an intermediary, that makes all the difference to ethical difference, resisting its hegemony.

We have returned to ethical difference. We may hear it in another antinomy, Whitehead's extraordinary understanding of the relation between public and private.

> The theory of prehensions is founded upon the doctrine that there are no concrete facts which are merely public, or merely private. The distinction between publicity and privacy is a distinction of reason, and is not a distinction between mutually exclusive concrete facts. The sole concrete facts, in terms of which actualities can be analysed, are prehensions; and every prehension has its public side and its private side. (Whitehead, PR, p. 290)

Here without question is another indeterminate dyad, in close proximity with sexual difference, even as we may wish to resist outright identification. For men and women have always inhabited public and private places. What if we associate public places with "the masculine," private with "the feminine"? We have understood every place as elsewhere. On this understanding of place, close to Whitehead's, any place is located elsewhere, everywhere, but an everywhere that circulates the "re-" and "dis-" of place, not a place for All. The All is not a place, certainly not a Place, No Place. To be anywhere is to be somewhere else. Nature's univocity echoes throughout, from dyad to dyad.

Whitehead's view of actual entities' placement is in place and elsewhere. Each actual entity is somewhere and everywhere—but not "precisely" everywhere, or anywhere.[7] Somewhere and anywhere remain indefinite, to be determined, an excess of circulation that belongs to any and every place. Actual entities circulate, atoms of becoming. While they creatively and freely "preside over their own becoming," they are anything but self-sufficient, because they circulate among themselves, publicly and privately, circulate repeatedly in dyads.[8] The circulation of goods circulates the number two, or three, or another number, or many other numbers, all intermediates, limits, and unlimits.

Setting Whitehead aside for a moment, setting him in his place so that we may find his thought in other places, we may consider other dyadic figures of displacement in the circulation of intermediates beyond limits. Dewey, for example, speaks of means and ends, divides experience and nature into means and ends, two pairs of dyads, yet reunites them.

> "experience" is what James called a double-barrelled word [James, *ERE*, p. 10]. Like its congeners, life and history, it includes *what* men do and suffer, *what* they strive for, love, believe and endure, and also *how* men act and are acted upon, the ways

> in which they do and suffer, desire and enjoy, see, believe, imagine—in short, processes of *experiencing*. . . . It is "double-barrelled" in that it recognizes in its primary integrity no division between act and material, subject and object, but contains them both in an unanalyzed totality. (Dewey, *EN*, p. 8)

> experience is *of* as well as *in* nature. It is not experience which is experienced, but nature—stones, plants, animals, diseases, health, temperature, electricity, and so on. Things interacting in certain ways *are* experience; they are what is experienced. Linked in certain other ways with another natural object—the human organism—they are *how* things are experienced as well. Experience thus reaches down into nature; it has depth. It also has breadth and to an indefinitely elastic extent. It stretches. That stretch constitutes inference. (Dewey, *EN*, pp. 4a–5)

Dewey speaks of one dyad after another, experience and nature, what and how, means and ends, doing and suffering, act and material, subject and object; and with each dyad, the pair dissolves into a circulation that contains them both. Experience is a plenitude, a many, that stretches, that reaches into nature, which is also a plenitude that stretches and expands indefinitely. The key word for Dewey is "indefinitely." It matches James's "blooming, buzzing confusion." It unmeasures every measure.

Dewey does not let his one or many dissipate the dyad. Inference and representation stretch into nature along paths of intermediaries. Some intermediate pairs are neglected by Dewey: man and woman, human and animal, human and machine. I will come back to them, again and again. For if experience is what *men* do and suffer, love and endure, is this humanity undivided by sexual, species, or technical difference? Kindred difference may be something Dewey does not imagine or hear. For in what may be his most interesting development of the idea of experience as a term of excess and plenitude, he describes three levels of experience and context, undivided still by sexual or kindred difference. Ascribing his idea of context to the anthropologist Malinowski, Dewey says:

> Examination discloses three deepening levels or three expanding spheres of context. The narrowest and most superficial is that of the immediate scene, the competitive race. The next deeper and wider one is that of the culture of the people in question. The widest and deepest is found in recourse to the need of general

> understanding of the workings of human nature. (Dewey, *CT*, pp. 108–9)

The three—not a two but still an intermediate number—compose the moment, the people, and humanity. What of the dyad, man and woman? What of other dyads, man and animal or man and machine?

Postponing this concern for a moment, this concern with a human nature in which none of the intermediates divides humanity, we see an unmistakable concern for intermediaries in Dewey, twos or threes, or others. Experience offers itself, with nature, as a plenitude in which we are led along paths of meaning, relations of means and ends, to intermediate numbers.

But another theme echoes in Dewey, in the dyad that defines his major work and may define ours. For to the question of whether experience and nature are one or two, composing a circle, Dewey says the following:

> There is a circularity in the position taken regarding the connection of experience and nature. Upon one side, analysis and interpretation of nature is made dependent upon the conclusions of the natural sciences, especially upon biology, but upon a biology that is itself dependent upon physics and chemistry. . . .
>
> The other aspect of the circle is found in the fact that it is held that experience itself, even ordinary gross macroscopic experience, contains the materials and the processes and operations which, when they are rightly laid hold of and used, lead to the methods and conclusions of the natural sciences; namely, to the very conclusions that provide the means for forming a theory of experience. (Dewey, *NE*, pp. 246–47)

Experience and nature compose a dyad, as if each represented a restricted economy, this the human, that the natural. Yet they define a circle in which we find the natural sciences, as if they composed another general, excessive economy. Science, for Dewey, composes general economy, whereas its practitioners claim that science works in restricted economy. What general economy means here is that science's sovereignty explodes into the uselessness of any scientific rule.[9] It also means that experience and nature circulate in the general economy of representation.

Dewey says about this circling pair, experience and nature, "[t]hat this circle exists is not so much admitted as claimed. It is also claimed that the circle is not vicious; for instead of being logical it is existential and historic" (Dewey, *NE,* p. 247). Now being "logical" might on my reading belong to the general circulation of experience and nature, though we would have to add its excessiveness. But Dewey says, as explicitly as possible, that if we understand logic to be restricted to measure, the existential and historical exceed any standards, do not compose a pair, but fall apart into general circulation. Experience and nature do not belong to each other in an identity of two that is really one. Experience and nature are each a plenitude, a circulation of goods and things, of judgments and representations, excessively, another pair expressing general circulation.

In the dyad, then, Dewey finds a third, but without reconciliation, giving voice to nature's ethical difference.

> This theory [of means and ends] is actually a theory about nature. It involves attribution to nature of three defining characteristics. In the first place, it is implied that some natural events are endings whether enjoyed or obnoxious, which occur, apart from reflective choice and art, only casually, without control. In the second place, it implies that events, being events and not rigid and lumpy substances, are ongoing and hence as such unfinished, incomplete, indeterminate. Consequently they possess a possibility of being so managed and steered that ends may become fulfilments not just termini, conclusions not just closings. . . . In the third place, regulation of ongoing and incomplete processes in behalf of selected consequences, implies that there are orders of sequence and coexistence involved. . . . (Dewey, *EN,* p. 159)

Nature's indeterminatenesses unfold into the restricted economy of regulation and selection, the control of consequences, but compose general economy. Nature expresses the general economy in every restricted economy.

We find that general economy cannot be represented by one, or many, or two, or three, and so on, but is represented for us in the movement Socrates describes in *Philebus* in which the limit, the unlimit, the one, the many, and the intermediate numbers circulate madly among themselves to express the excessiveness of general economy. On this reading, the dyads of sexual–animal–technical difference belong to general economy.

To close this discussion, we may consider another figure of general circulation caught up in the number two. I am speaking of Lyotard's figure of "linking" [*enchaîner*], together with its neighbor, *le différend. Le Différend* repeats the chorus of the *intervalle* and *entre,* falling between; linking repeats the intermediary theme in judgment. Even here, we find another *entre,* between one *différend* and *Le Différend,* between a restricted and general economy of *aentres.*

> As distinguished from a litigation, a differend [*différend*] would be a case of conflict, between [*entre*] (at least) two parties, that cannot be equitably resolved for lack of a rule of judgment applicable to both arguments. (Lyotard, *DPD,* p. xi)

> The title of this book suggests (through the generic value of the definite article) that a universal rule of judgment between heterogeneous genres is lacking in general. (Lyotard, *DPD,* p. xi)

> By showing that the linking of one phrase onto another is problematic and that this problem is the problem of politics, to set up a philosophical politics apart from the politics of "intellectuals" and of politicians. To bear witness to the differend. (Lyotard, *DPD,* p. xiii)

The *Différend* (with its definite article) generically expresses the heterogeneity of genres, of *régimes* and rules, circulating in the endless movement of goods and judgments, without rules, endless betweens, *aentres* and *intervalles, différends.* Judgment, always circulating in the heterogeneous plural, circulates, as Irigaray and Kristeva suggest,[10] a musicality to the general economy of the circulation of judgments and goods, always the *Stabat Mater.* The circulation of judgments and goods composes, echoes, ethical difference. Lyotard calls it political, emphasizing the law. I emphasize the impossibility of the law—still law, together with its general impossibility—as ethical difference, the endless circulation of heterogeneities. I emphasize something Lyotard says, but does not dwell upon, something which is forgotten in English.

For he approaches this general economy of circulation in speaking of three things besides (that is, together with but on the side of) (*Le*|*les*) *différend*(*s*): linking, temporality, and economy. The obligation, the responsibility, to bear witness to *le différend* reflects in starkest terms Lyotard's understanding of the event in Heidegger, described by Lyotard as *Is it happening?* [*Arrive-t-il?*] This upsurgence of an event without a rule—circulating, upsurging, appearing—is the general economy of, first, time, then linking, always in the *entres* and *intervalles* of *différends.* Put another way, we find ourselves always circulating together with what cannot be said by rules, but what imposes responsibility for saying and bearing witness to what cannot be said, bearing witness to *le différend.* One *différend* after another. With a certain necessity (that we may find incongruous): "[f]or there to be no phrase is impossible, for there to be *And a phrase* is necessary. It is necessary to make linkage. This is not an obligation, a *Sollen* [an ought to], but a necessity, a *Müssen* [a must]. To link is necessary, but how to link is not" (Lyotard, *DPD,* p. 66). We may think of linking as circulation of goods and judgments without rules, in heterogeneity. And surely, without question (and with a certain necessity), linking contains, enfolds, the number two. Yet as we say that to link is to join, to bring together two, we know that two frequently makes three, and more.

This necessity without necessity, which disappears from two to three to four and more, withstands the movement from two to infinity (and unlimit cannot be counted to infinity, cannot be counted at all), because the movement from two or any other intermediate number to unlimit, back to limit, to one, is no movement, is no necessity. How are we to know the necessity of *enchaîner* as a *Sollen* but not a *Müssen? Loi* but not *droit,* both law? How are we to know the necessity of time's refusal to be chained, except without necessity? Put another way, can we resist the necessity of the number two, or three, of any rule or measure, without sending it away without necessity? The movement from the intermediate number to unlimit resists necessity again and again. That would appear to be the force of *le différend.* And the force of time. "There is no moral diachrony. Pure ethical time is the now of the phrase which, with one stroke, presents the obligation and the obligated one (and perhaps the obligating one, the *I am able to*), each in their own way" (Lyotard, *DPD,* p. 126).

The narrative of diachrony and heterogeneity is told in the now, the *entre* of the event between, the interval, the rest, between the obligation and the obligated (a two that might pass into three, through the intermediation of the obligator). But how, in this moment of rest, do we know heterogeneity except as an unending circulation of judgments and goods? Linking is circulation, from two to three to general economy, told in a voice without rules—nature's song. *La réalité comporte le différend.*[11] Nature, reality, is made up of *différends,* of multiple and heterogeneous kinds with their representations. The *entre* is no place of a pure ethical time, but a mobile circulation in general economy. Time represents the flow of circulation as if by a certain necessity, though every effort, every work, seeks to hold it up. The endless flow of time, of *enchaîner,* goes on by a certain necessity from two to some other intermediate number to . . . rest.

> 248. Money can make advances in time because it is stocked-up time. (Lyotard, *DPD,* p. 176)

> 253. The economic genre's hegemony over the others can certainly put on the garb of an emancipatory philosophy of history. More wealth, more security, more adventure, etc., there's our answer to the canonical phrase of political ethics: *What ought we to be?* This ethical question is not asked, however, in the economic genre. In it, you don't gain (you don't grab onto the stakes) because you listened to the obligation and welcomed it, but because you've gained some time and are able to gain even more. Thus, the economic genre of capital in no way requires the deliberative political concatenation, which admits the heterogeneity of genres of discourse. To the contrary, it requires the suppression of that heterogeneity. (Lyotard, *DPD,* p. 178)

With this theme of stocking time, holding it up in its intermediate state, we return to the opening theme of our discussion (minus a note to be recalled momentarily): the circulation of goods in an exchange economy. For the economic genre, defined as stocking up time under the *régime* of money, twice fails to know the event, the *arrive-t-il,* in the *entres* of the endless circulation of goods, always in rest, never at rest, and in the necessity of the link, of time. "The differend is reborn from the very resolution of supposed litigations. It summons humans to situate themselves in unknown phrase universes, even if they don't have the feeling that something has to be phrased. (For this is a necessity and not an obligation.) The *Is it happening?* is invincible to every will to gain time" (Lyotard, *DPD,* p. 181). The general circulation of judgments and goods is unmasterable by any restricted economy. Even here, where the *Is it happening?* destroys every two, every expression comes back to two: *Sollen* and *Müssen;* necessity and obligation; stocking and releasing time.

We began this discussion with the social contract, the exchange of women. Culture, politics, ethics, all circulate and exchange women among the goods and judgments staked against . . . , according to Lyotard, the necessity of time. Exchange assaults a heterogeneity that cannot be destroyed, that resists every attempt to gain time. The economic genre (restricted not general economy) engages in exchange and substitution to hoard, stock up, reserve time against its heterogeneous movement, against the ethical|political. "With capital, there is no longer a time for exchange. Exchange is the exchange of time, the exchange in the least possible time ("real" time) for the greatest possible time ("abstract" or lost time). Anything at all may be exchanged, on the condition that the time contained by the referent and the time required for the exchange are countable" (Lyotard, *DPD,* p. 177). Exchange, substitution, circulate in restricted economy based on measure, on the counting of time.

The movement of this or any economy, because it circulates judgments and goods, imposes a debt. Yet in general economy, the debt circulates endlessly along with the goods, circulates within judgment and judgment's judgment. This gives us a criterion, if we need one. "In an exchange, the debt must be canceled, and quickly. In a narrative, it must be recognized, honored, and deferred. In a deliberation, it must be questioned, and therefore also deferred" (Lyotard, *DPD,* p. 178). Ethical difference circulates along with goods and judgments in a debt beyond time, beyond satisfaction, but not beyond a restitution that circulates together with it promoting one deferral after another. Yet deferral imposes another injustice, another debt, if we are speaking of victims and oppression. We must end oppression and save the victims as quickly as we can, throwing us into exchange. If we are to redeem oppression, we must work in restricted economy. Women's freedom cannot wait. Yet redemption belongs to general economy.

All these "musts" haunt us, as if every one of them imposes another victimization. The *Is it happening?* is invincible to every will to gain time. What if it were not invincible, by a certain necessity, but rather by a certain resistance? "Are you prejudging the *Is it happening?*" (Lyotard, *DPD,* p. 179). What if we could not avoid prejudging when we judge, prejudging within the circulation of judgments? What if the circulation of judgment always imposed injustice's debt?

This returns us to the note passed over as I attempted to trace in Lyotard the themes of this chapter, linking between, *entre* and *intervalle,* time and circulation, all dyads, intermediate numbers, intermediary judgments that circulate from two to three to . . . Yet the dyad with which we began scarcely enters into the goods and judgments circulating around time and the *arrive-t-il?* except in the play of death. The dyad is the exchange of women, sexual difference, perhaps the most frequently repeated, overwhelming attempt to gain time. Women are exchanged in the service of death, though men call it life. Death here, something that happens to one, turns into a dyad of gender. This may be due to biology, though perhaps, just perhaps, a one-celled organism may not die, nor a multiple-celled society of organisms, whereas the individual members do. What of the possibility that the dyad of sexual difference represents the general economy of death?

Lyotard's movement around *le différend,* the *arrive-t-il?,* and the gaining or stocking of time repeats Heidegger's view of the *Gestell* as *Bestand* [standing reserve]. In neither do we recognize the dyad of sexual difference, not even of love, though Lyotard calls "the jews" to our attention as Europe's (and Heidegger's) Forgotten. And what if the name of the Forgotten always were a forgetting, forgetting another dyad, here of gender?

For the exchange and circulation of women, if it stocks up a time against death that cannot be stored, does so by circulating them more quickly, expeditiously, with as little obstruction as possible. Women are to be available freely of their own volition, something modern technology at its very best (so far) cannot bring about in machines. We want our machines to love us, to gain their *jouissances* at our service, just like women are expected to do. Women's *jouissance* calls us to know something we do not want to know. We do not want to know the *jouissances* of animals.

Against the stocking up of time, the stuffing of time into the stocking-up of *régime* and genre, the exchange of women, the circulation of women, together with animals and machines and all the goods of the earth, seems to know no restrictions. The circulation of women knows countless oppressions, but may know no restrictions. This, it seems, is the message of the invincibility of time, that as we impose one restriction after another on sex, we find women, lacking their place, disturbing one place after another. Not least, indeed, as Irigaray suggests, because in the absence of their place, women disturb every place, because there cannot be a place for Man without Woman.

The exchange of women, upon which society draws its rules of mastery, is not restricted but general economy. The dyad of gender echoes every binary, every opposition, every intimacy, and every linking. The place of gender is everywhere even where we refuse heterosexuality. Women homosexuals are not men homosexuals; lesbians are not women, are not gays, are not men, are . . . supposed to know something else. The place of women is nowhere and elsewhere, as is the place of men, who may not know it (but then, women may not know it). The general economy of men and women is a dyad filled with the infinite, God, unlimit. The general economy of men and women, engendered and embodied, is general economy, the rests of the earth, together with machines and animals and plants and things, all caught up in twos, all exceeding their intermediate numbers.

This discussion concerns the ways in which the number two expresses general economy, the rests of the earth, as nothing else can (except some other number), not even Dionysus, unlimit (and he is two with Apollo). We think in two (or three) because we think, not because of the law of noncontradiction, which is a certain way of taking up the number two.[12] The profusion and proliferation, the fragmentation and disruption, of the earth, at rest, break down, halt, trace the remains in musical silence, of twos: oompah, oompah; one oompahpah followed by another oompahpah. Two and two make three, or four, or more. Heterogeneity is unmeasured, but not because there is no measure of two.

This discussion resists the possibility of escaping from a dyadic logic to a multivalued logic, a logic of profusion and excess, another mastery of judgment. For such a logic repeats the number two as it multiplies it. Logic belongs to two, logical and illogical, rational and irrational, proper and improper, true and false, and . . . Two remains within the and . . . Logic belongs to measure.

Ethical difference emerges from the hold of measure on us, on the earth, resting on the earth in every attempt to throw the intermediate number away and to pass into the harmony of the spheres.

Let us briefly return to Whitehead's general circulation, understood as the general economy of ethical difference. Such an understanding has two sides, one we have seen—"an ideal peculiar to each particular actual entity" (Whitehead, *PR*, p. 84), which I interpret as pertaining to whatever circulates, whether they be individuals, events, and kinds. To circulate is to possess an ideal, a good, not in the sense of a perfection against which the event falls short, but in a sense close to Spinoza's. To be is to be an ideal and to strive to circulate as an ideal. The circulation of events is a circulation of goods in an excessive and inexhaustible plenitude. This circulation is ethical difference, belongs to nature, to humanity, and to the number two, including mastery and opposition. This same circulation is a circulation of evils. For these ideals cannot all coexist, and mutual obstruction is evil. This pair, this dyad, of good and evil, is a coexistence, not an opposition, though in many places it works in opposition.

We recall what Dewey says about the relation between experience and knowledge, given a somewhat different meaning in the present context. "For things are objects to be treated, used, acted upon and with, enjoyed and endured, even more than things to be known. They are things *had* before they are things cognized" (Dewey, *EN,* p. 21). One reading is that Dewey understands knowledge to emerge from practical and instrumental relations, that these relations provide the measure of knowledge. On the understanding that experience and nature circulate in general economies, disturbed as well as restored by each other, then knowledge here, including ours and Dewey's knowledge, all philosophic knowledge including knowledge of general economy, all knowledge comes too late and belongs to restricted economies: restricted, technical, instrumental circulations of things circulating wildly, speedily, madly, beyond any calculation and measure. The things that circulate, in experience and in nature, include rocks and stones, atoms and molecules, plants and animals, human beings and their instruments, numbers and measures, including the number two, and three, and other intermediate numbers.

Numbers and instruments, the representations that do *technē*'s work, do not cease to circulate madly in general economy when they are taken into restrictive economies. That is what Dewey says, and it is what Lyotard may mean by the invincibility of the question. The triumph of *technē* does not violate the general circulation, though it may disturb it. Irigaray says something similar of Woman, who in having no place, disturbs the places that she is for man, disturbs every place. Returning to the echoes of place and rest, we note that neither nature nor humanity nor man nor woman nor the number two, under *technē* or not, under *poiēsis,* in nature, none of these can find a place that is not a place of rest, of remains and traces and disturbances, circulating excessively, in place. Each of these and the others circulate in their places, somewhere and everywhere, where the latter is no place, the place where woman is not, everywhere and nowhere. No place circulates in every place that *technē* imposes its hold, and everywhere else.

The sense that things, each thing among the others, every thing including intermediates and techniques and instruments and human beings and animals, including men and women among the countless other pairs, circulate excessively, inexhaustibly, is cherishment. Cherishment is the cacophony of inexhaustibility, the music of the spheres among countless other spheres. We have heard it as the rests of the earth, listened to its song. This song I understand as ethical, the sense that each thing, every thing and kind, is inexhaustible, precious in its general circulation beyond all circulations. But the circulation as a whole offers no ideal. I do not take Leibniz's step toward the goodness of the total circulation, but find that ethical difference knows a heterogeneity and general circulation that do not stop with God. When Dewey says that things are had before they are known, the two ordinary words given extraordinary force here are "had" and "before." I understand the having not as ours, our experience, belonging to human beings, because no line of exclusion can be drawn between experience and nature and because experience does not belong to us, to anyone, is not owned (Dewey, *EN*, pp. 20, 234–35). The having that is "before" is the circulation of goods, of things and judgments. Judgments circulate in practical and aesthetic and other affairs, in desire and will and joy, before they are known. Knowledge, as the general circulation of judgment, is always after, always emerges from a wider general circulation. This wider, wilder circulation in which, enfolded, judgments emerge, thereafter to circulate excessively, is the "before." This "before" is excess. The excess of excess, as the before of before (or limit of limit), is the general circulation in which we find ourselves under every restricted economy, every instrumentality, surrounded by *technē*.

General circulations of goods compose ethical difference as cherishment. The impossibility of a total ideal within this heterogeneous circulation is sacrifice. Plenishment takes this circulation of precious things, of joy and pain and care and love, as the overarching narrative of place and displacement, another dyad. And in this pair, of place|unplace, we find the emergence of restricted economies. Things (and we) work in places in a certain disturbance. Restricted economy is not a port of safety surrounded by disturbance, but is endless disturbance, injustice's debt to heterogeneity.

I will now explore other kinds of heterogeneity: first, in chapter 7 with its rest, the general economy of nature's plenitude, our relations to animals and other natural kinds; then, in chapter 9 and rest, the erotic side of heterogeneity, expressed in sexual difference, obscured in the mark of gender: face to face with the other in proximity; leading to witches in chapters 11 and 12.

CHAPTER 7

Carnaval

Irigaray asks Levinas, "is there otherness outside of sexual difference?" (Irigaray, *QEL*, p. 178). She answers:

> The function of the other sex as an alterity irreducible to myself eludes Levinas for at least two reasons:
>
> He knows nothing of communion in pleasure. . . .
>
> . . . he substitutes the son for the feminine. (Irigaray, *QEL*, pp. 180–81)

I ask, does the heterogeneity of the others—animals, insects, rocks, sky, mud, "jews," et cetera et cetera, nature's plenitude—as alterities irreducible to myself and the others elude Levinas and Irigaray, perhaps in different ways, because they know nothing of communion in pleasure with nature, with animals and plants? Because they substitute the human for the Other, continue to speak in a human sacrificial voice? This (ecological feminist) question resonates somewhere between the dyad of sexual difference and nature's plenitude, inexhaustible other dyads, other heterogeneities. I understand difference to inhabit dyads that neither disappear into the All or One without a trace, into nature's plenitude, nor remain in domination and exclusion. I hope to listen to the rests of nature's voice.

If "the [male or heterosexual] society we know, our own culture, is based upon the exchange of women," (Irigaray, *WM*, p. 170)[1] then without a doubt, far more pervasively, the (human) society we know is based upon the exchange and circulation of animals. Heterosexual society would collapse, would cease to reproduce itself, to have a future, if women no longer participated in reproductive exchange. But human society would collapse on the spot, dissipate into dust, if all products made from nonhuman animals were abolished. Every space of human social life is filled with animal products. Every cranny of human life is occupied by animals, microorganisms and insects—who live where human beings live and carry on human work, planned and unplanned—and with products made from animals who are designed to carry on human work.

We have entered the place, listened to the voice, where the face-to-face dyad of ethical responsibility opens to irreducible alterity. On the one hand, the dyad of the ethical appears in Levinas beyond all others in the resonances of the one for the other, a beyond that takes us to unlimit. "That the glory of the Infinite is glorified only by the signification of the-one-for-the-other, as sincerity,[2] that in my sincerity the Infinite passes the finite, that the Infinite comes to pass there, is what makes the plot *[intrigue]* of ethics primary, and what makes language irreducible to an act among acts" (Levinas, *OB,* p. 150; *AÉ,* p. 235). The dyad of the ethical appears in an affair of love *[intrigue]*, heterogeneously, a dyad in which the infinite comes to pass. In Levinas, the ethical demands a dyad in which the saying *[dire],* the voice, of the infinite resounds, the two passing away into unlimit, one and many.

On the other hand, the two becomes three, was always three: the supreme and dangerous truth of the dialectic, which in its movement from two to three seems to abandon the movement to unlimit, except obliquely, obscure within the Absolute. So Levinas can say that before the third party, face to face with another neighbor,[3] the dyad of the one for the other explodes into another unlimit beyond the infinite. "In the proximity of the other, all the others than the other obsess me, and already this obsession cries out for justice, demands measure and knowing, is consciousness" (Levinas, *OB,* p. 158). To what unlimit, how far, how long (O Lord), does our obsession with all the others take us? All! In what intermediary voices may we sing of all the others? You and I may hope that Levinas pursues our inexhaustible movement from proximity to the rests of the earth, yet we recognize the obstacle that remains in subjectivity. For he names the other as brother *[frère]* to men *[hommes],* not women, giving force to Irigaray's reservations.[4]

And when he continues within a movement that we hope to take us from the one for the other to the plenitude of nature, to all the others that obsess me in the other, in a beautiful, haunting movement, Levinas returns to the masculine, if in the neuter, and to the precedence of male bonds before any other kind, as if disinterestedness might first be masculine.

> All the others that obsess me in the other do not affect me as examples of the same genus united with my neighbor by resemblance or common nature, individuations of the human race, or chips of the same block. . . . The others concern me from the first. Here fraternity precedes the commonness of a genus. My relationship with the other as neighbor gives meaning to my relations with all the others. All human relations as human proceed from disinterestedness. (Levinas, *OB,* p. 159)

We recognize this Kantian movement, this traditional movement in a thought that would echo in an immemorial voice, of the disinterestedness, the unsituatedness, of ethics, of our obligations and concerns, an unsituatedness that is always already situated as male, in fraternity. Yet we may hesitate at the abandonment of place, as if we could be ethical without knowing our places, somewhere and elsewhere. I hesitate at an otherwise that cannot rest in its place.

We recall the identity and reciprocity of substitution. "In proximity the other obsesses me according to the absolute asymmetry of signification, of the-one-for-the-other: I substitute myself for him, whereas no one can replace me, and the substitution of the one for the other does not signify the substitution of the other for the one" (Levinas, *OB,* p. 158). In a movement that would go from the dyad of the one for the other to the others without resemblance or commonality, the other as neighbor is both masculine and human, representing neutrality. Irigaray addresses this neutered masculinity of humanity when she says that she will never be in the place of a man nor a man able to replace her. There can be no substitution or replacement between men and women, one and the other, face to face, but there can be responsibility and love. Caught up in the subjectivity of the one, the absolute and irreducible heterogeneity of the other that would explode into others beyond others, already present in any love for the other, comes up short into substitution and fraternity, repeating the hold of the human on ethics, however disinterestedly, especially disinterestedly.

Even in Levinas, then, who gives us an ethics of heterogeneity, of responsibility face to face with an other who is not I and toward whom I may bear no resemblance and commonality, the reach of the ethical toward the others halts within commonality and resemblance, within the human, if not within the rational, essential, or said, replaces displacement with disinterestedness and substitution. The general circulation of dyads of ethical difference collapses before substitution. I insist that ethical difference exercises an unlimited obsession with and responsibility toward heterogeneous other kinds in virtue of the impossibility of reciprocity, symmetry, and substitution. This impossibility resists impartiality. To the contrary, we need to know where we are, know our place, our kind, here and elsewhere, to know the demands of heterogeneity upon us, to know our own heterogeneities. For our responsibilities to others are anything but the same, unreachable from disinterestedness and substitution.

The reach of the otherwise in Levinas, as Irigaray suggests, within my obsession toward the other does not reach the heterogeneous. I take up her movement, from the one sex to the other, but cannot stop at that (essential) mark of heterogeneity that echoes in gender. All the others that obsess me face to face with heterogeneity represent a profound beginning for ethics because each of us, all of us, in our skins, find it difficult to reach, to know, to care for all the others, to find our way to cherishing all the other kinds in nature, except through our face-to-face, body-to-body, relations with some. In cherishing the other as other I experience the demand and the impossibility of cherishing the others. And conversely, perhaps more crucially, I cannot cherish any without cherishing some. Responsibility to all the others imposes on me an unlimited responsibility to care for, touch, some in my proximity. The reach of the neighbor is everywhere, in proximity. Cherishment depends on a sense of place, somewhere and everywhere, resting in place. The return to place, from elsewhere, returns us from the unlimit of plenishment to the intermediate number, in proximity, face to face.

Levinas recoils in the movement from the dyad to unlimit, retaining the limits of the third and the Infinite. I understand the movement to unlimit and its return in a more dangerous and catastrophic way. But I leave Levinas for the moment to retrace a far-reaching hesitation, of the same kind, reaching out, as Levinas does not, to animals, within a similar recoil before their inexhaustible heterogeneity. I reach out to animals across the otherwise of their alterity on the way to nature. I ask us to think first of animals and their liberation in analogy with women's liberation, understanding the movement from rights and liberation to plenishment as analogous to the movement from measure and intermediate numbers to unlimit. I return to feminist readings of nature's plenitude upon coming to rest. I will later extend our ethical responsibility to other kinds.

Peter Singer asks us to think of animals ethically in a way that Westerners tend not to do, placing animals together with women and people of other races (Singer, *AL*). Animal Liberation joins Women's and Black Liberation as the movements of our time. In a juxtaposition that seems close to Irigaray's understanding that the question of our age is the question of sexual difference as a liberation of women from oppression, Singer adds animals to women and to the children of slaves.[5]

I will retrace this movement into heterogeneity, but let us first leap into the breach we have opened in Levinas, where we wonder where the face to face leaves off, our cherishment toward all the others who obsess me in the neighbor. For Singer opposes what he calls "speciesism" in the language of the speciesists, using a different criterion. And he makes the criterion the mark of the good. He speaks with combined affection and distaste, with a rational aversion, of St. Francis.

> It was not only the sentient creatures whom St. Francis addressed as his sisters: the sun, the moon, wind, fire, all were brothers and sisters to him. His contemporaries described him as taking "inward and outward delight in almost every creature, and when he handled or looked at them his spirit seemed to be in heaven rather than on earth." This delight extended to water, rocks, flowers and trees. (Singer, *AL*, p. 205)

Singer shows his distaste, contempt, for such a delight in every creature and thing, first calling it "reminiscent of someone who, in more modern terms, is 'high'" (Singer, *AL*, p. 205), then appealing to "rational reflection."

> While this kind of ecstatic universal love can be a wonderful foundation of compassion and goodness, the lack of rational reflection can also do much to counteract its beneficial consequences. If we love rocks, trees, plants, larks, and oxen equally, we may lose sight of the essential differences between them, and most importantly, the differences in degree of sentience. We may then think that since we have to eat to survive, and since we cannot eat without killing something we love, it does not matter which we kill. (Singer, *AL*, p. 205)

You and I may hesitate at such an argument, may bear a very different proximity to ecstasy and love.[6] Singer's project is to show that we can regard animals ethically, striving to avoid their unnecessary suffering, and still make important distinctions between one kind of animal and another, distinctions involving circumstances. His project remains an ethics distinguishing good from bad, excluding some from ethical consideration.

We may find here several issues relevant to plenishment: (1) Singer distinguishes ethics from love, from compassion and goodness, from ecstasy; (2) he has no patience for an ethic of compassion that is not based on "rational reflection," although reason has been the traditional Western ground for the mistreatment of animals; (3) the only criterion he accepts is sentience, and even here, only part of sentience, the capacity to suffer; and finally, (4) it is a sentience like ours. Singer's ethics begins with humanity and extends its reach to animals, asking how far the likeness stretches. We wonder whether he knows of any alterity irreducible to himself. "If a being suffers, there can be no moral justification for disregarding that suffering, or for refusing to count it equally with the like suffering of any other being. But the converse of this is also true. If a being is not capable of suffering, or of enjoyment, there is nothing to take into account" (Singer, *AL,* p. 176).[7] Yet nothing in Singer's argument justifies this converse. His entire approach concerns the relevance of suffering to ethics, with nothing whatever to say where joy and suffering are absent but gravity and beauty are present, where a forest provides shade for beautiful flowers, or where there exists something entirely unimaginable to us, something heterogeneous. The law of noncontradiction works here in a destructive way: to exclude. Singer repeats the form of the argument that if the woman or person of color or animal is not rational, is incapable of language, does not suffer, or whatever, then nothing (ethical) is present to take into account. They are thereby excluded from ethics. Existence, life, beauty, relevance, the unknown, all bear no ethical weight. He repeats the form of the argument that only that which is like us is ethical. Perhaps the good is where there is nothing like us, but still we bear responsibilities toward it. Perhaps my responsibility for the other is where the other bears no relation to me of the same.

I will trace the development of Singer's argument through three movements in which he retrieves the ethical relevance of animals but denies the ethical relevance of plants and stones, of everything in nature. Only some things are ethically relevant, belong to the good. The entire ethical movement in this book has been to undertake the question of sexual difference as giving rise to an ethic of inclusion in which such a denial cannot be sustained.

1. Singer tells us he is not interested in animal love but in animal rights.

> This book is not about pets. It is not likely to be comfortable reading for those who think that love for animals involves no more than stroking a cat or feeding the birds in the garden. It is intended rather for people who are concerned about ending oppression and exploitation wherever they occur, and in seeing that the basic moral principle of equal consideration of interests is not arbitrarily restricted to members of our own species. The assumption that in order to be interested in such matters one must be an "animal-lover" is itself an indication of the absence of the slightest inkling that the moral standards that we apply among human beings might extend to other animals. No one, except a racist concerned to smear his opponents as "nigger-lovers," would suggest that in order to be concerned for mistreated racial minorities you have to love those minorities, or regard them as cute and cuddly. So why make this assumption about people who work for improvements in the conditions of animals? (Singer, *AL*, pp. x–xi)

You and I may have many hesitations when reading this passage, even where we accept Singer's goal that we should end the oppression and exploitation of animals and women and racial minorities wherever they occur, and possibly the exploitation of the earth as well, wherever it occurs. Those who share their homes with animals, and love them, do not think that their relationship is no more than stroking or feeding. A life shared with an animal, or in proximity with animals, plants, streams, and forests, is a tending and concern and passion. It is not incongruous to care for other animals because one cares for one's own, and because they care as well. The argument against exclusion moves as persuasively from pets to other animals as from humans to animals and to natural habitats.

More important, the suggestion that ethics has nothing to do with love, with care, concern, with cherishment, represents an assumption that an ethic of inclusion must regard with suspicion.

"Nigger-lovers" is a term of opprobrium; it contains a word of hate. At other times and places, we might speak with similar revulsion of "sheeny-lovers," of "fag-" and "dyke-lovers." "Animal-lovers" is a different idea. Christ said that we should love others as we love ourselves, and to love people of other cultures and experiences may be neither irrelevant nor antagonistic to ethical difference. In the ethic of sexual difference out of which I hope to echo ethical difference, one of the conditions of the dyad is love, whether heterosexual or other. The dyad that we cannot relinquish, the face to face, is closer to love than anything Singer has to offer. This may include love for animals and their love for us.

Singer tells us that "[t]his book makes no sentimental appeals for sympathy toward 'cute' animals" (Singer, *AL*, p. xi). And perhaps we must resist our natural sympathy for cute or beautiful or powerful animals just because we incline so forcefully in that direction, as we must resist our sympathy for beautiful women or virtuous men as the only objects of our ethical concern. But we must wonder if such a resistance is because these sympathies are irrelevant to ethics, or because they are too relevant, too important to us, to our feelings toward other people, our neighbors. For we must consider others, and still others. To the extent that we must act where we are, in our places, then we must accept the truth that the cute and cuddly animals who share our homes, or the baby animals toward whom we feel affection, or the people we love, erotically or affectionately, open wide the doors of cherishment. Singer's repudiation of pets and cuddly animals is analogous to Kant's and Levinas's disinterestedness. We must join the others, but must begin with the feelings we have in our proximity. We cannot disdain the ethical force of love.[8] In the considerations that enable us to distinguish those for whom we will risk our lives, those for whom we care but must forbear sacrifice, and those we may respect but cannot care for, love and compassion, relations of propinquity and kinship, are of utmost relevance. Many of us do not care for an ethic in which our children and beloveds, our closest neighbors, are on a par with those we do not know, those far away. We need to take our places into account as we come to know that those far away are close at hand. We need a more nuanced and complex account of situation and place, especially of the relation between heterogeneity and proximity.

2. Singer tells us that the good is not bound with compassion

and love but with rational reflection. Yet nothing has been more destructive to animals in the history of the West than this rationality, both as instrument of reflection and as criterion. Singer's project may be understood as a repudiation of the historical standard of rational reflection, marking the ethical, of the view that only creatures who can reason deserve ethical consideration. Those who suffer also deserve consideration! What then does reason serve, since it does not tell us what marks the good, except as an instrument of deliberation, among other deliberations?

Though Singer does not consider the extreme possibility, marked by Nietzsche, that reason belongs to ethics, belongs to the will, and therefore cannot give us ethics, he considers the proximate possibility twice, that is, that reason is captive, first to our love for animals, second to our stomachs. For in relation to animal experimentation, with its brutal horrors, far exceeding anything German doctors did to concentration camp inmates, Singer states the unqualified truth (concerning animals and Jews) that "[a]t present scientists do not look for alternatives *simply because they do not care enough about the animals they are using*" (Singer, *AL*, p. 78). Or Jews.[9] Before all rational reflection, before all ethics, he seems to know and say that we must care about and for the animals and others, must cherish them. But we do not do so, he shows, as revealed in many of the arguments throughout the West against animal rights, "testify[ing] to the relative strength of desires that emanate from the stomach and those that are based on compassion in a country [Britain] that has a reputation for kindness to animals" (Singer, *AL*, p. 107). We kill and eat animals, neglecting any ethical concerns, because we like to eat meat. We (men) hoard and exchange women, neglecting the good, because we desire to control our domestic and reproductive activities. We do what we do with the things around us because we desire to control them.

The strength of the desires of the palate in relation to compassion and love are shown by Singer in another important context that does not serve reason well, that is, religions with dietary laws that pertain to killing and eating animals. For the laws that govern eating tend to replace compassion among Jews, for example, representing God's word, so that in the animal rights movement repeated discussions take place about whether Jews face special dietary and ethical difficulties. According to Jewish law, animals must be slaughtered when healthy and moving, conscious; however quickly the animal is killed, the law of the ritual replaces compassion. Singer summarizes the only ethical conclusion he and I can defend: "[i]f, to preserve religious laws intact, a choice must be made between the taste for meat and the agony of millions of animals, surely it is justifiable to ask those who follow the religious laws to do without meat" (Singer, *AL*, p. 156). Orthodox Jews regularly do without meat when they travel or visit other people's homes, at certain meals, and under many circumstances when they cannot ensure that dietary laws are in force. They do without whenever the law commands, but not when compassion toward animals beseeches.

This is not a point about Jews' immorality—I am Jewish—but about the rule of the law in the Greek–Judeo–Christian tradition. Derrida summarizes it beautifully:

> there was a time, not long ago and not yet over, in which "we, men" meant "we adult white male Europeans, carnivorous and capable of sacrifice." (Derrida, *FL*, p. 951)

> carnivorous sacrifice is essential to the structure of subjectivity, which is also to say to the founding of the intentional subject and to the founding, if not of the law, at least of law *(droit)*. (Derrida, *FL*, p. 953)

Sacrifice presents an ethical truth we cannot avoid. I am still exploring it. I am concerned for the moment with the carnivorousness under which animals are used by us for our purposes. "Shorn of all brutality and cruelty, quick, clean, and technically efficient, slaughter at its best still is based on the attitude that animals are means to our ends . . . " (Singer, *AL*, p. 157). I will speak of the formation of the subject presently. It is a far more important subject for us to lay to rest.

If domestic animals do not reason, but cherish and care for the people among whom they live their lives, are they not ethical twice, once in how they treat us, second in how they ask to be treated? Dogs and cats save their human companions' lives, sometimes at great risk to their own. Animals risk their lives for their offspring. Could it be possible that ethics and ethical consideration lie in joy and suffering and sacrifice more than reason, law, and justice?

3. Singer speaks of animal rights, but the criterion he employs

is sentience: we are obligated to consider the interests of those who can experience joy or suffering. You may be reminded of *jouissance* and *souffrance,* for the point made earlier was that these were not the same for different people, and might not be the same for different creatures. Spinoza claims that they differ with the minds and souls of those who experience them. Moreover, Singer's criterion is suffering, despite the added qualification of enjoyment: he gives no arguments derived from joy. He agrees with Bentham: "[t]he question is not, Can they *reason?* nor Can they *talk?* but, *Can they suffer?*" (Bentham, *PML,* chap. 7, in Burtt, *EPBM,* n. 11, p. 847; quoted in Singer, *AL,* p. 8). Singer adds:

> The capacity for suffering and enjoyment is *a prerequisite for having interests at all,* a condition that must be satisfied before we can speak of interests in a meaningful way. It would be nonsense to say that it was not in the interests of a stone to be kicked along the road by a schoolboy. A stone does not have interests because it cannot suffer. Nothing that we can do to it could possibly make any difference to its welfare. (Singer, *AL,* p. 8)

Suppose we were to paraphrase his own words of a page or two earlier, modifying this criterial and exclusive sense of interests, speaking of wellbeing rather than of interests.

> The basic element—the taking into account of the [well-being] of the being, whatever [that well-being] may be—must, according to the principle of equality, be extended to all beings, black or white, masculine or feminine, human or nonhuman, [animate or inanimate]. (Singer, *AL,* p. 6; [modifications in brackets])

We cannot be sure that there is no relevant sense of well-being that pertains to things that do not suffer, though suffering and enjoyment are ethically relevant for creatures that feel, relevant to their well-being.

The ethical distinctions we seek among different kinds of creatures may not depend on them alone, but may depend on us, on those who make ethical judgments and their situations, having to do with our relations to the world, to others, to ourselves, to our places, and to our powers. Not all distinctions that pertain to us and our circumstances need divide different species from the good, but may have to do more with what is possible for us to pursue and what is important where we are.

4. With the thought that Singer does not seem to know that

ethics pertains to alterity and heterogeneity rather than the same, even to an alterity irreducible to humanity, we may reexamine the entire course of his argument. Even his beginning, which on one side seems truly caring, betrays a certain—dare we call it?—speciesism.

> This book is about the tyranny of human over nonhuman animals. This tyranny has caused and today is still causing an amount of pain and suffering that can only be compared with that which resulted from the centuries of tyranny by white humans over black humans. The struggle against this tyranny is a struggle as important as any of the moral and social issues that have been fought over in recent years. (Singer, *AL,* p. ix)

The struggle for an ethic of sexual and other differences of kind may be the most important ethical struggle of our time, of our world. But the calculation is unintelligible of what may be more or most important ethically and politically. Ethical difference may know nothing whatever of such a calculation, may know only of a cherishment without measure.

The fundamental measure echoes in Singer's phrase, echoes doubly, that the tyranny of human over nonhuman animals has caused "an amount of pain and suffering that can only be compared" with human pain and suffering. I will not go into the measure embodied in an amount of suffering, though that returns later in a remarkable way, when he compares the amount of pain a horse may suffer to the suffering of a human baby.

> If I give a horse a hard slap across its rump with my open hand, the horse may start, but it presumably feels little pain. Its skin is thick enough to protect it against a mere slap. If I slap a baby in the same way, however, the baby will cry and presumably does feel pain, for its skin is more sensitive. So it is worse to slap a baby than a horse, if both slaps are administered with equal force. But there must be some kind of blow—I don't know exactly what it would be, but perhaps a blow with a heavy stick—that would cause the horse as much pain as we cause a baby by slapping it with our hand. That is what I mean by "the same amount of pain" and if we consider it wrong to inflict that much pain on a baby for no good reason then we must, unless we are speciesists, consider it equally wrong to inflict the same amount of pain on a horse for no good reason. (Singer, *AL,* p. 16)

We may hesitate at the possibility that this view, in part because of the irrelevant and repugnant idea of amount of pain, in part because of the comparison with humans, is as unethical a view, as speciesist, as anything Singer opposes. The wrong echoes not in the amount of pain, but in the treatment, the context, the oppression and domination. Horses and babies may both be slapped in ethical ways. The strange ethics Singer describes, based on amounts of suffering, permits him to emphasize suffering more than joy and more than killing. "This does not mean that to avoid speciesism we must hold that it is as wrong to kill a dog as it is to kill a normal human being" (Singer, *AL*, p. 20). When he speaks of killing for food, he says something far more ethical. "If we are prepared to take the life of another being [or harm it in any way] merely in order to satisfy our taste for a particular type of food, then that being is no more than a means to our end" (Singer, *AL*, p. 164).

This more Kantian description, with its deficiencies, is much closer to the ethic we are pursuing than Singer's, though they overlap in many ways. But once we open the door to an ethic that is not restricted to rational human subjects, it can never be closed. Singer himself approaches this understanding, stopping on the threshold. "What we must do is bring nonhuman animals within our sphere of moral concern and cease to treat their lives as expendable for whatever trivial purposes we may have" (Singer, *AL*, p. 21). We must bring everything that rests in the earth within our ethical concern and treat nothing as expendable for our own trivial purposes. But we may have important purposes. As may they. And we may cause harm no matter what we do.

Ethical difference insists that nothing is to be treated merely as a means, even if it cannot suffer or know joy. Nothing, nothing. Nothing is mere; nothing can be treated merely, in any way, whether as a means or ends. Especially, treating something merely as a means is unethical. This understanding is cherishment. Cherishment does not distinguish subjects who matter ethically from objects who do not. Everything is precious in its ways, and our ethical responsibility is to cherish it immeasurably. But everything is a means as well as an end, regardless of our ethical responsibilities, and we cannot treat everything as an end, merely as an end, cannot because everything is also a means. This impossibility is sacrifice. The conjunction is plenishment, ethical difference. But enough of this for the moment.

For we have not struggled enough with Singer's founding of ethics on the human, extending it by continuity and likeness to the nonhuman, stopping somewhere. His ethics is an ethics of the same. The title of the first chapter of *Animal Liberation* is "All Animals are Equal . . . ," based on the following: "*[t]he principle of the equality of human beings is not a description of an alleged actual equality among humans: it is a prescription of how we should treat humans*" (Singer, *AL*, p. 5). Singer does not consider the possibility that we may bear a greater ethical responsibility toward creatures and things unlike us, insofar as they are unlike us, perhaps because there are too many people like us, too many human beings or Westerners, or whatever, for us to worry very much about them, and too few lions or lizards or frogs or certain trees and lava deposits, or even elements. Our responsibility not to waste and destroy rare and precious things, works of art and beautiful insects, may indeed be ethical, if not only or predominantly ethical. And that responsibility is what ethical difference entails.

As for stopping the ethical somewhere, so that some things, even creatures, are excluded from ethical consideration, that insistence promotes my major reservation with Singer's discussion of animals, so great a reservation that I wonder if the line he draws between the ethical and nonethical, if any line drawn anywhere between the ethical and nonethical, can be ethical, a repudiation of the *aentre*. Singer recognizes this possibility as he repeatedly draws such a line, betraying a profound ethical ambivalence. In speaking of ceasing to eat meat, for example, he discusses the question of the line in ethical terms.

> How far should we go? The case for a radical break in our eating habits is clear; but should we eat nothing but vegetables? Where exactly do we draw the line?
>
> Drawing precise lines is always difficult. I shall make some suggestions, but . . . You must decide for yourself where you are going to draw the line, and your decision may not coincide exactly with mine. (Singer, *AL*, p. 174)

In terms of suffering, we should eat nothing but vegetables, though that can also raise serious ethical difficulties, involving the clearing of forests for cultivation, the use of plants for human consumption, and wounds that plants surely feel. But if we ate only vegetables, we would still be surrounded by animal products, in everything we do and own, in the fabrics we wear and the materials we employ. Everywhere. We could not draw a line if we wished to between living by the use of animal products and avoiding them altogether. Nor can we eat vegetables, use and eat plants for our purposes, with ethical impunity.

One conclusion, favored by some despite its evils, is that we may then do whatever we please, and since we must kill some animals to live, we may kill them all without compunction. And why not human beings as well, at least young and tender ones? The other conclusion is that not eating meat would save countless (really *countless!*) animals suffering and abuse. Add the practice of avoiding animal experimentation except when clearly directed to specific and immediate human benefit. Animals, but also plants and inanimate things, are to be treated as precious wherever possible, to be cared for, cherished, to be allowed to live rich and rewarding lives. If we cannot save them all, we save the ones we can, care for those we can.

And here the criteria, first, of suffering break down, but second, of not utilizing animals and things as means. They break down in part because we cannot avoid suffering: to live is to suffer. To live, to exist, is to be means as well as end, to employ means as well as caring for ends. More important, animals and plants, like human beings of any gender, race, color, or cultural background, pursue happiness in different ways. This is the truth of *jouissance,* of sexual difference, that irrupts into ethical difference, heterogeneity: every creature, in its alterity, knows something, a joy, a truth, that no one, nothing else, knows, perhaps the truth of its experiences, perhaps the truth of its feelings and sensibilities. Leibniz and Whitehead understand this joy and knowledge to belong to everything, everywhere. However incipiently, everything knows what and where it is in relation to some other things, some neighbors, is in its place and elsewhere, everywhere. To be itself, in place, it must inhabit inexhaustible relations—the indefinite dyad again, a different indefiniteness of dyads. Every thing in relation relates to its neighbors dyadically, knows its neighbors and itself indefinitely and inexhaustibly but, I insist, nonmetaphorically—or rather, both metaphorically and nonmetaphorically, lives in relation to the good. Singer insists on a strict nonmetaphorical sense that cuts some things and creatures off from any ethical consideration, from any possibility of joy or truth. Yet he tells us a deeper ethical truth. "We have to speak up on behalf of those who cannot speak for themselves" (Singer, *AL,* p. xiii). We have to do more than this, but even under this restriction, you and I may understand, as Singer seems to deny, that we have to speak up for the earth because it cannot (or when it cannot) speak for itself (in our language) of countless hidden, subjugated truths. And joys.

The practical|ethical line Singer draws is between the shrimp and the mollusk. "Those who want to be absolutely certain that they are not causing suffering will not eat mollusks either; but somewhere between a shrimp and an oyster seems as good a place to draw the line as any, and better than most" (Singer, *AL*, pp. 178–79). Better than most may be the best we can ever achieve, but I believe there can be no compelling ethical reason under the sun to eat oysters raw but not eat shrimp. And is this not the point, that we make our ethical decisions from compelling reasons based on our circumstances and conditions, not on the traits of others alone? Our powers and conditions are relevant to ethics, if not on the side of cherishment then on the side of sacrifice. If we are stranded on a desert island with only shrimp and perhaps some fish to catch, then probably we will catch and eat them, will have to do so to survive, and may do so ethically. But such a practice may be closer to cannibalism than we may be comfortable acknowledging, may place us in proximity to injustice.

This discussion of difficulties in Singer's treatment of the ethics of animals must not give the impression that I think there is a better practice toward animals than the ones he proposes, but rather, seeks to augment his understanding of the good by consideration of ethical difference in a way that does not begin ethics with human beings and does not end with sentience. Before exploring the good in relation to natural things and kinds beyond pain and suffering, we may consider another account based on ethical distinctions we know and respect, rather than on the possibility that the good imposes impossible responsibilities upon us to know and respect what we do not and cannot know at all.

Comstock offers a powerful ethical discussion of animals within the repeated assumption that we already know what it is to be ethical, seeking its measure (Comstock, *PP*). We may discover, in Comstock's reading, especially his reading of Taylor's respect for nature, something close to cherishment (Taylor, *RN*). But not quite. Comstock's strategy, initiated by the general question, "[i]s it in God's will to raise and eat pigs?" (Comstock, *PP*, p. 121), is to test all relevant and compelling ethical principles he can find against the possibility that it is wrong to kill pigs for food. His arguments traverse the following line, all concerned with how we may justify denying care and respect to pigs or other animals:

1. "[P]igs experience pleasure and pain, . . . have emotions, desires, wishes, preferences, and a family life" (Comstock, *PP,* p. 122). "Pigs are intelligent, affectionate, and social animals" (Comstock, *PP,* p. 122). This is a far stronger condition than Singer's sentience, defined by suffering. Pigs know joy and care. Moreover,

2. "The daily activities of hogs clearly suggest that they possess desires, preferences, pleasures, pains, and social lives" (Comstock, *PP,* p. 123). Moreover, hogs possess a *telos,* an end: "Not forgetting sleeping and investigating and eating and mating and playing, rooting must be one thing for the sake of which God made hogs" (Comstock, *PP,* p. 123). Hogs have their work, their task, their sense of nature's plenitude.

3. Ethics is restricted by many philosophers to creatures with language, creatures which unlike machines can take an interest in something they represent to themselves, for "without concepts the animal cannot represent its interests to itself" (Comstock, *PP,* p. 123). Comstock asks, from within a traditional line dividing humans from animals, "[d]o pigs possess language?" (Comstock, *PP,* p. 123), and answers, "[p]igs may indeed possess language, and may have the conceptual ability to take an interest in their future. But if they can take an interest in their future existence, they may have a moral right to that future. And if they do, our killing them violates their most basic right" (Comstock, *PP,* p. 124). Singer describes pigs screaming at their impending death in the slaughterhouses (Singer, *AL,* p. 157). They may know their death without language, as if in a dream.

4. Pigs can take an interest in their future, but many human beings—too young, too old, too infirm—cannot. "[T]o think that 'the way is open' to killing any being that lacks moral rights is to think in terms of an unacceptable conceptual paradigm" (Comstock, *PP,* p. 124). Here Comstock, in understated language, expresses the ethical impulse of inclusion, as if we, in our conceptual wisdom, might succeed in drawing perfectly acceptable lines that would justify, open the way to, killing beings that do not possess a certain something, thereby grounding ethical rights. Rights and sentience operate in this space of dividing nonethical from ethical beings so that we may use and destroy the first, as if they had no intrinsic worth. An ethic of inclusion grants intrinsic worth to nature and natural things everywhere.

5. Comstock quotes what he calls the theocentric perspective of his teacher, James Gustafson, "[b]e enlarged in your vision and affections, so that you might better discern what the divine governance enables and requires you to be and to do, what are your appropriate relations to God, indeed what are the appropriate relations of all things to God" (Comstock, *PP,* p. 124). You and I may hesitate before the exclusions within the idea of appropriate relations, but we may endorse the possibility that all things bear relations to God and other things that we are called upon to know and care about.

6. Comstock's theocentric reading of this approach turns on God's commandments defining "appropriate relations." This takes us to Biblical passages concerning the place of animals in relation to God, for example, surrounding the manger at Christ's birth (Comstock, *PP,* p. 125), and the passages in *Genesis* and elsewhere, to which we will return in this chapter, giving humanity "dominion over the fish of the sea, and over the fowl of the air, and over the earth, and over every creeping thing that creepeth upon the earth" (*Gen.* 1:28).[10] Yet Isaiah tells us that when God returns to judge,

> 6 The wolf also shall dwell with the lamb, and the leopard shall lie down with the kid; and the calf and the young lion and the fatling together; and a little child shall lead them.
>
> 7 And the cow and bear shall feed; their young ones shall lie down together: and the lion shall eat straw like the ox. (*Isaiah,* 11)

In the words of the hymn, "God's eye is on the sparrow" (Comstock, *PP,* p. 126). To God's words to Noah, giving every creature to humanity as food (*Gen.* 9:21),[11] Comstock responds, "[t]o me, the passage reads more as a grim prediction of what will happen or, perhaps, as an unavoidable curse God lays, grudgingly, on the world" (Comstock, *PP,* p. 126). I understand this curse in terms of sacrifice, as an inescapable and unjust penalty for acting in the world, responsible under the call of the good for avoiding injustice within the impossibility of doing so. On this reading, God does not enjoin human beings to kill and eat animals, does not compel them to do so as if that were the good, but allows them to do so because in the impossibility of the world, it may be required, may be, sometimes, unavoidable.

7. Comstock's solution draws upon Taylor's account of the inherent worth of things in nature, emphasizing "wild living things in the Earth's natural ecosystems as possessing inherent worth" (Comstock, *PP,* p. 128; Taylor, *RN,* p. 81). On Comstock's reading, Taylor seems, like many other writers, to restrict this sense of worth to wild animals, treating livestock as a special case, totally under human dominion, brought into being by human power (Comstock, *PP,* p. 128; Taylor, *RN,* p. 55). I wonder why we do not bear a greater responsibility toward animals we have placed completely in our power, why power and care do not go together. And that is how I read Taylor, who seems to me not to approve of the ways in which "[w]e hold them completely in our power. They must serve us or be destroyed" (Taylor, *RN,* p. 55). For he says that

> when we raise and slaughter animals for food, the wrong we do to them does not consist simply in our causing them pain. Even if it became possible for us to devise methods of killing them, as well as ways of treating them while alive, that involved little or no pain, we would still violate a prima facie duty in consuming them. They would still be treated as mere means to our ends and so be wronged. (Taylor, *RN,* pp. 294–95)

> anyone who has respect for nature will be on the side of vegetarianism, even though plants and animals are regarded as having the same inherent worth. (Taylor, *RN,* pp. 295–96)

I wonder why Comstock rhetorically places himself in a subservient position vis-à-vis Taylor and others, as if he must accept their analysis or something like it, as if being ethical demands authority. I wonder at his rhetorical strategy. For he refuses to follow Taylor's emphasis on wild living things, though perhaps Taylor uses that notion in a more generous way than Comstock may recognize. The sense of subservience to authority repeats mimetically the subservience to rules that Taylor insists is the structure of ethics. And within that subservience, we may find that Taylor draws an absolute line around living rather than dead things. For he insists on five "formal conditions, which are now widely accepted in contemporary ethics" (Taylor, *RN,* p. 25), as if such acceptance granted ethical worth rather than repeating the exploitation of nature against which Taylor's arguments are directed. The formal conditions define a "set of rules and standards to constitute a valid normative ethical system" such that the rules and standards

(a) must be general in form;
(b) must be considered to be universally applicable to all moral agents as such;
(c) must be intended to be applied disinterestedly;
(d) must be advocated as normative principles for all to adopt; and
(e) must be taken as overriding all nonmoral norms. (Taylor, *RN*, p. 27)

The possibility that the generality, universality, and disinterestedness of ethical judgments work against respect for natural things and have historically worked against women, animals, and slaves does not enter Taylor's thought. These traits have seemed to most readers historically to define a reciprocity and rational judgment pertinent only to certain kinds of human beings. To foster natural things, to plenish the earth, may require an attention to heterogeneity, to multiple kinds of things, that can be neither general, universal, nor disinterested, but may flow from a cherishment more pertinent to our particular places in the world.[12] I am considering the possibility that disinterestedness is a contaminated ethical category and am seeking to replenish it with cherishment and mourning for sacrifice.

The possibility that formal conditions work to exclude emerges in Taylor, for he repeats the structure of thought that bars certain natural things from inherent worth even as he extends its scope. For "the term 'inherent worth' is to be attributed only to entities that have a good of their own" (Taylor, *RN*, p. 75), and only animate things have a good of their own. A pile of sand, inanimate things, have no good of their own (Taylor, *RN*, pp. 60–61). He does not consider the possibility that the things that surround us, inanimate things, insofar as they compose habitats of living things, might be goods, not usefully or instrumentally, but in composing the earth we and they inhabit and share. He restricts the concept of inherent worth to a class of goods. Cherishment and plenishment address unknown, unthought, unimaginable goods, possibilities of goods, and kinds of goods, unknown and unimagined injustices and destructions. They resist any knowledge of the good that might measure it and any possibility of its completion.

I resist drawing a line between creatures and things toward

which we bear ethical responsibilities and those toward which we do not, those we may use for our own profit. I resist dividing animate from inanimate creatures and things, bearing a responsibility akin to God's toward every thing and every creature, a responsibility borne by each of us as best we can, in the ways we can.

8. Taylor offers five priority principles to resolve conflicts among our ethical responsibilities toward living things, which are grounded in the principle of species-impartiality. The priority principles are:

(a) The principle of self-defense.
(b) The principle of proportionality.
(c) The principle of minimum wrong.
(d) The principle of distributive justice.
(e) The principle of restitutive justice. (Taylor, *RN,* p. 263)

He makes a forceful claim: "I believe these five principles cover all the major ways of adjudicating fairly among competing claims arising from clashes between the duties of human ethics and those of environmental ethics . . . they do not yield a neat solution to every possible conflict situation" (Taylor, *RN,* p. 263). Comstock discusses them as follows:

> (a) *Self-defense:* "[i]t is permissible for moral agents to protect themselves against dangerous or harmful organisms by destroying them" (Comstock, *PP,* p. 132; Taylor, *RN,* pp. 264–65).
>
> (b) *Proportionality:* distinguishing basic from nonbasic interests of human beings, "[g]reater weight is to be given to basic than to nonbasic interests" (Comstock, *PP,* p. 132; Taylor, *RN,* p. 278) regardless of species.
>
> (c) *Minimum wrong:* "[t]he actions of humans must be such that no alternative ways of achieving their ends would produce fewer wrongs to wild living things" (Comstock, *PP,* p. 132; Taylor, *RN,* p. 283).
>
> (d) *Distributive justice:* "[w]hen the interests of parties are all basic ones and there exists a natural source of good that can be used for the benefit of any of the parties, each party must be allotted an equal, or fair, share" (Comstock, *PP,* p. 132; Taylor, *RN,* p. 292).
>
> (e) *Restitutive justice:* "[w]hen harm is done to humans, animals, or plants that are harmless, some form of reparation or compensation is called for. The greater the harm done, the greater the reparation required" (Comstock, *PP,* p. 132; Taylor, *RN,* p. 304).

I have resisted every proportion and measure, understand the good to impose a struggle with the injustice and evils of every measure and proposition, every exclusion, principle, rule, and criterion. I am not sure that we are justified in destroying harmful organisms in our interests, where the harm is small and the destruction is great. I am not sure whether the line between basic interests and nonbasic ones always holds even in human life. I do not know how to count wrongs and rights; I do know with some assurance that every effort to count has led to immense destruction. I wonder how we might allocate limited food and water to animals and plants when human children are dying. I am not sure that species-impartiality is good, given our special relation to other human beings and certain animals, our concern for fostering certain human communities—provided that we remember other species' communities. Questions of kinds impose an endless struggle with our own and others' identities. Most of all, I understand restitution not as a principle of ethical work, as Taylor's principles are, but as the immemorial call of the good, the endless debts imposed by endless injustices, including the injustices of every principle and rule. I understand these principles to bear this weight of responsibility toward our own and others' injustices, to seek to do the good against the constant threat of harm. This responsibility is required by the threat of sacrifice, its profound contamination.

Such an understanding of restitution brings us to question why wild living things might take precedence over dead domestic things, why we have the right to abuse, destroy, things we own, such as machines, artifacts, clothing. Why destroy anything that we or others might cherish? That creatures feel pain is not decisive. That creatures experience joy is perhaps more relevant, but again not decisive. The call of the good knows no lines between what imposes responsibilities on us for cherishing it, for plenishment, and other things, knows no lines that place these kinds of things within the good and those others outside it. Property rights are rights to cherish, not to destroy; they constitute intermediary figures.

I extend Taylor's and Comstock's respect for the inherent worth of things in the earth everywhere in the earth, the cherishment of things everywhere, giving rise to the impossible obligation of plenishment in the earth. Not without harm. That would be impossible. Not without sacrifice, without evil and injustice. But without self-aggrandizement and self-righteousness, without ethical justification for exclusion, for our injustices, for the harm we do. In our responsibility for plenishment in the earth, we must refuse every exclusion of something in nature within the call of the good. We suffer endless responsibilities toward the good everywhere without the solace of rules. Yet we cannot live without the guidance of rules. We must refuse the cut of exclusion, an exclusion Taylor and Singer—possibly Comstock as well—cannot think of ethics without.

Singer tells us exactly, within his understanding of ethics, why we should extend ethics to animals, regardless of how they relate to human beings. "If the recommendations made in the following chapters are accepted, millions of animals will be spared considerable pain. Moreover, millions of humans will benefit too" (Singer, *AL,* p. xv). We should stop eating and abusing animals, because we will then spare them pain and benefit human beings as well. From my understanding of ethical difference, I respond that we should stop using animals because they may then live their animal lives experiencing their own knowledge and joys, in the best ways they can, following the good, in the different places the good may take them. We cherish animals and things, owe them infinite responsibility to care for them, because of their possibilities of fulfillment, not ours. Such responsiveness and responsibility is known to many people, echoing for example in the songs of whales and dolphin dreams.

Here it seems that Singer and Heidegger share a movement going back to Aristotle, even as both resist that movement. For Singer speaks of human and nonhuman animals as his fundamental categories (Singer, *AL,* p. xiv), and Heidegger in many places speaks repeatedly with contempt of thinking the essence of the human as rational animal (Heidegger, *LH,* p. 202). For both—the one employing this premise as the basis of an ethic of animal liberation, the other implying the outright denial of such a liberation—the human is placed in a relation of similarity rather than difference, and difference is used to cut away animals and other natural things from ethical and spiritual consideration.

If we return to the quotations with which our discussion of Singer began, we find a repeated cluster of terms all of which exist to exclude.

> As I said in the first chapter, the only legitimate boundary to our concern for the interests of other beings is the point at which it is

> no longer accurate to say that the other being has interests. To have interests, in a strict nonmetaphorical sense, a being must be capable of suffering or experiencing pleasure. If a being suffers, there can be no moral justification for disregarding that suffering, or for refusing to count it equally with the like suffering of any other being. But the converse of this is also true. If a being is not capable of suffering, or of enjoyment, there is nothing to take into account. (Singer, *AL*, p. 176)

The words that repeat themselves throughout Singer's discussion are "legitimate," "boundary," "accurate," "literal" and "nonmetaphorical," "interests," "strict," "equality," and "capable," implying that across a divide we have nothing ethical to consider. The form of Singer's argument repeats the arguments he opposes: that ethics pertains by nature to some, human, rational, sentient, to members of certain kinds but not to others. Aristotle's and Spinoza's ethics do not include slaves and animals among others. The idea of reason seems to entail, for Singer, an ethic of exclusion, when he says, for example, that "we need to see, first, exactly why racism and sexism are wrong" (Singer, *AL*, p. 3).

If we did not see this wrong exactly, would racism and sexism be right, or are they wrong regardless of reason's exactness? The exact criterion Singer offers is equality, again excluding what is not like the others. Ethical difference includes all creatures in its purview, in many cases in virtue of their strangeness. We must refuse to limit ethics to the familiar, understand ethics to inhabit the intervals and rests of the strange and unfamiliar. Singer offers an extended ethics, from human beings to animals, but ethics still exists for him as something that excludes, right from wrong, good from bad, ethical from unethical. I am pursuing the possibility of an ethic of inclusion. And still we hope to tell right from wrong.

Thomas tells stories of lions and Juwasi Bushmen in the Kalahari Desert, summarizing their relationship as one of mutual respect, neither harming the other (Thomas, *L*).

> All of us assumed that the people, not the lions, determined the events.
>
> But the lions also had a share in shaping the relationship. A truce if ever there was one, the people–lion relationship wouldn't have worked unless both sides had participated. (Thomas, *L*, p. 82)

The Juwasi and the lions could easily have killed each other; leopards killed Bushmen and were killed by them, were shown no respect. Yet,

> The truce was quite remarkable. While we were in the Kalahari, we knew of only one person who had been injured by a lion . . . among fifteen hundred deaths recalled by the hundreds of people whose testimonies I was able to examine, only one death was said to have been caused by a lion. . . .
>
> We knew of no lion killed by a Bushman. (Thomas, *L,* p. 83)

This relationship no longer holds, as lions no longer live side by side with Bushmen.

Above all, Thomas tells of what lions may know, of us, or at least the Juwasi, that we, the Juwasi, may not know of them, even as the lions must be supposed by us and them to know.

> On several occasions, lions seemed to have strong feelings about us, about something we had done or were doing. As I look back, the interesting thing about the episodes is not that they were frightening, which they were, or dangerous, which they could have been, but that the lions seemed to be trying hard to communicate with us, perhaps simply to give expression to their feelings, perhaps to make us do something.
>
> Unlike the lions, who correctly understood, and even obeyed, the spoken and gestured commands of the Juwasi, . . . we human beings were not able to understand the lions. (Thomas, *L,* p. 89)

> At about ten o'clock that night, a lioness suddenly appeared between the two camps and began to roar. The loudness of lions cannot be described but must be experienced. . . .
>
> . . . She roared intermittently for almost thirty-five minutes. Then she left, with swift, impatient strides. And there the episode ended. She never came back, and no one ever knew what it was she had wanted of us. (Thomas, *L,* p. 92)

Gilbert tells of crows, who roost in groups that range in size from hundreds to millions (Gilbert, "Crows"). Why do they do so? Perhaps to provide warmth, safety, genetic diversity, or a shared rich food habitat.[13] A Bengali friend offers another possibility, "[b]ut of course, it also appears they come here to give *adda*":

> At predetermined times and at regular intervals, Bengali men and women meet and talk with congenial companions. This is always described as giving—never as having or taking—*adda.* "When

giving *adda* we talk a great deal, often all at the same time. The attraction is hearing, seeing, being in touch with each other. I expect the point is that it has no point except being together. Giving *adda,* I should think, would not make sense to many Americans but perhaps it does for your crows." (Gilbert, "Crows," p. 111)

Or something else, otherwise, that belongs to crows. In these tales we sense a respect, a reverence toward, a knowledge and an experience in other creatures, their joys, that we will never know.

Compared with an ethic that insists that we owe responsibility to those who resemble us, these tales of lions and crows who might be and know and enjoy something so different from us that we will never understand it, these tales suggest a deeper responsibility: to know, to understand, the possibility of a knowledge and a feeling, a way of belonging to nature, resting in the earth, that we will never know or understand, and caring for it, cherishing what we cannot and never will understand or experience. I have spoken of "rest"; we may also speak of awe. Ethics includes this rest, this awe, includes respect and awe before what we cannot know or feel but recognize as demanding immeasurable cherishment and responsibility. Ethics knows wonder at nature's heterogeneities and excesses, wonder and love at what we know we will never know, but may still love. The good includes its own excesses, and what exceeds those excesses, plenishment toward what exceeds the possibility of limit. Singer seems to know nothing of this impossible inclusion, reduces ethics to what we already know, already share.

When Sacks describes his patients, he expresses a breathtaking sense of their alterity, their human difference (Sacks, *MMWH*). One of his postencephalitic patients describes her movements and freezing by saying, "[i]t's not as simple as it looks. I don't just come to a halt, I am still going, but I *have run out of space to move in* . . . You see, *my* space, *our* space, is nothing like *your* space: our space gets bigger and smaller, it bounces back on itself, and it loops itself round till it runs into itself" (Sacks, *A*, p. 339). He describes two twins who seem to communicate with each other in arithmetic terms, but relate to numbers far from any human measure.

They do not approach numbers lightly, as most calculators do. They are not interested in, have no capacity for, cannot comprehend, calculations. They are, rather, serene contemplators of

> number—and approach numbers with a sense of reverence and awe. Numbers for them are holy, fraught with significance. This is their way—as music is Martin's way—of apprehending the First Composer. (Sacks, "The Twins," in *MMWH,* p. 208)

These strange tales portray a heterogeneous humanity, filled with capacities and knowledge that "normal" people will never know, even as they may know, with Sacks, that there is such knowledge. They also portray a heterogeneous sense of space and time, and numbers. Heterogeneity, in Sacks's portrayals, bears the astonishing sense of Lacan's sense of the *jouissance* of the woman, that we can know that we will never know what the woman or these patients know, but we do suppose, indeed we know, with Sacks, that they know.

And so indeed with lions. And beyond the lions, crows, oysters, spiders, and cockroaches, and plankton, and amoebas, viruses and protoviruses, and . . . All are heterogeneous kinds toward which we bear infinite and impossible responsibilities in virtue of their heterogeneity, in which we know that unlimited knowledges and truths rest, in the earth. All of nature, all of human life, is souled, filled with heterogeneous, irreducible, creative, and moving creatures whose very presence is perfection, not a perfection that measures in or out, up or down, but a perfection that asks to be cherished. God's eye is on the sparrow and the rock, as well as on you and me. Our response flows from an ethical responsibility, an infinite responsibility for ethical difference, that cannot be heard in Singer.

Nor in Heidegger, who thinks the essence of "man" to exclude humanity at the very least from animals. Man is not a rational animal because He is not an animal at all. Well, that may be so for Man, but women and men are different. Sexual difference, sexual bodies, refuse this possibility absolutely.

We have come to another digression, vital in the movement of this book, intimately relating sexual difference to ethical difference, through Derrida's readings of Heidegger on the theme of *Geschlecht,* where in German gender joins the essence of humanity and the domination of nature. This links an ethic of natural kinds, replacing *Geschlecht* with kinds and genders, with kindred difference. The idea of kindred difference, and its relation to ethical difference, represents the heart of this book, the movement to an ethic of inclusion. The theme of ethical difference pervading nature continues with the discussion of ecological feminism in chapter 8. Echoes of the slaughter of animals continues below, after this digression.[14]

What Heidegger says of humanity rests in the gift of language, cutting off animals and other creatures without tenderness, wisdom, and patience.[15]

> Mortals are they who can experience death as death. Animals cannot do so. But animals cannot speak either. (Heidegger, *OWL,* p. 107)

> In the common view, the hand is part of our bodily organism. But the hand's essence can never be determined, or explained, by its being an organ which can grasp. Apes, too, have organs that can grasp, but they do not have hands. The hand is infinitely different from all the grasping organs—paws, claws, or fangs—different by an abyss of essence. Only a being who can speak, that is, think, can have hands and can handily achieve works of handicraft. (Heidegger, *WCT,* p. 357)

Derrida responds to this last claim—he calls it, "seriously dogmatic"—in terms of a cluster of ideas closely related to ethical difference, all organized around the German word *Geschlecht,* a word that always appears as "ours": *unser Geschlecht.* One is that of monstrosity, which in French falls between (*aentre*), in the interval of, *monstre* and *montre,* between the monstrous and demonstration, closely related to the inexhaustible resonances of *le propre.*[16] "The hand is monstrasity [*monstrosité*], the proper of man as the being of monstration. This distinguishes him from every other *Geschlecht,* and above all that of the ape" (Derrida, *G2,* p. 169). In the idea of the *logos,* of reason, proof, and showing, of language and *poiēsis,* there sounds a monstrosity that must be discarded in the name of propriety. In the name of the gift of language, Heidegger excludes animals entirely from our *Geschlecht,* in an eminence without compassion.

I cannot avoid wondering whether the *Geschlecht* (in German, certainly in Heidegger) that divides man from animal so completely that the essence of man is animal in no way whatever, also divides German from Jew, again without compassion. For cherishment, care for others rather than oneself and one's *Geschlecht,* is lacking in Heidegger's infamous remark in 1949, his only known remark on the concentration camps. "Agriculture is now a mechanized food industry; in essence it is no different than the production of corpses in the gas chambers and death camps, the embargoes and food reductions to starving countries, the making of hydrogen bombs" (quoted in Lyotard, *HJ,* p. 85). Now the murder of millions of people in gas chambers, millions of Jews among others, is indeed in many ways like mechanized food production, especially in the treatment of animals. With compassion, care, with ethical wounding for the others, we might weep for the murdered people and for the millions of slaughtered and abused animals no one remembers. Animals suffer in the mechanized food industry in unimaginable ways. Their corpses litter our lives, our tables, haunt our souls. But with all our cherishment and responsibility, animals are different from people, and plants are different from animals, and we must and will cherish them differently, with or without criteria. Though those who revere Heidegger may deny it, the same lack of cherishment toward animals he evinces because they lack "the gift" carries over into a lack of cherishment toward people destroyed in the name of our *Geschlecht,* because they are not like us.[17]

A second idea, inseparable from *Geschlecht,* is that of embodiment, human and animal materiality. We touched on it briefly and obliquely in relation to Heidegger's denial that the essence of humanity (of the human *Geschlecht*) is that of an animal, however rational. One side of this denial is a withdrawal from the rationality of the essence of *Dasein.* But the other, clearly present, is that man is higher than animal. Man is not the animal with the gift of language, but is not an animal at all, not even in body. The human hand is not a paw, fang, or claw, is not embodied, material. It is never two, but only *the* hand. "Apes have prehensile organs that resemble hands, the man of the typewriter and of technics in general uses two hands. But the man that speaks and the man that writes with the hand, as one says; isn't he the monster with a single hand? . . . What comes to man through *logos* or speech (*das Wort*) can be only one single hand" (Derrida, *G2,* p. 182). The Hand represents, in the name of the gift, and within the body, a denial of flesh and blood embodiment, that is, being in matter with two hands, two eyes, flesh and blood, and sexual organs, mixed up and sometimes crazy sexual organs. The gift represents an exclusion based on a refusal of intermediate numbers, including the dyad of gender.

For *Geschlecht,* around which this entire discussion turns, is the German word for gender, sexual difference, reintroducing the central link between sexual difference and animal difference. It is an extraordinary word in German.[18] The essence of man echoes the interval between men and women, in the *entre* (and certainly *antre*), of sexual difference, in German in the name of our *Geschlecht.* The essence of humanity echoes the interval between human beings and animals or other creatures, in the *aentre* of the beast, the monster, again in the name of our *Geschlecht,* of our gender. kind. The essence of our *Geschlecht,* in which all the movements of ethics and politics move, the ethics|politics to which w|e belong, men and women, excludes "dogmatically."

What can save us from this dogmatism, when those who speak of our salvation repeat the movement of dogmatism? Perhaps nothing can save us from dogmatism because the *aentre* we inhabit in ethical difference is a forgetting. We struggle incessantly to remember that it is a forgetting. We struggle to cherish what we have forgotten, remembering our injustices and the injustices of others. I read Anaximander's fragment, describing the ordinance of time as restitution for the immemorial and unending injustices of things to each other, as imposing an inexhaustible responsibility toward everything everywhere, enacted in place, where we rest, always elsewhere. This remembering, living between a forgetting and a remembering, is plenishment, cherishment and sacrifice, ethical difference. It seems to be something Heidegger forgot, even as we gained the idea of the Forgotten from him. At least, that is what Lyotard says.

From the humankind of *Geschlecht,* but repulsing the dominion of The Human and The German, I ask you to consider the English language's "kind," sometimes restricted to Our Own Kind:

The Oxford English Dictionary lists the following principal meanings of *kind* (Old English *gecynde*), in two groups: (1) (a) what belongs to one by origin, birth, or nature, including place, property, and quality; (b) one's own, properly, by nature; (c) nature in general, generically; a class possessing attributes in common; (d) a race, or class, of creatures, also family, tribe, clan, kin, kinfolk; therefore, offspring, progeny, descendants, kin and kinfolk; family, stock, ancestry; (e) bread and water in the Eucharist; leading to *kind of,* the class, family, tribe etc. to which an individual belongs, a sort,

> sort of, vulgarly, to some extent, in a way; then *in kind,* alluding to goods or property; (2) (a) natural, native, inherent; (b) proper, appropriate, fitting; belonging by right of birth; (c) well-born, of good kind; (d) benevolent, bearing good will, generous and caring, agreeable, pleasant, thankful; (e) soft, tender, easy to work with.

This dyadic, heterogeneous kindness may express an ethic closer to nature's heterogeneity than we have so far considered, closer to sexual and ethical difference.

Derrida, in a remembering of sexual difference that I hope to echo,[19] another remembrance, asks us to remember that sexual difference cannot be forgotten when neutralized. Still restricted to Heidegger, but with the entire world, at least Western world, ringing in the wings, Derrida notes that the absence of *Dasein*'s sex . . . , Heidegger's silence on sex . . . , means . . . :

> Of sex, one can readily remark, yes, Heidegger speaks as little as possible, perhaps he has never spoken of it. Perhaps he has never said anything, by that name or the names under which we recognize it, of the "sexual-relation," "sexual-difference," or indeed of "man-and-woman." (Derrida, *G1,* p. 65)

> But insofar as it is opened up to the question of being, insofar as it has a relation to being, in that very reference, *Dasein* would not be sexed. (Derrida, *G1,* p. 66)

The point to which Derrida leads us, acknowledging the possibility in it of extreme violence, is that the neutrality of *Dasein, Dasein*'s lack of sexual difference, is sexed. The question of ethical and sexual difference for us is how nature, everywhere, is sexed, heterogeneous, filled with known and unknown kinds.[20]

We have heard in *unser Geschlecht* another exclusion of animals from the privileged realm of humanity, another animal sacrifice. Animals cannot speak. Animals cannot experience death as death (Heidegger, *OWL,* p. 107). Derrida speaks of this silence that excludes animals in what he calls his fourth discussion of *Geschlecht* (Derrida, *G4*). Beginning with the passing and cryptic words in *Being and Time,* "as in hearing the voice of the friend whom every Dasein carries with it" (Heidegger, *BT,* §34, p. 206),[21] Derrida returns us to a neutrality devoid of body, materiality, and sex, this invisible and disembodied friend. "The friend has no face, no figure. No sex. No name. The friend is not a man, nor a woman" (Derrida, *G4,* p. 165), certainly not an animal, who has neither ear nor voice nor hand, does not know its death. So Heidegger says, and Derrida asks us to reconsider, though not by representing the animal as voiced, with Care, within a certain negativity and silence, still resisting Heidegger's exclusions.

> The animal has no friend, man has no friendship properly so called for the animal. The animal that is "world poor," that has neither language nor experience of death, etc., the animal that has no hand, the animal that has no friend, has no ear either, the ear capable of hearing and of carrying the friend that is also the ear that opens Dasein to its own potentiality-for-being and that . . . is the ear of being, the ear for being. (Derrida, *G4*, p. 172)[22]

Here, in *G4,* we return to the primordial in *Being and Time* in terms of the ideas of voice and friend, leading, Derrida tells us, to the blow, the curse again, under the name of *polemos*. First, the primordiality.

> Dasein's opening to its *ownmost* potentiality-for-being, as hearing the *voice of the other as friend,* is absolutely originary. This opening does not come under a psychology, a sociology, an anthropology, an ethics, or a politics, etc. The voice of the other friend, of the other as friend, the ear that I prick up to it, is the condition of my own-proper-being. (Derrida, *G4,* p. 174)

Certainly, this friend, as *philein* and *logos,* is not an animal or a woman. Nor is the ear an animal ear (Derrida, *G4,* p. 175).

Yet something primeval echoes in the animal voice and ear, excluded by Heidegger's absolutely originary and primordial refusal of anthropology, sociology, ethics, and politics. Perhaps, in the refusal of ethics an ethics can be found toward animals and other natural things, as in the refusal of *Dasein*'s sex a certain sexual difference remains, a double and triple and quadruple blow. And perhaps another blow strikes in the profound and far-reaching granting of the animal voice, if only under the sign of death. For Heidegger says that animals do not know death as death, as they do not know language as language.[23] Hegel understands the triangle of voice, death, and animal in a profoundly haunting way. For in the early and unpublished work in which he speaks of death "in terrifying terms," Hegel speaks of the animal voice.[24]

> Every animal finds a voice in its violent death; it expresses itself as a removed-self (*als aufgehobnes Selbst*). (Birds have song,

> which other animals lack, because they belong to the element of air—articulating voice, a more diffused self.)
>
> In the voice, meaning turns back into itself; it is negative self, desire (*Begierde*). It is lack, absence of substance in itself. (Hegel, *JR II;* Agamben, *LD,* pp. 44–45)

If we do not emphasize death, loss, alienation and sacrifice, the animal voice still speaks, out of itself, in the plenitude of nature and reality, in the plenishment in the earth. It is worth comparing Aristotle, on "man alone" and the voice.

> Nature, as we often say, makes nothing in vain, and man is the only animal whom she has endowed with the gift of speech. And whereas mere voice is but an indication of pleasure or pain, and is therefore found in other animals (for their nature attains to the perception of pleasure and pain and the intimation of them to one another, and no further), the power of speech is intended to set forth the expedient and inexpedient, and therefore likewise the just and the unjust. And it is a characteristic of man that he alone has any sense of good and evil, of just and unjust, and the like, and the association of living beings who have this sense makes a family and a state. (Aristotle, *Politics,* 1253a)

For Aristotle follows this chapter immediately with a discussion of masters and slaves, husbands and wives, father and children. Voice and its unique relation to the just and unjust founds ethics and the state, on the corpses we may say, of animals, who can scream but cannot say that their deaths are unjust.[25]

It seems that the blow that strikes sexual difference, its curse, curses animals more bitterly, that in the silence of their death, in their screams, because they do not speak in consonants or grammar, we are ethically, morally, in service to the good and God, sure that we treat them well to kill them and eat them, to use them for our purposes. The blow under which women, slaves, and other races fall, falls repeatedly and devastatingly on animals. You and I may struggle with the idea that this primordial blow, originary *polemos,* works to the destruction of one or another kind of creature or human, when we know in our heart of hearts that to destroy a kind is to commit the worst possible crime.[26] I understand Heraclitus's *polemos* in terms of Anaximander's *adikia* to say again and again that we find ourselves surrounded by injustices that we must resist and against which we must seek endless restitution, knowing that every restitution works unjustly.

This brings me to my infinite difference with Heidegger, however close we may be on the idea of sacrifice.[27] For I understand the injustice of the strife, archaic injustice, to impose a double blow, described by Foucault in his reading of Nietzsche as the domination of domination and the infliction of violence on violence (Foucault, *NGH,* p. 151).[28] The contamination, the injustice, of *polemos,* of justice, truth, and law, of every work of the good in the world, is endless. Sacrifice is contaminated, unjust, violent, and destructive. An ethic of plenishment seeks to sacrifice sacrifice as much as possible in the contamination of contamination, the injustice in justice. The form this injustice takes is the destruction visited on certain individuals and kinds in the name of glory, bliss, community, self-protection, and the good. Ethical difference knows that there is always an enemy, and warns us to beware of ourself as that enemy, beware of our own injustices. In Derrida's words, we hope to have the ear to hear the endlessly repeated question, the question Heidegger seems never to hear directed at him, "[w]hen will you stop sacrificing me?" (Derrida, *G4,* p. 215).[29]

The suggestion to which we are led, the thought that contaminates Heidegger within every gesture we may make to remember his thought of forgetting, is that the idea of the ontological, primordial, originary, the Clearing in which *Dasein* receives its comportment, makes it impossible to think of the plenitude of nature, nature's movement, contingencies, events, as a heterogeneity of kinds. Kinds in Heidegger seem to know only beings in their assembling together, kinds divided, dispersed, in profusion. *Dasein*'s neutral, neutered dispersion comes before kinds, before sexual, generic, specific kinds, before species and genera. The innocent and challenging truth that being knows no genus, no species, turns out to be deaf to the oppression and destruction of one species after another. The innocent and challenging truth that in striving to know, we strive to know and to order kinds of beings, turns out to strive in a mode of domination. These two moments of heterogeneity, of the plenitude of the kinds of beings there are in being, in nature, *physis,* the plenitude without which we cannot plenish the earth, belong together pervaded by cherishment. To belong to the earth is ethical in a cherishment of beings, individual beings and kinds of beings, genera and species, of beings together with other beings from which they receive their sustenance, identities, goods, in whose circulation we find the general economy of the earth. The structure of Heidegger's thought makes this ethical difference, kindred difference, in kinds, impossible to think primordially, belonging to beings rather than Being. This may be the thought embodied in *Geschlecht* of the highest, over animals and sexual difference, the thought of highest spirit, contaminated, not just by superiority and propriety, but by the neutrality that Irigaray understands to mask the masculinity of the subject. Our *Geschlecht,* of The Human, denies the plenishment of other kinds, with their *jouissances,* knowing nothing of superiorities and proprieties. For us here, the primordial, immemorial, works against the propriety of any rule, against the sovereignty of any privileged thought of nature, any privilege that any kind of thought of nature may bear, without historical and kindred, that is, ethical responsibility.[30]

We may now retrace the forgotten shaping of our Western *Geschlecht* as a monstrosity toward animals, a digression historically tracing Western culture's exclusion of nonhuman creatures from the good, to be followed in chapter 8 by an ecological feminist understanding of this exclusion. Where should we begin this digression but with the Garden of Eden?

> 24 And God said, Let the earth bring forth the living creature after his kind, cattle and creeping thing, and beast of the earth after his kind: and it was so.
>
> 25 And God made the beast of the earth after his kind, and cattle after their kind, and every thing that creepeth upon the earth after his kind: and God saw that it was good.
>
> 26 And God said, Let us make man in our image, after our likeness: and let them have dominion over the fish of the sea, and over the fowl of the air, and over the earth, and over every creeping thing that creepeth upon the earth.
>
> 27 So God created man in his own image, in the image of God created he him; male and female created he them.
>
> 28 And God blessed them, and God said upon them, Be fruitful, and multiply, and replenish the earth, and subdue it; and have dominion over the fish of the sea, and over the fowl of the air, and over every living thing that moveth upon the earth.
>
> 29 And God said, Behold, I have given you every herb bearing seed, which *is* upon the face of all the earth, and every tree, in the which *is* the fruit of a tree yielding seed; to you it shall be for meat. (*Gen.* 1)

Every living thing is brought forth in its own kind, but humanity is created in God's own image, male and female. And humanity is given *dominion* over every other creature, though, at least in the Garden of Eden, human beings do not eat other animals, but eat seeds and fruits.

Everything depends on how we understand the word "dominion." And in this understanding, we take up the question of how cherishment can, faced with evil, avoid encouraging oppression. For verse 29 suggests, and has been read by many to support, the possibility that every living creature, including human beings, may live in peace without destroying other creatures. The dominion of man, here, may be closer to God as shepherd and judge of the good, far from the idea of using animals for human purposes. Socrates speaks repeatedly of shepherds and the art of shepherding as having the good of the sheep as its goal, not the benefit of the shepherd. Both of these images of dominion have been contaminated by later historical developments: all despotisms, however benevolent, seem in the end to serve the interests of the ruling class; the continuing pressure of instrumentality, *technē*, is toward specifiable goals. In the latter senses, any political dominion that is not democratic is despotic, and any purposiveness is instrumental, for the good of the agent.

Yet if dominion is not equated with political rule, but with God's, then it bears a closer relation to plenishment. God's purpose is the goodness of all things together in the Garden of Eden, under human dominion as the agent of God, in the likeness of God, bearing the same responsibilities toward the good as God's, responsibilities betrayed. And with that betrayal, with that sin, humans took on the burden of injustice, clothed by God in animal skins, sent forth from the Garden with the words:

> 17 . . . cursed *is* the ground for thy sake; in sorrow shalt thou eat of it all the days of thy life;
>
> 18 Thorns also and thistles shall it bring forth to thee; and thou shalt eat the herb of the field;
>
> 19 In the sweat of thy face shalt thou eat bread, till thou return unto the ground; for out of it wast though taken; for dust thou *art*, and unto dust shalt thou return. (*Gen.* 3)

We may read the Garden forward into the Flood, and later to God's dietary laws, as if every living creature belongs to humanity for its use. Yet Noah finds favor in God's eyes, not least because he has saved every living thing from destruction, God's destruction, and has counted them, pair by pair. "I will not again curse the ground any more for man's sake; for the imagination of man's heart *is* evil from his youth; neither will I again smite any more every thing living, as I have done" (*Gen.* 8:21).

> 1 And God blessed Noah and his sons, and said unto them, Be fruitful, and multiply, and replenish the earth.
>
> 2 And the fear of you and the dread of you shall be upon every beast of the earth, and upon every fowl of the air, upon all that moveth *upon* the earth, and upon all the fishes of the sea; into your hand are they delivered.
>
> 3 Every moving thing that liveth shall be meat for you; even as the green herb have I given you all things.
>
> 4 But flesh with the life thereof, which *is* the blood thereof, shall ye not eat. (*Gen.* 9)

Man's dominion becomes domination.

We may read the Garden instead as cherishment, as the work of God present in all living things, toward which, in their dominion, human beings bear the greatest responsibility for maintaining, fostering, preserving. All living things, all things, are precious in God's eyes, the fruits of his work. As God cherishes humanity, tempered with justice and mercy, humanity must cherish animals and other living creatures, all things, tempered with justice and mercy, surrounded by sacrifice. Others have read Eden as cherishment:

> Man walk'd with beast, joint tenant of the shade;
> The same his table, and the same his bed;
> Nor murder cloath'd him, and no murder fed.
>
> . . . .
>
> Heav'n's attribute was Universal Care,
> And Man's prerogative to rule, but spare.
> Ah! how unlike the man of times to come!
> Of half that live the butcher and the tomb;
> Who, foe to Nature, hears the gen'ral groan,
> Murders their species, and betrays his own.
>
> (Pope, *Essay on Man,* 3, 4:152–164)

Eden's utopia is impossible, was impossible long before Eve sinned; and again, this story of the good, of gardens and animals, cannot be told without recapitulating sexual difference. It is impossible because lions who lie down with lambs will probably die, because animals and things cannot all exist together. This incompatibility is what Whitehead understands as evil. Eden represents cherishment without sacrifice, goodness without pain and suffering. But ethics falls into the *aentre* of plenishment, cherishment, and sacrifice together. On the one hand, represented by Eden, we live with impossible responsibilities toward the good, of cherishing all, every living and nonliving thing, the inexhaustibility of their presence and promise. On the other hand, represented by the Flood, we live with memories of inexhaustible injustices and wounds, deaths and destructions, everywhere among living and nonliving things. Noah saves every living creature from destruction, from God's sacrifice, and receives in return their bodies for his use, another sacrifice. But no sacrifice can dull the memory of the good, where nothing is sacrificed to anything else, especially not to human beings, who can live with fewer rather than greater sacrifices of other creatures and things.

This is so important that I wish to repeat it. Many animals cannot live without destroying other animals and living things. They know no other way. Their bodies may demand sustenance that can be provided in no other way. But humanity knows many other ways and can frequently provide these requisites for itself and others in other ways. These other ways turn sacrifice upon itself, revealing its evil side. We might take responsibility for the institution of God's goodness, everywhere, as commanded in the Garden of Eden to do as best we can. But we humans have not chosen to save animals and ourselves from the destructive side of sacrifice, have chosen instead to magnify oppression and destruction.

Humanity's Edenic dominion over the earth is one of caretaking, cherishment, an economy of gifts, taking care of every precious thing as far as possible, receiving precious goods from the earth, circulating them as humanity's gift to the earth. Humanity's reach over the earth is limited, punctuated by floods and famines, by breaches in the earth and by human evil. Plenishment of the earth, ethical difference, falls into injustice, from oppression and domination to sadness and grief. Let us think of Noah's right to kill animals with the grief and wounding it deserves, a mark of the Flood, a wounding of the earth, to be avoided wherever possible, though avoiding it may be impossible. The goodness, the rests, of the earth demand it. God gives humanity permission to kill and eat other animals, to destroy other things, in the name of sacrifice. But this permission belongs to sacrifice. It belongs to the serpent's monstrosity.

For we have not thought deeply enough of the place of animals in the monstrosity of *le propre* and our *Geschlecht*. From the beginning of Western thought, madness and monstrosity have marked the limits of our *Geschlecht,* of our rationality. When Hecuba discovers that her son, Polydorus, has been murdered by Polymestor, whom she trusted as a friend, she speaks in madness' language of monsters and betrayal: "O awful crime! O deed without a name! beggaring wonder! impious! intolerable! Where are now the laws 'twixt guest and host? Accursed monster! how has thou mangled his flesh, slashing the poor child's limbs with ruthless word, lost to all sense of pity!" (Euripides, *Hecuba,* p. 823; 709–12) After she has blinded Polymestor, he speaks of animal monsters made so by ethical monstrousness—his and Hecuba's: "Ha! hush! I catch their stealthy footsteps here. Where can I dart on them and gorge me on their flesh and bones, making for myself a wild beasts' meal, exacting vengeance in requital of their outrage on me?" (Euripides, *Hecuba,* p. 834; 1070–73) Polymestor curses Hecuba to become mad as a dog, though again, she is already mad: "[t]hough wilt become a dog with bloodshot eyes)" (Euripides, *Hecuba,* p. 838; 1265). The voice of vengeance echoes the monstrosity of animals. Archaic injustice represents the wild unspeakableness of authority and goodness, echoing for us as the monstrosity of beasts.[31]

In the monstrosity of our *Geschlecht,* we find that humans, as always, represent the proper measure of justice where animals represent the measure of monstrosity. The natural consequence is animal sacrifice. Animals bear the mark of ethical difference, inhabit the *aentre* of ethical difference, as almost nothing else does or can, in the roars of monsters and the screams of their sacrifice. We may read the tale of the Garden of Eden as a narrative of this place of kindred difference.

We may compare this interval between cherishment and sacrifice, the Garden of Eden and the Flood, with Aristotle's unambiguous view of slavery, unambiguous at least in his *Politics.*

> Hence we see that is the nature and office of a slave; he who is by nature not his own but another's man, is by nature a slave; and he may be said to be another's man who, being a human being, is also a possession. (Aristotle, *Politics,* 1254a)

> Where then there is such a difference as that between soul and body, or between men and animals . . . the lower sort are by

> nature slaves, and it is better for them as for all inferiors that they should be under the rule of a master. (Aristotle, *Politics,* 1254b)

But Aristotle has said much the same thing of women, said it "dogmatically," without the slightest uncertainty. For he begins his *Politics* with the family, says that politics begins with sexual difference. "In the first place there must be a union of those who cannot exist without each other; namely, of male and female, that the race may continue . . . " (Aristotle, *Politics,* 1252a). This beginning is followed immediately, without the slightest interval, by the question of domination, who shall rule and who obey. "For that which can foresee by the exercise of mind is by nature intended to be lord and master, and that which can with its body give effect to such foresight is a subject, and by nature a slave" (Aristotle, *Politics,* 1252ab). The head rules, the body obeys: subjecting slaves, women, and animals. This triangle rings of the domination of these together, as if the first thought of each were subjection.

Yet a distinction rules between women and slaves, if not between slaves and animals, a distinction based on *technē,* or rather, on a certain view of *technē* and of nature's kinds. "Now nature has distinguished between the female and the slave. For she is not niggardly, like the smith who fashions the Delphian knife for many uses; she makes each thing for a single use, and every instrument is best made when intended for one and not for many uses" (Aristotle, *Politics,* 1252b). This idea of a single use of human beings (and animals, and women) underlies the entire idea of a ethical good based on *technē,* an idea resonating in Plato's *Republic,* but which I believe is countermanded there by a complex view of virtue [*aretē*].[32] It is closely allied, I believe, with this triangle of superiority, *aentre* women, slaves, and animals, all subordinated to the superior kind's dominion based on a single, technical criterion of superiority. Where virtue, human or natural excellence, is inexhaustibly complex and heterogeneous, as we understand to follow from ethical difference, superiority and inferiority vanish without a measure. Indeed, the measure of human and natural superiority and inferiority resonates with the idea of *Geschlecht.* That is what we hear in Aristotle.

But something deeper, more nefarious, works in this triangle of Aristotle's politics. For in the beginning, giving rise to the family, is the juncture of sexual difference and slavery, repeatedly thought together.

> Out of these two relationships between man and woman, master and slave, the first thing to arise is the family. . . . Every family is ruled by the eldest, and therefore in the colonies of the family the kingly form of government prevailed because they were of the same blood. As Homer says:
>
> "Each one gives law to his children and to his wives." (Aristotle, *Politics,* 1252b)

The beginning of politics is the family, emerging from sexual difference, based on the rule of the eldest man over his children and wives, men over women, from the very beginning, echoing the rule of men over animals and masters over slaves, while women and animals and slaves are all different, with different individual and unique excellences, "uses." Each has its use, and all are determined and fostered in their use by their masters. On this reading, I question where Irigaray says that women have no place. They have this place precisely, a place of use, men's, rulers', masters' use, which is their own. "The family is the association established by nature for the supply of men's everyday wants" (Aristotle, *Politics,* 1252b). With some certainty we know that the wants are men's and not women's.

In a discussion that begins with property, Aristotle repeats this triangle of slave, animal, and sexual difference. The discussion begins, "[l]et us now inquire into property generally, and into the art of getting wealth, in accordance with our usual method, for a slave has been shown to be a part of property" (Aristotle, *Politics,* 1256a). He ends the discussion with an analogy between (*aentre*) the "master of the house and the ruler of the state" (Aristotle, *Politics,* 1258a). In between (*aentre*), all things are useful to their superiors, for the benefit of their superiors (something Plato repeatedly denies).

> In like manner we may infer that, after the birth of animals, plants exist for their sake, and that the other animals exist for the sake of man, the tame for use and food, the wild, if not all, at least the greater part of them, for food, and for the provision of clothing and various instruments. Now if nature makes nothing incomplete, and nothing in vain, the inference must be that she has made all animals for the sake of man. (Aristotle, *Politics,* 1256b)

Here, unambiguously, based on a movement from nature's wild and multifarious excesses to the single predominant usefulness of natural things, Aristotle concludes that animals and plants, some human beings, and women all are useful to men, are ruled (and destroyed) to the benefit of their rulers, not to their own.

This idea reaches its excess of perfection in Aquinas, who makes Aristotle's ugliness uglier. For if we can imagine the possibility in Aristotle that nature, *physis,* knows of something other, provides another ethical movement than the use of things by men, Aquinas dissipates every other sense of that other.

> There is no sin in using a thing for the purpose of which it is. Now the order of things is such that the imperfect are for the perfect . . . things, like plants which merely have life, are all alike for animals, and all animals are for man. Wherefore it is not unlawful if men use plants for the good of animals, and animals for the good of man, as the Philosopher states (Aristotle, *Politics,* 1.3).
>
> Now the most necessary use would seem to consist in the fact that animals use plants, and men use animals, for food, and this cannot be done unless these be deprived of life, wherefore it is lawful both to take life from plants for the use of animals, and from animals for the use of men. In so far this is in keeping with the commandment of God himself. (*Gen.* 1:29–30 and *Gen.* 9:3 as referred to in Aquinas, *ST,* 2.2.Q64, art. 1)

This seems an exact portrayal of one side of Aristotle and of *Genesis,* with the addition of two ideas, perfection and lawfulness. Aquinas and Aristotle agree that plants and animals have their use, apparently a single use, for if these uses were plural, if animals had uses for themselves and others as well as human beings, then these might conflict, might resist superiority. But the greater perfection entails the rule and use of the lesser. And if something is lawful it is good.

I reply that it remains to be seen, in Aristotle and Aquinas, whether human perfection entails the right to use or, instead, the responsibility to save. I reply as well that because something is lawful, that does not make it good, but rather, the good may be in constant turmoil with the law.

But Aquinas becomes more and more oppressive. "[I]t matters not how man behaves to animals, because God has subjected all things to man's power . . . and it is in this sense that the Apostle says that God has no care for oxen, because God does not ask of man what he does with oxen or other animals" (Aquinas, *ST,*

2.1.Q109, art. 6).[33] The possibility, in Plato, that the sovereignty is one of care, for the good of the object used, that use is an ethical relation, vanishes in Aquinas's view of nature. I reply that I do not believe that God (if there be one) rules over humanity in the interests of God. I reply that in God's eyes—looking everywhere in nature for the good, in the rests of ethical difference—everything matters infinitely, inexhaustibly; nothing "matters not."

Aquinas's ideas carry forward virtually unchanged, to Kant. "[S]o far as animals are concerned, we have no direct duties. Animals are not self-conscious, and are there merely as a means to an end. That end is man" (Kant, *LE,* pp. 129–40). With this idea of means and ends I cease this historical recapitulation. For we have understood Kant to open to us the possibility that nothing whatever can be anywhere merely as a means. The burden of the teleological judgment is that nature always falls under ends.

An ethic of inclusion enters at this point, where nothing can be treated merely as a means, not because of our ethical ideals, but because nothing is a means and not an end. I take this from Dewey. Ethical difference rests upon the conviction that nothing can be treated merely as a means because nothing is merely a means. Ethical difference knows nothing of the "merely," refuses every "merely" that implies superiority. As Dewey says, everything is a means, in relations that link together composing projects, and everything is an end. Moreover, everything that is a means is also an end, with a certain inexhaustible finality, and everything that is an end is a means and can be used as a means, again inexhaustibly. Means and ends are not closures, oppositional, but to the contrary, each expresses inexhaustibility, excess, while the two together, the dyad, expresses another inexhaustibility of intervals, betweens, *aentres,* and envelopes of identity.

Moreover, the inexhaustibility is precious. "To know, means that men have become willing to turn away from precious possessions; willing to let drop what they do not as yet own, however precious, in behalf of a grasp of objects which they do not as yet own" (Dewey, *EN,* p. 131). I hesitate at the idea that we own objects unqualifiedly, ours to use and abuse. And Dewey denies that we own anything unqualifiedly, leaving the ethical implications aside.[34] The ethical implications are that even when we own something, we do not own it for our use alone, as if it were not inexhaustibly precious. Things in nature are what they are, precious and inexhaustible, with inexhaustible promises. Ethical difference cherishes this inexhaustibility beyond all cherishment, refusing every "merely." The form of judgment that expresses this ethical truth most irresistibly is art. Yet art finds its own ways to pass from cherishment to subjection, through the voice of art for art's sake, merely for art, neglecting the inexhaustibility of sacrifice.

Ethical difference irrupts in the turmoil of sexual difference, each an unlimited, indeterminate dyad rather than binarity, opposition, or domination, each repeatedly giving way to these where the unlimitedness of the dyad collapses into the intermediate number, the pair, into *technē*. Here woman as man's place is situated at multiple sites of inexhaustibility: man's inexhaustible limits, woman's disturbances, displacements of every place, inexhaustible places throughout nature. Sexual difference expresses the inexhaustibility of place, of being in place and of being elsewhere, related elsewhere, ends and means. Things as ends—not just "concretes" and "particularities," but nations, kinds, composites, harmonies, whatever—compose cherishment and emerge in *poiēsis*. For *poiēsis* is the coming to be of things in their inexhaustibility, cherished for the unending promises, possibilities, openings belonging to them, cherished for their coming to be. Art expresses cherishment, the inexhaustibility of things; art is *poiēsis*. But it is not the only form of *poiēsis*, nor the most precious form. Nor does it own cherishment. Everything we do, as Dewey says, is permeated, surrounded by, qualities, ends, finality, inexhaustibility. Things are inexhaustible. Nature is inexhaustible. Human experience is inexhaustible. All are inexhaustibly precious. To know, to participate in, to feel, to experience, to encounter inexhaustibility, is to cherish. Cherishment is our opening into nature's inexhaustible movement. It is the soul of ethics. It is soul.

Yet within this opening's movement toward inexhaustibility, unlimit, are relations and directions. Nature moves inexhaustibly out of itself in an ethical movement that belongs to everything everywhere, nature's inexhaustible places. To be in place, to have a place, an inexhaustible presence, finality, is to be in other places, elsewhere, related elsewhere as inexhaustible means. We cherish things inexhaustibly as ends. We use things inexhaustibly as means because they are means, are situated here and elsewhere, in relations. As cruel as it is to recognize it, temporal ekstasis, being outside oneself, belongs to *technē* in the form of sacrifice.

All this is heard in Dewey. Means and ends are everywhere, in experience and in nature. Existence—nature and being—possesses the qualities and relations we find in experience. "[T]he world of empirical things includes the uncertain, unpredictable, uncontrollable, and hazardous" (Dewey, *EN*, p. 42). These qualities and feelings, ascribed in Western thought to human experience, belong to nature, to natural things and creatures. And further, "[m]an fears because he exists in a fearful, an awful world. The *world* is precarious and perilous" (Dewey, *EN*, p. 42). This uncertain danger of the world bears resemblance to Nietzsche's sense of the Dionysian, promoting the understanding that Apollo and Dionysus represent indefinite dyads of nature and being, which humanity forgets in its passion for order, its fear of disorder.[35] The world is precarious and perilous, but also regular, patterned, and fulfilling. Nature is filled with qualities, with ends and finalities, some of which are glorious, rewarding, others of which are terrifying, disturbing. Dewey emphasizes the precarious because, like Nietzsche, he takes the Western tradition to have overemphasized the value of security.[36]

I understand ethical difference to inhabit the places where ends meet means, order meets disorder, *poiēsis* meets *technē.* I call it the *aentre,* emphasizing the places between one gender and another, one human kind and another, humanity and animals, human beings and nature, among heterogeneous kinds, unthinkable without sexual difference. Like sexual difference, ethical difference pursues the place(s) of men and women, human beings and other things, in nature and experience, where placement is both limit and unlimit, somewhere and elsewhere. Dewey emphasizes this elsewhere again and again, like Nietzsche in the form of the perilous and unstable, the disorderly. And, like Nietzsche, he suggests that ethical difference entails a certain unity, integration, of order and disorder, stability and hazardousness. "The union of the hazardous and the stable, of the incomplete and the recurrent, is the condition of all experienced satisfaction as truly as of our predicaments and problems. While it is the source of ignorance, error and failure of expectation, it is the source of the delight which fulfillments bring" (Dewey, *EN*, p. 62).[37]

We have noted Dewey's expression of the limits of *technē:* things are had before they are known; things are ends before they are means; things are unlimit before they are limit, and unlimit after they are limit. The intermediate numbers emerge from unlimit and pass away into unlimit. The plenitude of nature, in its qualities and irreplaceable things, frames the movement of *technē*. From the standpoint of ethical difference, havings and endings are the forgotten of *technē*. Our endeavor, in ethical and sexual difference, is to remember the forgotten in *technē*. If we think of women as instruments of men for holding death at bay, places for men, then women are the forgotten plenitude that makes such an instrumentality possible. This is true even, or especially, where women are oppressed.

Dewey does not speak of women and their oppression. But he does deny that things may be treated as means alone. And he explains what such a treatment means.

> In responding to things not in their immediate qualities but for the sake of ulterior results, immediate qualities are dimmed, while those features which are signs, indices of something else, are distinguished. . . . The very conception of cognitive meaning, intellectual significance, is that things in their immediacy are subordinated to what they portend and give evidence of. (Dewey, *EN*, p. 128)

Women, as instruments, places for men, lose their immediate qualities, are subordinated to how they may be used. They become objects, Irigaray says. Dewey points out that objects too may be used so as to lose their immediacy. The use of natural things destroys, dims, their qualities as individual things. Their preciousness disappears into the relations of what they portend.

On this reading, *technē* represents the meanings and uses of things and is of profound importance in how we are to live at our very best, yet nonetheless is framed by *poiēsis*, by things in their being and becoming. Art and *poiēsis* express the being and becoming of things, a profoundly ethical event. But ethical difference cannot accept what art can accept, cannot cherish things in their immediacies and finalities without their relations and instrumentalities. Ethical difference bears a responsibility to work that art interprets differently, an ethical responsibility for consequences and results, a responsibility to employ *technē* in relation to cherishment. Here *technē* belongs to sacrifice. Again, I speak not of a union but a juncture, an *aentre*, a circulation of things in their means and ends, in our representations, cherishing them and using them, using them as we cherish them. Cherishment and sacrifice together are plenishment, where the "together" repeats unending, inexhaustible circulation of the *aentre* between means and ends.

This *aentre* is where women and animals are found in place, the *aentre* of nature, alongside if in different places from men. With this understanding, and with the understanding that ethical difference and an ethic of sexual difference inhabit the heterogeneous places *aentre* humanity and nature, humanity and world, humanity and machine, *poiēsis* and *technē*, I will let our discussion of women and animals pass away for just a moment while we come briefly to rest in the deep ecology of sexual difference.

CHAPTER 8

Rest

Warren and Cheney describe ecological feminism in words frequently repeated.

> We take ecological feminism to refer "to a sensibility, an intimation, that feminist concerns run parallel to, are bound up with, or, perhaps, are one with concern for a natural world which has been subjected to much the same abuse and ambivalent behavior as have women." (Warren and Cheney, *EFEE,* p. 180)
>
> . . . the common thread that runs through ecofeminist scholarship is that the domination of women and the domination of nature are "intimately connected and mutually reinforcing." (Warren and Cheney, *EFEE,* p. 180; the quoted material is from King, *EFFE,* p. 18)

The movement here, from an ethic of sexual difference to ethical and kindred difference, follows the trajectory of ecological feminism, with a difference. I began with questions of sexual difference as questions of our age, understanding such questions to inhabit a movement from sexual to ethical difference, a movement in heterogeneity, understanding such questions to make a far-reaching difference in our age, in u|s, in our histories, in how we think about whatever pertains to us and our age. I understand these questions of the age, questions of sexual and ethical difference, to lead (back) to nature, to kindred difference. Questions of ethical and sexual difference are questions of nature's heterogeneities, understanding nature in terms of place, interval (*aentre*), circulation (restricted and general economy), and rest: all sexed, all embodied and represented as embodied, including skin, scales, fur, and membranes, and more. All questions of different kinds. Ethical difference sings the rests of the earth in a musical voice. This song follows the themes of ecological feminism, with a difference. I now take up the task of marking this difference.

We may begin with two conditions Warren and Cheney add to

ecological feminism, wondering why they do so, wondering if the addition resists the movement from sexual to ethical difference, resists the song of the earth.

> All ecofeminists endorse the view that an adequate understanding of the nature of the connections between the twin dominations of women and nature requires a feminist theory and practice informed by an ecological perspective and an environmentalism informed by a feminist perspective. (Warren and Cheney, *EFEE,* p. 180)

> What makes ecofeminist ethics feminist is a twofold commitment to critique male bias in ethics and to develop analyses which are not male-biased. (Warren and Cheney, *EFEE,* p. 180)

Our project here links the question of sexual difference to the earth, to natural things everywhere, in relation to mastery, to domination. Yet if the domination of nature and the domination of women are intimately linked, if we cannot understand the one without the other, if we cannot undertake a liberating practice toward one without pursuing a liberating practice toward the other, what further conditions do we impose in insisting on a feminist perspective and a critique of male bias?[1] Do Warren and Cheney imagine that there is a liberating ethical perspective that might fail to link the domination of nature and women, animals and women, that might link nature to machines but forget women, as Warren and Cheney seem to forget race and slavery in the dyad of women and nature, forget women's as well as men's slavery? Such a perspective seems unlikely. The bias may be male, and more; the bias may be evident from feminist and from other perspectives; ecology may be feminist at heart. Plenishment in the earth may fall between, *aentre,* the domination of women and the domination of nature, and more. In the more we resist exclusion.

Warren and Cheney may mean to enforce the priority of a feminist perspective in ecological feminism, resisting a deep ecology that subsumes the oppression of women under the oppression of nature or under the oppression of "mankind" in general.[2] I have strongly resisted that subsumption in a different, still I hope, feminist way, dwelling on the dyad of gender, refusing to let it pass away into the profusion of nature, another exclusion. Gender circulates throughout the other circulations of humanity and animals, humanity and machine, soul and body, goods and representations, circulates excessively, disturbs the equanimity and displacement of other dyads. Sexual difference expresses heterogeneity and excess, and more, for its dyads move so quickly among the others that none can remain in place without it, safely contained by it, perilously undermined by it. Dyads, intermediary figures, belong to the general economy of nature's rests, all sexed. Gender is an intermediary figure circulating everywhere in nature's plenitude.

I have dwelled on the idea of place, especially Irigaray's concern with the *aentre* of women's place, women and animals in the interval, at rest. I seek to understand an ethic of sexual difference—one I hope is truly feminist, and more—in the rests of the earth. But I believe that women inhabit nature's rests, as witches and gorgons, somewhere and elsewhere, always. And I believe that this elsewhere, of witches and gorgons, cannot be separated from the displacements of animals and other living creatures, extending to the bowels of the earth. From blood and kin.

This idea of place as displacement and replacement, every place as somewhere and everywhere, representing women's place and no place (inseparable from men's and animals' places and displacements), echoes forcefully in relation to the general economy of the earth. It reverberates so far and loud that we may wish to think of it beyond any critique of male bias, beyond its exclusions. This is not to deny male bias, again and again, but to consider that Western ethics is biased in more than male ways, twisted against much more than women, twisted by women as well as others against the rests of the earth. It is also to consider that questions of sexual and ethical difference concern matters deeper and more pervasive than bias or oppression. Questions of our age, even those of sexual difference, may not primarily concern the domination of women and nature, but the heterogeneous and unknown possibilities of the good everywhere, unacknowledged, excluded, buried and silenced, deep in the earth, as a result of that domination and more, inscribed on women's bodies and elsewhere.

Questions of our age, asked by Irigaray of Levinas, are questions of alterity, of what we may understand by kindred difference. I understand, as Irigaray does, that radical alterity, heterogeneity, brings us face to face with the gender, sex, or *Geschlecht* of the other, with another kind. The other toward whom we bear infinite responsibility belongs to other kinds within its singularity. Ethical difference confronts radical heterogeneity in ways inexpressible in individual terms alone. The positive side of this understanding, of our cherishment of the earth, including women and animals and other creatures and things, has little to do with male bias and domination, for it is sometimes present within the domination of biased males and sometimes absent among women and animals and other creatures and things. It has to do with heterogeneity and impurity.

The question of the relation between feminist and ecological ethics circulates repeatedly throughout ecological feminist writings. One approach is nurtured by an ethic of care, close to ethical difference. I first pick up the theme of ecological feminism and its feminist perspective.

> Ecofeminism is the position that "there are important connections—historical, experiential, symbolic, theoretical—between the domination of women and the domination of nature." It argues that the patriarchal conceptual framework that has maintained, perpetuated, and justified the oppression of women in Western culture has also, and in similar ways, maintained, perpetuated, and justified the oppression of nonhuman animals and the environment. (Curtin, *TEEC,* p. 60)

The quoted passage is from Warren (*PPEF,* p. 126). Yet Curtin follows the trajectory of ethical difference without exclusory conditions pertaining to male bias and a feminist perspective, except for the word "patriarchal." Women and animals have been oppressed in similar ways, under similar theoretical and political conditions, closely related to the use and destruction of the environment. Along with others. Curtin adds the word "justified," an important supplement, for the use and abuse of women and nature has been maintained and perpetuated by force, but it has been justified as ethical and good. The importance of ethical difference turns on the change it marks in our understanding of the good, in relation to women and nature, but also to machines and other things. The dyads, man–woman, man–animal, and man–environment, circulate around each other profoundly and deeply, circulate in the general economy of things together with their representations. In every case, the man, the male, is privileged, following the trajectory of masters and slaves. But having spoken of the rule of the master, we must include the dyads men–men and women–women, of different colors, races, and cultures. And we must include the dyads human–machine and machine–nature. All these heterogeneous dyads circulate in the general economy of practice as represented and justified as good.

I wish to suggest at this point, without undermining (but perhaps slightly displacing) a feminist perspective, that the dyadic echoes are more profuse and distorting than expressed by the pair, domination of women (by men)–domination of nature (by men). The dyads belong to, circulate within, the general economy of nature. Even where we agree with Irigaray that the "subject" has always been appropriated by the "masculine," so that the human subject who dominates animals and nature is masculine, we must add quotation marks. This "masculine" subject may not be male, be men, though men (some men, men in general) impose and profit from the domination and subjection. The masculine subject is not owned by men, may not even be male (though "male"), belongs to the social and historical construction of the dyad of gender. The neuter subject displaces women, gives them no place, substitutes the neuter for the masculine, which knows its place as woman. The (masculine) subject succeeds in passing itself off as the only subject by defining its own place elsewhere, in and as woman. Men and women, "masculine" and "feminine" subjects, places, are displaced, replacing each other. Place for both is somewhere and elsewhere, inexhaustibly. The universal neuter may be more dangerous than the male, dangerous even for men of different races and cultures. Even the possibility of a "male" bias and "male" oppression is a tremendous advance in the thought of ethical difference compared with a neutral universality that dominates both men and women, places men and women in subordinate positions, as if unknowing of their displacements.

Does this sense of inexhaustible displacement resist the idea of male domination, of the oppression of women, for example, by suggesting that some men too were oppressed or that in the oppression of women men displaced themselves? Such questions recall the founding question of ecological feminism: whether including the dyad women–animals undermines the thought of the oppression of women, works against a feminist perspective by dragging animals in. Ecological feminism especially as expounded by Curtin, insists that women's and animals' domination and oppression are inseparably linked. I have traced the movement of thought in which the idea of such oppressions belong to an instrumentality and an idea of use under which women and animals have historically been subjected, the idea that only men (mankind, the neuter) have souls. Or rather, that men in their infinite souls get cantankerous if they do not rule their women and children and get to eat their animals. At least, that is what Spinoza seems to say. Or else, that the oppression of women and children and animals is inseparable from slavery even in a world in which slavery has been abolished. At least, that is what some people say, abolished.

In the understanding here of place with its displacements, things always somewhere and elsewhere, dyads circulate together with other dyads in a general economy of the circulation of goods. This circulation is the general economy of the world, nature's rests. The subordination of women is linked inseparably with the subordination of animals and other natural things, and men, with subordination everywhere, displacing the subordination and subjection of men, of each dyad, by the others and multiply. The link between the domination of women and the domination of nature is not a mirror, as if there were no differences between women and nature, though it may reflect infinite mirrors, filled with displacements and representations. I have represented, expressed, the subjection of women in sexual difference as a pair *aentre,* expressing the places where women and animals meet in a radical heterogeneity neither kind can express alone, a monstrosity women cannot bear upon themselves alone, as it is cast upon them. I regard this radical heterogeneity to give rise to ethical difference, an ethic of cherishment and sacrifice. My concern here is with the difference between cherishment and care.

Let us return to the ethic of care within ecological feminism. We may hear the echoes of another dyad, or several dyads, circulating within and around an ethic of care. One is expressed by Warren, quoted by Curtin. Ecological feminism

> "involves a *shift* from a conception of ethics as primarily a matter of rights, rules, or principles predetermined and applied in specific cases to entities viewed as competitors in the contest of moral standing" to an ethic that "makes a central place for values of care, love, friendship, trust, and appropriate reciprocity-values that presuppose that our relationships to others are central to our understanding of who we are." (Curtin, *TEEC,* p. 61; Warren, *PPEF,* pp. 141, 143)

An ethic of care contrasts with an ethic of rules, rights, and principles, with an exclusionary, competitive ethic, and emphasizes love, nurture, trust instead of conflict. This is one dyad, framed in this context by the dyad of sexual difference. Corresponding to men and women are two ethics, of justice and nurture.

This is an important dyad, corresponding to a certain understanding of the dyad of sexual difference. As sexual difference divides men and women into a dyad, the dyad of gender, there are two ethics in which we find ourselves, corresponding to the difference of gender. This is the intermediate number two with a vengeance, not least because we might suppose that in the history of the West there were multiple ethical differences, multiple understandings and pursuits of the good,[3] but also because we do not imagine radical alterity in the idea that men and women have different ethics. To the contrary, the radical for us (men) may lie in the possibility that the ethics that may be revealed in feminist studies and in ecological feminism expresses something that men cannot live without, must suppose to know and be true, have always known as true. We, men and women, have always known injustice. The hold of sexual difference upon the dyad of justice and care expresses a measure of the good we cannot allow ourselves to accept as a measure, cannot allow ourselves to be forced to choose between. Such a between knows nothing of the places *aentre*.

In relation to an ethic of care, we may find another dyad, still framed in the language of conflict:

> Marti Kheel claims that much of the discussion of environmental ethics has failed to make "the open admission that we cannot even begin to talk about the issue of ethics unless we admit that we care (or feel something). And it is here that the emphasis of many feminists on personal experience and emotion has much to offer in the way of reformulating our traditional notion of ethics." (King, *CN*, p. 75; quoted from Kheel, *LN*, p. 144)

We are listening to the echoes of two different dyads (or dyads of dyads), one pairing in opposition justice and care, the other pairing, perhaps in opposition, perhaps in harmony, care as the possibility of ethics and care as the practice of nurture, trust. Both members of the latter dyad may derive from women's personal experiences and emotions, perhaps also from men's. One dyad concerns practice directly, asks us to choose in practice between justice and care. And perhaps we should make such a choice when we hope to act ethically; perhaps we cannot justify such a choice in relation to the good. I will argue against understanding the relation between justice and care, in ethical practice, as a choice.

But this discussion, this dyad, calls forth another contrast, between care in practice and the care, the feeling, from which ethics or the good emerge. Caring in practice is, for example, nurturing and fostering. Sometimes too much nurturing can be bad for children or for the caretaker. Another care inheres in the possibility of ethics, that one cares about, cares for, loves, the good in things, the others. This sense of care as cherishment bears no conflict or opposition within itself, even against the other kind of care, for it cannot replace it, cannot be chosen instead of it. I have understood it, for this reason, as an ethic of inclusion rather than exclusion. Yet Kheel and King seem unable to speak of a care that has no opposition, no conflict, within itself, no sense of being against.

I will now follow the first track of the oppositional dyad, the resurgence of conflict and opposition between an ethic of care (instead of conflict) and an ethic of rights and rules, prevailing within a world of conflict and exclusion. I will subsequently return to cherishment and sacrifice.

The oppositional dyad is given to us in two works typically read to give rise to a feminist ethics of care, Gilligan's *In a Different Voice* and Nodding's *Caring*. Gilligan claims that

> The moral imperative that emerges repeatedly in interviews with women is an injunction to care, a responsibility to discern and alleviate the "real and recognizable trouble" of this world. For men the moral imperative appears rather as an injunction to respect the rights of others and thus to protect from interference the rights to life and self-fulfillment. (Gilligan, *IDV*, p. 19)

Nodding is more prescriptive about ethical caring in relation to the good, but still matches it to femininity: "feminine in the deep classical sense—rooted in receptivity, relatedness, and responsiveness" (Nodding, *C*, p. 2). This dyad retains the force of opposition and conflict, not so much within itself, replacing conflicts of rights and duties with nurture and responsiveness, but between this ethic and the other ethic, care and justice, two ethics in opposition. In the extreme, we may be led to repudiate rights and duties as relevant to ethics in any way, even as destructive to ethics, for example: "I suggest that this and all of the difficulties mentioned in this essay could be solved by presuming that the relationship between rights and cares is neither additive nor competitive, but eliminative. We need to take the hard step of denying that rights exist" (Rigterink, *W*, pp. 42–43).

This conflict, between one ethic and another, repeats the structure of the conflict that pervades Western ethical thought from the beginning. I wonder if such a conflict repeats the exclusions of a patriarchal ethic against which an ethic of care is marshaled. Indeed, an ethic of care does not provide an ethic of inclusion when situated in opposition. Understandably, if we demand that an ethic present us with a course of action, when we choose one we must exclude the other. That is what it means to choose. Yet that we must exclude by choice is not equivalent with an ethic of exclusion. Hoagland expresses this insight in relation to self-sacrifice.

> We tend to regard choosing to do something as a sacrifice. I want to suggest, instead, that we regard choosing to do something as a creation. From heterosexualism we tend to believe that any time we help another, we are sacrificing something. . . . But these acts do not necessarily involve self-sacrifice. Rather, they involve a choice between two or more things to do. Often we have choices and we will have reasons for any choice we make. But that we have to make choices is not itself a matter of sacrifice. (Hoagland, *LEFA*, p. 162)

This insight, ascribed to heterosexualism, pertains to many Western views of altruism, viewing it as the sacrifice of one's interests to the interests of others, as if our interests always conflicted with those of others. Hoagland replies that we may benefit ourselves in benefiting others when we are in relation to them. This important understanding of the possibility of ethical practice without conflict, of fulfillment through pursuit of the good, still bears the structure of opposition, between homosexual and heterosexual, self-sacrifice and self-fulfillment. Hoagland institutes another opposition as she repudiates the opposition between choice and sacrifice. "Under the heterosexual model of femininity, the feminine virtues are self-sacrifice, vulnerability, and altruism. Female actions are to be directed toward others, thus the female ability to act is located in others. Consequently, the primary mode of female agency is manipulation" (Hoagland, *STC*, p. 246).

The language of self-sacrifice, vulnerability, and altruism echoes Levinas, a language as far as possible from manipulation. I have questioned whether the difference lies in subjectivity's relation to agency, if Levinas's subject acts toward the other, face to face, from the subject himself, in the masculine, whereas Hoagland's heterosexual woman acts toward the other, the man, subservient to the other. Here the only agent is the man, the only subject is masculine, repeating Irigaray's understanding that the Western subject is always appropriated by the "masculine." The self-sacrifice, vulnerability, and altruism of the heterosexual woman are not hers as a subject, as an agent, but given over to the man. That actions are directed toward others does not entail that they be located in others unless the direction is from the subaltern to the dominant, where the latter defines agency.

I do not share Levinas's understanding that the site of ethical agency lies in the ("masculine") subject, but understand agency and subjectivity in more dispersed and displaced terms. I understand Hoagland's language to reflect in self-sacrifice, vulnerability, and altruism not a displacement of ethical concern but a replacement of the woman's agency by another agency, another criterion, the man's. Men have passed off their standards as the universal standards of ethics. A caring woman cares for a man who may not care in return, may not reciprocate, and may not accept a caring ethic. "The anglo-european model of male ethical agency is that of one who is isolated, egoistic, competitive, and antagonistic" (Hoagland, *STC,* p. 247). If these are the standards for men, then care and altruism place women in subordination. Yet cherishment disperses, from one to multiple sites, imposes a debt from an other to inexhaustibly many others, pluralizes vulnerability, if always dyadically face to face. There is, then, for cherishment, no particular site. It rests everywhere in the earth, certainly not in men alone.

Hoagland resists a nonreciprocal understanding of care based on maternity as lacking respect for both the carer and the other. "When I have no real expectation of an intimate, when I have certain standards of caring for myself that I do not apply to the other, for example, then I am not showing respect" (Hoagland, *STC,* p. 254). Respect for the other and myself is another standard of maternity. How is it possible that maternity in Levinas can fail to subvert the respect that Hoagland finds essential, except perhaps that Levinas begins with a (male) subject–agent whose autonomy presupposes that care for the other engenders respect, begins with autonomy, whereas Hoagland begins with women's subordination? Alternatively, we may consider the possibility that ethical practice, the work of the good, depends on respect among equals, upon building trust and mutual responsibility, but that something closer to care, something unmeasurable by equality, reciprocity, respect, precedes all the work that these can do. Unless we cherish the other in ways beyond measure, all of the standards of ethical practice fail to know the good.

The respect of which Hoagland speaks insists on reciprocity from the other as a condition of ethical regard, imposes a standard of law upon human interactions. I understand the good to fall upon us, wounding us, with or without a measure, troubling every measure with immemorial injustice. This difficult and troubled regard for the other, disturbed by the good, allows us to say of another, ethically, "you do not respect me; you do not care for me; you do not pursue the good."

In a world of gender inequality in which women are subordinated to men; in a world of inequality where men and women of color are subordinated to differently colored men and women, an ethic of care passes into an altruism of subjection. "I am not convinced that a child, especially a male child, who experiences one-caring from his mother [or others with the role of caretakers] will ever learn to be one-caring himself" (Hoagland, *STC,* p. 254). "Recipients of unconditional loving—children and husbands—combine in exploiting mothers . . . " (Hoagland, *STC,* p. 258). I have added the possibility that caring is frequently given role classifications. This repeats the point that care, when understood as a measure, defining role identity with certain kinds of people as caretakers and other kinds as cared for, imposes sweeping and profound injustices, domination and subjection. Care in a woman whose role as a woman is to care, whose role is assigned to her to care for men and children who do not care in return, expresses profound abjection. Cherishment knows nothing of roles, measures nothing, faces heterogeneity heterogeneously. Before we assign any roles, we must cherish our places and the places of others. This cherishment precedes sacrifice, precedes conditions, is unconditional. An unconditional love rests at the heart of ethics, but it can work only under conditions, only through selections and measures. Ethical respect is the form cherishment takes under the sacrifice of the good imposed by measure.

Hoagland describes such a measure.

> If an ethics of caring is going to be morally successful in replacing an ethics located in principles and duty, particularly within the context of oppression, then it must provide for the possibility of ethical behavior in relation to what is foreign, it

> must consider analyses of oppression, it must acknowledge a self that is both related and separate, and it must have a vision of, if not a program for, change. In my opinion, care stripped of these elements isn't a caring that benefits us. (Hoagland, *STC*, p. 261).

It is unlikely that caring will replace principles and duty, especially in public spaces. It is likely that we will find ourselves in the future participating in a more complex ethics|politics, expanding the hegemony of rules and obligations with nurture and care. Ethical difference in the form of plenishment replaces nothing, does not inhabit the spaces of duty and principles except where these are understood to define the good. Ethical difference occupies the foreign, heterogeneous spaces in which the good rests in the earth. Here injustice, oppression, others and their differences, rest in the very soul of the good, giving rise to change, to resistance to oppression, in the reverberations of multiple heterogeneities. Ethical difference rests in the *aentres* of heterogeneity, of differences of kind.

The view of cherishment and sacrifice that gives rise to an ethic of inclusion pertains to our places everywhere, at rest, in place and displaced, responsible everywhere, fulfilled everywhere through cherishment demanding sacrifice, selection and choice, because not all things are possible together. But our greatest responsibility is to refuse to undertake a destructive choice, in relation to others or ourselves, without pursuing beyond all other pursuits the possibility of coexistence. We struggle to explore the possibility that the crucial and obligatory opposition of women to their oppression by men can take place within an ethic of cherishment without repeating the forms of conflict ascribed to a masculine ethics from which women have been excluded.

This issue represents the force of the discussion in this book, to seek an ethic of sexual difference that makes so profound a difference in how we think of ethics, sexuality, and gender, how we think of humanity and nature, that we displace, if we cannot eliminate, the course of oppositional thinking, of exclusion, that has defined Western thought and especially Western ethical thought. The point, however, as I have traced throughout my discussion of the indeterminate dyad, the recurrence of the number two throughout these discussions, is that we cannot and do not wish to eliminate dyadic thought, but to displace it to its unlimit, to understand that the places of dyads are elsewhere as well as somewhere. We do not wish to, and cannot, succeed in eliminating the dyads of gender and humanity and nature. But we must resist the hold of oppositional and exclusionary thinking on the foundations of our relation to the good.[4] Analogously, the thought of rights and duties has its place, as does a thought of care and trust, a local place and inexhaustible displacement. Both an ethic of care and an ethic of rights seem, in the places assigned them above, not to know that their place is elsewhere.

Let us continue to pursue this discussion at this level, before we return to the other, inexhaustible dyad, between (*aentre*) two cares. Curtin describes the recurrent qualification of an ethic of care: "In a society that oppresses women, it does no good to suggest that women should go on selflessly providing care if social structures make it all too easy to abuse that care. The injunction to care must be understood as part of a radical political agenda that allows for development of contexts in which caring for can be nonabusive" (Curtin, *TEEC,* p. 66). In relation to ethical practice, as contrasted with a practice of justice and law, caring for others who do not reciprocate respect and care risks abuse for the caretaker. This idea of a caretaker who may not be taken care of by others seems to echo the self-sacrificing mother who frequently becomes grotesque, mirroring the unassuagable guilt of infinite sacrifice. Caretaking here is a practice, contrasted perhaps with a practice of disinterested judgment, and must be evaluated in relation to the good. Here Kheel's understanding echoes cherishment: to be ethical we must care about something. We cannot praise or criticize caretaking without caring for the caretakers and others. There is a cherishment prior to becoming a caretaker that makes it possible to judge the work of an ethic of care. There is cherishment before the work of ethical practice that makes it possible to measure the danger of abusive care. Similarly, there is sacrifice in the very best undertakings we pursue, the inescapability of injustice, in the institution of any measure of the good. Against this inexhaustible sacrifice, self-sacrifice knows nothing of the good.

Another danger is frequently ascribed to Gilligan's work: "[t]here is a danger, however, for ecofeminism to reify unwittingly an 'ethic of care' or 'women's ways of knowing' as universal and biologically determined qualities (and thereby imply that women are limited to these) by dropping them into ecofeminist theory without the historical and cultural contexts in which they developed" (Lahar, *ETGP,* p. 39). An ethic of care can be combined with a biologically feminine view of nature, Mother Nature, with dire consequences for women and nature.

> Mother in patriarchal culture is she who provides all our sustenance and who makes disappear all of our waste products, she who satisfies all of our wants and needs endlessly and without any cost to us. Mother is she who loves us and will take care of us no matter what. The last thing the environmental movement [or women's movement] should do is encourage us to think of the environment in these terms. (Roach, *LM,* p. 49)

Again, this critique of overlapping views of mothers and nature belongs to a liberating practice, a practice that must involve choices in how we think and act. The reason why the last thing we should do is to think of mothers and nature as infinitely giving and self-sacrificing is that we thereby destroy them both. Now we can oppress and destroy women and mothers, children and animals. We can destroy forests and species. But perhaps we should pause before the idea of destroying nature. I do not think we can destroy nature, insofar as we understand it as the general circulation of goods and judgments. We cannot impose restrictions on nature to limit its general economy, forcing it into a restricted economy. Nature will not "resist" our attempts to subjugate it, will not resist our destructions in the sense that the animals and species we destroy will return, but there will be nature and general circulation in any case, however bleak we may succeed in making it. And so, if I may say so, with women. And animals.

Sexual and ethical difference pertain to restricted and general economies, circulate under rules and guides as well as more rapidly, excessively. Moreover, restricted economies cannot succeed in replacing general economies, cannot succeed in mastering their own excesses. They can only delude themselves into thinking they have done so. And thereby, they displace themselves. The attempt to define a place (for men, for Man) displaces itself into the terrors of the woman and the monstrosities of nature. The terrible fact of this displacement is that women suffer subjection and physical abuse, that animals suffer in every way humans can devise. Women and animals suffer endlessly in their endless circulation in every human and natural economy, suffer our endless failures to master the good.

Curtin appeals to Gilligan's work to speak of women's experience and thereby to criticize traditional ethics. One example is where she says that "[t]here may be contexts in which it would be helpful for feminists to present the case for moral treatment of animals in terms of rights. However, I would argue that there is nothing distinctively feminist about this approach" (Curtin, *TEEC*, p. 65). Another example, more extended, is:

> Whereas the rights approach tends to emphasize identity of moral interest, formalistic decision procedures, an adversarial understanding of moral discourse, personhood as autonomous, and a valorization of the nonbodily, Gilligan's research indicates that women's moral experiences are better understood in terms of recognition of a plurality of moral interests, contextual decision making, nonadversarial accommodation of diverse interests, personhood as relational, and the body as moral agent. (Curtin, *TEEC*, p. 65)[5]

It is as if we are to judge ethical convictions in terms of women's experiences and feminist insights even when drawn from an oppressive society, and where we seem not to criticize these experiences in depth. It is as if we are to decide what is right and wrong about ethics based on feminist insights. It is as if women's experience gives rise to feminist insights that women, at least feminist women, must employ in their ethical practices. But we do not know, as Curtin implies, that these experiences and insights are true and right. I do not know if these experiences and insights of women are true and right for men, for me. Curtin speaks of a "distinctively feminist ethic" (Curtin, *TEEC*, p. 69) as if that of itself might produce a different ethic, though in the passage in question, the conclusion is that such an ethic "should include the body as moral agent" (Curtin, *TEEC*, p. 69). I wonder why this does not represent a profound ethical insight, masculine or feminine.

Are feminist insights true or false, right or wrong, and for whom, for men as well as women? I have sought to displace this question, resisting the oppositional and dichotomous structure of the dyads. Are feminist insights radically heterogeneous relative to men's experiences? Is traditional Western ethics an ethics for and by men, based on men's experiences? Must we choose between men's and women's experiences in another opposition? Warren understands the extent to which domination permeates the very structure of Western thought. "Warren defines a 'logic of domination' as 'a structure of argumentation which leads to a justification of subordination'" (Slicer, *DD*, p. 114; quoted from Warren, *PPEF*, p. 128), though she does not seem to consider the logic of her own preferences to reenact such a subordination or exclusion.

We may read the repeated references to such insights as a dismantling of the oppositional relation to truth that rationality has seemed to presuppose in the Western ethical tradition. Yet in an analogous way, insights derived from women's as against men's experiences seem equally oppositional. We may read feminist insights instead as insights that derive from women's but also men's experiences, from the entire history of ethical thought and practice, repeatedly forgotten and enacted, perhaps, more oppressively on women's bodies. Let us read women's experiences and feminist insights as the radically heterogeneous truths that men as well as women can know, must and do know in the form of the forgotten. In the realm of lived experience, of life in the *polis* and directed by *technē*, Western ethics has frequently been based on similarity with human beings, formal conditions of equality, conflicts and exclusion, nonrelational and autonomous agents, a disinterested rationality independent of emotion and will, and the unimportance of embodiment to the good and to ethical responsibilities.[6] Instead, we may hope to replace such an ethics with one based on cherishment of diversity, contextuality, dialogue and accommodation, relationality, thereby dismantling the privilege of rationality by emphasizing emotion, feeling, trust, and embodiment. We may hope to do so regardless of whether they are the result of women's experiences, because men also experience the destructiveness of traditional ethics. Even if Curtin's criticisms are the result of feminist insights, they are extremely damaging to traditional ethical views. They represent the *technē* of ethical difference. I am pursuing ethical difference elsewhere, otherwise.

Curtin pursues the *aentre* of our concern here with the place where an ethics of sexual difference meets other living creatures in the form of a procedural claim. "[A] distinctively ecofeminist defense of moral vegetarianism is better expressed as a core concept in an ecofeminist ethic of care" (Curtin, *TEEC*, p. 69). "There are important connections through food between the oppression of women and the oppression of nonhuman animals" (Curtin, *TEEC*, p. 69).[7] And the oppression of men, between the use of slaves and the use of animals for human purposes, for men's and women's purposes.

We may set aside the question of oppression for the moment, returning to the dyads of care. I distinguished a dyad of dyads, one between an ethics of cherishment and an ethics of care, corresponding to the dyad of *poiēsis* and *technē*. I have been closely following another dyad in relation to an ethics of care, an opposition between rights and care, justice and trust, with virtually all ecological feminists on the side of an ethic of care against an ethics of justice, with warnings about the dangers of abuse. Rigterink considers three possible relations between an ethic of justice and an ethic of care: additive—"By this I mean that both perspectives are legitimate, but they need to be added together in order to obtain a truly adequate account of morality" (Rigterink, *W*, p. 39); competitive—"in the sense that present equally legitimate moral claims that have to be adjudicated on a case-by-case basis" (Rigterink, *W*, p. 41); and eliminative—"We need to take the hard step of denying that rights exist" (Rigterink, *W*, p. 43).

We may question whether these represent all possible relations between one ethic and another. And we may question whether Rigterink's arguments are compelling for abandoning any consideration of rights. Even within an ethic of care, we may wish to hold that

> One might argue here that meeting some expressed needs might violate the moral minimums in our society. I am willing to grant that this can happen. If it does, we must remember that the rules do not have a life of their own, but are guides. They help us to formulate a caring response because they speak to us of what most of us would want as a caring response in a similar situation. (Manning, *JC*, p. 51)

Manning finds something to praise in rights, at least in public and anonymous spaces, guiding us to care in general. Rigterink argues that rights tend to justify a restrictive ethic in which if we have not broken a rule, we are regarded as acting ethically. Both understand rights to serve two important functions, one to assist us in our ethical deliberations, the other to foreclose too large a range of ethical considerations.

In other words, relative to an ethic of care, an ethic of rights belongs to restricted economy. The debate between Rigterink and Manning is between which ethic is better: one is good, the other bad; one right, the other wrong. I understand such an opposition, repeated throughout ecological feminist writing, to belong to restricted economy, while cherishment expresses the good as circulating excessively within general economy. I understand such an opposition to belong to measure, to the repeated oppositional measure of the number two, dichotomously, where we have two and must choose the better. I understand this choice to reflect the imperative of *technē* that insists that we find our place.

The dyad within an ethic of care as to which is better, care or justice, is a dyad within a restricted and instrumental account of the good, not the general economy of goods and judgments, circulating inexhaustibly and excessively. Although care is offered to replace dichotomies and instrumentalities, it functions in an oppositional and polemical way, halts the circulation. Caring is better instrumentally for women, representing their experiences and enabling them to overcome oppression. Care gives women a safe place to be and to act. And surely we agree, with some qualifications. One qualification is that caring lends itself to abuse, and care for others must be accompanied by care for self. "My actual obligation [to care for others] rests on the seriousness of the need, my assessment of the appropriateness of filling the need, and my ability to do something about filling it. But I must also recognize that I am a person who must be cared for and that I must recognize and respond to my own need to be cared for" (Manning, *JC*, p. 49). Such a care for self balances its interests against the interests and needs of others, measuring itself as a means in a restricted economy. Such a care for self makes the place of women safe, whereas they are never safe in a Western economy.

A second qualification is that where caring is absent, in public institutional spaces, certain minimum conditions are required, represented in rules of conduct. Rights do work in public institutional spaces, and perhaps cannot be eliminated or replaced by standards of care. Here either standards and norms of care or principles of justice are required instrumentally, required for the work of the good. Again, then, an absolute sense of justice and right gives way to the demands of *technē*. If ethics is to work at all in the competing demands of a pervasive restricted economy, certain norms must be strong and effective.

My practical working response to this dyadic opposition between justice and care is that the circulation of goods includes both, that women's experiences of subordination and subjection demand more than rights, but respect for care. All this is within *technē,* where we hope to do good work. But I am also concerned, in relation to sexual difference, domination, and the exploitation of nature, with the circulation of goods in a general economy of cherishment, something radical and heterogeneous that good work fails to know. Everything, everywhere, offers itself as something precious, to be cherished. This is not workable within *technē,* as it competes with nothing, not even the sense that things are nothing but instruments. It is expressed especially powerfully in art, but it belongs to experience everywhere, men's, women's, and animals'; it echoes throughout nature everywhere, the rests of the earth. Paraphrasing Kheel above, in order for us to know any good at all, we must cherish the inexhaustible things around us, undertaking a profound and unlimited responsibility toward them. An ethic of cherishment is unlimited, and our responsibility toward things is unlimited. Ethics is possible because we cherish whatever might impose a responsibility upon us, what makes a difference, especially for what is so different, heterogeneously, that we do not know it to work upon it. We are on the verge of a wounding, tearing, infinite responsibility, filled with loves and joys. This is ethical difference, an ethic of cherishment toward everything different and heterogeneous, but not an ethic of care.

For I understand an ethic of care to fall into and under *technē,* to belong to and move within restricted economy, under measure. An ethic of care arises where we must decide and choose, between one course of action and another, to favor one person or another, including ourselves, distinguishing right from wrong, good from bad, who will and who will not be cared for, and in whatever ways, seeking, struggling not to hurt one to help another, not to harm ourselves in caring for the others. Mothers do decide such things. So do fathers. And in such choosing, we may find helpful guidance in principles of justice and right, which inhabit the spaces of injustice, impose their own injustices insofar as they arise in exclusion. Justice always imposes a measure of evil, even when it is the best there is. This is a Greek understanding: that we may do the best we can and still do evil—still the best, and the only good.[8]

In this sense, the relation between rights and care within *technē* is additive, competitive, and eliminative, all of them and more, depending on the contextual and historical demands of *technē.* The relation between cherishment and the dyad, rights and care, introduces another dyad, between the general circulation of goods and restricted economies under regulation, domination. Cherishment does not belong to *technē*, is represented and expressed through *poiēsis*, but surrounds us, places us in nature where we find ourselves and at the same time disperses us elsewhere. Where we find ourselves, in place, we must act according to the best measures of the good we can determine, under *technē*. There is no alternative. The intermediate number issues forth as the possibility of work. But insofar as we are always elsewhere, the intermediate numbers and measures pass away into the general circulation of the good, into ethical difference.

The subjection of women, domination and oppression, and the use and abuse of nature all convert nature's general economy, the circulation of endless and inexhaustible goods, into restricted economies, attempting to measure the good. Such measurement is unavoidable if we are to live, if we recognize that living is sacrifice of others and ourselves, that it entails endless injustice. Care and justice are both sacrificial, in this sense immemorially unjust, evil. We cannot avoid imposing measures of the good. We cannot avoid falling into evil. We cannot avoid enacting the good, circulating the good, amid the evil. For that is our responsibility.

I conclude this encounter with ecological feminism, in proximity, with a recapitulation of my understanding of ethical difference. Lahar describes her understanding of ecological feminism in words that mirror my reading of Whitehead, again with a difference. "Ecofeminist theory aspires to an integrated and intersubjective view of human life and society in/as part of nature. Ultimately, this is an encompassing natural philosophy that we should think of not as a blueprint to be developed by one or two utopian thinkers but as a cultural revolution" (Lahar, *ETGP*, p. 34). The strength and sweep of this cultural revolution depend, I believe, on the extent to which we understand this integrated and intersubjective view of human life and society to belong to nature. Yet we have seen that even in Levinas, where all the others that obsess me in the proximity of the other, my subjectivity brings otherness to a halt before radical heterogeneity. In the same way, if intersubjectivity is Ours, it will inevitably build Our *Geschlecht*, and we will extend our reach into nature only as far as we care, as we know that we care.

> At the core of the expanded concept of nature that I advocate is the rejection of a subject/object split at its root—the opposition of human consciousness and a mechanical nature—and the

> adoption, instead, of an ontology of nature as *fundamentally material and subjective.* This acknowledges different types of subjectivity in natural phenomena that include (but are not limited to) human life and mental processes. In these terms human consciousness is a specialized form of subjectivity but in no way exclusive or original. (Lahar, *ETGP,* p. 37)

You and I may remind ourselves that in such a view as Whitehead's, subjectivity defines nature's general economy, not just humanity. Nature is filled with subjectivity, and intersubjectivity, everywhere, with feeling and care, with knowledge and truth, inseparable from matter everywhere and from embodiment. Humanity's bodies are no more subjective than any other bodies, than matter everywhere. The way in which human life and society is part of nature is that the radical heterogeneity on which human subjectivity is built, based upon respect for and proximity with the other, exceeds any limits of any kind we can impose on it. In this sense of the excessive, wild circulation of goods and works, we find ourselves in nature, part of its wildness.

Lahar professes a concern that such a view, seemingly as far as possible from practical concerns, be part of an active emancipatory political agenda.

> I offer the following four points of focus to help create and maintain a firm ground for social and ecological responsibility and political participation. These are that we (1) treat ecofeminism as a moral theory, (2) engage in the project of working out an integrated philosophy of humanity and nonhuman nature, (3) view this theory as a living process inseparable from the individuals and groups who think and practice it, and (4) maintain an active political and participatory emphasis that is both deconstructive (reactive to current injustices) and reconstructive (proactive in creating new forms of thinking and doing). (Lahar, *ETGP,* p. 36)

I understand an ethics of sexual difference to give rise to ethical difference, and in this movement to express the most important issues of our age.

CHAPTER 9

Tango

When Irigaray asks Levinas, "is there otherness outside of sexual difference?" (Irigaray, *QEL*, p. 178), she answers that

> The function of the other sex as an alterity irreducible to myself eludes Levinas for at least two reasons:
>
> He knows nothing of communion in pleasure. (Irigaray, *QEL*, pp. 180–81)

We have listened to the reverberations of the "alterity irreducible to myself," man and woman, sexual difference, heterogeneity, heard the echoes of measure and unmeasure in sexual difference. We have gone from a restricted economy of sexual difference to its general economy, passing from the dyad to unlimit, from sexual to animal to kindred difference. We have not paused in the communion in pleasure, in love, of which Irigaray speaks, though we have heard her and Lacan speak of *jouissance*, especially the *jouissance* of ~~The Woman~~. We have begun to explore what it means to speak, to know, to hope to know what we can never know, the *jouissance* of alterities irreducible to myself, women, other peoples, and animals, nature's heterogeneous *jouissances*, the call of natural things, the rests of the earth. I will now retrace the movement from sexual to ethical difference along the line of heterogeneity opened up by Levinas and Irigaray as the face to face of love. We experience plenishment face to face.

I have noted Lacan's movement in the resonances of *jouissance*, somehow unknown in Levinas, named as love. "He whom I suppose to know, I love" (Lacan, *GJW*, p. 139). He, she, it, or the others. I take the face to face of Levinas to be nothing ethical without the love that marks the truth I must suppose to know in the other I do not and may never know. This love, this truth, this *jouissance*, represents ethical difference, my *jouissance*, and yours, and the others. Here, at least, we do not speak of love for all, *agapē*, for ~~The Woman~~, she is not all. Ethical difference rests in the *jouissance* of what is not all. Face to face.

I now ask Irigaray's question of Levinas differently, perhaps, not at first of radical alterity or heterogeneity, not of sexual difference as heterogeneity and alterity, though we cannot escape them, but of love, the one for the other, in proximity. Does Levinas, in the infinite responsibility face to face toward the other, in substitution and proximity, does he know love? Does he know a love that may not be common, a love which is not the same for the one and the other? Does he know of erotic ecstasy, out of the one toward the other? Can the good be thought, as proximity and responsibility, without love, without an other love, a different joy? And further—at risk of being heard to reinstate the tyranny of heterosexuality—can gender, sexual difference, be faced without erotic love? I do not disregard the love of man for man, woman for woman, nor of people for animals and its reciprocation, heterogeneous, sensual, carnal loves. These need not involve genital and procreative relations to be fleshed and erotic loves. I mean, rather, to question whether love can belong to the same, to repetition and substitution, following Lacan's thought of radical alterity. The one whom I suppose to be heterogeneous, another kind, I suppose to know. The one whom I suppose to know, I love. Or hate. The one I love I face heterogeneously, "heteroerotically." I am speaking of a more radical "hetero|sexuality" (heteroeroticism, heterogender, haetera| sexuality) than between men and women, the altereroticism of proximity: love's excesses.

Here we must pause, brought up short by something Irigaray says in relation to the radical alterity of the other, something I refuse as strongly as possible, even as I share her thought otherwise. For she follows her thought of a love across the borders of alterity to relate alterity directly to gender. "Pleasure between the same sex does not result in that im-mediate ecstasy between the other and myself. It may be more or less intense, quantitatively and qualitatively different, it does not produce in us that ecstasy which is our child, prior to any child" (Irigaray, *QEL,* p. 180). This is so terrible a thought that I resist it as strongly as I can.[1] She seems in this moment to associate radical alterity with given kinds, and even more, with gender's instituted kinds, men and women, suggesting that erotic ecstasy depends on heterosexual heterogeneity. And this despite acknowledging a very different possibility: "'I love you' is addressed by convention or habit to an enigma—an other. An other body, an other sex. I love you: I don't quite know who, or what. 'I love' flows away, is buried, drowned, burned, lost in a void. We'll have to wait for the return of 'I love'" (Irigaray, *WOLST,* p. 206). I think of altereroticism as that intimate relation in which the erotic faces us with heterogeneity, ecstatically, wherever we encounter it, in every face to face. I do not know quite who or what. Experience, face to face, is altererotic, ecstatic, between men and women, or between men and men or between women and women; and between us and any thing to which we relate intimately, face to face. Love is intermediary, between the one and the other.

This *erōs* we experience in the face of the other, this other we experience ecstatically in the face of love, expresses a proximity against the slightest whisper of substitution, against the hold of the same, to the point where the risks and dangers of the shared "hetero" in heterosexuality and heterogeneity, joined perhaps as heterodoxy, radical alterity, pose a profound threat on both sides of gender. What is shared or expressed by *erōs* and hetero|eroticism-geneity-doxy is the indeterminateness of the dyad we have heard as an intermediate number, the number two passing into three and beyond: proximity and responsibility. I now turn back to the dyad of gender as erotic proximity to listen to the echoes within it of unlimit, belonging to love and radical alterity. I have spoken of radical alterity as heterogeneity without emphasizing enough that its subject, for us, is sexual difference, gender, genera, and kinds, all sexed, mixed and unmixed, pure and impure. We have not faced up enough to Irigaray's question of whether heterogeneity belongs to gender's sexuality, where sexual difference meets and disturbs place. Can we think of nature's places without a thought of sexual, now erotic, difference, without sorcerer love?[2] The inexhaustible plenitude of natural things and kinds is organized from the beginning by sexual difference.

Proximity disturbs me, tears my skin, my clothing, from my body.

> The face of a neighbor signifies for me an unexceptionable responsibility, preceding every free consent, every pact, every contract. It escapes representation; it is the very collapse of phenomenality. Not because it is too brutal to appear, but because in a sense too weak, non-phenomenon because less than a phenomenon. The disclosing of a face is nudity, non-form, abandon of self, ageing, dying, more naked than nudity. It is poverty, skin with wrinkles, which are a trace of itself. (Levinas, *OB,* p. 88)

We die, we age, sometimes without neighbors, suffer the poverty of our being in the world, embodied, with and without the proximity of others. But we abandon ourselves to the others, we expose ourselves, our poverty and wrinkling, together with the others we love. This language of proximity, of the places of proximity for human beings and others, expresses an exposure known most to us, men and women or others, as love, as *erōs,* even where our actions seek to obscure the terrors and flayings of love.

I hope to speak of love as intermediary in every embodied face to face, but I find myself caught in the toils of gender, speaking of sexual difference, as Irigaray suggests, in order to acknowledge heterogeneity. We belong to gender in order to suppose to know and love heterogeneity, the other gender, kind. How in the world are we going to face other sexualities, genders, and kinds if we insist on interpreting heterogeneity as first of all between women and men, enveloping women and men? Instead, let us imagine that heterogeneity imposes on us a wounding, a nude embodiment, organized, first, around genera, genders, kinds, then, second, from the other calling profoundly into question the doubling of gender, all in the call of *erōs*. For while we may think of heterogeneity in terms of heterosexuality, men and women, such a thought seems safely domestic, far from the dangerous other. We will have to think about domesticity and privacy as far as we can, as figures of the other, against the possibility of safety. But here we may wonder if we are thinking of heterosexuality heterogeneously or homogeneously, as impure or pure. We come to the question whether, despite its name, heterosexuality is a dominion of the same.

That is Wittig's claim:

> the category "woman" as well as the category "man" are political and economic categories not eternal ones. (Wittig, *OBW,* p. 15)

> for us there is no such thing as being-woman or being-man. "Man" and "woman" are political concepts of opposition, and the copula which dialectically unites them is, at the same time, the one which abolishes them. (Wittig, *SM,* p. 29)

More important for us here is the possibility that "lesbians are not women" because " 'woman' has meaning only in heterosexual systems of thought and heterosexual economic systems" (Wittig, *SM,* p. 32). What is important is not what women or lesbians "are," or what are men—though these identities and others are at stake—

but heterogeneity in the production of sexual difference, gender, extended erotically to other kinds. If lesbians are not women, if "women" are produced and circulated in heterosexual systems of thought as another masculine dominion of the same, a reduction of heterogeneity, then lesbians are heterogeneous and impure where "women" are not. Perhaps there are women as well as "women" and Woman.[3]

I took up the number two in order to consider the possibility that something of heterogeneity resonated face to face that vanished in threes or more, in the passing away of the face to face from two to unlimit, required unlimit for its own heterogeneity, its excesses. Heterogeneity does not stop at multiple profusion, but insists on face-to-face proximity. We find ourselves repeating the movement we heard earlier, in a different tone, that of heterogeneity's face to face, a somewhat different dyad, the face to face of love's proximity. I have represented it as joy, the *jouissance* of the (erased and silent) woman who exists only in relation to man, whether man's dirty secret or the object of his oppression, or both. And more. The man can be himself, with his identity, only in virtue of a heterogeneity beyond all heterogeneities, instituted in heterosexuality, unknown to every homoerotic sexuality, that the other, whom I love, whom the man loves, I suppose to know something, a joy, that man, that I, will never know. This truth, of what I will never know, pertains not only to men who love women sexually, but to every proximity among men and women who themselves may not know their heterogeneity, who experience their heterogeneity among others, erotically, face to face with another kind. The experience of kindred difference reaches from the heterogeneity of humanity to proximity with animals and other natural kinds.

In a language of truth, heterogeneity demands that the extreme other may know or possess a truth whose very possibility I cannot imagine, cannot participate in, cannot share, but which I grant in granting the other. This theme of the unshared and unshareable haunts alterity. The Western idea of ethics, traditionally, turns on a shared and reciprocal set of duties and identities. We humans share ethics as we share our humanity, in the same movement. Except for women and slaves, who are not quite human, who share neither ethics nor (the highest) humanity. And except for animals, who are not human. And the rest.

I have traced this movement of unjust privilege repeatedly. I am speaking of, echoing here, something different: intimacy.[4] I am exploring the proximity of lovers as, in *Phaedrus,* they are bonded by *erōs* and *philia* within the mad and magical toils of alterity. For that is what *pharmakeia* entails, the movement of something other within *erōs* and *philia,* named by Socrates as *mania,* madness. Truth requires a poetic madness, a madness known only to poets. But it is present everywhere as *erōs,* love.

> "False is the tale" that when a lover is at hand favor ought rather to be accorded to one who does not love, on the ground that the former is mad [*mainētai*] . . . (Plato, *Phaedrus,* 244)

> in reality, the greatest blessings come by way of madness [*manian*], indeed of madness [*manias*] that is heaven-sent. (Plato, *Phaedrus,* 244b)

> the men of old who gave things their names . . . held madness to be a valuable gift, when due to divine dispensation . . . (Plato, *Phaedrus.* 244c)[5]

Love is face to face, heterogeneous and altererotic. It is an erotic relation to an other, radically heterogeneous, whether heterosexual, homosexual, or lesbian; it is face to face when communal, public, or orgiastic. Human love, perhaps any love, *erōs* or *philia.* is heterodox, heterogeneous, heterogenous, heterogonous, heterologous, heteromerous, heteronomous, heteroerotic, heterotopic, and so forth: alter, hetero, heterohetero, radically other, one of two, monstrous, mad, all intermediary figures. The figure of madness in Socrates' climactic speech in *Phaedrus* expresses the heterogeneous heterogeneity, the impure impurity, of love, the inexhaustible alterity of the indeterminateness, unlimitedness, of the face to face as madness, and more.

For *Phaedrus* is permeated by one intermediary figure after another of heterogeneity and alterosexuality: *erōs, philia,* madness, magic, desire, writing, all circulating around the figure of the *pharmakon,* including *pharmakeus* and *pharmakos,* especially including Pharmakeia, playing with Orithyia, whose rape gives rise to the world.[6] For as we read the climactic erotic speech at the center of the dialogue, we find ourselves caught between Socrates and Phaedrus, homoerotically, and Pharmakeia, reminding us that an act of rape represents the central *poiētic* event of the dialogue and of the world. Yet within this figure of heterosexual violence—and we must not forget that such a violence, of the birth of the world, can only be between men and women, in that degraded sense of heterosexuality—echo the themes of Western philosophy: nature, knowledge, truth, *physis, epistēmē, technē,* and *poiēsis*. Pharmakeia's presence throughout the dialogue haunts knowledge and truth as well as writing.[7] Plato asks us to think of the divinity of nature, the beginning of the world, in intimate conjunction with the most violent act of male heterosexuality. The closest proximity, erotic intimacy, echoes the heterogeneous plenitude of nature in nearest conjunction with injustice, sexual violence, women's subjection.

For the story of Orithyia appears doubled in Greek, repeating the dyad's heterogeneity, repeated again as *pharmakeia:* once the story of Erechtheus, king of Athens, whose daughter Orithyia was carried off and raped by the north wind, Boreas, who then married her (Graves, *GM,* pp. 168–72); the second the story of Eurynome, the goddess of creation, whose union with Boreas brought order out of chaos (Graves, *GM,* p. 27). The story of Orithyia and Boreas represents *physis* in conjunction with *poiēsis,* bringing forth being from nonbeing, order from disorder, in the play of magic as menace and mystery, in the play of *Pharmakeia,* where the *pharmakon* expresses a plenitude of figures of heterogeneous hetero|sexuality: *pharmakeia* as medicine, drug, madness, remedy, poison, potion, agent, dye, pigment, color; *pharmakos* as sacrifice, scapegoat; *pharmakeus* as wizard; *pharmakis* and *pharmakidos* as sorcerers and witches. Desire circulates as poison and cure, madness and remedy, menace and magic, in the multifarious colors of light.[8]

I do not offer a reading here of *Phaedrus* in relation to writing's truth. That I have undertaken elsewhere.[9] Here I mean to consider a narrower reading, though we may expect it to burst out of its enclosure, like a hungry animal.[10] I am concerned, at least for the moment, with the heterodoxy of *erōs,* of sexuality and desire, for the moment at least unsure whether I wish to speak of hetero|sexuality or heterogeneity, or both, of heterogender and alter*erōs*.

For the climactic, orgasmic speech begins at the heights of erotic love, as we have seen, with the figure of madness, understood as an echo of heterodoxy, sexual cacophony, again the juncture of sexual desire with truth as madness and Pharmakeia. It is by no means "an invariable truth that madness is an evil, but in reality, the greatest blessings come by way of madness, indeed of madness that is heaven-sent" (Plato, *Phaedrus,* 244). The greatest blessings and truths, the greatest circulation of goods comes from a madness that is sent from the heavens, which exceeds any measure, any *technē*. I am thinking of a mad, insane heterogeneity that is the greatest blessing possible, the highest good, that can circulate among human beings as *erōs,* the mad cacophony of desire.[11]

On the verge of madly throwing ourselves into the heterogeneous climax of the dialogue, we may recall the extraordinary erotic figure with which the entire dialogue is framed, the private and, for the moment, homosexual place where Socrates and Phaedrus meet. Socrates and Phaedrus belong to the same colloquial gender, and if we read their encounter as an erotic event, in a private and beautiful place, it is between two men, with recurrent sensual references. The most striking occurs on this verge of an erogenous climax, begun by Socrates asking, "Where is that boy I was talking to? He must listen to me once more, and not rush off to yield to his nonlover before he hears what I have to say" (Plato, *Phaedrus,* 243e). This boy was Socrates' beloved, whose nonlover Socrates in his first and blasphemous speech pretended to be (Plato, *Phaedrus,* 237–42), but now no longer, now speaks openly to his beloved of love. But to whom was Socrates speaking? Phaedrus responds: "Here he is, quite close beside you, whenever you want him" (Plato, *Phaedrus,* 243e). What could be a more erotic response? Socrates and Phaedrus lie alone together, in a private spot far from the city, engaged in highly charged, erotic activities, pervaded by love and desire, interspersed with references to the intimacy of their friendship.

We are surrounded by love's madness, about to rise on crests of sexual passion, attracted by the irresistible lure of the good. Our first step toward the good, and love, is through the soul's immortality. "All soul is immortal" (Plato, *Phaedrus,* 245c). All soul. But some living things are called mortal and others called immortal, as some are inanimate and others animate (Plato, *Phaedrus,* 246b). And far more important, "All soul has the care [*hepimeleitai*] of all that is inanimate, and traverses the whole universe, though in ever-changing forms" (Plato, *Phaedrus,* 246b). This care, unlike the Care that *Dasein* shows for itself,[12] is a care of soul for its others, where both it and the others are everywhere, heterogeneously. For soul can live the life of the gods, or can shed its wings, and settle into an earthy body (Plato, *Phaedrus,* 246c), for which it cares, as it cares for all other inanimate things, becoming a mortal composite structure of soul and body, of care for the good and that which is cared for.

Soul is moved by itself, "and precisely that is the essence and definition of soul, to wit, self-motion. Any body [*sōna*] that has an external source of motion is soulless, but a body deriving its motion from a source within itself is animate or *besouled,* which implies that the nature of the soul is what has been said" (Plato, *Phaedrus,* 245e). What has been said is that soul moves itself and has the care of everything that is not self-moved, soulless, other, heterogeneous. Soul is everywhere and moves every thing. And whatever lacks soul is dead.

This moving picture echoes in one pair after another: animate and inanimate, mortal and immortal, soul and body, gods and humanity. Each pair portrays for us a heterogeneity that is repeatedly described in terms of the good, repeatedly described in terms of the impossibility of a crossing and of the care that the good demands in a crossing.

Yet I have neglected another heterogeneity, perhaps the one this entire discourse circles upon, that of hetero|sexuality, the radical alterity of sexual desire. For within the soul's immortality, its nature is as follows:

> Let it be likened to the union of powers in a team of winged steeds and their winged charioteer. Now all the gods' steeds and all their charioteers are good, and of good stock, but with other beings [*allōn*] it is not wholly so.[13] With us men, in the first place, it is a pair of steeds that the charioteer controls; moreover one of them is noble and good, and of good stock, while the other has the opposite character, and his stock is opposite. Hence the task of our charioteer is difficult and troublesome. (Plato, *Phaedrus,* 246ab)

Thus, we tell the story of desire for the good, figured by madness and Pharmakeia's magical ambiguities, in terms of heterogeneities, first, between humanity and the gods; second, between humanity and animals, two horses; then third, between one noble and good animal and the other opposite, in the souls of human beings, even winged, impure. This heterogeneity, this double and triple impure heterogeneity, steeped in altereroticism within its homoerotic frame, permeates and pervades the human soul, in general and everywhere. This profound heterogeneity within the soul of human beings, within their relation to the good, pertains to their winged souls and thereby to their materiality. The soul is a heterogeneous composite, an impure hybrid, of two conflicting steeds, sexually and ethically conflicted in relation to the good, in the winged soul itself, before it joins the body. The human soul is multiply heterogeneous and, given what follows, multiply altererotic, one erotic face to face after another. What is almost certainly denied in *Phaedrus* is that this eroticism divides only into male and female.[14]

For soul lives with the gods, among "many spectacles of bliss upon the highways where the blessed gods pass to and fro" (Plato, *Phaedrus,* 247), in a "place beyond the heavens" of which "none of our early poets has yet sung, and none shall sing worthily" (Plato, *Phaedrus,* 247c). Immortal soul lives where *poiēsis* cannot reach, in a place of which *poiēsis* cannot sing. So we too, and Plato, cannot sing its song, unless we imagine that we philosophers can sing of what the poets cannot say. We must consider the possibility that Socrates speaks here of something unspeakable, sings of something unsoundable, the good, the bliss, the gods, the other other, hetero|hetero, the good that gives the place to ethics. This soul stands on the back of the world, unknown to mortals, living the life of the gods and the good.

> For the souls that are called immortal, so soon as they are at the summit, come forth and stand upon the back of the world, and straightway the revolving heaven carries them round, and they look upon the regions without. (Plato, *Phaedrus,* 247c)
>
> Such is the life of the gods. . . . (Plato, *Phaedrus,* 248a)

This is the immortal but not human soul that stands on the back of the world and knows "veritable knowledge of being that veritably is" (Plato, *Phaedrus,* 247e). And so we must suppose, if we suppose that there is anything to heterogeneity, that the other, the woman, or god, or animal, knows something that we do not know, a truth precious beyond imagining, and that we may love the other in virtue of the knowledge, the truth, this other knows, thereby loving the good that we do not and cannot know. But we, men or women, humans or animals, in this case as we suppose the other to know, are ourselves the other, heterogeneously. This point, that we are the other, we must repeat, as Plato suggests, again and again. If there is heterogeneity, alterosexuality, alter*erōs,* if the good is heterogeneous, we are heterogeneous and we seek the good. More of that later.

For the moment let us return from the immortal souls whose animals within live the life of the gods to those heterogeneous souls, part of which "best follows a god" (Plato, *Phaedrus,* 248), and the other parts of which, though "eager to reach the heights and seek to follow, they are not able; sucked down as they travel they trample and tread upon one another, this one striving to outstrip that" (Plato, *Phaedrus,* 248b). We repeatedly hear the echoes of heterogeneity in the parts of the soul, the animate creatures that strive, suck, trample, and tread, the one horse and the other, the one relation to the good and the other—both relations to the good, oppositional and destructive relations to the good, at least for the other. But Socrates follows an explicit expression of heterogeneity: "with their charioteers powerless, many are lamed, and many have their wings all broken, and for all their toiling they are balked, every one, of the full vision of being . . . " (Plato, *Phaedrus,* 248b).

This striking image of the bleakness of heterogeneity inverts the movement we followed in Derrida (*G2*), where sexual difference is struck two blows, the one of gender, which we are still moving toward, the other from the *Schlag* in *Geschlecht* to sexual violence, opposition, *polemos.*[15] To the contrary, it seems in *Phaedrus* that the heterogeneity of mortal souls, their composition by one steed and another, one and the other, the presence of proximity, signifies, first, confusion, then opposition and rule. And within the confusion, before we struggle with the opposition as if we might avoid the rule of the good, we may imagine that only immortal souls,[16] who stand on the back of the world and live among the gods, can know bliss, can know the good, can know *jouissance.* All the others live in confusion. But that is not what Socrates says.

> For only the soul that has beheld truth may enter into this our human form . . . and such understanding is a recollection [*anamnēsis*] of those things which our souls beheld aforetime as they journeyed with their god, looking down upon the things which now we suppose to be, and gazing up to that which truly is.
>
> Therefore is it meet and right that the soul of the philosopher alone should recover her wings, for she, so far as may be, is ever near in memory to those things a god's nearness whereunto

> makes him truly god. Wherefore if a man makes right use of such means of remembrance [*hypomnēmasin*], and ever approaches to the full vision of the perfect mysteries, he and he alone becomes truly perfect. (Plato, *Phaedrus,* 249cd)

Souls that live among the gods can know true being and the good. But philosophers too, and only, remember being close enough to the gods to know the good, what makes a god truly god. Only those, philosophers, who remember can know the good and true being. These behold the beauty of the world and madly remember true beauty, their wings begin to grow, and they are called by others "demented" (Plato, *Phaedrus,* 249e), the fourth kind of madness, the philosopher's *poiēsis.* Yet not only philosophers may know this madness, this yearning, for "every human soul has, by reason of her nature, had contemplation of true being" (Plato, *Phaedrus,* 250a). The language of heterogeneity is a language of exclusion. Yet Socrates' narrative excludes no one from remembrance of the good, excludes no soul, anywhere or everywhere, from remembrance within the dangers and disturbances of heterogeneity. Rather, the dialectical movement repeats our understanding that we bear responsibility face to face with the other everywhere as heterogeneity, passing from it to the inexhaustible circulation of the good, unlimit, everywhere. This is an everywhere of heterogeneity, not an everywhere of universality, an everywhere of difference, alterity, not an everywhere of the same.

Around us, then, everywhere, not just in "earthly likenesses of justice and temperance and all other prized possessions of the soul" (Plato, *Phaedrus,* 250b) that are traditionally thought to represent Plato's view of the good, especially in *Republic,* but in beauty everywhere and anywhere, we recall the blessed vision of the good. And we recall it erotically, sexually, altererotically, beyond sexual activities between men and women.

> But when one who is fresh from the mystery, and saw much of the vision, beholds a godlike face or bodily form that truly expresses beauty, first there comes upon him a shuddering and a measure of that awe which the vision inspired . . .
>
> Next, with the passing of the shudder, a strange sweating and fever seizes him. For by reason of the stream of his soul's plumage is fostered, and with that warmth the roots of the wings are melted, which for long had been so hardened and closed up that nothing could grow; then as the nourishment is poured in,

> the stump of the wing swells and hastens to grow from the root over the whole substance of the soul. . . . Meanwhile she [the soul] throbs with ferment in every part. . . . Wherefore as she gazes upon the boy's beauty, she admits a flood of particles streaming therefrom—that is why we speak of a "flood of passion"—whereby she is warmed and fostered. . . . And behind its bars, together with the flood aforesaid, it throbs like a fevered pulse, and pricks at its proper outlet, and thereat the whole soul round about is stung and goaded into anguish. . . . At last she does behold him, and lets the flood pour in upon her, releasing the imprisoned waters; then has she refreshment and respite from her stings and sufferings, and that moment tastes a pleasure that is sweet beyond compare. (Plato, *Phaedrus,* 251–52)

This excessive figure of the soul's recollection of the good is given in an erotic figure of sexual arousal and release, of *jouissance.* Heterogeneity, the other world in its truth and goodness, exists for us and Socrates (or Plato) as hetero|sexuality, understanding this less as something between men and women than as inexhaustible and irreducible alterity, in the form of erotic desire. Plato cannot be accused, at least on the one side, of knowing nothing of irreducible, sexual, altererotic alterity. Or put another way, sexuality, desire, reaches toward heterogeneity, not to overcome it, for that would be impossible, a denial of itself, but to envelope heterogeneity inextricably.

For heterogeneity does not belong to sexuality only in relation to the pairs sexuality moves among, between man and woman, mortality and immortality, animate and inanimate, the dyads Socrates describes as composing the world, but is composed itself within sexuality. We return to the charioteer with his steeds, understanding more than ever that this three becomes two, that the charioteer is assigned the role of tamping the fires of sexuality, but does not do so. Socrates' description gives us the good and bad, in a figure we would do well to resist, of both race and rule.

> Now of the steeds, so we declare, one is good and the other is not. . . . He that is on the more honorable side is upright and clean-limbed, carrying his neck high, with something of a hooked nose; in color he is white, with black eyes, a lover of glory, but with temperance and modesty. . . . The other is crooked of frame, a massive jumble of a creature, with thick short neck, snub nose, black skin, and gray eyes, hot-blooded, consorting with wanton-

> ness and vainglory, shaggy of ear, deaf, and hard to control with whip and goad. (Plato, *Phaedrus,* 253de)

We may read this as a reference to race, from the southern Mediterranean to northern Africa. More important, and closely related, is the theme of rule. For this wanton animal must be controlled by force and violence. For, when "with head down and tail stretched out he takes the bit between his teeth and shamelessly plunges on . . . the driver, with resentment even stronger than before, like a racer recoiling from the starting rope, jerks back the bit in the mouth of the wanton horse with an even stronger pull, bespatters his railing tongue and his jaws with blood, and forcing him down on legs and haunches delivers him over to anguish" (Plato, *Phaedrus,* 254e).

In relation to the good, we must compel, force, overcome, cause evil and intemperate animals and people to suffer. In the name of the good. In the name of the good, we and others must suffer. "And so it happens time and again, until the evil steed casts off his wantonness; humbled in the end, he obeys the counsel of his driver, and when he sees the fair beloved is like to die of fear. Wherefore at long last the soul of the lover follows after the beloved with reverence and awe" (Plato, *Phaedrus,* 254e). But still pervaded by sexuality, hetero|sexuality for the other, altereroticism from which love for the other emerges. For the dyads of *erōs* are heterogeneous within and without, including the heterogeneity of humans and other humans, and of humans and animals. All the heterogeneous dyads coalesce in *erōs*'s heterogeneity, for every pair of lovers.

For they reach the good on either path, led by beauty and *erōs,* or rather, reach it heterogeneously through alterosexuality. And they reach it together without the third.

> And so, if the victory be won by the higher elements of the mind guiding them into the ordered rule of the philosophical life, their days on earth will be blessed with happiness and concord, for the power of evil in the soul has been subjected, and the power of goodness liberated. . . . (Plato, *Phaedrus,* 256b)
>
> But if they turn to a way of life more ignoble and unphilosophical, yet covetous of honor, then mayhap in a careless hour, or when the wine is flowing, the wanton horses in their two souls will catch them off their guard, bring the pair together, and choosing that part which the multitude account blissful achieve

> their full desire. . . . When death comes they quit the body wingless indeed, yet eager to be winged, and therefore they carry off no mean reward for their lovers' madness, for it is ordained that all such as have taken the first steps on the celestial highway shall no more return to the dark pathways beneath the earth, but shall walk together in a life of shining bliss, and be furnished in due time with like plumage the one to the other, because of their love. (Plato, *Phaedrus,* 256de)

Sexuality is pervaded by light and dark, good and bad, conflicted and unconflicted, requiring the third, the mediation, of rule. Nevertheless, lovers of beauty shall walk together in bliss, whether philosophical or not, shall be granted bliss together, the same,[17] because of their love, in the altereroticism of their love. For the second love is sexual, erotic, face to face. And it can be love only insofar as it is heterogeneous, the one for the other, in their heterogeneous joys, without any intermediary's law.

I add at this point, I remind myself repeatedly, that the two animals with and without their driver compose a heterogeneity, a hybrid alterosexuality, inseparable from identity and self. A theme echoes in *Phaedrus* that I have not yet noted, repeated several times, closely related to self-knowledge, regarded by many as Plato's predominant theme. For in the context of the erotic place where Socrates and Phaedrus meet and share a private and highly erotic encounter, whatever the similarity of their gender, the theme of who they are echoes repeatedly.

For the dialogue contains repeated references to Phaedrus's and Socrates' identities and, moreover, to each of them knowing the other. "I know my Phaedrus. Yes indeed, I'm as sure of him as of my own identity [*hemautoū*]." (Plato, *Phaedrus,* 228b) "Beware. Do not deliberately compel me to utter the words, 'Don't I know my Socrates? If not, I've forgotten my own identity [*hemautoū*].' . . . " (Plato, *Phaedrus,* 236c) Socrates' and Phaedrus's identities share an insatiable, unsurpassable desire for discourse, for philosophy and truth, within their heterogeneities. The inscription at Delphi to know thyself joins *erōs* and *philia* as hetero|sexuality. Plato portrays heterogeneity repeatedly both in relation to erotic desire, heterogeneous sexuality, and in relation to self-knowledge and self-identity.

It follows that hetero|sexuality—the heterogeneity of sexuality, of desire—expresses the heterogeneity and impurity of self and self-knowledge. The Delphic inscription never passes identity of self into the same under the rule of Ideas, but rather, finds the good in heterogeneous movements from the intermediate numbers to the unlimit of the good. Throughout *Phaedrus,* and throughout sexuality, we find ourselves caught up within, formed and constituted by, repeatedly accounting for, one dyad after another, within an inexhaustible, unending, excessive general circulation of kinds and genders and sexualities. The dyad of gender is indeterminate, impure, heterogeneous, canonically represented in *Philebus* as the passing away from the number two to unlimit, but not too quickly, that is, not by giving up the face to face of intimacy within the general circulation of goods. Ethics here inhabits the interstices, the intervals, rests, and *aentres,* moves in the intermediaries, defines the envelopes of identity heterogeneously. The dyad of gender defines a heterogeneity that reverberates as a face to face, resonates as embodied sexual difference, where these cannot be allowed to pass away into inexhaustible proliferation "too quickly," but give rise nevertheless to inexhaustible heterogeneity and profusion, all in relation to desire, expressed in *Phaedrus* by Eros, madness, and Pharmakeia. Mad desire, altereroticism, belongs to the heterogeneity of sexual difference. This heterogeneity is what we may understand of love, altererotic hetero|sexuality. The question of sexual difference is a question of heterogeneity, between men and women, and more, as gender, then as desire's erotic, corporeal excess, again Eros, madness, and Pharmakeia.

In this way, and others, magically, madly, love pervades the heterogeneity of responsibility for and toward the other. But the heterogeneity of erotic desire is not restricted to the other sex, men or women. The other gender or sex, people and animals of other sexes, genders, and kinds than mine and yours, circulate among the known and unknown sexualities of the natural and human worlds, among embodied relations face to face. That is what I mean, in part, by general economy, the heterogeneous others, always plural, impure, always unlimited, other kinds, madly and excessively, heterogeneously. In this way there remains the question of gender, where gender seems to speak of two, insisting that in this pair we do not forget the kind of the woman, passing away with intermediaries into the unlimit of identity and desire. Irigaray suggests that radical alterity grants something of the two, rather than the one, erotically. For there remains the feminine and the *jouis-*

sance of the woman. I will now undertake the task of unearthing the heterogeneity of gender as woman when we have come to understand how deep the alterity may be in sexuality, passing away to endless alterities of kinds, where we cherish other sexualities and kinds when we do not and cannot know them. I begin with gender separated from desire as Socrates speaks in *Phaedrus* of writing separated from madness. Lacking *erōs*, face to face, gender lacks something of heterogeneity.[18]

Ivan Illich speaks of vernacular gender in relation to the rise of industrial capitalism. Vernacular gender passes over into economic sex.

> I oppose the regime of scarcity to the reign of gender. I argue that the loss of vernacular gender is the decisive condition for the rise of capitalism and a life-style that depends on industrially produced commodities. (Illich, *G*, p. 3)

> I use gender, then, in a new way to designate a duality that in the past was too obvious even to be named, and is so far removed from us today that it is often confused with sex. By "sex" I mean the result of a polarization in those common characteristics that, starting with the late eighteenth century, are attributed to all human beings. Unlike vernacular gender, which always reflects an association between a dual, local, material culture and the men and women who live under its rule, *social sex* is "catholic"; it polarizes the human labor force libido, character or intelligence, and is the result of a diagnosis . . . of deviations from the abstract genderless norm of "the human." Sex can be discussed in the unambiguous language of science. Gender bespeaks a complementarity that is enigmatic and asymmetrical. (Illich, *G*, p. 4)

> The transition from the dominance of gender to that of [economic] sex constitutes a change of the human condition that is without precedent. (Illich, *G*, p. 4)

We have noted the claim that the exchange of women is the condition of every human society, that every society requires women as commodities.[19] I have responded that the circulation of women, together with other goods, composes general rather than restricted economy, an excessive circulation. This defines the juncture at which we encounter Illich's understanding of gender. For he presents the following notes of gender:

1. Gender, vernacular gender, inhabits every local, material culture.
2. Industrial societies transform vernacular gender, specific to a time and place, into social and economic sex in a genderless view of The Human.
3. This transformation, from vernacular gender to economic sex, is without precedent, perhaps the most compelling mark of the modern world.
4. Vernacular gender is enigmatic.

I will recount these numbered points, one after the other.

1. If we take the results of feminist explorations and resistances seriously, if we follow the line of thought we have taken in earlier discussions, the form of gender, sexual difference, that inhabits human culture has been predominantly, even in pre- and non-industrial societies, oppressive to women. We do not need to investigate whether there have been societies in which men and women share equally in the responsibilities and rewards of social life, nor whether there have been or may be societies in which women were predominant. Such societies are important but relatively rare. Vernacular gender opens a space between men and women in which women are typically oppressed, frequently violently. If gender is not the only or the predominant mark of domination and subjection, if race and slavery have coexisted in close proximity with gender, vernacular or not, it is enough to note that the blow, the *Schlag,* that strikes sexual difference "from the beginning," in Heidegger, of strife and opposition, is typically, as a class or kind, at the expense of women. I am speaking of subordination but also of extreme forms of sexual violence.

2. The genderless view of humanity, if it is a powerful force in modern industrial societies, Western and non-Western, inhabits Western thought from the Greeks as a norm against which women typically fall short, a masculine norm. As Wittig says, in an essay to which we will shortly return, "[t]he abstract form, the general, the universal, this is what the so-called masculine gender means, for the class of men have appropriated the universal for themselves" (Wittig, *MG,* pp. 79–80). The sexual difference at the heart of sexual indifference is passed off as objectivity, neutrality, disem-

bodiment, the masculine norm. This normativization of the "masculine" is problematized in a certain reading of Plato, especially in his *Republic,* where he halts his discussion of justice and the state, carried on as if gender could be ignored entirely, to take up questions of women and children, sexual difference and domesticity, suggesting that no *polis* can exist without resolving questions of sexual difference and reproduction.[20] We have seen that within the assumptions that "the one sex is far surpassed by the other in everything, one may say," and that "[m]any women, it is true, are better than many men in many things," Socrates proclaims that "[t]he women and the men, then, have the same nature in respect to the guardianship of the state, save in so far as the one is weaker, the other stronger" (Plato, *Republic,* 455d–456b).[21] If we hesitate at endorsing too strong a reading of "the same nature," out of concern for heterogeneity, reading this nature as privileging the masculine, if we read this nature as heterogeneous and impure, we must nevertheless read Socrates' argument to entail that there is nothing in principle that allows us to exclude women from any affairs of state.

The norm, at least for the guardians of the *Republic,* is the same for men and women, though perhaps not for all human beings, for cobblers and shepherds, for example. And it is a complex and heterogeneous norm, involving courage, fortitude, physical prowess, musical and medicinal capabilities, love of wisdom, and so on, drastically undermining the idea that each human being has a single virtue, as Aristotle says. Far more important, Plato suggests that to distinguish men's and women's activities and virtues based on gender is always to privilege one and subordinate the other. Every dyad circulates in relations of domination and subjection. And we cannot be sure, no dialectic guarantees, that this circulation will carry us from domination to reciprocation. All the evidence is to the contrary. Perhaps we can resist the privilege of men's work over women's only within a common norm of humanity, resisting all heterosexuality.

I am reading "the same nature" as heterogeneous, understanding the organization of *Republic* to represent the multiplicities and complexities of justice as heterogeneous questions of heterogeneity: the heterogeneity of human life, different *aretēs*; the heterogeneity of justice itself, always a "contested" and multifarious term, even within ourselves.[22] The heterogeneity of gender circulates among the heterogeneities of virtue and justice, displacing them, heterotopically. The same nature is heterogeneous, heterotopic, impure. The same place, of sexual and ethical difference, is other places.

3. This heterotopia intervenes at the place raised by the genderlessness of the modern world that against the possibility of a norm of The Human, gendered or genderless, a norm of measure, the univocity of gender expresses heterogeneity. This brings us up short before Illich's idea of vernacular gender, as if it did not retrace the oppression of women. For Illich's understanding is that there is something unprecedented, fundamental, about the transformation of gender in modern society, something fundamentally economic or restricted, even if we do not share with him the potentially utopian sense of vernacular gender, however enigmatic.

Genderlessness in the modern state imposes a norm at the expense of women, a norm that justifies the exchange of women. But the exchange of women, we are told, composes the very possibility of a state, modern or otherwise. And there is something unmistakably true about this, true about the unique and engendered status of women, without whom there could be no state, no humanity. There cannot be a state composed solely of men. But men compose the state, publicly and powerfully, regulating the circulation of women.

Nevertheless, within this perhaps universal regulation of women, something fundamental occurred with industrialism, fundamental to gender. Illich describes genderlessness as an economic precondition. "There could be no competition for 'work' between men and women, unless 'work' had been redefined as an activity that befits humans irrespective of their sex. The subject on which economic theory is based is just such a genderless *human*" (Illich, *G*, p. 10). This unisexed work seems given support by Socrates' arguments in *Republic*. And it is a dangerous idea to resist when the resistance is virtually always accompanied by the public sense that women's work has no human and public value, diminishing the identities of women.

What, then, do we understand to be the industrial sense of gender, transforming sexual difference without precedent? We may note something more fundamental in industrial societies than unisex, that women are always paid less than men. And they are nearly always paid less for both the same and for different work than men, and for work in occupations typically their own. Women compete with men genderlessly, at the expense of men overall, always at the expense of women. And women compete economically with men divided by gender, always at the expense of women. Economic gender reminds us repeatedly and pejoratively of women's work, of women who work as secretaries, seamstresses, nurses, those who care for children and sick people.

It also reminds us of something antagonistic, it would seem, to unisex and genderlessness in modern industrial societies, something almost universal, it would seem, remarked by Freud who was taken to task for it by Irigaray. "When you meet a human being, the first distinction you make is 'male or female?'" (Freud, *F,* p. 113; Irigaray, *SOW,* p. 13) This "almost universal" trait is repeated and praised by Illich with no trace of an awareness of "the problem," stated by Freud immediately preceding these words. For Freud opens the paragraph saying to his medical audience, "Nor will *you* have escaped worrying over this problem—those of you who are men; to those of you who are women this will not apply—you are yourselves the problem." (Freud, *F,* p. 113) Illich seems to think that not to know men from women is a problem. "From afar, the native can tell whether women or men are at work, even if he cannot distinguish their figures. The time of year and day, the crop, and the tools reveal to him who they are. . . . To *belong* means to know what befits *our* kind of woman, *our* kind of man. . . . Gender is in every step, in every gesture, not just between the legs" (Illich, *G,* pp. 67–68). Yet Freud closes the paragraph by questioning this certainty: "you are bound to have doubts as to the decisive significance of those elements [ova or semen] and must conclude that what constitutes masculinity or femininity is an unknown characteristic which anatomy cannot lay hold of" (Freud, *F,* p. 114). Where anatomy cannot tell us, where we cannot distinguish sexual figures, we can tell from other, cultural clues. Work tells us the truth of gender, that it is assured and certain but not just between the legs. It is out there in the world, enigmatically and everywhere.

It seems that we must know, must be able to tell with assurance, who are the men and who are the women, at least, who are our women. And if we cannot do so, we are among strangers, we have a problem. And the problem, at least in Freud, however repugnantly, is women, women are the problem. And perhaps, since they are the problem for men, it is not women who need to tell the men from the women, but the men. All dressed up in pink and blue, at least in our culture, to make sure the stranger can tell, the women tell the men what the men need to know.

Perhaps what the stranger can tell, what the native can tell, with great assurance, remains enigmatic, at rest. But still they and we insist on being able to tell. The enigma of gender, of which Illich and Freud speak, coexists, rests together with, the assurance of being able to tell with certainty what no one knows. Illich does not once question the possibility that all these indigenous cultures repeat the astonishing and widespread (if not universal) opposition of gender that turns the indefinite movement of unlimit, human and natural, into a definite dyad. My orientation is to reverse this movement from unlimit to two, from the indefinite to the definite, to reverse it without giving up the dyad. My concern, belied by being able to tell with assurance what cannot be told at all, is that gender is two, and will remain two, as it proliferates beyond any imagination. It is two at the expense of women.

4. Gender, vernacular or otherwise, is enigmatic. We have seen this enigma throughout our discussion, especially in the inexhaustible heterogeneity of the dyad of gender. Economic sex inhabits an enigmatic place I have described as the general economy of the circulation of goods and work. The circulation of women, within the circulation of gender, with its norms and heterogeneities, composes general and excessive economy in which the forms of homogeneity, the rules of economic exchange, the conditions of work, work heterotopically: displaced, replaced, constantly disturbed. The enigma of vernacular gender seems to deny within itself all the oppressions and subjections we have seen belong to women, thereby to men and humanity. I understand gender instead, sexual difference, to compose and to be composed by heterogeneous heterogeneities that cannot be expressed even in metaphors, but are present and represented everywhere, where everywhere is heterotopic.

What Illich says of vernacular gender we must say of gender even in industrial societies: "[g]ender is something other and much more than sex. It bespeaks a social polarity that is fundamental and in no two places the same" (Illich, *G*, p. 68). Yet the social polarity is everywhere, and must perhaps be resisted, if not by turning everything into the same. And perhaps industrial society, which through its technical capabilities constantly changes social life, has given birth to a mythology of the normal that it imposes everywhere, at the same time that it has given rise as well to the idea of the general circulation of gender. In the name of vernacular gender, Illich touches on the heterogeneous in the name of heterosexuality in a way unprecedented for us or for anyone else we have read, including Irigaray. "Kinship is possible only between what we conceive as men and women; it only specifies the fit between gendered people. What we perceive as men and what we perceive as women can meet and fit not only because but in spite of the unique contrast between them. They fit like the right fits the left" (Illich, *G*, p. 70). Homosexuals and lesbians typically cannot be recognized, have no standing, in such vernacular kinship relations, are neither right nor left. Is that not another reduction of heterogeneity, of alterosexuality?

There is something profoundly heterogeneous, Illich says, about vernacular gender, about gender in kinship societies. There is something heterogeneous about sexual difference, something that passes beyond men's and women's differences to other kinds of sexual relations among human beings, other kinds of erotic relations among humans and nonhumans, to the natural world, including inanimate things. Sexual difference knows a heterogeneity, a "unique contrast," unknown to any other difference. And homosexuality knows another heterogeneity, another unique contrast. And other sexualities; other erotic relations, other kinds in proximity.

Unprecedented in the modern world is the way in which the general circulation of goods and people has been brought under the norms of restricted economy, of monetary and financial norms, norms of industrial production and the distribution of goods. "While under the reign of gender women might be subordinate, under *any* economic regime they are *only* the second sex" (Illich, *G*, p. 178). Unprecedented as well is the sophisticated and vernacular resistance to this restriction, divided by ethnic and sexual and other heterogeneities. Of this, Illich has much less to say. The juncture where sexual heterogeneity meets natural heterogeneity is the site where the most far-reaching work is being done today. Such work I hope to undertake here. For the moment I am concerned with the heterogeneity of the face to face. I respond to Illich's view of vernacular culture in terms of heterotopia. "Everywhere, girls and boys seem to grow into their respective genders early on. By the time they are weaned, they use unmistakably different gestures" (Illich, *G*, p. 127). What of the heterogeneities that this unmistakable difference destroys? What of the inexhaustible diversities that have already vanished? What of the destruction wreaked at the local site by sexual opposition, especially the destruction to girls and women? Too many are dead. And too many have suffered sexual violence. Even in vernacular cultures or in cultures that hope to be vernacular.

Illich aroused a storm of fury in his reading of gender, oblivious to the vernacular of women's oppression, oblivious to his reduction of women.

> Your argument, Ivan, flows (Noah's-ark-like) in a procession of twos, of pairs, of dualisms: Vernacular Gender vs. Economic Sex; spoken language vs. taught mother tongue; asymmetrical, ambiguous complementarity vs. unisex competition; patriarchy vs. sexism; and, once again, gender vs. sex role. Underlying these paired key words lie other only hinted at and implied normative dualisms, for this is a very moral universe that you are constructing: spirit vs. flesh (as in "genderless sex"); wholeness vs. fragmentation; order vs. chaos; communitas vs. societas; and, finally and perhaps inevitably, good vs. evil. (Scheper-Hughes, *VS*, p. 28)

In this overwhelming attack on Illich for taking over the question of sexual difference without granting its importance to women, especially feminist women, in these justified and important criticisms, we find a disregard for certain of his truths. "Illich is primarily interested in his history of scarcity, and gender study is for him one step along the way"; "The preceding essays show, once again, I think, that gender is central study which cannot be subsumed under other studies" (Bowles, "Conclusion," *FI*, p. 38). I agree, I take the question of sexual difference to be, perhaps, the burning question of our age, marking all other questions with the mark of gender, and thereby consider the possibility that that question leads from itself, leads from sexual difference to an ethical difference inscribed everywhere in the rests of the earth, erotically and heterogeneously.

Gender is dualistic, giving us our struggle here with its heterogeneity, the possibility that heterosexuality, with its repressiveness, represents a certain important heterogeneity. And sexual difference is ethical, as Irigaray suggests, ethical not as falling into traditional dichotomies between good and evil, but disturbing every such dichotomy, something that Illich does not seem to know. Finally, industrial societies do not invent sexual difference, do not invent gender as a distinction that oppresses women, for women are oppressed nearly everywhere, in the vernacular and in the technological. But something unprecedented does occur in industrial societies.

What is unprecedented, Illich shows, is the transformation economic conditions work upon sexual differences, not demonizing beneficial vernacular gender relations, for they fall unduly upon women, but in the ways in which sexual differences permeate the signs and activities of industrial culture. In this way, gender expresses a far-reaching condition of contemporary social life, explaining why we may pursue the question of sexual difference as the question of our age. But gender has had a far-reaching role in every society we know, and from the beginning of Western thought. And, perhaps against Illich's understanding, gender and sexual difference together have always played a role in a genderless environment of thought and norms. Here we may find it useful to return to Derrida's writings on *Geschlecht,* in Heidegger, where certain reverberations of gender's dyadic inexhaustibility can be heard, apparently unknown to Illich.[23]

Before we do so, however, we may consider a different approach to questions of gender, almost a polar difference from Illich, an approach that focuses less upon enigmatic and local but allegedly universal relations between men and women marking gender difference. Against the establishment of another gender identity, vernacular or feminist, Butler speaks of "gender trouble," the trouble with gender, promoting the question, "[w]hat [is the] best way to trouble the gender categories that support gender hierarchy and compulsory heterosexuality?" (Butler, *GT,* p. vii). I understand the categories of gender to be "troubled" from the first, never free from trouble, understand sexual hierarchy and restrictions on heterosexuality designed to legitimate sexual relations exclusively between men and women to express another, deeper, more pervasive alterosexuality, altereroticism, or alterogender, throughout nature and human history. Gender speaks from itself, its "trouble," of uncontrollable heterogeneities, differences of kinds and erotic proximities. Established categories of gender represent a restricted economy imposed on the general economy of face-to-face, erotic heterogeneity.

Butler finds feminist theory caught up in establishing the gender identity of women so as to promote the feminine in feminist theory, while the results of feminist theory promote instability and heterogeneity.[24]

> Precisely because "female" no longer appears to be a stable notion, its meaning is as troubled and unfixed as "woman," and because both terms gain their troubled significations only as relational terms, this inquiry takes as its focus gender and the relational analysis it suggests. Further, it is no longer clear that feminist theory ought to try to settle the questions of primary identity in order to get on with the task of politics. Instead, we ought to ask, what political possibilities are the consequences of a radical critique of the categories of identity? (Butler, *GT,* p. ix)

Our ethic of inclusion moves within the possibility that ethical and political difference belongs to displaced places of identity, to heterogeneity, alterogender, and other, displaced sexualities. I am exploring the possibility that such displacements of identity circulate in relations between the one and the other in the erotic displacement of sex throughout different natural kinds meeting face to face. All this I understand to be the rests of the earth, the displaced and heterogeneous places in the earth in which gender's inexhaustibility coexists with the different dyads into which it falls, again and again.

In this sense, I seek to extend Butler's critique of the categories of identity. "[T]he question of women as the subject of feminism raises the possibility that there may not be a subject who stands 'before' the law, awaiting representation in or by the law. Perhaps the subject, as well as the invocation of a temporal 'before,' is constituted by the law as the fictive foundation of its own claim to legitimacy" (Butler, *GT,* pp. 2–3). This image of standing before the law reminds us of Kafka's doorkeeper in *The Trial* and the man for whom the door is open for him alone, never to be crossed. And Kafka's image is more troubled than that of the dissolution of the subject instituted by the law, troubled perhaps to the point where as we dissolve the subject, we constitute ourselves and the others as subjects, with joys and truths we suppose to know. If women or ~~The~~ ~~Woman~~ are not a woman subject, a pure kind of subject, except as subjected to the law, still they are subjects for whom the trouble with gender, alterogender, offers a possibility of liberation—or not, given that gender is always fragmented, displaced, impure. Butler speaks of this circular displacement.

> It would make no sense, then, to define gender as the cultural interpretation of sex, if sex itself is a gendered category. Gender ought not to be conceived merely as the cultural inscription of meaning on a pregiven sex (a juridical conception); gender must also designate the very apparatus of production whereby the sexes themselves are established. As a result, gender is not to culture as sex is to nature; gender is also the discursive|cultural means by which "sexed nature" or "a natural sex" is produced and established and established as "prediscursive," prior to culture, a politically neutral surface *on which* culture acts. (Butler, *GT,* p. 7)

I understand gender to be the disturbed and heterogeneous site of *Geschlecht* at which humanity and nature have been instituted, nature in general and everywhere, productive and reproductive nature, human and otherwise, everywhere and every kind. The plenitude of nature is sexed, gendered, reproductive (by repetition), kindred, throughout. The "social constitution" of gender offers a limited reading of this aboriginal upheaval of sexual difference within the heterogeneities of nature.

Butler offers a glimpse of this aboriginality, giving a hint, perhaps, of a more extreme movement.

> Gender is a complexity whose totality is permanently deferred, never fully what it is at any given juncture in time. An open coalition, then, will affirm identities that are alternately instituted and relinquished according to the purposes at hand; it will be an open assemblage that permits of multiple convergences and divergences without obedience to a normative telos of definitional closure. (Butler, *GT,* p. 16)

I add that this permanent deferral works: first, everywhere as gender, that gender is one of the pervasive and fundamental sites of heterogeneity, impurity, and deferral; second, that this deferral is fundamentally ethical, ethical difference, that is, a primordial and pervasive relation to the good, that again, gender is not just something that lacks identity, but one of the sites where heterogeneity appears as kindred difference; therefore, third, that the face to face in which heterogeneity appears, before the other, is erotic as well as gendered, in enigmatic, deferred, mad and magical ways.

This understanding, this intimate proximity of gender with heterogeneity, is brought up short within Butler's understanding of the hold of traditional heterosexuality upon gender, in a way more analogous perhaps to Illich than Butler might like, the Illich who understands the enigmas of gender to disappear in economic sex but to be maintained in vernacular cultures. Gender is enigmatic, heterodox, in vernacular and industrial societies. Butler agrees. But she hesitates to endorse this truth without qualification in traditionally heterosexual societies.

> Gender can denote a *unity* of experience, of sex, gender, and desire, only when sex can be understood in some sense to necessitate gender—where gender is a psychic and/or cultural designation of the self—and desire—where desire is heterosexual and therefore differentiates itself through an oppositional relation to that other gender it desires. The internal coherence or unity of either gender, man or woman, thereby requires both a stable and oppositional heterosexuality. (Butler, *GT,* p. 22)

It all depends on what "unity of experience" means, unity of sex, gender, and desire. If it means a stable and oppositional identity of gender, of men and women, it seems impossible that any society, however conventionally heterosexual, has ever produced an identity of gender, or two identities of gender, has ever stabilized man and woman, even as categories of domination. Western societies have always worked by placing different genders, different kinds of people, at the edges of the *polis,* frequently and typically women, as Clément repeatedly shows, but also or in addition, witches, spinsters, unmarried men, adolescent males, drug addicts, criminals, mad men and women, freed slaves, and so on, as we have seen in Foucault, people whose kinds and sexualities are always problematic relative to mainstream social sexual roles. And there are plants and animals whose genera are filled with weird genders, heterogeneous heterogenders. Of all ideas, that desire might be a unity when infinite, inexhaustible, excessive, among men in relation to women, in total domination and control of women, as Irigaray says, seems impossible to think anywhere, in an oppositional heterosexuality or elsewhere.

The point, perhaps, is that gender can be stably oppositional only when it is oppositional, where sexual difference is not multiply alterosexual, altererotic, heterodox, but this one and that one and no more, that is, where the dyad is definite and does not pass away, promoting what Butler calls "the heterosexual matrix" (Butler, *GT,* p. 35). She demands that the oppositional dyad of sexual difference pass away into complexity. I am pursuing that thought with the difference that I hope to let gender pass away into unlimit, into nature's plenitude, away from human complexity into other kinds in nature's rests.

For she seems to retain The Human within the displacements of gender.

> Are there ever humans who are not, as it were, always already gendered? The mark of gender appears to "qualify" bodies as human bodies; the moment in which an infant becomes humanized is when the question, "is it a boy or girl?" is answered. Those bodily figures who do not fit into either gender fall outside the human, indeed, constitute the domain of the dehumanized and the abject against which the human itself is constituted. If gender is always there, delimiting in advance what qualifies as the human, how can we speak of a human who becomes its gender, as if gender were a postscript or a cultural afterthought? (Butler, *GT,* p. 111)

I respond with the extreme thought that gender's mark is inscribed in nature, far beyond the human, together with sexuality and *erōs.* I respond with the thought that human being finds itself already sexed in an already sexed and gendered Being, a Being already divided by sexual re-production. I respond with the following words:

Are there ever any natural creatures and things that are not, as it were, already gendered, sexed? The mark of gender seems to qualify bodies, any material bodies, as male or female or neuter (not male or female, but something else). Those material creatures who do not fit into one of the categories of gender are unnatural, monstrous, perhaps angelic, perhaps demonic, reimposing the subjugation and subjection inscribed upon the bodies of the abject and impure—women, freaks, mad people, primitives, and animals—against which The Human in its spirituality and privilege is constituted. If gender is always there, even within its neutrality, delimiting in advance what qualifies as being, how can we speak of something "becoming" its gender? How can we speak of something "becoming" its kind?

This reading of the mark of gender suggests that Being is always divided by gender, by a gender indefinitely deferred, thereby a Being unified as well as divided by gender.[25] The univocity of being, against the dominion of identity, is marked by sexual difference and gender.[26] Yet Butler criticizes Wittig's understanding that to overcome the mark of gender demands two things: one, the possibility in language "as a whole" of reinscribing heterogeneity against the oppositions of heterosexuality; the second (in Butler's words), "an ontological presumption of the unity of speaking beings in a Being that is prior to sexed being. Gender, she [Wittig] argues, 'tries to accomplish the division of Being,' but 'Being as being is not divided'" (Butler, *GT,* p. 117; quoted from Wittig, *MG,* p. 81).

I read Wittig differently, read the undividedness of Being as its impurity and heterogeneity, perhaps its univocity. She speaks of reappropriating the universal against its appropriation by men, perhaps of reappropriating the universal or univocal against any class's appropriation. Most of all, she speaks against the way "[s]ex, under the name of gender, permeates the whole body of language and forces every locutor, if she belongs to the oppressed sex, to proclaim it in her speech" (Wittig, *MG,* p. 79). Her concern is with the possibility of releasing the hold of gender on everyone who falls under it, on how it is possible for women, including lesbians, to be released from gender. She describes this as a release to the universal, to what Butler calls the unity of being rather than the dividedness (into two, by gender and sexual difference) of being. In this space, between the unity and dividedness of being, heterogeneity appears, in this moment as the gender of the other, face to face with the erotic other. I join Butler in hesitating before the universality of gender and at the possibility of release to universality. Yet I pause in the univocity of gender.

Wittig says, as universally as possible, that "[g]ender is an ontological impossibility because it tries to accomplish the division of Being. But Being as being is not divided. God or Man as being are One and whole" (Wittig, *MG,* p. 81). Being is not divided and language is not divided. As such. But language and being are always heterogeneous. The "as such" may be heard as indefinite deferral. "Language as a whole gives everybody the same power of becoming an absolute subject through its exercise" (Wittig, *MG,* p. 80). May we hear the undividedness, universality, and absoluteness as univocity, heterogeneity, general economy, and plenitude? Wittig does not consider the possibility that the inexhaustible plenitude of language, God, and being that makes them "One," a oneness I interpret as heterogeneous, as a movement against the same, is altererotic. Of course, this must be true if lesbians can erase the mark of gender, if Wittig (in *The Lesbian Body*) and we can "attack the order of heterosexuality in texts and assault so-called love, the heroes of love, and lesbianize them, lesbianize the symbols, lesbianize the gods and goddesses, lesbianize men and women" (Wittig, *MG*, p. 87). Being, the world, must admit, contain, circulate altereroticism, another face-to-face sexuality that lesbians know, individually or as a group, that others perhaps know, and still others.[27] The undividedness of Being is heterotopic, pervaded by desire and desire's excesses. I wonder if the mark of gender wears Zorro's masks. I wonder if gender always wears masks. I read Butler as sharing that wonder, from which emerges the extreme thought of the erotic heterogeneity of (un)divided Being.

I have resisted the thought that Being is undivided as I have resisted the thought that *Dasein* and its relation to Being, primordially, is not sexed. I find Being divided and sexed, but I do not understand divided sexuality to repeat the opposition between men and women, one gender and the other. Rather, I understand the sex and gender of Being to be hetero, alter, kindred: heterogeneous, heterogender, heterodox, heterotopic. The univocity of Being undermines the dominion of identity in virtue of its heterotopicality, its inexhaustibility, something so excessive, something so far beyond trouble and complexity, passing to unlimit, that gender passes into genera, the kinds of nature, nature's plenitudinous rests, joins animals and other natural creatures. The univocity of Being is its unlimit, passing from the dyad of gender.

Wittig may be read as suggesting that lesbians and other homosexuals do not participate in traditional heterosexuality, that they are not women and are not men. This is an important possibility to consider, though because homosexuals and lesbians inhabit societies pervaded by gender oppositions, it offers a limited and qualified truth. They cannot escape defining themselves as men and women in the societies in which they reside. But they mark the possibility of other sexualities, many other sexualities. They open the curtain that obscures other sexualities with the mark of gender, reveal the possibility of other kinds of gender. Men and women homosexuals express and mark the oppressiveness of oppositional heterosexuality. Butler rejects "the radical disjunction posited by Wittig between heterosexuality and homosexuality" (Butler, *GT*, p. 121) as based on a coherent heterosexuality and a coherent homosexuality, another oppositional dyad. She insists that what I call the univocity of gender, its inexhaustible deferral, opens other spaces of difference, heterotopic spaces. I extend her reading to ethical and kindred difference, everywhere, human and other spaces, a univocity that dismantles identity in virtue of its incoherence, heterogeneity, heterotopicality. I extend her reading to include intimacy, ecstasy, love.

Irigaray criticizes Levinas as knowing nothing of radical alterity, in the face to face of proximity and substitution, nothing of communion in pleasure, of shared sexual *jouissances,* in the plural. Sexual difference inhabits the places of joy and pleasure as well as suffering, in private as well as public. This is certainly one of its most disturbing and terrifying features. Gender, sexual difference, is not found only in the fields, at work, found there in the forms of sexual harassment and sexual violence, everywhere in all these forms if not at every moment. Women suffer physical and sexual violence and subjection, wherever they are—in their homes, in the streets, at work—far more than men, in different ways than men. The dyad of gender, vernacular gender, includes not only women's work but women's pain, suffering and pain, and joy. Illich seems to know nothing of women's intimate joy, and little of their pain, even in the vernacular. Something of heterogeneity unfolds in women's intimacy. Something of responsibility for the other unfolds in proximity, as love.

Speaking of "God" (who may not be God, though Other) and of the "soul" (who as feminine [*l'«âme»*] may also be woman, *la mystérique*), Irigaray speaks of a desire given by ecstasy, by fusion with an other, heterogeneously, a fusion that cannot be unity, a love that is outside itself, something of heterogeneity that desire knows, that knows desire:

> Thus "God" has created the soul to flare and flame in her desire. And if beyond this consummation He/she endures, it is because He/she is nothing but adoration of that warmth, passion for the heart that none can appropriate, light suited to that lone mirror, *and* its virtual reduplication. . . . "God" goes beyond all representation, however schematic in its approximation. (Irigaray, *M*, p. 197)

He/she, from within desire, represents a heterogeneity beyond all representation. Even more powerfully: "I know, now, that both height and depth spawn—and slit—each other in(de)finitely. And that the one is in the other, and the other in me, matters little since it is in me that they are created in rapture. *Outside of all self-as-same*" (Irigaray, *M,* p. 200). In rapture! Enraptured! Ecstatic!

I am exploring the face to face of erotic sexuality as the heterotopicality of ethical difference, leaving aside for the moment my discussions of sexual difference inhabiting public places. What we may acknowledge in the movements we have heard in Illich's, Wittig's, and Butler's understanding of gender, vernacular and economic, economic and political, is their publicity, if not their naturality. There is nothing in gender's public relation to its place and work that embodies a face to face, even in relation to sexuality, that knows intimacy. I wonder if such a public relation to work, in the fields where we can tell, with certainty if we are not a stranger, the gender of the figure in the field, wonder if such a telling's anonymity knows anything of ethics, of heterogeneity, if it might be devoid of ethical responsibility for difference, as economic sex's unisex.

In this way, even the vernacular, concerned with sexuality, with the dyad of gender, every generic heterogeneity, takes on ethical|political neutrality, the same neuter character as *Dasein*'s relation to Being, the indifference of gender. This understanding—that to be silent about sexual difference, gender, *Geschlecht,* is already to have said too much, to have been steeped in a difference forgotten within its neutrality—repeats itself everywhere, even where gender and sexual difference are (or is) the topic. Gender's unisex, neutrality, the availability of work in industrial societies for members of any sex is false, and assumed to be true at the expense repeatedly of women. Women bear the brunt of women's work, of being paid less, and the brunt of competing with men for men's work, bringing down the wages of men. And they bear the major penalty of that competition, in the workplace, but all the more, in the home. And it is the home that we now find ourselves entering, hesitating on the threshold, the places where men and women share intimacy together, and others share with them and among themselves. For not all domiciles are shared by people of different genders, but all domiciles are, in the sense I am pursuing, altererotic, in proximity, face to face with the other, heterogeneous and sexual, hetero|topi|sexual. Domiciles are, like public places of work, heterotopic and alterosexual, places where heterogeneity joins sexuality, places where we must work through different joys and different kinds of joy. This has something to do with men and women. It has little to do with conventional heterosexuality except as repetition.

I retrace Derrida's reading of the sexual neutrality of *Dasein* to link sexual difference with animals and love. We will return to gender in chapter 10, complicating its altereroticism.

Derrida observes that Heidegger does not speak of sex, of sexual difference and gender. With Derrida, I wonder if it is possible not to speak of sex, of gender and sexual difference, when speaking of something else, anything else, especially anything "more fundamental." Perhaps nothing is more fundamental than sex, than being sexed, engendered, in heterogeneous proximity, and if so in a very different way from being sexed in public, in valley and field, if being sexed is heterogeneous, enveloping multiple unknown kinds. Perhaps our debt to Freud lies in his recognition that nothing is more fundamental than sex; yet we may resist joining him in locating that truth in the phallus, defining the problem of woman, rather than locating it everywhere, heterotopically and heterogeneously.

It seems that Heidegger insists of *Dasein* that "insofar as it is opened up to the question of being, insofar as it has a relation to being, in that very reference, *Dasein,* would not be sexed" (Derrida, *G1,* p. 66). Yet this impressive silence must be heard to speak, implicitly and explicitly, of sex, of sexual difference, gender, *Geschlecht,* possibly of love. For the fundamental question, of Being, that fundamental question from which the analytic of *Dasein* emerges, would have it that *Geschlecht* does not belong to *Dasein* fundamentally. "Hence the consequence could be drawn that sexual difference is not an essential trait, that it does not belong to the existential structure of *Dasein*" (Derrida, *G1,* p. 67).

The question of sexual difference as the ethical question of our age here becomes, what sexual difference is heard in the denial that *Dasein* is fundamentally and existentially sexed, erotic? Postponing the ethical question for the moment, we note that Derrida calls our attention to Heidegger's Marburg lectures in Summer 1928 (Derrida, *G1,* p. 68), where Heidegger, in order to emphasize the "neutrality" of *Dasein,* names it from the first as not *Mensch,* not sexed. "For the being which constitutes the theme of this analytic, the title 'man' (*Mensch*) has not been chosen, but the neutral title, '*das Dasein*'" (Derrida, *G1,* p. 69). This statement is followed immediately by the explicit claim that sex is on Heidegger's mind, however obliquely and silently. "That neutrality means *also* [Derrida's emphasis] that *Dasein* is neither of the two sexes [*keines von beiden Geschlechtern ist*]" (Derrida, *G1,* p. 69).

Dasein, the opening from humanity to Being, is in its fundamental nature neutral, a neutrality that means, in its fundamental nature, from the first, not sexed, not *Geschlechtern.* This sense of *Geschlecht* is German, the conjunction of gender with sex and folk—"sex, genre, family, stock, race, lineage, generation" (Derrida, *G1,* p. 69)—the vernacular indeed and repeatedly, related to the world of natural kinds in English. This conjunction may be German, however vernacular and consequently local, may still be German. But the neutrality of the human is precisely in Heidegger (or especially there) gendered, *Geschlechtern,* if only in the thought of its denial. In Derrida's words, "it is sexual difference itself as binarity, it is the discriminative belonging to one or another sex, that destines or determines to a negativity that must then be explained" (Derrida, *G1,* p. 72). The denial of sexual difference is a denial of *Dasein*'s *Geschlecht,* that is, a denial of gender along with genre, family, stock, race, kind, and so on. Not to be sexed in a world divided vernacularly by gender is a negativity to be explained. Not to be *Geschlechtern* in a world divided by *Geschlecht* is to be . . . what? Derrida's question, bringing us back to our dwelling upon the indeterminate dyad of gender, is "[w]hat if 'sexuality' already marked the most originary *Selbstheit?* If it were an ontological structure of ipseity? If the *Da* of *Dasein* were already 'sexual'?" (Derrida, *G1,* p. 74). And he ascribes these suspicions to Heidegger, who says that "ipseity is therefore 'neutral' with respect to being-me and being-you, 'and with all the more reason with regard to "sexuality"'" (Derrida, *G1,* p. 74). What, as I understand Derrida to suggest, can this remarkable emphasis on *Geschlecht,* "all the more reason with regard to *Geschlecht,*" betray but the profound possibility that sexual difference enters being, nature, humanity from the first, primordially, every nearness and proximity, every kind, that being is dispersed into heterogeneous kinds? Does this possibility echo gender everywhere and also echo sex, sexuality, *erōs,* love, face to face, everywhere? These questions echo heterogeneity, again in the language of gender, and again in the endless dyads of the one and the other, the hetero, kind or gender, the other places. Derrida's questions, together with Irigaray's, confront the possibility of an Other, however Forgotten, a heterogeneity that is at its heart sexual, erotic.

I wish to take up this absurdity in all its perversity. I wish to wallow, so to speak, in the possibility that heterogeneity in its most fundamental nature, at bottom, is sexual, gendered, erotic, however absurd that may be. For that absurdity belongs to the question of sexual difference, and for us here, ethical difference. We go from difference in general back to sexual difference then to the other differences, other kinds of differences, the movement of the dyad from definiteness to indefiniteness. We see it in Freud. And perhaps Freud says something profoundly true, that the problem of difference, of heterogeneity, of enigma and the uncanny, is the problem of sexual difference. But not just the problem of the place of women.

For Derrida calls our attention to another difference, dissemination, dispersion [*Zerstreuung*] in Heidegger's view of *Dasein*, a dispersion in *Dasein*'s body [*Leiblichkeit*]. Now "every proper body of one's own is sexed, and there is no *Dasein* without its own body" (Derrida, *G1*, p. 75), thoroughly sexed, thoroughly and properly sexed and different from other bodies with other sexes, other genders. But *Dasein* is originally neutral, especially with respect to sexuality, gender, while "it is its own body itself, the flesh, the *Leiblichkeit*, that draws *Dasein* originally into the dispersion and *in due course* into sexual difference" (Derrida, *G1*, p. 75). Of which Derrida comments, "[t]his 'in due course' (*damit*) insists through a few lines' interval, as if *Dasein* were supposed to have or be a priori (as its 'interior possibility') a body found to be sexual, and affected by sexual division" (Derrida, *G1*, p. 75).

We might ask, at this point, in relation to this proper body, in relation to every fleshy body, what color is *Dasein*'s own proper body? Is it brown or yellow or white, or something else? If we are certain, as we must be, that humanity in general, neutral or other, must be in its flesh, and if that fleshed embodiment must be sexed, must fall apart into sexual difference, we are equally certain that it must fall even further apart, along different lines of cleavage, into rainbow colors, races, nations, cultures, bloods, and kinds. What hue is *Dasein*'s proper blood? Here is where *Geschlecht* in its rainbow polysemic polymorphism presents us with sexual difference's heterogeneity. For sexual difference, in the body, throws us into the profusion of skin and blood, while race, nation, community, every "we," throws us into the dyad, however unlimited, of gender.

I have discussed the alleged neutrality of nature, humanity, and rationality as containing within itself a forgotten sexual difference, a sexual difference in closest proximity to ethical difference. In this context, in relation to Heidegger, I imagine that the neutrality of *Dasein* may be a symptom, if not a cause, of Heidegger's inability to grasp that his understanding of *Dasein,* in its flesh, is fundamentally ethical. To be, to be in nature, animate or not, is to be in embodied, erotic relations, whatever sexuality and eroticism may be. The relation is the one Socrates describes in *Phaedrus,* that "[a]ll soul has the care of all that is inanimate, and traverses the whole universe, though in ever-changing forms" (Plato, *Phaedrus,* 246b). All animate soul has care for, stands in ethical relation to, all that is inanimate, all the rest, as Adam was placed in care of all living things and the earth. To be placed in care is to be responsible for and vulnerable to, not in charge or sovereign over. Similarly, *Dasein,* in its flesh, is fundamentally and ethically responsible for its body's relations to other bodies, human and otherwise, in the ways that bodies relate, sexually and otherwise. Bodies relate to other bodies in the form of desire, erotically, giving rise to the possibility of different erotic, intimate joys. Sex, *erōs,* desire, is inseparable from body, matter, flesh, their altererotic heterogeneity.

If we sexual beings must know whether that other figure is man or woman, from the first, then we must know whether that other figure is human, embodied in the flesh, so that we may know whether it is man or woman, whether it is sexual. The world surrounding us is divided into things we may sexually know in order that we may know some of these things sexually, may experience them madly and erotically. The world surrounding us is divided into different kinds of things altererotically, reflecting the heterogeneity of desire.

My concern at this point is not to repeat the movement from the sexual neutrality of nature to heterosexuality, but to displace this abstract movement of body and matter to ethical proximity. That is the point of the discussion in this chapter, to move from the abstraction of ethical difference to place, to proximity, to the private places where we come face to face. The movement here is again with the unlimited dyad, as a face to face, in proximity. I put my concern as follows. I do not know how it may be possible for any creature to be face to face, in proximity and love, how any natural thing may love another, any other, if not divided sexually, alterosexually, altererotically. *Erōs* must, from the first, break up the original univocity of the differences of Being as cherishment, as love, if there is to be responsible response to Being. Sexuality must, from the first, reenact the kinds, the genres, the generations, the *Geschlechtern,* in heterogeneity, must erotically reenact heterogeneity's heterogender. Which is to say that heterogeneity without sexuality, without *erōs*, intimacy, face to face before the other, does not know ethical difference or love, *philia* or *erōs,* does not know its responsibilities face to face. Heterogeneity demands the unlimited dyad of being face to face in a private place, where we encounter the other as another sex and that sex as other.

My concern is with the implicit, private, original (and mad) eroticality in the alleged neutrality of humanity and truth. For with this private movement of thought, we find ourselves inverting what Derrida suggests may be the extraordinary possibility in Heidegger's (and his) thought. "[M]ay one not begin to think a sexual difference (without negativity, let us clarify) not sealed by a two?" (Derrida, *G1,* pp. 82–83). Our inversion, turning on the movement of the indefinite dyad into proximity, leads me to ask whether every such two is not profoundly at its heart sexual, altero|dyado|sexual. Do we wish to think of sexual difference as three or more, orgiastically, communally? Do we wish to think of sexual difference as dispersed everywhere, abstractly or in general? Or do we find sexual difference in every thought of two, or one, or three, in every thought of ethical difference, face to face, however obscurely, *erōs,* intimacy, in every proximity, unknown, multiple, erotic, heterogeneous desire?

Derrida comes much closer to the question of the sexuality of ethical difference as proximity when he asks: "[h]ow is difference deposited among two? Or again, if one kept to consigning difference within dual opposition, how can multiplication be stopped in difference? Or in sexual difference?" (Derrida, *G1,* p. 83). How does one allow oneself to move within the indefiniteness of the dyad, in the face to face of heterogeneity, neither resisting the number two absolutely nor reinstating it against its inexhaustible movement? That has been our concern with sexual difference, the passing away from two to unlimit, the passing away within the double mark of gender, never losing sight of the dyad, resisting the hold of its rule.

We find this mark, which we cannot let ourselves overlook, in ethical difference, like Levinas, face to face. But we may traverse another line of *Geschlecht* in Derrida to come more closely face to face with this face to face. For I have followed the trace of Derrida's second reading of *Geschlecht* through the themes of ethical difference to sexual difference, monstrosity [*monstrosité*] and propriety [*le propre*], without pursuing the ethical within propriety, especially without coming face to face with proximity. That is my concern now.

For Derrida remains at this fundamental, primordial, and abstract level of ontology, the level at which we may say no natural or human thing can rest, when he reminds us of the untranslatability of the word *Geschlecht,* of which nevertheless, to feel its force, we must know that "it can be translated by sex, race, species, genus, gender, stock, family, generation or genealogy, community" (Derrida, *G2,* p. 162). The word takes us directly from the dyad of sex to the family and community of "we": *unser Geschlecht.* It takes us from proximity to community, from face to face to blood. This movement traces the line of contamination in which sexual difference reverberates throughout the human and natural world, reverberates in every echo of heterogeneity. The other is always, however individual, an other kind, and we, in our kind—humans, men, or Germans—stand in our kind over and against the others, the other kind, steeped in blood. Heterogeneity means flesh, matter, blood. Even in relation to spirit. And love.[28]

I follow Levinas's face to face, from proximity to all the others that obsess me in my infinite responsibility, from a face to face of charity to nature's profusion, and back. I follow Levinas from the good to proximity. "Justice is impossible without the one that renders it finding himself in proximity" (Levinas, *OB,* p. 159), perhaps the theme of my understanding of ethical difference, except for heterogeneity. This chapter, on the intimacy of heterogeneity, is an examination of proximity, face to face, perhaps in a way unheard by Levinas. But even so, it echoes his understanding of the place of ethics, if not the heterogeneity and altereroticism of difference. It echoes his understanding of place and something else, heterotopically.[29]

The circulation of goods, in general, takes place face to face, in proximity. And every such encounter, every experience, in its indeterminateness, brings us face to face, in closest proximity, to heterogeneous kinds and desires, to another person, thing, creature, or kind, in desire's excessive madness. But the world is not made up of individuals only, and face-to-face relations obsess us in the list of kinds that resonate in *Geschlecht*—"sex, race, species, genus, gender, stock, family, generation or genealogy, community"—and others. And they frequently do so etched in blood. My concern here is with tracing something unsaid in Levinas's understanding of all the others that obsess me in the other, all the other kinds, of the impossibility of a justice without proximity: the bloodiness of proximity, the monstrous madness of injustice.

For I agree with Levinas, in the movement we have traced, that responsibility and obsession in proximity to the other are an irresistible component of justice. I disagree with him in three ways: first, that he knows too little of heterogeneity; second, that he does not seem to recognize the erotic proximity of the other; and, third, that he fails to know that the possibility of justice always emerges from and in the places of injustice. This is Anaximander's truth, at the heart of my reading of injustice. This means that in obsession and proximity is always injustice, immemorially, with justice the work of restitution. Injustice belongs to proximity in exceptional ways, monstrously marked for us by heterosexuality.

I understand ethical difference to emerge from an inexhaustible and unlimited sense of the inexhaustibility of things and kinds, of each and every kind of natural creature and thing, imposing upon us an inexhaustible responsibility face to face with each and every thing and kind, a cherishing of, a love and respect for, its inexhaustible preciousness, a responsibility toward it as other to ourselves, heterogeneous. This inexhaustible responsibility is cherishment. From this ethical relation to nature, everywhere and in every thing, we face the impossibility of any fulfillment of the ethical demand, emerging from cherishment and heterogeneity themselves, to select and choose, to bear the force of incompatibilities in intimacy and proximity. In our face-to-face experiences, we encounter wounding. This is sacrifice, but it bears cherishment within itself, a sense of the immemorial and unlimited injustice in things and ourselves. It is related to what Whitehead calls "evil," understood face to face. Cherishment, together with sacrifice, is plenishment, ethical difference put into work, where that work intimately is obsessed by an inexhaustible responsibility toward injustice and evil, by the necessity to employ sacrifice against sacrifice.

Here I understand the movement of ethical difference, the circulation of goods together with our responsibilities, to move from and around the species and kinds of things to face-to-face proximity. I understand ethical difference to bear an unlimited and obsessive responsibility toward heterogeneity that encounters another heterogeneity, another, unknown kind, face to face with another person or creature, other in person and singularity, other in species, kind, or genus. Heterogeneity, between genera and kinds, falls repeatedly into proximity, bears the weight of immemorial injustice in proximity. I understand this as alterosexuality, altereroticism, face to face. Obsession with the other, heterogeneously, is always altererotic. But heterogeneity is always generic, if never universal, always between kinds, human beings and animal beings, animate beings and inanimate beings, and that is where we find erotic desire stretching: in the circulation of heterogeneous goods, stretching from the other person to the other creature, face to face, in proximity, then to other things and kinds. Cherishment and sacrifice take on special meaning face to face, the mad *erōs* of obsession and wounding.

I have traced this movement from the other human being, man or woman, to animals and throughout nature, as the movement of ethical difference into heterogeneous kinds we cannot begin to imagine. Here we understand, as we could not before, why Singer's rejection of our love for cute and cuddly animals, for pets, as crucial within our ethical relation toward them, must be harshly rejected in turn. For ethics always comes down to, works erotically in the place of, proximity. Animals are deeply heterogeneous for us, thereby in our love for them, hetero|sexual for us, heteroerotic, where we do not and will never know what this means, except that it does not mean just human sex and human *jouissance*. Eroticism proliferates together with gender, with endless heterogeneities. In our love for our pets and for other cute animals, for the animals that live in our proximity, face to face, our neighboring animals, whether cats and dogs, or chickens and goats, we love and know other embodied joys and sufferings than we can possibly know within ourselves and other human experiences involving men, women, or children. Ethical difference opens up into another love, a joy, a knowledge and truth we will never know, but may know that we suppose to know, and care for, regard as infinitely precious.

And still, within our deepest and most obsessive ethical care for the preciousness of the world around us, we must sacrifice ourselves and others, must undertake the work of justice as one injustice after another.[30]

CHAPTER 10

Rest

"Sexuality is to feminism what work is to marxism: that which is most one's own, yet most taken away" (MacKinnon, *FMMS1,* p. 515).[1] In this way, MacKinnon echoes certain notes of the ethic of inclusion here: the place of sex and sexuality in relation to personal and group identity and to the surrounding society and world. For work in marxism defines not only the human individual, but that individual's relation to, first, the spheres of production in which that individual participates, then, to the natural world in its materiality to which those productive spheres belong. I do not wish to pursue here, at this time in our history, either the extreme emphasis on material production in marxism or the possibility of a science of work. My analysis is concerned with the ways in which injustice and sexual difference represent and express something older than science or *technē,* embodied in a work closer to *poiēsis,* giving birth to a besouled materiality, face to face. I hope to do this, to remember ethical and sexual difference as a forgotten in work, something marxism does not know of sexuality, even in MacKinnon, though she speaks of it as a feminist.

Sexuality is to feminism, but possibly also to human life in general, and to nature, perhaps to these always and everywhere, but not in general, that which is most . . . but perhaps not one's own, since the proper of one's own delimits another point of exclusion. I have been pursuing a different sense of sexuality's place in and around human places, in proximity, face to face, disturbing every place. My reading of sexuality in human life and nature, drawn from feminism, is heterotopic, disturbing the places in which we and other creatures find ourselves, in which we inhabit nature. I understand these proximities and intimacies, heterogeneously, as sexed, as hetero|sexual, altererotic, in a deeply displaced way, certainly not just between men and women, males and females, and not owned. But we cannot abandon the heterogeneity between men and women, turning away, for example, to unisexuality, to another purity. Rather, I am exploring the sexuality of intimacy and proximity, of *erōs*. I add to Levinas something Irigaray says he does not seem to know, as Heidegger seems to know but refuses: the possibility that the face to face of ethical difference is at heart gendered, sexed, heterosexed, but again, not restricted to men and women; the possibility, expressed in *Phaedrus,* that heterogeneity is dyadic and that dyadic proximity is erotic. If we know this, we know it in other proximities, for example, face to face with works of art, seeking beauty, truth, and the good, in proximity with animals and works, perhaps in every face to face.

MacKinnon pursues one side of our encounter here with sexual difference, something I have understood from Irigaray, embodied in the question of sexual difference. MacKinnon gives it a Wittigial twist.

> the molding, direction, and expression of sexuality organizes society into two sexes—women and men—which division underlies the totality of social relations. Sexuality is that social process which creates, organizes, expresses, and directs desire, creating the social beings we know as women and men, as their relations create society. (MacKinnon, *FMMS1,* p. 516)

This powerfully repeats Wittig's claim that "for us there is no such thing as being-woman or being-man. 'Man' and 'woman' are political concepts of opposition, and the copula which dialectically unites them is, at the same time, the one which abolishes them" (Wittig, *SM,* p. 29). It is important to hear another difference here in relation to sexual difference: that sexuality and gender create men and women as well as relations between them, institute their circulation. These relations inhabit the places I have been pursuing as the sites of ethical and sexual difference. But the places where there are men and there are women, together or apart, are historically and socially constructed spaces, places of the unequal distribution of power.

I have discussed this circulation of men and women in society in general, the circulation of women among men, and men among women, along with the circulation of goods. In this circulation in general we hear the general economy of social life, heterogeneously and hetero|sexually. But I do not understand hetero|sexuality to be, first of all and only, between (*aentre*) men and women, in private or in public, sexually and erotically, nor first of all and only, between the legs. I understand hetero|sexuality as altereroticism, where desire meets the other face to face, where *erōs* circulates madly in proximity. Further, then, I understand the strains and dangers of sexuality in relation to ethical difference, to infinite responsibility toward the other, to belong to erotic intimacy and proximity in unknown ways, always excessive and deferred. This is where sexual difference introduces into the general economy of power and desire something forgotten in their public works. For power and desire exist in public, but they work in private, especially upon women's bodies. They define human bodies, materialities, invested with desire and power, working in face-to-face proximity, even in public. Human bodies work, in proximity, erotically and excessively, giving rise, in certain social and historical configurations, to men and women, dominant and subordinate, thereby engendering the human, in general, in public, again dominant and subordinate. Men and women and others meet in public, carrying the excessive materiality of erotic face-to-face proximity. This materiality, the gravity of embodiment in general, composes ethical difference.

MacKinnon speaks of this movement from the social dispersion of sexuality into men and women, sexed and gendered human beings, in public and in intimate relations in proximity, in powerful and compelling ways. First, our language, English, archaically knows that sexuality is domination, and perhaps that domination is sexual, for "the relations in which many work and few gain, in which some fuck and others get fucked, are the prime moment of politics" (MacKinnon, *FMMS1,* p. 517).[2] The sexual politics in which women are sexual objects in private, objects of sexual violence as well as love, makes them sexual objects in public and frequently objects of sexual violence. The word we must not say in public, when speaking of sexuality, is said again and again in public, speaking of domination. Women are fucked by men, and some men are fucked by other men, speaking of nothing (homo)sexual. Or perhaps domination is precisely (hommo)sexual, in Irigaray's words, whether toward men or women, or animals.

The relations in which women are dominated and subject to sexual violence, in the home and on the street, closely parallel the relations in which men bond with and dominate other men, as if our society of men and women organizes itself into sexual violence twice, once against women, the other against allegedly inferior men and women. Superiority plays itself out, as we have seen in

Aristotle, inseparably from slavery, and where slavery is abolished, inseparably from economic and political subjection.

But where there are both women and slaves, there are two forms of subjection in the home, in private, women and slaves in the home, and women as slaves. Women and slaves are both subjected in the home, in closest proximity, to erotic subjugation, historically to sexual exploitation. The point of this discussion is that even where men and women in the home are subjected to oppression, but not to genital contact, the activities in which they circulate, in the home, in private, are sexual, heterosexual, gendered, including the circulation of men together with men and women with women, in the home. Sexual desire and sexual subjection cross, not only between men and women, but across lines of class, race, and culture. Many who work as domestics in the home are people who cannot get other jobs, doubly and triply subjugated, with nowhere to go if they fail but to the streets, people of other races, new immigrants, illegal aliens. Heterogeneity, otherness, works in the home, in closest proximity. The home, face-to-face proximity, is a place of profound sexual injustices, of intense domination and subjection. The places of *erōs* and *philia* are places where the greatest injustices and oppressions work.

To this complicated and difficult sense of domesticity, places where many of the most oppressed and disadvantaged members of society, those afflicted both financially and culturally, work, we add the impossible burden of women as sexual objects in a culture of gender inequality.

> women notice that sexual harassment looks a great deal like ordinary heterosexual initiation under conditions of gender inequality. . . . If sex is ordinarily accepted as something men do *to* women, the better question would be whether consent is a meaningful concept. . . . As women's experience blurs the lines between deviance and normality, it obliterates the distinction between abuses *of* women and the social definition of what a woman is. (MacKinnon, *FMMS1*, p. 532)

With Andrea Dworkin, MacKinnon denies that a clear and supportable distinction can be made in a society of gender inequality, our society, between heterosexual intercourse and rape, between "normal" sexual relations between men and women and sexual violence. The violence permeates the society, under conditions of oppression and subjection, to the point where erotic activities undertaken by a "man" or "woman" are filled with violence, coercion, with subjection, more perhaps, with women's abjection. We might include homosexual and lesbian activities as well, to the extent that the members of these groups inhabit the same societies. In a society with gender inequality, the work of sexuality is organized around women's subjection and abjection.

My concern here is somewhat different, for I am following a line that MacKinnon touches obliquely. Her social analysis of sexual oppression and inequality so completely overwhelms the possibility of sexual love without violence between men and women in our society that she neglects the erotic points of proximity between men and women (or other points of proximity, between women and women, men and men). These are places of ethical difference. For I am still concerned with two things obliquely present in MacKinnon, but which we may say permeate her thought. One is the theme of proximity as an essential place at which ethical difference and justice work. This means that gender inequality along with the sexual violence directed primarily toward women are not just residues of evil in an otherwise ethical society, but are the source of pervasive and recurrent injustices.[3]

The second is the primary theme I am echoing at the moment: the theme of sexuality as a place of proximity, dyads of meeting face to face, undertaking unlimited responsibilities. If proximity is heterogeneous, altererotic, a site at which we meet radical alterity face to face, then it is profoundly and multiply dangerous. It is also profoundly and multiply fulfilling, heterogeneously fulfilling. And that is another factor in its danger. I am speaking of joy, multiply heterogeneous joys and truths unknown as such to the one who is face to face, joined with the other, but known nevertheless. Such a heterogeneity of joy and truth is expressed by Irigaray in "*La Mystérique*."[4] Here joy and suffering express altereroticism together with the dangers that emerge from the heterogeneities and multiplicities of desire, far exceeding the dangers of suffering.

In particular is the danger of ethics itself, face to face, obsession, and the danger of destruction in close proximity, the danger of extreme wounding, far beyond, perhaps, other suffering. Taking as contaminated an example as possible, from MacKinnon, that speaks to the dangers and violence of heterosexuality, where sexual and ethical difference cross from the general to proximity: "[r]ape is only an injury from women's point of view. It is only a crime from the male point of view, explicitly including that of the accused" (MacKinnon, *FMMS2,* P. 652). This insight represents an institutional perspective, perhaps overstated, for some men care about women's injuries, from their point of view as individual men. MacKinnon speaks of injuries and crimes in general within a society based on gender inequality, especially between men and women, and the social and institutional conditions of sexual violence.

If rape is indistinguishable in general, institutionally, from sexual intercourse except in terms of ambiguous and indeterminate conditions of social interaction, especially ambiguous in a society based on gender inequality, then sexual intercourse between men and women in general (but perhaps not in every case) inhabits a sphere of sexual violence, crosses in the most intimate and face-to-face conditions from care and love to violence and suffering. In other places, MacKinnon elaborates on this crossing, first from men's point of view: "men who are in prison for rape think . . . they were put in jail for something very little different from what most men do most of the time and call it sex. The only difference is they got caught. That view is nonremorseful and not rehabilitative. It may also be true" (MacKinnon, *FU,* p. 88). She speaks directly to women, attempts to express their point of view in relation to sexual intercourse when surrounded by sexual violence. "To women I want to say: what do you really want? Do you feel that you have the conditions under which you can ask yourself that question? If you feel that you are going to be raped when you say no, how do you know that you really want sex when you say yes?" (MacKinnon, *FU,* p. 83). If women are in danger of sexual violence all of the time, in every proximity with men, then how can they be free to participate in a sexual relation free from violence? How can they be free from violence in a world in which every proximity is dangerous, altererotic, organized around the abjection of women?

The question of sexual difference brings us face to face here with the impossible thought, certainly for women (who live with it constantly), and for men, that in the proximity of sexual relations between men and women, there is no difference worth mentioning, no measurable difference, between sexual intercourse and rape, between physical intimacy and physical destruction. MacKinnon asks us to consider the reasons for this under Marxist headings, especially unequal distributions of power. Those who care about women, men and women, those who concern themselves with questions of sexual and ethical difference, must hope that the pervasive gender inequalities of Western societies, perhaps most societies worldwide, may be transformed into gender equalities. "We do not need more fear. We need to make fear unnecessary" (MacKinnon, *FU,* p. 83). This need haunts every moment of our ethical lives.

Yet we may also listen to other notes of ethical difference, other notes of danger inescapable in proximity. For MacKinnon's arguments, forceful in relation to gender inequality, may embody a deeper, more pervasive possibility. For the rapist and his victim are face to face, and there is no safety in such proximity. Similarly, battered and abused women and children are beaten and violated by those closest to them, in greatest proximity, directly face to face.

I am following a line of thought from Levinas that justice is impossible without proximity, face to face, and I am struggling with the heterogeneity of desire, the altereroticism of relations face to face, the madness and wounding of proximity. I am considering the possibility that altereroticism enters every proximity, between man and woman, but also between man and man, between woman and woman, between human and animal, between human and thing, and more, circulates to excess. *Erōs,* desire, inhabits all our face-to-face relations, looking into the face, the eyes, touching in close proximity, relations with our neighbors, human and inhuman, animate and inanimate. If sexuality is constructed socially, in our society under gender inequality, also in other societies, in a dream perhaps, of gender equality, of other sexualities, then we do not know what sexuality may be except an embodied relation to an other, face to face. We may know face-to-face embodiment as erotic, proximity as sexuality. There is nothing, no relation, we can think of or relate to, that is unsexed.

But a deeply contaminated danger echoes in this understanding of the indeterminateness of sexuality, the pervasiveness of sexual difference, intimately related to our dyads of proximity. What MacKinnon says of a society in which women are oppressed and sexually violated may be true of every erotic dyad, including gender equality, that there is no measurable difference, no difference under law, between sexual violence and sexual intercourse. This is not to say that there are no differences, for women may say yes or no, men may be more or less violent, in or out of marriage. More important, it is women in general who suffer sexual violence, men occasionally; women in general who are obligated to perform sexually, obligated to be sexual objects even if they incline otherwise, men occasionally. Men protest, rightly, that they suffer from gender inequality, from sexual violence, in different ways from women. They especially suffer sexual abuse as children from women who were themselves abused. Nevertheless, the brutality of sexual violence is visited predominantly on women's bodies.

All these differences, based on women's consent and terror, are unmeasurable. The difficulty of getting battered women to accept the truth that there is no acceptable level of physical violence that they are required to accept in domestic relations, the difficulty of getting police and social agencies to treat domestic violence as they would treat any other violence, reflects a terrible truth. In proximity, face to face, in ethical and sexual difference, we are in profound danger, we and the other, before the otherness of proximity and the sexuality of otherness. Heterogeneity, face to face, is altererotic, meaning that we do not know what forms of desire, what ecstasies, we may find inspiring, what threats may exist as we place our identities in jeopardy, in relation to others. If we are haunted by an immemorial injustice, if our ethical relations contain monstrous threats of violence and domination, they work especially face to face. In proximity, we are all in danger, and women suffer sexual violence as a kind.

That women suffer the brunt of gender inequality and sexual violence in most societies is a harsh and uncompromisable truth. An ethics|politics of sexual difference must insist on something akin to gender equality, perhaps more subtle and ramified than equality, in which men and women may both participate in social and institutional relations in personally and socially fulfilling ways, safely and rewardingly, free from coercion and violence. This is, we may say, a public reading of erotic joy, organized around its opposition to suffering. This is one possibility of sexual difference, one reading of feminism, that our society might undergo a public transformation under the pressures of sexual difference.

Yet this version of an ethics|politics of sexual difference lacks Levinas's understanding that the ethical emerges from proximity. And here we understand the face to face of intimate sexual relations, not only between men and women, but any intimate dyadic relations, to open possibilities of desire and identity that we cannot begin to imagine. Here we may emphasize the otherness of the other individual, Levinas's other, but also other others, especially other kinds in heterogeneity, passing into heterogender. Before the other, face to face—for example, in the home or in the street or in the forest or beside the stream or under the tree—we encounter not only the other person, creature, or thing, but other kinds whose fulfillments, joys and sufferings, open other worlds of experience, feeling, and truth. We encounter these worlds of experience, but may not share them. We encounter them, but may not know them.

Can we guarantee that every such relation will be safe or non-violent? How could it be? A greater safety might come with the destruction of heterogeneity, a safety filled with danger. An example is how we deal with the creatures who most threaten human hegemony over the earth, the insects, who we destroy wherever we can but never succeed in dominating. The possibility that they represent not only another form of life that might share the earth with us, but another fulfillment of God's work, a richer joy than ours (measurable or not), another cherishable joy, filled with truths we do not and will never know, appears here and there in literature, but fails to touch most people's lives. Yet we speak of the wonder with which philosophy begins, love toward the other kind as other.

I share MacKinnon's Marxist view that men and women possess identities formed in public, by sexuality and work, in general. But I understand the relation between public and private differently. First, I share Arendt's understanding of the public even as I reject her view of the private realm. For Arendt set her model of the *polis* in Greece, and never grasped the horror of slavery or the acute oppression of women in private. "The institution of slavery in antiquity, though not in later times, was not a device for cheap labor or an instrument of exploitation for profit but rather the attempt to exclude labor from the conditions of man's life" (Arendt, *HC,* p. 94). The pervasive degradation of the soul in slavery and especially of women in private, in Greece and almost everywhere thereafter, the oppression of women in the proximity of sexual heterogeneity, seems unknown to Arendt.

Yet she expresses a deep concern with heterogeneity, at least in public, and a remarkable sense of this public.

> The term "public" signifies two closely interrelated but not altogether identical phenomena:
>
> It means, first, that everything that appears in public can be seen and heard by everybody and has the widest possible publicity. For us, appearance—something that is being seen and heard by others as well as by ourselves—constitutes reality. (Arendt, *HC,* p. 45)
>
> Second, the term "public" signifies the world itself, in so far as it is common to all of us and distinguished from our privately owned place in it. This world, however, is not identical with the earth or with nature, as the limited space for the movement of men and the general condition of organic life. It is related, rather, to the human artifact, the fabrication of human hands, as well as to affairs which go on among those who inhabit the man-made world together. To live together in the world means essentially that a world of things is between those who have it in common, as a table is located between those who sit around it; the world, like every in-between, relates and separates men at the same time. (Arendt, *HC,* p. 48)

This public world, the world itself, is the world of work. It is what I understand as the circulation of goods, extending its reach beyond fabrication and artifacts to nature and general economy. Arendt acutely describes it as the circulation of heterogeneity.

> the reality of the public realm relies on the simultaneous presence of innumerable perspectives and aspects in which the common world presents itself and for which no common measurement or denominator can ever be devised. . . . Being seen and being heard by others derive their significance from the fact that everybody sees and hears from a different position. (Arendt, *HC,* p. 52)

> The end of the common world has come when it is seen only under one aspect and is permitted to present itself in only one perspective. (Arendt, *HC,* p. 53)

We may consider the extreme possibility that Arendt's writing, as magnificent and truthful as it is, knows nothing of ethical and sexual difference, nothing of the heterogeneity of proximity or the subjection of intimacy. Heterogeneity for her exists and circulates in public, within the common world, rather than within the private realm. Her understanding of privacy seems alien to the question of sexual difference, unknowing of the terrible dangers to women that exist because there is not and has never been a private life in which the public stakes of danger were not enforced on women by oppression and violence. Arendt seems to know nothing of what MacKinnon tells us, of the impossibility of private safety in a world of gender inequality. In this sense, Arendt seems to write from a certain Greek nostalgia, after Heidegger. I have understood it to fall under a certain contamination, of Our *Geschlecht*.

> To live an entirely private life means above all to be deprived of things essential to a truly human life: to be deprived of the reality that comes from being seen and heard by others, to be deprived of an "objective" relationship with them that comes from being separated from them through the intermediary of a common world of things, to be deprived of the possibility of achieving something more permanent than life itself. (Arendt, *HC*, pp. 53–54)

I add two things, the nostalgia for the control of time that would demand the achievement of something more permanent than life itself at the expense of pain and suffering, and the reality that there is and has never been an entirely private life for women. Or rather, there has never been an entirely private life; public and private are, like men and women, categories of domination. But women in general, and members of other races and classes as well, have suffered subjection. Oppression belongs to certain kinds and not others.

The nostalgia is stronger when Arendt tells us of the safety of the private world.

> mass society not only destroys the public realm but the private as well, deprives men not only of their place in the world but of their private home, where they once felt sheltered against the world and where, at any rate, even those excluded from the world could find a substitute in the warmth of the hearth and the limited reality of family life. (Arendt, *HC*, p. 54)

Here "men" is surely a gendered word, describing those who have the right and standing to live in public and who build shelters around the hearth where they may live safely. For women, who lack public standing, this safety has been an illusion and a lie.

But Arendt's concern, if we give up the nostalgia, is for the heterogeneity of the public world. My understanding of public and private is closer to Whitehead's than to Arendt's or MacKinnon's:

"there are no concrete facts which are merely public, or merely private. The distinction between publicity and privacy is a distinction of reason, and is not a distinction between mutually exclusive concrete facts. The sole concrete facts, in terms of which actualities can be analysed, are prehensions; and every prehension has its public side and its private side" (Whitehead, PR, p. 290). Everything in circulation circulates in general economy and in multiple restricted economies. I understand the general circulation of goods to take place face to face, in proximity, goods circulating dyadically. This is my understanding of ethical difference. The public, common world is, as Arendt says, a world filled with heterogeneity, a world that would disappear if it became the same. But it cannot be reduced to a single perspective within general economy. Only the dream of restricted economy, under a single teleology, can offer the illusion of a single perspective within multiple circulation.

But I follow Whitehead further to understand that the heterogeneities that inhabit the common world belong to multiply complex and ramified places in private, face-to-face relations. Heterogeneity shows itself in its radical alterity, face to face, in proximity. This is Levinas's point and pervades my understanding of ethical and sexual difference. From the standpoint of the unequal distribution of power between men and women, where women suffer the sense of their difference most is not (I believe) being paid less for the same work, or being excluded from certain work by men, but face to face, with lovers, with men and other women, and with employers, and not just with other people, but in relation to other things and possessions, in closest proximity to their bodies and their bodily powers.

I understand the private realm to be the place where the heterogeneities of the public world do their work, have their places. I understand the multiple circulations of heterogeneous goods in general economy to work in indeterminate and inexhaustible proximities. And within this understanding, I arrive at a different reading of the idea of "one's own," far from Arendt's and Heidegger's sense of safety, alien to Hegel's sense of the world as property, of mastery,[5] and Derrida's reading of one's own as "proper," as property and propriety. I understand the public world as the "common world" of heterogeneity. But I understand that we can belong to that public world, can circulate among the goods that circulate around us, only in face-to-face relations, the relations in which we make these others "our own": our selves, our bodies, our friends, our lovers, our domiciles, our surroundings, all our own not as our possessions but in our proximity.

Human beings, men and women, live in a world of other human beings, creatures, and things, surrounded by natural plenitude. But they do not experience the plenitude "in general," as it and they circulate together, or do so momentarily in passing.[6] The general economy works in dyadic form, from this to that proximity, face to face. In these face-to-face encounters, proximities, we make other beings our own, and make us theirs, not in the sense that we own them, nor in the sense that we impose rules of propriety upon them—though we recurrently and shamefully do both of these things. The sense of "our own" that inhabits the spaces of proximity, face to face, is that in which we find our places, inhabit our envelopes, at rest, between. That place where my identity, who I am, is at stake, is where I am at rest, the multiple places at which I (and you) remain at rest, excessively and heterogeneously. The places where I find myself as my own are the dyadic places where I am in proximity, within my intimate experiences.

I have added to this far-reaching sense of "my own place" the understanding: that every proximity, face to face, is erotic, sexual, sexed, and gendered, in unknown, potentially unimaginable ways; that the heterogeneity of an encounter with the other is an experience face to face, one and the other; that this encounter is a responsibility for and toward the other's otherness; that this otherness is not only a difference of that other individual but, more deeply and radically, of that other's kind, species, *Geschlecht,* gender, unknown and perhaps unknowable kinds, circulating in general economy. I understand questions of sexual and ethical difference to circulate so deeply and profoundly into every encounter as to call into question every gender, species, kind, or nation, to call into question their nature and durability, raising impossible questions of production and reproduction. Questions of ethical and sexual difference challenge the imposition of every form in every face to face, therefore especially all the gendered forms in which men and women meet erotically, and the durability of every form, of other relations face to face, with other kinds.

On my reading of *Phaedrus,* every proximity is erotic, permeated by desire and power, by mad excess. Here *erōs* belongs to general circulation, pervaded by the excesses of desire and longing, including possession and mastery. We yearn, infinitely and excessively, from within desire, *erōs*'s inexhaustible longing for the good, surrounded by necessities demanding mastery. We find ourselves before others, other men and women, but also face to face with animals, as they are face to face with us and others. We hope to be face to face with still other animals, wild animals, and leave the city in order to be in proximity with trees and flowers. The close encounter with a work of art is another proximity in which our very being is at stake, the possibility of our transformation brought to the fore, in ways we cannot begin to imagine until their inception. And then there are the other encounters. In this way, as Whitehead suggests, every thing is in proximity, where every public kind meets others face to face.

These ways in proximity, in our inexhaustible responsibilities before the others, face to face, represent ethical difference. There is no place for love or ethical difference, no place of safety, no hearth where men and women, or men and men, or women and women, can meet erotically apart from the general circulation. Rather, the general circulation is a circulation of intimacies, of families, of reproductive units for procreation and regeneration.[7] In private, we are in public; in public, in the work of the public, we encounter each other and encounter other creatures and things, intimately, erotically. This, I believe, is the truth of *Phaedrus:* that to make anything our own, we must relate to it face to face and in proximity, in love and friendship, with cherishment, filled with desire and madness. These proximities, face to face, are the living truth. But the living truth is Pharmakeia, in her terrible ambiguities and complexities. It is also the truth of the places of lovers in proximity to the unworking of work. "For the community, lovers are on its limit, they are outside and inside, and at this limit they have no meaning without the community and without the communication of writing: this is where they assume their senseless meaning. Reciprocally, it is the community that presents to them, in their very love, their singularities, their births, and their deaths" (Nancy, *IC*, p. 40).

Levinas speaks of the face to face as a place of wounding, obsession, and exposure. I have not undertaken our exposure, in our materiality and temporality, to the other as inhabiting the hearth of ethical difference. I have spoken of wounding and obsession as ethical moments. Yet exposure in our bodies, exposure to others in their bodies, in our kinds and in theirs, is an exposure to time, aging, wrinkling, and decay, and an exposure to desire and power. In the materiality of our bodies, face to face with an other of a very different kind, with a very different truth and joy, we are exposed down to the very rests of our souls, remain exposed in every proximity. Face to face is embodied.

Face to face is the place where the work of the world transpires, ethically, filled with the terrible dangers of such work, dangers of failure and dangers of oblivion. With these words we return to MacKinnon, to retrace the inseparability of rape from erotic love. She ascribes this inseparability to gender inequality. I have approached a more dangerous, possibly more contaminated place. For I understand the meeting of men and women (restricting myself to these dyads for the moment) as taking place in dangerous erotic proximity. And especially, accepting both MacKinnon's and Wittig's understanding that gender is a socially and politically constructed category, I understand that one of the most dangerous moments in erotic proximity, between men and women, terrifying and without any safety, is the indeterminateness of gender. "When you meet a human being, the first distinction you make is 'male or female?'" (Freud, *F,* p. 113; Irigaray, *SOW,* p. 13). What if no distinction could be made between male and female, no distinction of gender or *Geschlecht,* that was not a political distinction, a distinction of power? With what safety might we find ourselves in erotic proximity, especially in an age of AIDS? What safety can we find when women, in erotic proximity with men, are taken up as reproductive property?

The abortion debate in the United States today is shaped as one of life and death (always of the fetus, sometimes of the woman) versus women's choice. If women are given life and death choice over the lives of their unborn, are they not blasphemous? Yet the condition of women's bodies, procreative and reproductive, visited upon women's bodies everywhere, is oppressive everywhere there is gender inequality. Reproduction is an oppressive condition when it is not an individual woman's choice—for women in general may also impose reproductive rules on other women. In this light, the abortion debate is a debate over women's bodies.

> unless procreative choice is understood as a desirable historical possibility substantively conducive to every woman's well-being, all debate regarding abortion is morally skewed from the outset. (Harrison, *RC,* p. 102)

> I have never read a word of moral discussion on abortion that recognizes the complex history of women's efforts to control and shape their own power of reproduction. (Harrison, *RC*, p. 104)

You and I may hesitate at the standard of well-being Harrison interposes before the responsibility of life and death.[8] We may care more for suffering and joy, understood as an opening onto heterogeneity. But at stake is control of life and death, not of one life and death but of humanity, whether women or men or some neuter society controlled by men, control and shape human reproduction. The importance of abortion is the importance of sexual and reproductive control, placing it in closest proximity to rape. The abortion debate and the impossibility of eliminating rape derive from the same impossibility, both based on gender inequality. There is no safe place for women, especially sexually and procreatively. Others have a stake in every woman's sexuality and procreation.

In a *régime* of gender inequality, women suffer oppression, the oppression of that gender inequality, of being "Women," in their most intimate, face-to-face relations. Or rather, they suffer that oppression especially poignantly, forcefully, in an encounter with a man in relation to whom they are "a woman," in their most sexual, erotic activities. MacKinnon describes this in terms of the meaninglessness of the distinction between rape and erotic love between men and women. I interpret it in terms of heterogeneity in proximity. In proximity, we place ourselves at risk before the alterity of the other, who may differ from us and from what we take that other to be not only individually but as an unknown kind. In proximity, we experience the terrors and joys of encounters with unimaginable alterity. And we pass from face-to-face heterogeneity, pass away from proximity to the general circulation of dyadic heterogeneity. The passing away gives us, in general economy, the possibility of a public world, of a politics. We let the number two pass away from dyads to unlimit, to general circulation, in relation to nature. But we cannot let the dyads disappear, cannot relate to heterogeneity except in proximity. That is the truth of ethical difference, brought home to us through questions of sexual difference. It is also the truth of kindred difference, manifested throughout history in face-to-face encounters with different civilizations and with animals, something men and women have always sought.

Here we confront a terrible contamination. For if erotic proximity is dangerous and terrifying where we meet the other, heterogeneously and altererotically, then why is it a surprise that there should be sexual violence? We cannot distinguish rape from love except in terms of unmeasurables; why should we be able to measure the distinction between erotic love and sexual violence?

There is something to this question, something within this question that relates profoundly to sexual difference, to *jouissance*. But it is no minor point that women suffer the brunt of sexual violence, that the dangers of heterosexuality are visited upon women especially, and especially female children (though male and female children are another recurrent point of subjection). Here altereroticism, the multiplicities of intimacy and gender, are reduced to sexual violence against "women." In most societies based on gender inequality and in most societies, including vernacular societies, based on stereotypical gender identities, the eroticism of the other passes into sexual domination, gender oppression. Sometimes this takes the form of physical violence, rape or domestic abuse. But as Wittig and MacKinnon emphasize, sexual violence has already taken place in the determination of gender that reduces the excesses of altereroticism and, above all, reduces the dangers of altereroticism by force and violence.

Here we may pass from sexual relations between men and women, by force and violence, to other obsessions and desires, between men and men, women and women, and across species and genera. Here we may understand our relation to nature, to other creatures and natural things and kinds, as erotic and embodied if not procreative. The understanding of erotic desire in terms of genitals is reductive and indefensible, and endlessly repeated. Erotic desire belongs to us in our bodies, throughout our bodies, at different points of bodily encounters. At this point in history, still, procreation takes place between men and women, however interpolated by society and technology. If procreation does not define sexuality—and it does not for homosexuals and lesbians—then it does not for human beings whose erotic relations fall outside human relations, those who live entirely alone in the desert, those whose fulfillments are with natural things.

Some people love animals, love them as their companions. Others exploit and abuse them. Some people love streams and twilight. Others exploit and use them. We, as subjects, relate face to face with everything around us, cherishing things in our proximity, cherishing other things with which we might be in proximity, cherishing the others who obsess us in every proximity. Every such relation, of proximity, of cherishment, is erotic, a heterogeneous relation of uncontainable yearning, a dyadic encounter in which identities risk profusion. The risk in every face to face belongs to everyone, men and women. Sexual violence—and I understand sexual violence to be a violence that men suffer as well as women, even when they are its perpetrators—is a violence to one's being, a hardening and destruction of one's identity, in proximity, face to face. But it is a violence whose pain and destructiveness falls disproportionately, extremely, upon women. Nothing can justify that sacrifice, that pain and suffering. And in addition, beyond that impossible lack of justification, nothing can justify the destruction to women, and men, and sexuality, and love, and human identity, that such violence imposes.

I add that nothing can justify the destruction to natural things and creatures that human violence imposes, blind to the ethical imperatives cherishment demands in every face-to-face encounter with any creature or any thing.

We have returned to rest, in relation to domesticity, if I may use this word to describe not every proximity, but the proximities that express our private, day-to-day activities, erotic activities, organized around sexual difference.[9] We return to rest through understanding that ethical difference belongs to domestic proximity, face to face, to the one and the other together, heterogeneously and altererotically. And we understand that people and things come together, face to face in proximity, in certain places, need places for face to face encounters, for erotic encounters. These are places of rest, in the sense in which rest disturbs the tranquility of every place, remains disturbed by erotic excess. We understand in this way the general economy in which we and others circulate in erotic dyads, indefinite dyads, always finding places of rest.

Phaedrus and Socrates find their place of rest away from the city:

> Upon my word, a delightful resting place, with this tall, spreading plane, and a lovely shade from the high branches of the *agnos*. Now that it's in full flower, it will make the place ever so fragrant. And what a lovely stream under the plane tree, and how cool to the feet! . . . And then too, isn't the freshness of the air most welcome and pleasant, and the shrill summery music of the cicada choir!" (Plato, *Phaedrus*, 230bc)

The cicadas madly sing, reminding us of *erōs*'s madness, of altereroticism's excess, in a voice of music.

> The story is that once upon a time these creatures were men—men of an age before there were any Muses—and that when the latter came into the world, and music made its appearance, some of the people of those days were so thrilled with pleasure that they went on singing, and quite forget to eat and drink until they actually died without noticing." (Plato, *Phaedrus,* 259c)

The places of altereroticism, the places where ethical and sexual difference do their work in proximity, are places of rest, private places, where lovers and companions can meet as others face to face away from the crowd, and where they cannot help but be obsessed by them along with all the others. But they meet, erotically, in a face to face in which heterogeneity reaches a crux, indefinitely, inexhaustibly, and erotically. Such erotic places of rest, where lovers and friends meet daily and repeatedly in private, are the domiciles in which we live together, sometimes men and women, sometimes men and women and children, more frequently than before perhaps men and men, women and women. But men and women have always lived among members of the same sex and gender, at least in the West, when unmarried or under certain circumstances, economic and otherwise—at war, for example.[10]

Domiciles, where people meet in domestic relations, where we rest in domesticity, need not be houses, homes, despite the etymology, but may be delightful resting places away from the crowd. But they are away from the crowd, away from the public, even when they are crowded; they are places of rest, if not always delightful; and they are, if not delightfully, erotic. This point, about desire within proximity, needs as strong an emphasis as I can give it. I am following the line of thought in *Phaedrus* that suggests that what friends and lovers do in private is to pursue the good in erotic proximity. They need not do so through procreative relations, though many do. The immortal soul and the philosophers who remember their souls' immortality undertake as erotic and ethical a relationship as possible to the good. But others, in sexual passion, also walk together in a life of shining bliss. They walk together altererotically in close and intimate proximity because of, in, and through their love. They know the attraction of the good in ecstatic union with each other.

All such dyads, in relation to the good, are indefinite, excessive, mad, inspired, but also altererotic, the one together with the other erotically. Sex as penetration, genital contact, is one erotic form in human life. But dyads, human and other dyads, are permeated by desire, erotically, filled with desire, with yearning, for the good, for fulfillment, together, madly and excessively, throughout their bodies and everywhere. The good sprouts in this soil of mad, excessive, altereroticism where one and the other meet to face each other as other in unimaginable and unthinkable kinds and ways. Who the one and the other are remains indefinite, indeterminate, determined within the circulation of desire's excesses. Our general economy, the general economy of nature, circulates goods and things dyadically and erotically.

We turn away from Singer's image of cute and cuddly pets to a much more erotic and engendered image of face to face proximity before animals. When we live together with a dog or cat, in closest proximity, we know that they own a soul of a very different kind from ours and that they possess another kind of madness. Animals live and yearn; they yearn for us, they care for us, and they gain fulfillments we will never know, may never know enough to judge, good or bad, high or low. Face to face with cats and dogs, or turtles and fish, we encounter *erōs* and *philia* at work in mysterious ways, souls at work in closest proximity, ennobling us insofar as we and our desires are placed at risk before their heterogeneity.[11] Face to face with trees and the dark, impenetrable faces of great peaks, as we place ourselves in proximity to them, we find that we and the earth move before them, move in the joys and fulfillments, the yearning and striving before the good that Spinoza called *conatus,* which the Romantics felt immensely as transcendent, a heterogeneity which we experience as belonging to others. I call it "cherishment," and identify it with the enigmas of inexhaustible fulfillments and joys, permeated by desire. Joy is erotic, returning us to the *jouissance* of the woman, who bears the brunt of otherness in our world, standing in this respect for the others. I suppose that the woman who is not-all experiences a joy for the others.

We find another interpretation of the passing away from the intermediate number, the indefinite dyad, to unlimit, as the movement from sex, face to face between men and women, to the unlimit and excess of desire for the good, disturbed unlimitedly by heterogeneity, into the general circulation of goods and things and kinds, in nature, altererotically.

With this insight, I return to that point of extreme contamination to where women, at rest in domestic relations, suffer continual oppression, ranging from subjection to outright sexual violence and abuse. If domiciles, where men and women meet in proximity, are places of rest, erotically, they are dangerous, violent. Ethical difference, like sexual difference, is a struggle with the good that does not know that violence is always wrong. Murder, assassination, always take place face to face, even (or especially) terrorist actions. I deny, totally and unequivocally—and I hope you join me—that any justification of any kind whatever can entail that women or children or animals or any members of any particular kind shall bear the brunt of the dangers of proximity and, especially, bear the violence of proximity. Sexual difference, not as men and women, but as altereroticism, works at rest where love and care and peace themselves are in closest proximity to opposition and strife. Erotic places, domiciles, proximities, are where injustice works, face to face, where justice is strife, *polemos*. I am concerned with whether the disturbances and dangers of rest, places in private where we are at rest, can justify sexual violence.

Irigaray says that women, having no place of their own, are dangerous to men, disturb men's places. And men, in return, are violent toward women. But nothing can ethically justify, no justice in the world can support, that women must suffer sexual violence and abuse in the greater part, while men must suffer dreams of castration and disempowerment. No people or kind is chosen to suffer. To the contrary. The ethical consequence of proximity, of altereroticism, of hetero|sexuality, is cherishment, and the sacrifices demanded belong to general economy. Sacrifice belongs to justice as restitution for immemorial injustice. Face to face, in proximity, we hope to cherish each other in our unknown and unknowable heterogeneities.

Only in the world, under *technē*'s law, are we called upon to sacrifice ourselves and others. In this world is gender inequality, unequal distribution of power, and women suffer violence and abuse. In this world is species hegemony, the triumph of *homo sapiens* over other kinds of creatures, who along with their habitats suffer destruction at human hands, suffer destruction as if they do not matter, without the least reverence for their heterogeneity. Without altereroticism there cannot be ethics. But the work of ethics moves from domiciles, in private, to public spaces where we live together with the others. This movement, one of sacrifice, resists the violences of an ethic of nurture and care. In proximity, care is cherishment of the other as something strange, therefore not just as man or women. In public, in circulation, we undertake responsibility for and to each other in kinds and groups, always struggling with the reduction of heterogeneity, the reduction of *erōs* to *technē*, to mastery and control. This struggle, this mating of charity with sacrifice, is plenishment. Plenishment remembers cherishment. Sexual violence renders it abominable, enforces the abjection of women. And men.

CHAPTER 11

Walpurgisnacht

A man of quality, Faust is willing, with enthusiasm and love, to bring, to force, a vulnerable woman to destruction, to eternal damnation. But he recoils from dancing with a beautiful young witch, when a red mouse springs out of her mouth. In a certain voice, we might wonder whether Faust's affair with Gretchen in the name of Spirit could be any more beastly. I do not utter that voice here, resisting its monstrosity. In another voice, we may ponder the destructiveness of Spirit, may wonder if it bears any superiority to a tiny red mouse. Here sexual difference and animals meet in the figure of the witch. For witches have animal familiars, mice and cats especially, but in Goethe's *Walpurgisnacht* are surrounded by the teeming profusion of nature.[1] In the figure of the witch, women join nature's plenitude, partake of life with joy. Why should we regard the sterility of Faust's study as higher?

Shall we hear this natural plenitude as belonging to the Devil, as Faust suggests, with books and human laws belonging to God? Or shall we think of what Mephistopheles says in response to Faust's revulsion at the shocking color of the mouse: "One must not so squeamish be; So the mouse was not gray, enough for thee"? (Goethe, *F*, Part 1, scene 11, p. 160). We may wonder at the color red, may identify the witch's beauty with the red mouse and, if we do so, we may think of the beautiful witch, with or without the Devil or the dead or dying God, as beautiful in virtue of the disquietude she evokes out of nature's richnesses and the teeming lives circulating within. Witches represent intermediary figures of general economy: nature's plenitude and desire's excess. For the relationship Faust disdains, with the beautiful witch who has a red mouse in her mouth, might be one of equals, an unpredictably dangerous, erotic relationship of equals, inscribed on, filled with, the inexhaustible plenitude of nature, teeming with animal life, teeming with the unexpected. Gretchen's exploitation is altogether predictable.

I have taken up this relation of nature's plenitude to sexual difference in various ways, dyadically, carnivorously, and more, circulating profusely in nature's general economy. For the moment, I spin the subject of ethical difference around the figure of the witch, conceived broadly, inclusively. I conceive of ethical inclusion, the inclusion of everything in a teeming, inexhaustible natural plenitude, as falling within the circulation of goods and judgments, as a disturbed figure: first, of women, mostly but not altogether women, for wizards have always been together with the witches; second, of animals, for animals have always joined the witches and wizards; then, third, of nature's plenitude. Ethical difference includes everything precious in nature's plenitude, cherishes the preciousness of nature's plenteousness, passing through witches and wizards and animals, through sexual difference and gender, through animals and other natural differences of kind, heterogeneity and alterogender, including differences by race, color, culture, history, geography, sexual preference, all human and natural differences of kind. In the figure of the witch we find the resurgence of questions of ethical, sexual, and kindred difference, of heterogeneity. The witch is an intermediary figure.

But I conceive the figure of witches broadly, inclusively. Especially, I include women together, their lips touching together. Especially, I include other kinds we may have overlooked.

Of *The Lesbian Body (Le Corps Lesbien)*, Wittig says, in her Preface to the English translation,

> "I" [*Je*] conceals the fact that *elle* or *elles* are submerged in *il* or *ils*, i.e., that all the feminine persons are complementary to the masculine persons. The feminine "I" [*Je*] who writes is alien to her own writing at every word because this "I" [*Je*] uses a language alien to her; this "I" [*Je*] experiences what is alien to her since this "I" [*Je*] cannot be "*un ecrivain*." . . . If *I* [*J/e*] examine m/y specific situation as subject in the language, *I* [*J/e*] am physically incapable of writing "I" [*Je*], I [*J/e*] have no desire to do so. (Wittig, *LB*, pp. 10–11)

In "The Mark of Gender," she calls this process "lesbianization," claiming that the *J/e* in *LB|CL* can attack "the order of heterosexuality in texts and assault the so-called love, the heroes of love, and lesbianize them, lesbianize the symbols, lesbianize the gods and goddesses, lesbianize men and women" (Wittig, *MG*, p. 87).

Perhaps she means something different, more wicked, of lesbianization, something we will come to momentarily. But in a gendered language, not just French, German, Latin, or Greek, but also English, in a language in which the One is Man, in the pronouns of writing, in writing out of personal experience, one speaks of *ils,* of men and mankind and humanity, in every I and One that is not singular. The individual can pass in grammar as unsexed; the group is always male, masculinizing the "unsexed," despite linguistic neutrality. Only lesbians as a kind can speak of themselves as *elles,* in English as *they,* without having to say, we mean not men, we are not masculine. Only lesbian women are not not-men, as women, as a group of women. Lesbianization, grammatically, in relation to the *J/e,* which silently contains an *elles,* expresses a female identity that does not pass through male identity to be female. Only without men can women be women, Wittig says. Women are women as a kind in a way that only lesbians can say, perhaps (though I hesitate at the repetition of "without men"; hesitate at the possibility of being a woman without men under conditions of gender inequality, even for lesbian women). Wittig insists on saying something of women's identity, as women, in a way that resists thinking or saying, women as *elles* as men have always been *ils,* without neutrality or hegemony. Something of the identity of women, of human beings, of anything, belongs to the group, the kind. I think of it as hetero or alter: hetero|sexuality, altereroticism, heterogeneity, alterogender. I think of heterogeneity as a profusion of kinds.

This thought of women as women must fail as a thought while it expresses something of gender inequality and of gender equality. I am speaking again of gender inequality in which women are subordinated to the male. Only without their male rulers can women find their identities to be not subordinate but, instead, heterogeneous. Yet the analogy in relation to other kinds—for example, that Africans can be African only in the absence of Europeans, that postcolonial means pure African—fails both by extreme nostalgia and by history. And the analogy that animals—for example, lions and elephants—can be what and who they are only when pure, in the absence of human beings, fails again in the wild, for the proximity of humans and animals, the *aentre,* reveals something of the one and the other—for example, the lions and the Juwasi. Perhaps lesbianization is what is needed for women to be women in proximity to men where language belongs to the masculine. But we must not give up the thought of proximity, face to face, of heterogeneity, in the identity of *ils* or *elles*, between women and women, possibly men and men. Wittig places us in closest proximity, in Levinas's language. "*I* watch [*regarde*] you, *I* watch you, *I* cannot refrain from crying out" (Wittig, *LB*, p. 65). "You are alone as *I* am with you face to face" (Wittig, *LB*, p. 67). Face to face is altererotic, heterogeneous, *aentre*.

The thought of women without men must fail to express heterogeneity and altereroticism, proximity and exposure, as completely as human without pig or cat. Something of the human belongs in the *aentre*, the displaced places of being the one and the other, the one with, face to face with, exposed to, the other of a different kind. Perhaps the relevant thought is not of failure, the failure of the thought of women without men, humans without animals. Such a thought does not fail, may indeed succeed in providing a certain liberation for women, and for men, but nevertheless lacks something of heterogeneity, sacrifices heterogeneity in its purity. I have repeatedly echoed the theme of the indefinite dyad as a movement at the heart of heterogeneity, the endless circulation of dyads around and away from themselves, face to face, passing away into the general economy of circulation. I understand the plenishment of the earth as a general economy of dyads, *aentre*, at least of certain intermediate numbers, where the face to face, with the other, transpires in a place of difference, a difference of the one, the singularity of the individual, and also of the other, the different kind of the other, which I understand as gender, and more, the excesses and impurities of sexual difference, *erōs*. Heterogeneity is alterogender, face to face, body to body, with the other, exposed to the wounds of the other, the space of ethical difference. I understand it to be altererotic, kindred difference, in a special way.

Women without men would reduce this alterogender, the impossibility of and in ethical difference, in an economy of the same, repeating—at least, that is my fear—the economy of the same that has ruled male societies, in a different voice, the alterogender men inhabit but do not know in their proximity with men, including homosexual men. Women without men, lesbianized—if that is what "lesbianization" means, without men, rather than women who do not need men in order to be women—would escape the difficulties of ethical difference, the impossibilities of the other organized around hetero|sexuality, in the sovereignty of the same, passing from the dyad to the one, but not away into the unlimited, not into plenishment in the earth, nature's inexhaustibility face to face. This idea of women without men knows hetero|sexuality as any face to face knows altereroticism. It is one of the astounding achievements of *LB|CL* to portray for us an incredible hetero|sexuality, a profusion of other sexualities, within the lesbian world. Perhaps too different, too incredible. Even so, the possibility of women without men remains obscure, analogous perhaps to the idea of human beings without animals, including the animals we devour, or of nature without any of us: men, women, animals. Our—I speak of men and women—humanity diminishes in the disappearance of animals, the humanity that finds itself in the heterogeneity of the other, that tells its truth in relation to the other, heterogeneously, otherwise. And to the others.

Yet women with men, in nearly all human societies, occupy intolerable spaces of subjection, frequently violently. Lesbianization opens the possibility of an *elles,* a womankind, that is not subjected to the *ils*. Men do not, at least in this pronominal movement, require subordination before they can be men, before they can be an "I." Even so, we have seen that authority and injustice haunt the spaces in which the subject forms, lording it over women and animals as well as workers and slaves, truth and law lording their sovereignty over subjects. The subject is a site of subjection, the "I" a site of abjection—the male or neuter "I." The *elles,* then, the *J/e* of lesbianization, delineates a space in which women—but others as well, other subjections, including men the lords and masters, as they abjectly subject themselves to rational rule—might circulate among altererotic others without an identity forged in the shadow of subjection.

This is how I read *LB,* more accurately how I read *CL,* for the original French text expresses something the English translation struggles vainly to know. I propose to read a text in which the sexuality of human and other bodies, the proximity of desire and writing to bodies, materializes in other erotic spaces than those of conventional heterosexuality. I read *LB|CL* as a man who discovers in it, not its truth—not at least the truth it may have for *elles-nous,* we women, nor a truth it may have for *ils-nous,* we men, certainly not we humans—but a site of heterogeneity, the kinds of the others, the plenishment of the earth, in bodily form.

I say that I read *LB|CL* when many readers may wonder if I, a man, any man or men, can read it at all, especially from within its lesbianization. What can I, a man, know of the lesbian body? This question repeats the question of sexual difference, the question I understand as that of ethical difference. I am in relation to others that I must suppose to know and to experience, to feel, a joy, that I cannot know, experience, or feel, but must know, experience, and feel to be true and to belong to the others, to other individuals and other kinds. This knowledge, experience, and feeling, this granting of the others' alterities, is the responsibility face to face that I understand as ethical difference, a different understanding of ethical respect that knows nothing of moral law. That I do not and may never know the lesbian body, in whatever sense it materializes in *LB|CL,* is the truth that I must know and experience as ethical, know and experience in the endless responsibilities toward that heterogeneity that we understand to be our general economy, face to face with the other, caring for and respecting its erotic heterogeneity.

I return, then, to this face to face with the lesbian other, I return to the other in a way that a woman may not be able to return, especially in a way that a lesbian woman may not be able to know, return out of my own heterogeneity. I discover in the lesbianization of women's bodies something of my self and kind that I could not otherwise know, even as I discover something that I cannot know of the other. For when I read *LB|CL,* in English or French, I encounter monstrous, alien themes. I list some of them, the ones that call us to the witches, in our *Walpurgisnacht,* the red of blood, the wildness of the mouse.

> not one will be able to bear seeing you with eyes turned up lids cut off your yellow smoking intestines spread in the hollow of your hands your tongue spat from your mouth long green strings of your bile flowing over your breasts, not one will be able to bear your low frenetic insistent laughter. . . . The gleam of your teeth your joy your sorrow the hidden life your viscera your blood your arteries your veins your hollow habitations your organs your nerves their rupture their spurting forth death slow decomposition stench being devoured by worms your open skull, all will be equally unbearable to her. (Wittig, *LB,* p. 15)

This is at the very beginning, the very first paragraph. It opens in several directions.

1. The unnamed narrator, the *J/e* (who cannot appear in English, who cannot be heard in French, who disappears in English into the undivided *I,* whereas in French reflexives divide again and again, profusely, for example, in "*j//arrive; j//atteins; j//arrache*" [Wittig, *CL,* p. 9]), this *J/e* repeatedly names the parts of her unnamed lover's body,[2] opens the altererotic body in its profusion and plenitude, by naming.[3] Flesh, tissues, blood, excrement, rotting, vomit, all the moving impulses of living bodies, living in proximity to death and age and rot.[4] This nominal profusion of bodily parts—French and English parts, inwards, organs, materials, tissues—shares a heterogeneous space between (*aentre*) languages and the immateriality of embodiment,[5] an erotic, fleshy space. Anatomical science is one of the forms by which nature's profusion may be known erotically. Nature's plenitude opens to us through the opening of language and work, of representation.

2. The profusion and plenitude of nature enters the flesh, the body, in all its crevices, organs, tissues, and materiality, in the form of love. We love each other, we know (if we are lesbians, lesbianized) a love incarnate, embodied, that does not impose a transcendental signifier, that does not glorify a single organ or site, but pervades, permeates, suffuses, sometimes in terrible, awful ways, the lover's body, everywhere in nature, refusing to stop at the skin. Penetration takes on another meaning, not the entering of one privileged organ into another, again and again, one organ, one act, repeated endlessly, but a profusion of penetrations and permeations, along every fold of flesh, including folds we cannot know, do not know, may never know, including lines of biology and anatomy that romantic love, romantic male lovers, disdain. Even Merleau-Ponty:

> I am my body, at least wholly to the extent that I possess experience, and yet at the same time my body is as it were a "natural" subject, a provisional sketch of my total being. . . . let us look closely at what is implied in the rediscovery of our own body. It is not merely one object among the rest which has the peculiarity of resisting reflection and remaining, so to speak, stuck to the subject. Obscurity spreads to the perceived world in its entirety. (Merleau-Ponty, *PP,* pp. 199–200)

This body that I am, that I pervade and that pervades my whole being, this body in whose proximity I live, I live in everywhere, in every tissue, sinew, fluid. Something profoundly excessive in this proximity, this inhabitation, this placement in and with our bodies, far surpasses its and our obscurity. Something close to music's kindredness.

I would like to read *LB*|*CL* as portraying, as dramatizing to the extreme, excessively, this belonging to and with the body that Merleau-Ponty describes, to the point that men may not know such a belonging. For the body that is described in such excessiveness is not the narrator's, not m|y relation to m|y own body, in which *J*/*e* find my place, but the beloved woman's body, permeated, penetrated, pervaded. This excessiveness, this inexhaustible permeation, disrupts, displaces every sense of my subjectivity in my or my beloved's body, destroys the unitariness and grounding of our fleshiness.

And destroys as well the unitariness and originariness of our sexuality, gender, bringing sexual difference upon us in the form of a heterogeneity, an awful otherwise, that casts us into our bodies in an enigmatic way far exceeding Merleau-Ponty's neutered account of our sexuality.[6]

3. The inward fleshiness of the lover that the unnamed narrator portrays, describes, inhabits, is a space, many spaces, that lovers cannot inhabit without language and without violence. This is not men's violence against women, but it is no less shocking, intimidating.

> *I* discover that your skin can be lifted layer by layer, *I* pull, it lifts off, it coils above your knees, *I* pull starting at the labia, it slides the length of the belly, fine to extreme transparency, *I* pull starting at the loins, the skin uncovers the round muscles and trapezii of the back, it peels off up to the nape of the neck, *I* arrive [*j*//*arrive*] under your hair, m/y fingers traverse its thickness, *I* touch your skull, *I* grasp it with all m/y fingers, *I* press it, *I* gather [*j*//*atteins*] the skin over the whole of the cranial vault, *I* tear off [*j*//*arrache*] the skin brutally beneath the hair, *I* reveal the beauty of the shining bone traversed by blood–vessels, m/y two hands crush the vault and the occiput behind, now m/y fingers bury themselves in the cerebral convolutions, the meninges are traversed by cerebrospinal fluid flowing from all quarters, m/y hands are plunged in the soft hemispheres, *I* seek the medulla and the cerebellum tucked in somewhere underneath, now *I* hold all of you silent immobilized every cry blocked in your throat

> your last thoughts behind your eyes caught in m/y hands, the delight is no purer than the depths of m/y heart m/y dearest one [*m/a très chérie*]. (Wittig, *LB*, p. 17)[7]

The permeation everywhere in the body is described in destructive, cruel, cataclysmic terms, resolved into intimacy, proximity, love.

How, if we bear endless responsibilities toward the good, if we remember countless violences toward women, can we join the thought of women face to face together in such a violent way? How do we avoid ethical contamination? What are we to make of such sadomasochistic language, when most sadomasochistic events are directed destructively at women? Perhaps we would prefer a more harmonious accompaniment.

We must wonder, when we read *LB|CL* as opening a truth concerning our belonging in flesh, our materiality and embodiment, not just lesbians' embodiment, and understand the theme of violence as part of that belonging, if we may avoid recapitulating the oppression and subjugation of women, their physical destruction. Perhaps violence belongs to desire. Perhaps we may celebrate its Dionysian side. Yet as we do so, we must wonder if the unnamed woman who narrates *LB|CL* might be celebrating a destruction and violence too conventional, too masculine, too repetitive for us to bear ethically. Yet we cannot read *LB|CL,* in its shocking violence, without a profound sense of cherishing the beloved's body.

Perhaps under conditions of gender inequality, only lesbians, only women together, can cherish every morsel of the other's body, beyond any considerations of domination and oppression. For the beloved remains beloved and always comes back together. Perhaps there is, in a Nietzschean way, a celebration of every facet of life and body, including suffering, grief, and mourning, that is closed to men in relation to women because of gender inequality. Perhaps the Dionysian that Nietzsche describes cannot be celebrated between men and women, cannot enter the spaces between men and women, because of women's historical subjection. That, at least, is the conjecture I offer here in response to the violence of *LB|CL* that never destroys. I will offer another possibility momentarily.

4. The language of *LB|CL* is violent, but it is especially and repeatedly violent in animal form. Wittig bridges in the materiality of embodiment, in the lesbianization of humanity, a close affinity with animal flesh and animal soul.

> You stand upright on your paws (*pattes dressées*) [raised paws] one of them intermittently scratching the ground. Your head weighs on the nape of m/y neck, your canines gash m/y flesh where it is most sensitive, you hold m/e between your paws, you constrain m/e to lean on m/y elbows, . . . you rip off m/y skin with the claws of your four paws, a great sweat comes over m/e hot then soon cold, a white foam spreads the length of your black chops (*babines noirs*) . . . a moment comes when frenziedly you take m/e on your back m/y she-wolf m/y arms round your neck m/y breasts m/y belly against your fur m/y legs gripping your flanks m/y sex thrusting against your loins, you begin to gallop. (Wittig, *LB,* p. 22)

I add a partial list of animals and other corporeal places in nature that appear in *LB*|*CL:* worms, amoebas, spores, butterflies, monkeys, turtledoves, swans, flowers, bitches, water, wings, bats, birds, spiders, fish, mares, sharks, vegetables, snakes, finches, felines, gorgons. The *aentres* of women's *erōs* obtrude repeatedly in the form of paws, fangs, and claws, thoroughly against the exclusions of Heidegger's gift of language. Rather, language, the form in which all of these appear in their profusion, echoes animals and plants, reaches out toward nature's plenishment.

Death, sex, violence, corporeality all meet in the space, the *aentre* of the lesbian|woman|animal, meet on the island of Lesbos|Physis. Multiple women meet together, as *elles,* meet as many women may meet without men, as if they might be human, animal, whatever they are as women, together, heterogeneously|alterogenderedly, without men. Yet we know that men cannot be together as men without women, while they would pretend and speak otherwise. The form of the otherwise, for men and for women, we have seen, forcibly, violently, and mordantly displayed by Wittig, is the *aentre.*

She calls it lesbianization. And w|e who read her, especially we men (though some men may enter her lesbianization with less threat to their *ils* than some heterosexual women, under conditions of gender inequality, may know to their *elles*), must confront the question of what it is to read something of what we men can never know, the *jouissances* of women together in love. Nor can women know the *jouissances* of men, with the qualification that the theme of writing in the West incessantly, the incessant theme of writing's desire, has been said to manifest the *jouissances* of men and to pass them off as the human good.

The resurgence of the *elles,* where women love each other, at least in *LB|CL,* I take to open up a space of inclusion, including the profusion of women's bodies, other bodies, the profusion of nature's plenitude, animals, flowers, plants, everywhere in nature. Lesbianization includes what traditional heterosexuality excludes, includes alterities, heterogeneities, otherwise and other kinds, everywhere, because the wall, the barrier of the cut of sexual difference in a system of inequality, no longer holds. The *ils* collect everything under the obscure and masked hold of the man. The *elles,* dissolving that hold, open spaces of heterogeneity, of other kinds, face to face and in proximity. Women love each other in ways that are not defined by men, not defined by reproduction, not defined by genitals, still in proximity to bodily organs and pervaded by desire. Always excessively and heterogeneously. We men must wonder if we can become lesbianized, or whether it is something that only women may know. Or rather, we insist on being lesbianized, denying that only women may know it, as if they may know nothing else, reducing heterogeneity again. But in our lesbianization, we grant that lesbian women may know something that we cannot know. W|e desire excessively the excesses of lesbianization, heterogeneously, between *elle* and *elle,* and between *elles* and *ils* and *les animaux,* in the *aentre* of sexual difference.

The *aentre,* the lair of the animal, in whose proximity women meet altererotically, the lesbian love that offers another sexuality than either men's or heterosexual women's, opens in a space, an *aentre,* of animals in nature's profusion. I speak of plenishment in the earth, carried by Wittig into the plenitude of corporeality, a profusion of embodiment and materiality, realizable through language, writing. I hesitate to embrace this bond, as an *aentre,* between language and body, languages and bodies, where to love is to love another in her multiple and profuse embodiments, corporeality, materiality, giving us a profusion of excess in the form of materiality, through language. Wittig wraps her narrator's sexuality and eroticism in nouns and pronouns, the *elles* of women, the tissues, organs, plenitude of human and animal bodies. W|e men may hope to share this eroticism, this heteroerotic placement within our bodies' corporeality as the excessiveness of eroticism. All excess.

The body, bodies, corporeality, materiality, human and otherwise, all materialize in the form of excess, profusely embodying the fluids and tissues of altereroticism, that is, the other, the hetaera, the impurities, of eroticism, throughout the body, in its *aentres,* spilling out excessively, circulating throughout the general economy of the body's corporeality into nature's economy. The theme of general economy, the excess in which sovereignty is both instituted and dissolved, echoes in *LB|CL* in the form of the "entire body" (Wittig, *LB,* pp. 35, 129), an image that counters the sense that a single bodily organ, the penis|phallus, takes on the entire weight of the lack. Against the movement of lack, giving rise to general economy, an endless profusion of wants and lacks, all signified in the phallus, in a single place, Wittig gives us the entire body, opens onto nature's plenitude. Nature's profusion, plenishment in the earth, gives forth a profusion in corporeality, materiality, a profusion, we may say, that was always present in matter, in Aristotle's view of *hylē,* but that collapsed into regimentation under the weight of the human form, its masculinity.

The profusion of embodiment and materiality, here, in *LB|CL,* opposes the hegemony of the Form of the Human, the Perfection of Mankind, under whose dominion women and animals have been subjected. The *elles,* which opens the space for women together, without men, as if there were no men (at least in language), that opening moves with immense speed from the *entres* of women together to nature's and women's *antres,* the animality of women not understood as subjection to the rationality of men, but as relation to nature's plenitude. I speak of our relation to this plenitude as plenishment; I understand it to inhabit the heart of ethics, not singularity but profusion, multiplicity, impurity, heterogeneity, and altereroticism, pervading every pore of the body, every body and every kind. We can reach it, reach knowledge of the knowledge of the other through words, even as we cannot know that knowledge.

5. Wittig speaks, in *LB|CL,* of something that has no existence, cannot even be forbidden. "*Le Corps Lesbien* has lesbianism as its theme, that is, a theme which cannot even be described as taboo, for it has no real existence in the history of literature" (Wittig, *LB,* p. 9). We may wonder at the forgetting of women who love women, who live together with women, who have done so throughout Western history and throughout other places in the history and the world. If they did not write, if they did not say "I am lesbian," did they exist? Homosexuality, Wittig claims, was

named and written, but lesbians had no name. And still, in many countries of the world, women still live alone or together, but do not practice something called (in any language) "lesbianism." The kind asks for a name.

Wittig speaks, then, both of a silence, an unsaid, an unwritten, of some thing or kind that may not exist without its name, a concern of language and earth, of the place of anything in the earth unopened by language, and of a silent, masked, forgotten kind. The task is of bringing forth into being what, forgotten, has both always and never been present, a recapitulation of our thought of sexual difference. Sexual difference, I have struggled to say, belongs to the earth itself, which cannot be thought without gender, because the plenitude of nature reveals itself in natural and alterogendered kinds. The nonexistence of lesbians repeats the nonexistence, the forgetting, of what has always existed, has been said again and again, but spoken of in such a way as to vanish silently. Against this, Wittig speaks, writes, names not women, who exist in too close a proximity to men, subjugated, but women face to face with women, lesbians, who may be called forth by the *poiēsis* of words, the words of witches.

> The body of the text subsumes all the words of the female body. *Le Corps Lesbien* attempts to achieve the affirmation of its reality. The lists of names contribute to this activity. To recite one's own body, to recite the body of the other, is to recite the words of which the book is made up. The fascination for writing the never previously written and the fascination for the unattained body proceed from the same desire. The desire to bring the real body violently to life in the words of the book . . . (Wittig, *LB,* p. 10)

This infinite, endless, inexhaustible, excessive love of words passes into an infinite, endless, inexhaustible, excessive love of every crevice and pore of the female body, of the lover and her body, an altererotic image of love and woman and embodiment. And it passes from that woman's body, from the corporeality of *erōs* to the materiality and plenitude of the world, the circulation of every thing, everywhere, in nature, the infinite, endless, inexhaustible, excessive love of whatever belongs to nature, in profusion, the cherishment of every crevice, part, place in the earth, its plenishment.

Cherishment echoes in *LB*|*CL* in the names of the parts, organs, fluids, recesses of women's bodies, cherishment of the narrator's beloved, cherishing her collectivity. The individual woman is a member of a kind, of women, but as an individual is a collective of bodily parts and material fluids—vomit, blood, and pus among others. The individual is not juxtaposed against the collective, against the different kinds to which an individual may belong. The different kinds enter into individuality itself. Individuality echoes in *LB|CL* as a collective, a kind, that encompasses named and unnamed parts and organs. Heterogeneity is named by Wittig in naming the many different parts of the individual, which, as an individual, is a kind, each individual another kind, among multiple kinds of kinds.

If we take up this line, if we men are permitted to know nature's profusion in the writing of a love in which we will never participate, never share, but may know as heterogeneous nevertheless, a love that reveals our heterogeneity dispersed through every crevice and pore of women's and men's and others' bodies, a love whose profusion we may emulate in our own ways without succumbing to another privileged identity, then we are led in *LB|CL,* through its words and other words, through words and language, representation and thought, we may now say ethically, led by nature's plenitude first to cherishment of the inexhaustibility of the earth, then from this sense of preciousness to sacrifice, to the impossibility of fulfilling everything that we know is precious, from the good to injustice. Within this impossibility beyond measure, weighed down by endless responsibilities toward the good, we seek plenishment in the earth, everywhere, as our ethical work. W|e, not just women, but men as well. Here we men may know something from women that we seem unable to know of ourselves, the immeasurable, immemorial plenishment in the earth. We may know it and we may live it, heterogeneously, hetaera|sexually.

Perhaps, now, we may understand the violence, the unnerving, shattering violent images in *LB|CL,* the flaying, crunching, bleeding, not as a repetition of male violence, against other men but especially abusive to women's bodies, but as a portrayal of sacrifice. This portrayal gives us a sense of sacrifice that I have both failed to name, at least to this point, and refused to accept, wary of its contamination. The contamination is that we might accept sacrifice as the good, as an ethical necessity and thereby holy, as if destruction, war, *polemos,* even self-destruction, inevitably belonged to the good, as if through sacrifice we might arrive at the good, making sacrifice good instrumentally and absolutely. There is indeed a sense in which sacrifice belongs to the good, the sense in which pursuit of the good always finds itself stumbling into sacrifice. But I understand this sacrifice as immemorial and inescapable injustice, believe that cherishment imposes on us a sense of responsibility that we cannot avoid and cannot achieve without injustice, without sacrifice, giving rise to endless mourning. Without an inexhaustible sense of and haunting by the good, in every proximity and face to face, every dyad with an other of another kind, nothing ethical is possible. The joy of the good bears within it a wounding, exposure, haunted by endless grief.

I think of this endless haunting by the otherwise of the good as mourning. But not only mourning, for I understand all of time and history as endless restitution for sacrifice and injustice. I understand law and reason and truth and love as infinite and inexhaustible restitutions that cannot pay off and that endlessly impose their own injustices and sacrifices for inexhaustible sacrifice and injustice. It follows that grief and mourning, vengeance and retribution, repay past injustices, immemorial sacrifices, with other sacrifices and injustices, repay and restore and wound and oppress. Even so, they institute the good, the only good we can achieve, the only good we can bring into work, into the city,[8] a good without achievement, that works as endless injustice in justice. Such work is tempered at every moment and on all sides by the understanding that the good circulates in general economy, excessively, exceeding any restitution, any vengeance, work, thereby imposing endless and excessive responsibilities upon any restitution toward the good. Sacrifice is terrible and infamous, always unjust. It thereby does the work of the good.

The grief and mourning and despair of injustice, of sacrifice, fail to capture its entirety. For in our acknowledgment that the circulation of goods takes place dyadically—and *LB*|*CL* is a portrayal of that erotic circulation, throughout the islands and the women's bodies—we know that love, *erōs* and sexuality, appears, works dyadically, heterogeneously, and altererotically. The violence, the crunch of bones, the tearing of flesh, is always in *LB*|*CL* an act of love, an erotic act that opens the *aentres,* the limits, of corporeal love.

Men crunch women's bones, tear their flesh, rape them and kill them, in proximity. The contamination of which we must beware appears in this place, between (*aentre*) men and women, in the slaughter of animals, in the confrontation with immemorial injustices justifying retribution and destruction in the present, upon men, women, and animals, especially upon men and women of other races, colors, histories, religions. A profound and desperate ethical contamination works in the monstrosity of the good, the violent monstrosity of the impossibility of fulfilling the good, measuring the good. It is my subject here.

For I read *LB*|*CL* as witches' work, understanding women together, women writing and acting together (and apart) as witchcraft, disturbing the places of rest, the resting-places in the earth. I return to the rests of the earth, to disturbance and displacement, in the figure of the witch, the narrator of *LB*|*CL* as a witch, tearing open the body of her beloved in an act of violence that is an act of love, that does not harm her beloved, that destroys without injury.

> The women lead m/e to our scattered fragments, there is an arm, there is a foot, the neck and head are together, your eyelids are closed, your detached ears are somewhere, your eyeballs have rolled in the mud, *I* see them side by side, your fingers have been cut off and thrown to one side, *I* perceive your pelvis, your bust is elsewhere, several fragments of forearms the thighs and tibiae are missing. . . . *I* Isis the all-powerful *I* decree that you live as in the past Osiris m/y most cherished m/y most enfeebled *I* say that as in the past we shall succeed together in making the little girls who will come after us, then you m/y Osiris m/y most beautiful you smile at m/e undone exhausted. (Wittig, *LB*, pp. 79–80)[9]

This is a terrible violence in sexual difference that we must struggle to forswear. And yet, as extremely as the violence is portrayed, the unnamed narrator's unnamed beloved is never destroyed, neither of the lovers is destroyed, the pain belongs to their *erōs,* their joys.

I wonder again if we are in a sadomasochistic dyad, sex with pain, sex together with death. And here I ask a brutal question. What kind of difference would it, does it make (two different questions) that we think, experience love and intimacy in violent, animate, penetrating, terms between lovers under conditions of gender inequality? We are brought back violently to MacKinnon's question. I am struggling with the contamination of sexual intimacy under conditions of institutionalized gender oppression and with the the contamination of violence and the torments of the flesh under conditions of gender equality. Wittig makes us think of the possibility of an erotic, intimate relation between equals, an *erōs* not focused on a single, perhaps phallic or vaginal, signifier. She insists that we confront violence. I am interpreting this insistence as exposure to sacrifice.

But Wittig and MacKinnon tell us something of sacrifice that we might easily forget: the endless contamination that sacrifice brings, the thought that has infinitely contaminated ethics and politics throughout history. If we cannot live without destruction—and we cannot—then perhaps we must keep ourselves safe from despair by accepting violence and destruction as belonging to the good, as producing the good, as fulfilling the good, through law, reason, and judgment. We may then think of our joy as produced by sacrifice and may think of sacrifice as the just work of the good, especially the sacrifice of others in the name of the good, but in the case of women, historically, we may think of the sacrifice of women to men and children as woman's good, above all the sacrifice of animals to human beings as animals' good.

This sacrifice—the oppression and violence to which women, but also men and children, are subjected nearly everywhere, the destruction of human lives, men's and women's lives, but also of the things of the world, of other kinds and species, destroyed in the name of others' lives—is called "progress." I think of it as incessant injustice. We find ourselves in our endless responsibilities toward the good within a certain impossibility related to heterogeneity, with the contamination that to give way before the impossibility of realizing the good everywhere, to collapse into despair or spite, into a certain nihilism, is to avoid the responsibilities that bring forth that impossibility. Such a responsibility is for and toward other kinds, kindred difference. I read Nietzsche as defining for us another nihilism, where the impossibility is the soul of the good, with the danger that we will enjoy the violence, will accept the destruction and domination brought by the quest for the good as the good. That is again to avoid the impossibility of the responsibility.

Cherishment is toward the things of the world, each and every thing in each and every place excessively, nature in its enigmatic heterogeneities. Sacrifice is the impossibility this plenitude of the world brings within its profusion to realize the good within the call of cherishment. The two together compose plenishment in the earth, our response to the call of the good, endlessly haunted and enraptured by the preciousness of things, by the earth's teeming profusion. In *LB|CL,* the narrator's beloved's body appears in an endless profusion, anatomically and more, excessively, surpassing any sense of place or bodies or sexual and erotic joy, a joy that exceeds any joy, pervaded by, made possible by, grief, by sacrifice, by violence. It is a violence that does not destroy, a violence that faces up to the terrible destructiveness of sacrifice, faces up with joy, haunted by mourning and forgetting.

LB|CL is pervaded by a forgotten, the silence of the *elles,* pervaded by a task to bring forth and sound the *elles,* to unearth their places. But there can be no place of safety where women or any other creatures can live together, the lion with the lamb, without death, without violence, without sacrifice. The task of *LB|CL* is to say something that cannot be said in a gendered language, therefore, to say something violent in that language, unacceptable, mimetically reappearing in the violence of penetrating the corporeality of the beloved's body. But both violences are words, perhaps just words. The narrator does not corporeally tear open her beloved's flesh, cannot do so without destroying her. Perhaps language and other forms of expression allow us to struggle with violence, sacrifice, and death in a dark and terrifying way that sacrifices certain destructions by performing others. We cannot live without sacrifice, we cannot work for justice without injustice, seek the good without destruction, but we may seek destructions that do not destroy, violences that provide restitution for injustices, sacrifices that remember injustice without retribution.

Perhaps *LB|CL* overwhelms us with its violence to the point where we can find no continuing presence of the good. Or perhaps, the impossible work of the good, in the shadow of sacrifice, is to distinguish endless restitution from retribution, to belong to nature in the form of sacrifice and restitution without forgetting their contamination. For we remember countless terrible crimes, and have forgotten countless others. This, at least, is how I read the most violent passages in *LB|CL*: as a certain terrible memory that cannot bring itself to repeat the enormities it holds before it.

> *I* am the pitch that burns the assailants' heads, *I* am the knife that severs the carotid of the newborn ewe-lambs, *I* am the bullets of the submachine-guns that perforate the intestines, *I* am the pin-

> cers brought to red heat in the fires that tear the flesh, *I* am the plaited whip that flagellates the skin, *I* am the electric current that blasts and convulses the muscles, *I* am the gag that gags the mouth, *I* am the bandage that hides the eyes, *I* am the bonds that tie the hands, *I* am the mad tormentor galvanized by torture and your cries intoxicate m/e m/y best beloved the more that you restrain them. (Wittig, *LB,* p. 16)

For the passage ends with restitution, immediately following: "[a]t this point *I* invoke your help m/y incomparable Sappho, give m/e by thousands the fingers that allay the wounds, give m/e the lips the tongue the saliva which draw one into the slow sweet poisoned country from which one cannot return" (Wittig, *LB,* p. 16). There can be no good without the memories invoked by knives and guns and torture. What can it mean to be a woman, lesbian or otherwise, without these memories pervading the sinews of o⃒u⃒r⃒ bodies? Or a man.

We readers, men or women, are asked to engage, in the name of lesbianization, with this struggle of restitution as plenishment in the earth, with ethical, sexual, and kindred difference. The violence and destruction we understand through the figure of witches, their little red mice darting from their red mouths, the gift of mice instead of tongues. Or goddesses, all famous women. For Wittig speaks of one mythic woman after another, of one mythic figure after another turned into woman, witch or goddess: Ulyssea, Achillea, Christa, Zeyna, Sappho, Isis, Ishtar, Golgotha, Gorgon, Archimedea. Perhaps most of all, I think of these as figures of the Erinyes, or Erinyes|Eumenides, haunting us with memories of violence and injustice, making justice possible, not as repetition of injustice, but as countless memories from which we draw the possibility of working toward the good.

I read *LB|CL* as no lesbian, nonetheless hoping to be lesbianized in some ways, struggling to understand what lesbianization might mean, for me, for others. I trace it as a figure circulating around two themes, the excessiveness of embodiment, everywhere in m|y own and m|y beloved's body, against the privilege of a particular bodily site, a figure of soul and desire. The excessiveness of desire, of *erōs,* permeates the body, permeates nature, permeates the earth, plenishes the world. The second theme, from which we must recoil, yet cannot avoid, is the theme of violence, situated in and throughout the body and nature in two ways: one, another moment of its excesses, the thought that *erōs* pervades the body everywhere, excessively, in figures of violence and death, of penetration, intervention, blood, vomit, and guts; the second, the way in which we find violence inescapable in the body and throughout nature relates to sacrifice. For I understand the lesbian lover to cherish her beloved deeply, facing her plenitude in the form of sacrifice. Joy's heterogeneity brings us to loss, to mourning. The thought, the pain, of love bears a certain sacrifice, destruction, deep within itself.

I repeat that this is a remembered, recounted, written, represented destruction, a violence in writing and memory, not a destruction of self or kind. In heterogeneity, in altererotic or lesbian love, there is an other, an alterity, that cannot join us without pain, without loss, losses we mourn, injustices we remember and seek to have remembered. Death is not the silent event we know but once, but losses we remember endlessly, wounding and suffering. But these losses, destructions, sacrifices, exist for us in a restitution that refuses to repeat loss, sacrifice, destruction, violence, to whatever extent we can refuse, refuses as an act of love. We live with pain as our joy. We seek to transmute injustice into grief, into mourning, suffering into sadness. We arrive at a *jouissance* that knows something of *douleur*—a profoundly knowing joy that knows the sadness of injustices—as opposed to the unhappiness of despair—the suffering that knows no joy, the revenge that takes no care for its own oppressions.

The figure, the silent figure, of these sorrows is the Stabat Mater, the woman–mother–witch who bears the sins of the world on her shoulders, not in servitude toward men, nor toward her children, but in a conjunction of joy and sorrow, a mourning for the joys, the fulfillments, the goods she has lost, the goods she can know only knowing of their loss. In the general economy of the circulation of goods, of the excessive goods and representations that circulate everywhere, in nature and pervading every tissue and fluid of our materiality, there are losses, sacrifices, that we would do everything in our power to avoid, bear endless responsibility to avoid, yet which belong profoundly to our joys. There is a joy, a happiness, in and of the good, together with its sacrifices, a joy in plenishment. There is pain in the sound of music, the echoes of the *Stabat Mater.* Yet the mother remains a disturbing and disturbed figure, repeating the figure of the woman at the gate, the old woman down the lane, the figure of the witch, reminding us of God the Father.[10] It repeats this figure of the witch in its displacements and its sacrifices. We must not forget the thousands of women—and men, yet thousands more women—killed as witches, killed because they were women–witches. And the hundred million more killed as women, before they became witches, allowed to die, silently to die. We scream against the silence.

We hear the ride of the witches, their endless disturbances and displacements, screams and laughter, haunting us with memories of past and continuing injustices, with thoughts of displacement underneath every rule of order. We hear the witches' ride, disturbingly, in *LB|CL,* throughout the profusion of natural things and kinds with which it surrounds us, permeating the living body, but especially in cacophonies of violence and destruction. I hear these cacophonies as echoes of sacrifice, of the pain of life, but not as destruction, oppression, subjugation. The narrator's and her beloved's bodies remain loved and loving, restored, in the most disruptive of corporeal dispersions. Wittig writes and speaks in a certain violence, but does not commit a violence that destroys.

The view I struggle to evoke, the ethic of kindred difference in which I hope to participate, engendered by the women's movement and sexual difference, accepts a certain weight of history as fallen upon us. Witches pose for us, men and women, questions of whether we can accept, remember, live in memory of the disturbances of blood, desire, law, and power without committing other destructions, without imposing torture and suffering in the name of our memories, without committing injustices that are within our power to avoid. Can we live in memories of past injustices that we cannot repay and with present and future injustices that we cannot avoid, can we live in joy, mixed with grief, in love, mixed with anger, avoiding the injustices we can, undertaking the responsibilities we can, in the shadow of a sense of the earth in which we bear a responsibility and a bond? Can we live in justice without the endless pain of remembered injustices?[11]

The witches, heretics, madwomen demand that we remember the shedding of women's blood without reinstituting, as men always have, other murders, other destructions, countless murders of countless other women, and men, and animals.

CHAPTER 12

Rest

We hear, we see, the univocity of being, nature's unisons, echoing polyphonically, cacophonically, polychromatically, "[o]n a colored sky" (Trinh, *WNO*, p. 28). Colored witches and red mice, the gift of the tongue, speaking heterogeneously. Yet no comfort can be found for witches, especially red rather than gray, who would live in a male|neuter community, "in the world in which I move uninvited, profane on a sacred land, neither me nor mine, but me nonetheless" (Trinh, *WNO*, p. 1). The work of profanity disturbs culture's mastery, endlessly, in mixed hues.

> The story never stops beginning or ending. It appears headless and bottomless for it is built on differences. Its (in)finitude subverts every notion of completeness and its frame remains a non-totalizable one. The differences it brings about are differences not only in structure, in the play of structures and of surfaces, but also in timbre and in silence. (Trinh, *WNO*, p. 2)

Those who tell these stories, endless, silent, resonant, circulate in intermediary figures of wizards and witches, heretics, madwomen and men; also ordinary people, who inhabit intermediary places, mixed and impure; all subverting the Master's mastery, the hidden rules of the same, faced with the impossible task of writing under the rainbow, storytelling on a colored sky. "Neither black/red/yellow nor woman but poet or writer" (Trinh, *WNO*, p. 6), we must refuse to be any particular kind of thing even as our heterogeneity depends on being a kind of thing or person, on many different, plenishing kinds. This refusal to be one kind is a refusal of the taxonomy of subjection, refusal of a knowledge that would know any kind of thing in order to rule. To write, to speak in public, is to submit oneself to the law (Trinh, *WNO*, p. 8) while this public offers the only site at which one might not be "only" of one's kind, with a subjugated history.

> What is at stake is not only the hegemony of Western cultures, but also their identities as unified cultures. Third World dwells

> on diversity; so does First World. This is our strength and our misery. The West is painfully made to realize the existence of a Third World in the First World, and vice versa. The Master is bound to recognize that His Culture is not as homogeneous, as monolithic as He believed it to be. He discovers, with much reluctance, He is just an other among others. (Trinh, *WNO*, pp. 98–99)

The Master discovers painfully that His Culture is not homogeneous. My account here, from the beginning, of our relationship with nature, has been a disclosure of this heterogeneity, of the alterities, multiplicities, and mixtures of kinds. Nature is heterogeneous; our ethical relation to this heterogeneous plenitude is plenishment. We wonder why we should privilege safety. We wonder why our sense of order must be allied with safety, when we gain that order at others' expense, others whom we make unsafe in order that we be safe, we masters, as if we were permitted to sacrifice women for the safety of men, women and men of color for the safety (such as it is) of Master Women (if a woman may be Master), as if we gained safety by sacrificing animals, rather than depleting the store of the world, when order is unsafe. What can be the privilege of homogeneity when we are framed by heterogeneity on all sides? I have wondered on what basis, other than arbitrary sovereignty, homogeneity might gain ascendance, in the name of what safety and reliability. We still meet each other face to face, one kind face to face with another, with sorrow and joy.

The subject facing us is authority, the authority of safety, purity, and law. "As long as words of difference serve to legitimate a discourse instead of delaying its authority to infinity, they are, to borrow an image from Audre Lorde, 'noteworthy only as *decorations*'" (Trinh, *WNO*, p. 101). Infinity here is less a figure of time and history than of heterogeneity. Authority's delay works in relation to differences, ethical, kindred differences and plenishment, that do their work without authority, refusing the claim that authority's violence is good. Authority has no monopoly on violence and legitimates its violences in the work of exclusion. Some kinds are excluded from power, excluded from the good, may bear the brunt of the work of the state by exclusion. All of this may be necessary, but the culminating injustice is that this exclusion from the good is claimed by the state as its right to declare to be good. The delay of authority to infinity is the upsurgence of heterogeneity. I am speaking of witches and wizards, kinds and colors—color a representation of kind—belonging to other cultures than the Master's. And even His Culture is heterogeneous.

How do we think of heterogeneity within an understanding that we participate in heterogeneity in virtue of a certain forgetting, an unjust and painful exclusion? Speaking of the ways in which feminist theory does not, yet must, "notice" women of color, Lugones writes:

> But what would it be to be noticed? We are noticed when you realize that we are mirrors in which you can see yourselves as no other mirror shows you. When you see us without boomerang perception, to use Spelman's wonderful phrase. It is not that we are the only faithful mirrors, but I think we *are* faithful mirrors. Not that we show you as you *really* are; we just show you as one of the people you are. What we reveal to you is that you are many—something that may in itself be frightening to you. But the self we reveal to you is also one that you are not eager to know for reasons that one may conjecture. (Lugones, *OLPF*, pp. 41–42; quoted from Spelman, *IW*)

This understanding of what other people mean to us, of how our identities are constructed in relation to others, perhaps especially others who are different from us, represents a powerful truth of heterogeneity, but not quite as deep a sense as I hope to portray. I am unhappy with the visible image of mirrors, especially of "faithful" mirrors, when I understand heterogeneity to work in relation to distortions and uncertainties, to disturb and displace, to reach beyond light and sight, to sound and music, into the rests of the earth, where Lugones takes us.

Lugones preserves and enforces Trinh's understanding that in relation to the other's heterogeneity, we discover our own. We discover that we are not as homogeneous, pure, in our selves, our identities, our culture, as we thought and hoped to be. We discover that we are of different kinds and that we are among others. These are different thoughts of heterogeneity. The first is that identity itself is heterogeneous, multifarious, that heterogeneous others reveal to us our own heterogeneities, the different kinds to which we belong and which compose our multiple identities. This is Lugones's point, with the qualification perhaps that this revelation need have nothing to do with faithfulness or mirroring, but may be most poignantly felt where we do not find ourselves comfortably before the others, for instance, where we find ourselves awestruck before them or where we have no overriding identity to impose. Lugones's point seems to me that we must grant others a certain truth within their heterogeneities, a truth that bears on our own identities but may not come through us. Perhaps the other knows a heterogeneity that cannot stand in any relation between us, does not relate to me in a recognizable way or show me something of myself that I must accept or that I may use for myself, yet I must know, must accept, must acknowledge, must recognize nevertheless the other to be and to be heterogeneous.

The others' heterogeneity may echo in a different place than any I can occupy, thereby disturbing my sense of place, multifariously and pluralistically, but recognizably unrecognizable, unknowable.

> How more invisible than invisible can you be? And yet there is a quality of invisible invisibility which many of us women, feminists, of other than the dominant culture have. A *Feminista Hispana* is at home nowhere. . . . Society at large thinks of us as Hispanics and the majority of Hispanics think of us as women. Only among our very few is our name understood: FEMINISTA HISPANA. (Isasi-Diaz, *FH,* p. 51)

> Will they ever understand that it is not a matter of baking a cake? *Feminismo Hispano* is not one more ingredient to add. *Feminismo Hispano* is to be there as a motivating force, at the level of conceptualization, understanding, definition, planning, or the feminist movement in the U.S.A. will continuously betray itself. (Isasi-Diaz, *FH,* p. 58)

Beside the heterogeneity of women face to face with men and women is an endless supply of heterogeneities, of others of other kinds, here Hispanic women, Hispanic feminist women, who as women do not bear the weight of their cultural identity as Hispanic, but who disappear as women into a collective Hispanic identity.

These identities—of women, Hispanics, homosexuals, lesbians, of color, identities of language and place—work in multiple displacement. Trinh suggests that we may wish to preserve, if that is the word, to maintain the displacement, to delay the authority of any identity to infinity. Perhaps the idea of maintaining and preserving, even fostering, is the question, when we find ourselves in the flux and displacement of heterogeneity. What, if we hope for happiness and freedom from oppression, if we hope to achieve as well as undertake the burdens of the good, do we bear with this flux and displacement of identities?

Lugones offers another image of multiple identities in a gesture against its flux and fragmentation. Within the frame of "'outsiders' to the mainstream of, for example, White/Anglo organization of life in the U.S." (Lugones, *PWTLP,* p. 3), she speaks of an outsider "shifting from the mainstream construction of life where she is constructed to other constructions of life where she is more or less 'at home,'" (Lugones, *PWTLP,* p. 3). She offers this image of world traveling, of shifting place and identity, as loving and creative, as "ethical" in our understanding of ethics, in part. "As outsiders to the mainstream, women of color in the U.S. practice 'world'-travelling, mostly out of necessity. I affirm this practice as a skillful, creative, rich, enriching and, given certain circumstances, as a loving way of being and living" (Lugones, *PWTLP,* p. 3).

Women of color, rainbow witches, find themselves by necessity within a multiple displacement of identity and place, thrown into places of heterogeneity where they have no place. Lugones and other writers of color suggest that this displacement, this heterotopia, however painful, offers a deep, enriching possibility of living and loving. Against the possibility that the withholding of authority to infinity, endlessly delaying the hold of law, places women of color, even "us," in a dangerous place too close to heterogeneity, Lugones suggests that this image of safety is a colorless myth. People of color, especially women and especially lesbians, especially slaves, women slaves, have always been outsiders in multiple worlds, public and private, so that they know no safe place, if anyone knows any places of safety. Even so, they know the possibility of loving and creating in the demands of traveling, shifting, intermingling, from world to world, kind to kind. Heterogeneity, I have insisted repeatedly, knows sadness and grief, pain and suffering, but also joy.

Something else, in Lugones, is worth attention, something beyond the heterotopia of world traveling. This is the nature of the worlds she describes as "constructions of life," as ethnic|social|communal worlds, as heterogeneous places, especially heterogendered, alterotopic, altererotic. What makes her thought of world traveling ethical is that it moves from the places of displacement and heterogeneity in which women of color find themselves, where human beings and other creatures and things find themselves, surrounded and permeated by heterogeneity, images of danger, disruption, fragmentation, oppression, images of misery and pain, all caught up in histories and memories of suffering, to a thought of the creative and enriching—I do not say "fulfilling"—possibilities of heterotopia, place and displacement. This is our *Walpurgisnacht,* the dance in which the multiplicity of displacements moves from tragic displacement to joyful heterotopia. "I recommend to women of color in the U.S. that we learn to love each other by learning to travel to each other's 'worlds'" (Lugones, *PWTLP,* p. 4). Perhaps we may recommend to everyone something of this traveling, mingling, in relation to love and cherishment, but even more to heterogeneity. World traveling is an ethical relation to heterogeneity, an intermediary movement in different kinds of places. World traveling is an ethical relation to general economy, the constitution of identities and kinds through the excessive circulation of goods and judgments. Lugones's ethnic, social, and communal worlds are the environments in which we and others circulate, constituted as individuals and kinds by circulating representations.

If world traveling means being able to participate in multiple cultural and natural worlds, as if one belonged anywhere and everywhere, it knows nothing of heterogeneity. If world traveling means participating in other worlds, entering other places, masterfully, dominatingly, it is anything but ethical. If world traveling means participating in the rush to development in which heterogeneity is exchange and substitution, it gives way to empty mastery. Yet something ethical, belonging to the good, may be recognized in the multiple, hybrid, heterogeneous identities world traveling constructs and presupposes. "I am different persons in different 'worlds' and can remember myself in both as I am in the other. I am a plurality of selves" (Lugones, *PWTLP,* p. 14). Lugones's worlds are ethnic, social, and communal. "For something to be a 'world' in my sense it has to be inhabited at present by some flesh and blood people . . . A 'world' in my sense may be an actual society given its dominant culture's description of life, including a construction of the relationships of production, of gender, race, etc." (Lugones, *PWTLP,* pp. 9–10). I am pursuing this idea of heterogeneity into nature's inexhaustible kinds, into *natura naturata.* It does not mean "my" kind as against "yours," not even "ours," but a certain heterogeneity of kinds, mixed, impure.

I hope to extend Lugones's understanding of cultural worlds to nature, to nature's heterogeneity, plenishment in the earth. Lugones's worlds are ethnic, social, and communal. Similarly, she speaks of "being at ease in a 'world'" in social and human terms, speaks of different ways of being at ease.

> by being a fluent speaker in that "world." . . .
> by being normatively happy. I agree with all the norms. . . .
> by being humanly bonded. I am with those I love and they love me too. . . .
> one has a history with others that is shared, especially daily history . . . (Lugones, *PWTLP,* p. 12).

She speaks of playful traveling to address the incompatibilities of different worlds, for example, where one's identity is subordinate and diminished in one world, powerful and effective in another. There are worlds in which being playful is hard, even damaging to me. In these worlds, there are witches. We find heterogeneity everywhere, plenishing the earth, and we participate with a certain struggle, a certain frenzy, a love, a cherishment that remembers sacrifice.

A similar line of thought can be traced through non-Western witches, for Europe's witches are not all the witches there are, nor has every world tortured its witches, even when they were known as evil. Let us listen to some Western versions of non-Western stories.

> An outsider is not likely to spend more than a few hours in any Mekeo community without hearing some reference to "sorcerers" (*ugauga*) and their nefarious actions. One soon learns that these men—for no women are accused of such activities [in Mekeo, but typically elsewhere]—are not merely suspected by the rest of the community of wielding death-dealing powers; they are publicly recognized as the force backing the authority of the village leaders of descent groups, the *lopia.* (Stephen, *MS,* pp. 42–43)[2]

This example, where the powers and threats of witches and sorcerers sustain sovereign authority expresses something of the arbitrariness and dangers of every system of rule, of the most legitimate authority, something that Africans and other non-Western peoples know routinely, but that Westerners have lost in their reverence for rational law.[3] To take another, more indicative example that opens another dimension of the social:

> Though the sorcerer trafficks with powers beyond society and human morality, he nevertheless uses them *within* the moral order. The sorcerer himself may be the ultimately non-reciprocal man, yet it is apparent that the Nissan "master of terrible power," the Ilahita master artist and sorcerer, the Mekeo "man of knowledge" are all seen to exercise their powers ultimately in accord with the common good. . . .
>
> Control is a crucial aspect of the sorcerer's role. (Stephen, *CIP*, p. 271)

The sorcerer here—there are no female witches in Melanesian society—exercises a power that, while supernatural, works in close proximity with tribal leaders. The other thought Stephen engenders is of lack of reciprocity. The supernatural element in sorcery and witchcraft represents a good and a power at the edges, beyond the reach, of social and reciprocal activities.

Ideas of witches play as intermediary figures throughout the themes with which we have struggled in our account of gender and nature. Here is one summary, from a different place, of African witches:

> 1. Witches are female. Very occasionally one may find a man accused of witchcraft, but in such cases it is likely that Africans have themselves become confused about the distinction between the psychical and the magical. The "male witch" is best regarded as a wizard, magician, or sorcerer—someone who uses *magic* for malevolent purposes.
> 2. Such women meet in secret assemblies, at night. When travelling to these assemblies they take on the form of an animal and leave their physical bodies behind.
> 3. Witches prey upon non-witches who are neither deserving of nor responsible for the misfortunes they suffer.
> 4. Often the witch is thought to "consume" the body or spirit of its victim in some psychical and/or physical fashion. The physical symptoms of this in the victim are disease or any wasting, lingering illness.
> 5. Witches are sometimes thought to derive certain of their powers from a "witchcraft substance," either internal to the body of the witch, or kept by her in some external, secret

> place. (Hallen and Sodipo, *KBW*, pp. 93–94; from Parrinder, *WEA*)

If this powerful sense of the evil and gender of African witches is as strong as suggested here, we must struggle with the condition that in some African societies, rulers must exercise the power of witches and sorcerers.

> The Highest Beng officials make use of the power of witchcraft; indeed, the legitimacy of their rule depends on their obligatory (though circumscribed) practice of witchcraft. But other witches, who do not hold political office, are reviled and were at one time killed. Witchcraft for the Beng does represent the height of immorality, but it is not only practiced by immoral people, for all that. Kings as well as witches use this power, but witches use it unrestrictedly for their own benefit, whereas kings use it only for the political "good" . . . (Gottlieb, *WKS*, p. 264)[4]

With this forceful sense of disturbance that echoes around the place of sovereignty in Beng society, in intimate proximity with witches, typically women–witches, who work in utmost evil yet an evil that kings must employ, we address a side of the good that it would be too easy to allow to pass away unheard. It contains an evil, first, inseparable from nature. This is something African thought knows, for the proximity of the human and the natural is close, face to face, in much African thought. It is an evil, also, inseparable from the finest achievements of human beings. Here we may exercise a certain caution, though I have resisted Lugones's obliviousness to witches.

In the context of an essay that presents a warning to Western "African-oriented research methodology," Vernon Dixon describes what he takes to be established differences between African and African–American worldviews and European–American worldviews, what Lugones calls different "worlds" for the construction of identities, concluding with a startling principle: "[t]he researcher must be a full participant observer in the Black community" (Dixon, *WVRM*, p. 91), a thought that might well suggest that non-Blacks cannot travel from world to world, certainly not to African worlds.

Sandra Harding discusses Dixon's distinctions and analysis to show affinities between feminist worldviews and African worldviews, but also to highlight certain important criticisms. More important for her is the idea of deviance from the dominant discourse ascribed to African–Americans and women.

> Dixon outlines these world views in order to explain why it is that the economic behavior of Afro-Americans is persistently perceived as deviant when viewed in the context of neoclassical economic theory. Thus, his argument is that the "rational economic man" of this European theory is, in fact, only European. Aspects of Afro-American economic behavior that appear irrational from the perspective of neoclassical economic theory appear perfectly rational when understood from the perspective of an African world view. (Harding, *CCFAM*, p. 300)

Reason, rationality, irrationality, economic theory are all European. Harding does not consider the possibility that reason is European while something else, witches perhaps, may be African, or that reason is a stratum of European life, while witches and sorcerers work in both Europe and Africa. Dixon rules out the latter possibility, for as an African–American economist he cannot imagine that something other than reason might promote economic behavior, cannot imagine a general economy whose rationality is disturbed by excesses.[5]

Dixon retains a certain centering of the ethical upon the individual self and self-interest that I have sought to disturb, again in Harding's words. "Nature is an 'external, impersonal system' which, since it 'does not have his interest at heart, man should and can subordinate . . . to his own goals'" (Harding, *CCFAM*, p. 301). Or perhaps he does not retain that centering, but employs it to describe the Western worldview. For in the African worldview, there is, he says, no gap between the self and the world and no centering of the ethical universe upon the individual, but

> a narrowing of perceived conceptual distance between the observer and the observed. The observed is perceived to be placed so close to the individual that it obscures what lies beyond it, and so that the observer cannot escape responding to it. The individual also appears to view the "field" as itself responding to him; i.e., although it may be completely objective and inanimate to others, because it demands response it is accorded a kind of life of its own. (Dixon, *WVRM*, p. 61; quoted from Cohen, *ICR*, p. 46)

Homeland and overseas Africans

> view man and the phenomenal world as mutually interdependent, they experience man in harmony with nature. Their aim is to maintain balance or harmony among the various aspects of the universe. . . . According to this orientation, magic, voodoo, mysticism are not efforts to overcome a separation of man and nature, but rather the use of forces in nature to restore a more harmonious relationship between man and the universe. The universe is not static, inanimate or "dead"; it is a dynamic, animate, living and powerful universe. (Dixon, *WVRM*, pp. 62–63; from Mbiti, *ARP*, chap. 16)

We have a complex and troubled sense of a dynamic, animate, living, and powerful universe, filled with witches and demons, destruction as well as fulfillment, grief and sadness as well as harmony.[6] We may hear the themes of balance and harmony in Dixon as echoing another restricted economic measure, while the general economy of the earth rests in excess, disruption, and displacement. We may understand magic, voodoo, and mysticism less in relation to harmony, especially where they are employed by kings to certify their power,[7] and more to express the displacements and disturbances always present in the rests of the earth, in its animate powers. The souls of things circulate in an excessive and disturbing general economy. We also have a more complex and troubled sense of Africa, a continent filled with variety and multiplicity.

Harding develops her account of Dixon in words of dichotomy.

> For Europeans, knowledge seeking is a process of first separating the observer (the self) from what is to be known, and then categorizing and measuring it in an impartial, disinterested, dispassionate manner. In contrast, Africans "know reality predominantly through the interaction of affect and symbolic imagery" [Dixon, *WVRM*, pp. 69–70]. The interaction of affect and symbolic imagery, in contrast to intuition, requires "inference from or reasoning about evidence" [Dixon, *WVRM*, p. 70]. But in contrast to European modes of gaining knowledge, it refuses to regard as value-free what is known, or as impartial, disinterested, and dispassionate either the knower or the process of coming to know. The self's feelings, emotions, and values are a necessary and positive part of his coming to know.
>
> In summary, Dixon argues that the African world view is grounded in a conception of the self as intrinsically connected

> with, a part of, both the community and nature. (Harding, *CCFAM*, p. 302)[8]

She is concerned with three "conceptual problems" within each literature: ahistoricity, dichotomous contrasts (or oppositions), and metaphoricity. They amount to a strenuous critique of Dixon's dichotomies. "Feminine vs. masculine and African vs. European are contrast schemas. These particular ones originated primarily in men's and Europeans' attempts to define as 'other' and subhuman, groups they intended to and did subjugate" (Harding, *CCFAM*, p. 305). She looks for an explanation of the parallels between African (and African–American) experience and (European?) women's experience, rejecting the possibility that biology can be relevant, given that African men and Western women do not share similar life experiences except as subjugated.

> Historians have suggested that "the feminine" functioned as a "category of challenge" in eighteenth-century French thought. Perhaps this notion can be used more generally to conceptualize the similarities in the world views of women and peoples of African descent. We can think of both "the feminine" and "the African" as having important functions as categories of challenge. (Harding, *CCFAM*, p. 308)

She also insists that this notion of "challenge" "needs to be supplemented by the more concrete account of the differences in social activity and experience that make the dichotomized views appropriate for different peoples" (Harding, *CCFAM*, p. 308).

We may pause in this discussion to remind ourselves that the idea of dichotomized views belongs more within the dichotomized view Harding describes, dividing subjugated from subjugating, more to one pole of Western thought than the other. Dixon denies that it pertains to African thought and claims that African thought, homeland and overseas, avoids dichotomy. He thereby reinstates another dichotomy. Harding notes that much feminist writing seeks to avoid another dichotomized view, even within the dichotomy between dichotomous and nondichotomous worldviews. Harding's concern with asking why a dichotomous view pertains to European women's experience—and relating that to systems of oppression, which employ multiple levels of dichotomy in the service of racial and gender oppression—suggests that the dichotomies "feminine vs. masculine and African vs. European" repeat the dichotomies of oppression.[9]

My pursuit of an inclusive ethic has struggled with and against dichotomy, struggled with the possibility of an ethical difference that emerges within dyadic experience and thought in virtue of proximity and heterogeneity, that passes from the face to face to unlimit, from restricted to general economy, away from dichotomy without instituting another dichotomy, always threatened in its work by dichotomy, by measure and rule, within its dyadic heterogeneity. I hope to share a feminist and African experience in which self and world belong together (to speak in words that belong to neither), where belonging together is neither unity or dichotomy, but something closer to plenishment, to general economy, where one and two relate to each other not as measures but as excesses in proximity. But I understand belonging together, of humanity and nature, and excess, as unmeasured, giving rise to measure. Ethical difference inhabits the places where neither dichotomy nor unity works as measure, giving rise, for example, to equilibrium or harmony. To the contrary, I recognize the importance of choice and selection in the work that is demanded of us by the good, but understand it as a cut, a sacrifice, something we must do and something we must avoid whenever we can.

The difficulty is that feminine and masculine, African and European, belong to the history of the world, work as dichotomous measures, cutting people and things off, casting them away from the good, as if the good demanded exclusion as its sacrifice. The good calls for cherishment; its work requires sacrifice. But no one, no group, no kind of creature, is obliged to bear the work of sacrifice. That is injustice. Sacrifice is closer to haunting by grief and death, destruction and violence, than to justified destruction. Kindred difference bears responsibility for cherishing the kinds of the world against any possibility of singling out any to bear the brunt of sacrifice, to do the work of ethical difference.[10]

In the same volume as Dixon's, other African themes appear, perhaps closer to displacement. One example:

> in the African mind, the question of origins is a meaningless one. The world, to the African, has no origin. It just is; it just exists. This is one of the fundamental differences between European and African thought, and its effects can be found in virtually every area of life characterizing the two cultures. The European looks for causes, for motives in his world, whereas the African does not. (Clark, *SINC,* p. 105)

Origins here are causes, motives, circulating in a restricted economy. Origins for us, that is, ethical origins, point to no causal or fixed point, but to the immemoriality and plenitude of nature and the good. Another example:

> the European man is the only creature who attempts to demonstrate independence from the forces of nature. To be independent is to be just that; not dependent. To be dependent means that one is *somehow* related to the forces of nature. The African man has typically identified this relationship as one of interdependence. (Clark, *SINC,* p. 117)

I have interpreted this "interdependence" as a heterogeneous dyad, face to face, in general economy, as neither dependence nor independence, but proximity. And still another example:

> what we now view as science is Euro-American scientism infused with implicit racist and oppressive formulations. We must begin to understand, that perhaps, this is the best that this culture in its present direction can offer; that the distortions of science really define Euro-American man's individualism, atomism and mechanism are essential to his strategy of maintaining imperialistic exploitation if not inherent in his nature . . . (King, *ONCW,* p. 230)

This possibility, thought as deeply and harshly as possible, is the thought of ethical inclusion, understood now as a thought. As a thought that would include, science excludes where we have no other thought of inclusion. And when we introduce that other thought, we exclude science, European–American thought, as not ethical. The possibility that science bears profound injustices within itself must be thought from within science, even as we would modify it drastically. That at least is what we may hear the witches, including Harding, and the sorcerers, Dixon and King, say. For our thought is close to Dixon's, provided we attempt to join African witches, to travel to their worlds. "[T]here is no gap or separation of man, nature and supernature. One is simply an extension of the other" (Dixon, *WVRM,* p. 61). Understood as ethical, as nature's general economy, this is plenishment in the earth.

Among the forms in which Africans and other non-Westerners speak—which European–Americans have largely forgotten how to hear—are proverbs and stories (Dixon, *WVRM,* p. 72). First, a few Ethiopian proverbs:

> He who takes notice of his own fault, notices that of the others.
>
> He who bears what he cannot will miss what he can.
>
> The fruit of conscience is humility, and the fruit of humility is love.
>
> If you cannot control yourself, you cannot order others.
>
> The wise man enquires into all things great and small.
>
> Sorrow shortens life and love of money ends in sorrow.
>
> He who heightens his wish weakens his conscience.
>
> Life for fools is death. (Sumner, *SAP,* p. 31)

And a Yoruban story:

> You know, there are some trees—if you remove their bark, the bark will cover again. The kind of tree is *Obgunrunmundum.* This is the *emi* [life force or vital spirit of the person]. It goes and comes back. I've once explained that they [*emi*] come back to the world to become children. When its time is correct, it will become a child and a woman will give birth to it. (Hallen, *PEATT,* p. 74)

Here humanity's essence, life force, is thought through both natural things and women, as if nothing in man's nature separates him from and places him in ascendancy over nature or women. Moreover, the life force works by inclusion rather than exclusion. And so with death.

> When the snake drops off the old skin the real snake still exists somewhere else, still in a body. At the first sight of such an empty carcass of a snake a timid person can flee believing to have seen a snake. As the carcass of a snake resembles exactly a snake so also does the dead body of a person. To us human beings the corpse is a dead person, but to the *emi* it is merely a worn-out garment. (Hallen, *PEATT,* p. 77)

Hallen comments that "death is not my personal negation—the ultimate, meaningless absurdity that must inevitably crown my worldly exertions. For I myself am most importantly an immortal spirit or life force—*emi.* The body that dies and is left behind is a small thing by comparison with the *emi* that lives continuously, though alternately, in and out of body (*a para da*) as it proceeds through an indefinite series of reincarnations" (Hallen, *PEATT,* p. 77). We may think of such a reincarnation as bearing no weight of the singular individual, but as plenishment, everywhere in the earth.

Now listen to an aboriginal story entitled "The Strange Shape of Animals."

> When animals were brought to life from the frozen depths of earth by the sun goddess, who shall tell what they were like? There are some who say that they had the form of men and women, and others that they had many different shapes. We can be certain of only one thing . . . that after a time they grew tired of the forms Baiame had given them, and were seized by vague longings.
>
> Those who lived in the water wanted to be on dry land. Those who walked on the earth wished to feel the freedom of the sky. There was not a single animal that was not possessed by this strange discontent. They grew sad and hid themselves away from Yhi. The cheerful sound of their voices was no longer heard, and the green plants wilted in sympathy with their friends the creatures. . . .
>
> The story of these changes has been told round campfires for a thousand years. When men and women came to live in the great continent, and saw the creeping, crawling, jumping, swift-running, flying, burrowing wild life on which they depended for their food, they invented strange tales to account for the habits of the creatures that Baiame had given to them. As we crouch round the embers with them, sheltered from the wind by the low fence of woven branches, let us also listen to tales that have come from the heart of a people who are closer than we are to the gods of nature. (Reed, *MLA,* pp. 19–21)

Compare this with the story of the Garden of Eden, where Adam gains dominion over animals by naming and, perhaps, counting them. Certainly, if not in Eden, Noah counted the animals in pairs, counted them to save them and to use them. In the aboriginal story we have just heard, nothing can measure the panoply of nature, of living creatures, who refuse to stay with their names.

Let us now listen to another aboriginal story entitled "Baiame and the Land of Women."

> At the end of the world, beyond the mountain where Baiame the Great Spirit lived, there was once a land inhabited only by women. These women were famous for their skill in making weapons—spears, boomerangs, and nullanullas. They traded them with men for meat and possum skins which they needed for food and warmth, because there were no animals on the other side of Baiame's mountain. Hunters were equally glad to trade

> with them, for the weapons that the women made were the finest in the world. (Reed, *MLA,* p. 46)

A man named Wurrunah—speaking in a voice we have heard before—decided to steal the women's weapons.

> "It is ridiculous that men should be content to accept what women are prepared to give them," he complained to his brothers. "After all, they are only women, and men should be their masters. If no one else will do it, I will show them how they ought to be treated." (Reed, *MLA,* p. 46)

Wurrunah turned his brothers into swans. The women chased them. Wurrunah stole the weapons and, when the women chased him, multitudes of animals were released, surprising the women who had never seen such a sight before. But the men were arrogant, and were defeated by the elements and spirits. Crows saved the brothers in their form as swans.

> They [the crows] plucked the black feathers from their plumage and scattered them over the swans until they were warm again, and able to swim ashore.
>
> Baiame looked down and was amused at their temerity, and touched by their kindness to the swans; as a reward he allowed the swans to live and decreed that all the swans of Australia would have black feathers instead of white. (Reed, *MLA,* p. 48)

Here the women are powerful, too powerful for the men to defeat except by cunning. And nature is filled with multitudes of animals and spirits, human life is filled with spirits and animals, multitudinous and plenitudinous. These are the powers touched by the witches. Where men and women meet, where they join nature, the world is filled with multiplicity and heterogeneity.

Carol Adams tells a similar story, without ascription.

> In the early times men and women lived apart, the former hunting animals exclusively, the latter pursuing a gathering existence. Five of the men, who were out hunting, being careless creatures, let their fire go out. The women, who were careful and orderly, always kept their fire going. The men, having killed a springbok, became desperate for means to cook it, so one of their number set out to get fire, crossed the river and met one of the women gathering seeds. When he asked her for some fire, she

> invited him to the feminine camp. . . . She made him some porridge. After he had eaten it, he said, "Well, it's nice food so I shall just stay with you." . . . The second man set out, only to be tempted by female cooking, and to take up residence in the camp of the women. . . . The last man became very frightened indeed and besides by now the springbok had rotted. He took his bow and arrows and ran away. (Adams, *SPM,* p. 25)

A similarity of the stories lies in the need, far beyond sexual and procreative, of men for the powers possessed by women. A difference lies in relation to animals, for in the latter story, animals are present as meat, hunted and eaten by men, neither hunted nor eaten by women. The aboriginal story places men and women together and apart in plenitude and heterogeneity, a natural world filled with teeming profusion.[11]

To close this discussion of witches and Africans, I ask if we must choose "dichotomously" between European–American philosophy and thought—worldviews that emphasize the dividedness and exclusiveness of reason—and the fluidity, mobility, and spirituality of African and feminist thought—a thought symbolized by the witches and by Pharmakeia, in her ambiguity and confusion, in her violation and oppression.[12] To do so, to be forced to choose one or the other, would be to repeat the dyadic exclusions of the form of thought I hope ethically to resist. An ethic of inclusion includes rather than excludes in the community and the environment of nature, nature's plenishment. It does so in service to heterogeneity, to multiplicities of kinds, profusions of kinds and truths and desires. It does so in memory of endless sacrifices and losses, incompatibilities of heterogeneous kinds that cannot joyfully occupy the same places together.

If we refuse to choose, must refuse to choose in the light of the good between Western and African thought and practice, we may instead seek to bring them together. Yet the junctures we have considered fall apart into a Western and non-Western dichotomy, for example, between universality and totality. Instead, we return to the echoes of our juncture throughout, understood as the *aentre,* a between that links and joins but also opens a space of absence, silence, negation, excess, a between of forgetting and a between of profusion, plenitude. Perhaps our thoughts of the one as problem-solving, the other as experiencing, the one as linear, the other as topographic, do not divide exclusively, do not exclude each other, but share memories of the good, the one, perhaps belonging to *technē*, the other to *mythos* and *poiēsis*, but where *technē* and *poiēsis* compose no dichotomy.

To the contrary, perhaps, dichotomy belongs to measure, represents a definite dyad, and, for us, reduces heterogeneity in its proximity. Heterogeneity, as proximity, face to face, presents the indefinite dyad, immemorially remembering a forgotten good that has no measure, cannot be measured, but that circulates everywhere, imposing upon us and others endless responsibilities. With this possibility, that we think of the good under two signs, together and apart, with no choice between them except in response to our ethical responsibilities, we come to what it means to be ethical, to do ethical work, what it means to plenish the earth by those who find their places in it.

We return to the perhaps fantastic relation of native Americans to the earth, close to plenishment. "We know the sap which courses through the trees as we know the blood that courses through our veins. We are part of the earth and it is part of us. The perfumed flowers are our sisters. The bear, the deer, the great eagle, these are our brothers. The rocky crests, the juices in the meadow, the body heat of the pony, and man, all belong to the same family" (quoted in Krell, *DL,* p. 317).[13] Including Europeans.

CHAPTER 13

Rhapsody

The earth composes things and kinds in multiple relations, composes environments of environments and representations of representations, nature's general economy. Goods circulate as representations, mirroring, expressing, exceeding each other throughout nature, intermediary figures of place and displacement, purity and impurity. I sing of this commotion as the plenitude, general economy, cacophony, of things sounding, circulating together, harmonies and disharmonies, each resting in multiple places, complicating every identity, every kind, with inexhaustible excesses. Nature is the place of place, echoing multiple displacements, harmonies, disharmonies, rests. Each place in the earth is filled with multiple places, each place composing other places, displacing places, each kind dismembering every kind, each body remembering other bodies, every place filled with kinds representing themselves and other kinds. Each site echoes with multiple identities, multifariously, heterogeneously.

We may think of each place, every thing in its place, as a *locale,* a habitat, an environment, a rest, for other things, things that compose it, things it composes, things and kinds, each kind composed of other kinds. We may think of each locale as a profusion of *ingredients,* sounding, ringing, each ingredient another locale, another habitat, for multiple ingredients. To be, to rest, in the earth is to be in place—a locale—and to belong to, rest in, multiple locales, as an ingredient, multiply ingredient in any place, in multiple places, and to locate, provide places for, other ingredients. This multiplicity of locations, *locality,* is the plenitude of the earth, the general economy of nature, the harmonies, disharmonies, cacophonies, excesses, of the heterogeneous song of the earth.

The song of the earth is filled with the sounds of *unisons,* of things and kinds with displaced, heterogeneous identities inhabiting multiple places, echoing multiple resonances, composing every identity as profuse, every purity as impure, exceeding every identity and place. To echo in place, one place, is to sound in unison. But every unison resounds with multiple *resonances,* inexhaustibly multiple reverberations, echoing its heterogeneous rests. Each ingredient and kind in its place echoes as a unison constituted by other ingredients and kinds, by multiple environments, locales, to which it belongs; each ingredient echoes multiple and heterogeneous unisons, related and entwined, and moves among them. Unison expresses the local place in which something excessive and inexhaustible sounds at rest; resonances express the multiple and excessive places displacing every place of rest. The earth is the plenitude, general circulation, of unisons and resonances together composing multifarious and diverse identities, rests, individual and collective, public and private, harmonies and disharmonies. The plenitude of the earth is nature's *sonance,* the ring of representation, sounds and tones and rests composing habitats, environments, locales and spheres, of multiple identity.

I ring the plenitude of the earth in the triangle of *locality, inexhaustibility,* and *ergonality.*[1] Locality echoes place, every being resting in its place, an ingredient of a local place, a locale for other ingredients. Every ingredient in its place is an environment, a habitat, a place for others. Inexhaustibility echoes multiple places, every locus an ingredient, sounding in multiple places of rest, placed together with displacement, harmony with disharmony, profusely, multifariously, heterogeneously. Each locale, each symphony, defines a shared kind of place among its different ingredients, its different themes and tones. And each locale, in virtue of its multiple locations, resonates cacophonously with heterogeneity, multiple places and reverberations.

Ergonality speaks of representativity, the work and unwork that things and kinds, that loci, do in their multiple places, echoing their cacophony, the work of the good that plenishes the earth, that circulates the things of the earth in its musical economy, exceeding every work. The general economy of the good is the cacophonous rhapsody of the earth. In its place, in its places that remain at rest, everything bears a certain good, circulates, resounds, as the precious thing it is, precious also in the work it does, the work it has done, and in its inexhaustible promise of other work, circulates as excess. Ergonality, the work of things that plenish the earth, in their multiple places, rings of the good that things may do, may do of themselves, in what they are, their being and becoming, and in what they do and undo in echoing, representing, working toward others. Ergonality, work, and representation transform the plenitude of nature, locality and inexhaustibility, into the call of the good. Plenishment responds to that call.

Cherishment is kindredness, kindness, tenderness, compassion, unrestricted, unconditional love toward, care for, local and inexhaustible things, different and heterogeneous things together composing, representing, multiple kinds circulating together, excessively. It is a love, a kindness, closer perhaps to *philia* than to *erōs,*[2] but the gender, the sexual difference, in heterogeneity, in multiple kinds, is erotic as well as kind, altererotic in proximity, face to face with another kind. This face to face is a proximity in which each composes the other's kind and identity within the impossibility of taking the place of the other, a proximity giving rise to the general circulation of things and kinds composing and representing multiple hybrid environments. *Philia* and *erōs,* kind(red)-ness and desire, represent heterogeneity, are intermediary figures. Sacrifice is the impossibility of fulfillment in a world of local and inexhaustible things circulating together, the impossibility of subjecting this excessive cacophony to a single harmony, to an overarching good, or to precisely measured divisions and hierarchies. The inexhaustibility of things, heterogeneously, makes sacrifice inescapable, still within the call of the good, within endless cherishment, in the relentless contamination of injustice. Plenishment in the earth is our ethical and political response to this call, a response engendered by unending responsibilities called forth by cherishment, disrupted by sacrifice. It knows no rules, knows immeasurable joys and sorrows.

Cherishment and sacrifice are beyond measure, have no measure and fall under no rules. Cherishment is love for, kindness toward, all kinds of things in all kinds of ways, exceeding any capacity of fulfillment, an inexhaustible compassion for inexhaustibly heterogeneous kinds of things. Sacrifice is the immeasurable and immemorial loss that life and work in time and space impose, the impossibility of saving and fulfilling all things together, where the loss is infinite, unmeasurable, beset by grief, but where the good demands its work, bestows its joy. Sacrifice imposes a certain memory, mourning, grief, a sadness at death and destruction, at endless injustices, which cannot be avoided because sacrifice belongs to the call of the good as profoundly as cherishment. But sacrifice belongs to cherishment, does the work of the good as cherishment. If some must die that others may live, the deaths are unjust, must be remembered and mourned, must be repaid, will impose a debt. We may think of this sacrifice as tragic, but it knows joy, knows the possibility of the good in sacrifice. Tragedy and comedy together share the poetic space of finite sacrifice, *souffrance* and *jouissance*.

Foucault speaks of this sacrifice within the call of the good as value, in relation to wealth and exchange.[3] He speaks of genealogy as the "*insurrection of subjugated knowledges*" (Foucault, *2L*, p. 81), an endless struggle of restitution against sacrifice and loss. I understand this struggle as ethics. I understand the emergence of value as the work of the good in time, the sacrifices cherishment demands in order to do the work of the good. In this sense, value, but also justice, truth, and law, all emerge from death and destruction as sacrifice, the sacrifice of some goods for others, and not just for others, the death of some that others may live, but as well the destruction of some priceless goods for the institution of justice, truth, and law. These are instituted in the echoes of injustice. Plenishment is the entwining of cherishment and sacrifice in the work of the good, in memory that this work bears responsibility for endless injustices, endlessly resisting the injustices of subjugation, endlessly undoing the authority of work. Justice, truth, and law are restitutions for immemorial injustice, not repayments or retributions, but responses to the immeasurable debt they bear for the sacrifices they require. They endlessly call for insurrection.

This restitutive truth of justice, truth, and law may be expressed in relation to *technē*. The work of the good must be done repeatedly, repeated endlessly: first, in its immeasurability, under the call of the good, face to face, in proximity, within the indefiniteness of the dyad that bears the weight of heterogeneity, of inexhaustibly multiple kinds; second, in falling sacrificially into time, under law and rule; third, bearing the weight, the gravity, the memories and insurrections of the call of the good against any possibility of fulfillment, advance, or progress. Cherishment and sacrifice know no rules, exceed all measure, express the passing away of measure into plenishment in the earth, undo work's authority with memories of unwork (Nancy, *IC*). But they give rise, as they must, to rules, to measure and law, give rise because the work of the good is done by measure, enters time as selection, decision, exclusion, and bears responsibility for imposing exclusion while endlessly haunted by what exceeds measure. General economy circulates goods everywhere excessively, under the sovereignty of restricted economies. Plenishment circulates goods everywhere, inexhaustibly, under the rule of measure, where this measure is given birth by sacrifice in general economy. Plenishment, then, is the use, the implementation, of measure under *technē* toward the good, haunted by endless sacrifice, inspired by cherishment to seek endless restitution. *Technē*'s works contribute profoundly to nature's profusion, plenish the earth, as they threaten every profusion.

I do not contrast plenishment with *technē,* do not contrast *poiēsis* or *physis* with *technē,* do not understand *technē* as representation or *poiēsis* as spirit, as if the one resounded within the call of the good, whereas the other betrayed it, as if the one circulated in general economy, the other in restricted economies, as if the two composed a definite dyad. I do not describe a deeper, truer, more authentic way of being for human beings than *technē,* as if ethical regard were otherwise than being in the world or doing good work. The immeasurability of the good, the immemoriality of injustice, the unworking of work, does not separate the work of the good from the works of *technē,* inclusion from exclusion, but circulates these works together with the others, with the works of nature and the earth, excessively, displacing each other, inciting insurrections against exclusion. *Technē*'s works belong to nature and its general economy, to the general circulation of goods in teeming profusion together with other things and representations, adding to and supplementing the profusion. Cherishment calls upon us to know, to cherish, human works, *technē*'s works, works of art and craft and instrumentality, human things along with natural things, but also calls upon us to resist their sovereignty, the rule of measure, the authority of work, the sovereignty of exclusion. *Technē*'s works are beautiful, precious, but they do not measure the goodness of things. They exist side by side, heterogeneously, with others that displace them, unwork their work. They do not determine heterogeneity. They do not establish proximity.[4]

Plenishment in the earth—our ethical response to cherishment and sacrifice and to the demands of injustice in justice—knows no rules, but spends all of time imposing rules, seeking guidelines, principles, criteria, measures, doing work as *technē.* Plenishment in the earth knows that every rule, guideline, principle, or criterion, every measure, intermediate number, or dyad, calls forth its own injustices, is born in injustice and continues to bear injustice's fruits. Injustice haunts justice, undoes work. Plenishment knows this haunting and unworking of justice's work face to face, in proximity. In domestic, private places where we meet each other face to face, in love or friendship, in public spaces but still face to face, anywhere we are in proximity with others, we find the demands and burdens of the good, of heterogeneity. Where men live together with women or with men, where women live together with women or men or children, where men live in their homes or barracks, wherever *erōs* and *philia,* love, friendship, and kindness, impose responsibilities, we find the call of the good to show us our own and others' injustices under rule and measure. We may insist that we should bring our loved ones to justice under law, as Euthyphro does, but our love in such cases bears the burden of revealing law's injustices. There is no escape from injustice. But there is life and responsibility for and toward injustice, as well as a deep and profound joy in the ethical possibilities that we may realize surrounded by endless injustices, including our own. A joy consists in response to the call of the good from within the impossibility of its realization.

This joy, inseparable from mourning, owes its existence to the triangle of locality, inexhaustibility, and ergonality. For the call of injustice, immemorial injustice, arises in every place where we respond to the call of the good, in inexhaustible displacement. The work of the good, the work we find ourselves called upon to do, which constitutes our ethical responsibility, circulates everywhere in mobile and rapid displacement. The responsibilities time imposes on us, the works that fulfill our responsibilities, displace every place of the good with injustice, with wounding, but also displace every wounding, making us infinitely wounded everywhere, exposed to injustice everywhere, to a wounding and injustice that resists the permanence of scars. Said in a different voice, because this language of scars evokes Hegel, time is incompatible with the possibility that anything may heal all scars; time gives rise to an ethical responsibility and joy that is possible only in virtue of the memories of scars and in virtue of having responded ethically to scars, to wounds, to injustices, without committing other, heinous injustices or ripping open other wounds. But time is incompatible with endless memory.

What should we do, what are we called upon to do, how do we know what we are called upon to do, in our ethical responsibility for the work of the good? We, and others, human beings and others, have always done the work of the good, always struggled with our responsibilities, caring for others and for other things, with the sense of nature's worth. We have pursued the call of the good, against injustice, frequently paralyzed by weakness, sometimes surrounded by destruction. We have felt the responsibility of work toward the good. We have done the work of the good in every representation, in every identity and place. Even so, we have repeatedly and unjustly understood the call of the good to define us, to mark the human against the nonhuman, the civilized against the barbarian. We have understood the good to exclude. In this way, perhaps, we have hoped to limit the impossibility of our responsibilities toward everything in the earth, but have hoped in vain.

If we accept the truth that we human beings, together with other, perhaps all, beings and things, occupy nature in our our work together—working for the good, representing ourselves and others as individuals and kinds—then perhaps, in an abiding sense, we do not find the work the good imposes on us within an inclusive ethic—that is, an ethic that does not exclude anything from the call of the good, especially an ethic of heterogeneity, encompassing sexual and kindred difference—to be very different from work we have done in the past, but perhaps to be understood, thought, and felt in different ways and to evoke different relations to the good, to its multiplicity and heterogeneity. We hope to avoid injustice, to work for justice, to bring about the good, to pursue the truth. But we know that our best efforts are and will continue to be destructive and unjust and that in difficulty we may be led to heinous acts. We bear endless responsibility for the sacrifices that we impose in our responses to the call of the good. We bear endless responsibility for the wounds we impose in every judgment, for the sacrifices borne within our work toward the good.

Here the exclusions of the good, the cuts that cut off some of nature's kinds—animals, plants, women, barbarians, slaves—from cherishment, serve us in a doubled way. For the cut that seems to reduce the threat of the impossibility of our responsibilities for the good imposes an unjust, indefensible sacrifice upon some kinds of creatures and things. The exclusion destroys, defames, demeans the good in the representation of kinds. When we are as self-righteous as possible about our own superiority, individual and collective, we know in our heart of hearts that we are unjust. We know in our heart of hearts we are unjust when we claim the right to destroy other creatures and things in order for our kind to proper. That knowledge is cherishment. We know it as the call of the good. It calls upon us to know that the thought, the ordering, the representation of things of the world, the best knowledge and truth we can attain and the best lives we can live, even the idea of the best, is guided by a responsibility to the good that always fails it, brings forth injustices, works in sacrifice.

Cherishment demands that we take upon ourselves the burden of the worth of things and kinds together with the impossible burden of their incompatibility, of the inescapability of sacrifice, take on this double and impossible burden as the call of the good, and joyfully. Cherishment and sacrifice together compose an impossible burden, doomed to guilt. But guilt, a far-reaching and catastrophic sacrifice, defeats the call of cherishment, collapses our love toward and care for others into grim destructiveness, toward ourselves and toward others. Guilt in this sense cannot be plenishment, cannot give rise to plenishment. Rather, plenishment is a certain joy, love, exhilaration, kindness, compassion, inseparable from suffering, loss, grief, memory, mourning, in which we take up the memories of injustice and move on with them, not making them whole, not making ourselves whole, but circulating together with them within the good. This call of the good everywhere bears within its impossibility a joy.

Some memories of past injustices haunt and oppress us in such a way that, remembering our wounds, we wound others deeply, unjustly, mercilessly. Some memories of past injustices we cannot endure, must forget, cannot endure to mourn and we thereby cease to know and to care about their injustices. Some decisions we may be called upon to make in the present, or in the future, we cannot understand, we cannot bear to face. Ethical responsibility for others, heterogeneously, is a wounding and obsession, painful and disturbing.

But, in understanding that this disturbance and pain belong to nature, to the earth, that wounding is everywhere, that everything in the earth calls upon us to care, to pay attention, to take responsibility for and toward others in proximity, we may understand that the burden's very impossibility brings with it a joy inseparable from love, from *erōs* and *philia*—not a joy of relief, but an exhilaration, ecstasy, rapture, of responding with energy and dedication to a call, more Dionysian than Apollinian. It is the call of cherishment, everywhere. It is the call of heterogeneity, profusion, disorder, where we understand that locales and ingredients are different and heterogeneous kinds, kinds whose identities, unisons and resonances, and places in the earth are always displaced, so that we cannot order, control, give place to all the kinds.

We cannot give place, of ourselves, to all individuals and kinds. Nor can they find their places, all together. Yet in their multiplicity, their teeming profusion, excess, they plenish the earth. And we bear responsibility for plenishment insofar as we belong to the earth, insofar as we can think of, take responsibility for, expose ourselves to different and heterogeneous proximities. This responsibility, this call, is borne by everything in the earth, borne everywhere, by whatever lives and moves and inhabits the earth, by animate and inanimate creatures and things, borne by them differently, with different responsibilities, borne by them mobilely, with multiple displacements. We human beings bear endless responsibilities for plenishment, not more serious or more grave than, or superior to, the responsibilities and proximities of other creatures and kinds: for example, among insects, to move the earth; among bacteria, to clean the earth; among mountains and valleys, to glorify the earth; among the stars and planets, to give radiance to the earth; and so on. All these plenish, all do their work, and all bear a certain exposure to and wounding before the others that surround them and join their plenishment. All plenish the earth within a certain wounding, destruction, that we human beings magnify in our destructions beyond anything imaginable elsewhere and bear a certain consciousness of and toward.

Human beings bear a sense of love and kindness, know cherishment, know it and feel it. But so do animals and birds toward each other and their surroundings, and so do insects and flowers basking in the rays of the sun. Human beings bear a responsibility to care for the earth, but so do worms and bees, together with countless microorganisms. Human beings wield great powers, instrumental powers, and know great spirituality, plenishing the earth with works, poems, statues, buildings, monuments, working consciously and by means of complex representations. This work, this ergonality, is human plenishment, which is not to be diminished or reviled among the workings, ergonality, plenishment of the other things and kinds in the earth, as it is not the only plenishment we know. We know ergonality everywhere, working toward plenishment.

But within this plenishment of works is a darker and destructive side. For human works corrode, erode, destroy, limit possibilities for other goods as they expand other possibilities. Human works oppress, subjugate, restrict the possibilities of many other kinds of things, other works, in hidden, unknown ways. The ethics of human work, understood to fall entirely within human instrumentalities, *technē*, within a sense that the human good, the good for humans, is not the only good, but includes endless others, this restriction to *technē* excludes. Instrumentality, understood as the only good, is a desperate, destructive, oppressive good. When we measure the good by our humanity, we oppress and subjugate not only inanimate and nonhuman creatures, but human beings as well, throughout the earth. That is the repeated lesson of our injustices. Instrumentality, *technē*, institutes the work of the good but is not the only good we know. We know the good as breath; we know the good as air, reminded of this by Irigaray, and others.[5]

Irigaray speaks of sexed rights as the right to human dignity, the right of women to cease commercial exploitation of their bodies and images by institutional powers and to gain freedom over their own representations; the right to human identity, recognition of virginity and motherhood as components in female identity and worth, as defined by women; the mutual right to define mother–child relations independent of men; the right to life, place, and tradition independent of male law; the right to freedom from financial penalties as women; the equal right of men and women to exchange, to participate in the social contract; the right to equal representation and participation at all institutional sites (Irigaray, *WDSR*, pp. 86–89). These sexed rights are rights for women, who under conditions of gender inequality bear the weight of this inequality in every construction and presentation of their identity *as women*. The predominant right of women is to determine their own identities as women, rather than having them determined by men and by institutions governed by men.

We have seen that rights exclude animals and other creatures from ethical regard, exclude piles of sand and other natural things if rights are granted to living things. Moreover, rights impose measures that diminish the menaces of sacrifice, weakening the depth and reach of our responsibilities toward the good. They suggest, against the claims of cherishment, that if something is done or exists by right it cannot be wrong, cannot be criticized as evil. Yet that one may have the right to speak does not entail that one will not say hateful things. That one may have a right to bring up one's children as one sees fit does not entail that one will care for them. One may criticize evil within the very best of work.

Rights are inclusive in one respect: they may be claimed, and are claimed by those who profess to possess them. Again, this claim may work to exclude others who cannot exercise such a claim or whose claims are not recognized. Cherishment may suggest, perhaps too forcefully, that the one who cherishes and who bears responsibility for another has the obligation to nurture the good for that other. Yet where the other is human or, among animals, creatures that possess a good for themselves,[6] that can choose, that good may be claimed, if implicitly, silently. Inanimate things may be allowed to exist untouched; animate things choose and pursue their goods for themselves.

Irigaray's rights pertain to women who demand their rights as women. Others extend the idea of rights to animals, perhaps to other living things. But only so far. Piles of sand, mountain ranges, have no rights. Yet Heidegger speaks of *Gelassenheit zu den Dingen,* translated as "releasement toward things" (Heidegger, *DT,* p. 54), and of letting things be, though he refuses to understand this letting as ethical.[7] My discussion may be read as an account of what it might be to let all things be, and to understand this letting be as ethical–political, in this way following Levinas's belief that our primary relation to being is ethical, but rejecting the otherwise as taking us away from being, emphasizing the otherwise everywhere, in every proximity. Cherishment is letting be. Sacrifice is the impossibility of such a letting, where ethics is responsibility toward this impossibility. Plenishment is the ethical regard, the unlimited responsibility, the wounding borne by sacrifice in the reverberations of cherishment, the demand for and impossibility of kindness toward every kind, all kinds together, knowing that kindness recomposes kinds. This reemergence of kinds takes us back to Irigaray's understanding that an ethics of sexual difference is an ethic of sexual rights for and by women, constituted in the no place of women as kind. Possibly there is also an ethic of sexual rights for men, by men; perhaps also no place. But she is concerned with an ethic for women rather than an ethic for all, from which women have been historically excluded. I am dubious about any ethic for all from which other animate and inanimate creatures and things are excluded.

The identity of which Irigaray speaks, of woman as woman, is borne by women as individuals and as a kind, borne in a certain circulation and tension between them. It is not a question of women as individuals alone, as if they were not women. Gender inequality forms gender, as Wittig says, as a mark of subjection. Woman and man are categories of subordination and domination. Kinds are constituted by social and historical relations, by representations. Yet heterogeneity, face to face and in proximity, is realized not by individuals alone, in proximity, but by kinds, collectives, in juxtaposition. Heterogeneity is realized by the proximity of kinds in circulation, where the identities of individuals and kinds are always in question, where individuals are collectives, kinds, all circulating in the general economy of goods and representations. I call these kinds locales composed of ingredients, circulating as ingredients among other locales, in a world composed of kinds, collectives, of locales and ingredients, themselves locales, circulating in inexhaustible intermediary figures of representation.[8]

In *Adventures of Ideas,* Whitehead speaks of Beauty, Truth, Adventure, Art, and Peace.[9] He speaks of these as unsexed, ungendered. Perhaps that is why he does not ascribe an ethic to them. But he does speak of good and evil.

> Goodness is the third member of the trinity which traditionally has been assigned as the complex aim of art—namely, Truth, Beauty, and Goodness. With the point of view here adopted, Goodness must be denied a place among the aims of art. For Goodness is a qualification belonging to the constitution of reality, which in any of its individual actualizations is better or worse. Good and evil lie in depths and distances below and beyond appearance. They solely concern inter-relations within the real world. The real world is good when it is beautiful. (Whitehead, *AI,* p. 345)

If we speak in gendered terms, pertaining to and divided by heterogeneous kinds, we may find here ethical and kindred difference. For the beauty of which Whitehead speaks is as close as possible to plenishment.[10]

I take the earth to be composed of kinds, the general economy and circulation of things together, composing kinds, locales, collectives, composing individuals as envelopes of qualities, organs, affections, parts, ingredients. Nature is composed of poems, each composed of other poems, tones and chords, reverberating everywhere, with no individuals or simples or purities or totalities that end the circulation. The call of the good is the call of kindred difference, that is, the responsibility toward kinds in their collectivity and their specificity, especially in their ergonality, their representativity. Only kinds can be specific, and heterogeneity bears relation to different kinds, face to face, in proximity.

To the heterogeneity of the dyad, then, face to face with the other in proximity, to our boundless responsibility toward the others, I add the general circulation of kinds of things, of identities and kinds—of genders, species, types, identities—kinds, not just individuals in their consummate inexplicability, all circulating in representation. We do not know what it is to be an individual that is not composed of many kinds, that does not inhabit many realms, that does not participate in heterogeneity, its own and the heterogeneity of others, where heterogeneity pertains to kinds, to sexual, kindred, and other differences. We do not know an individual or a kind that does not represent and that we know without judgment. The song of the earth is the plenitude of individual things and kinds, of singular things as kinds, in their differences, genders and kinds, circulating in judgments. The call of the good is cherishment of these differences in their heterogeneity. The impossibility of realizing any goal that may fulfill heterogeneity, any goal at all but especially any particular measure of heterogeneity, without infinite and unmeasurable destruction, brings us to sacrifice. Plenishment is immeasurable responsibility for and work toward the good in the light of sacrifice, fallen under measure and law. Plenishment in the earth is the work of the good, under sacrifice, returning to cherishment and its inexhaustibility. The intermediate number, we recall, passes away to unlimit. The work of the good, of justice, truth, and law, is ethical and can be given ethical regard only where these pass away into cherishment and sacrifice, repeating the grief, sadness, and loss at injustice.

I hope in closing to offer guidelines to plenishment in the earth, instructions that give no measure, know no measure, but express cherishment and sacrifice, heterogeneity. We may think of these as representing the inscription of the song of the earth, where that song, plenishment in the earth, is written down within a certain impossibility of fulfillment and of bringing the general economy of the circulation of goods under a particular form.

1. We find ourselves belonging to many different kinds: mixed kinds, kinds belonging to other kinds, by birth, by history, by choice, and by the activities and representations of others. This is our ethical condition. We find ourselves surrounded by many different kinds, which we constitute by our activities and representations, and by which we and they constitute who we are, as human and as individuals. To be is to be individual among kinds, individual in virtue of complex and mobile kindred relations. Our ethical relation to the good is a relation to kinds, heterogeneous kinds to which we may belong, other kinds in our proximity to which we know we will never belong.

2. Everything, every individual thing and every kind, matters and is precious, infinitely, inexhaustibly, heterogeneously. Everything in the earth is precious, in its ways, known and unknown, in the kinds in which it participates. Everything sings its movement to the good. To cherish, love, revere the goodness of things is to let them pursue their own good, with three qualifications:

3. (a) they may not know their own good, though no one else can know it better; (b) such a good, one's own proper good, is multiple, heterogeneous, impure, bound to others face to face, constituted by memberships, practices, representations, and mobilities; (c) the kinds of the earth, human and other kinds, with their goods, belong everywhere in nature in fourfold relations: constituted by their members, constituting their members' identities, in virtue of their mobilities and circulations, and related heterogeneously. This heterogeneity of the good shows itself as the monstrosity of kinds. One's own good to and in proximity with others shows itself as monstrosity. It works by authority, gives rise to injustice.

It follows that:

4. Cherishment in time gives rise to the impossibility of fulfilling the good of heterogeneous things together and to the impossibility of a measure of fulfillment. This impossibility, sacrifice, knows no rules, demands judgment without criteria, is wounded by endless responsibilities toward the good. This responsibility and

this judgment bring with themselves a certain joy enriched by sorrow.

5. Among creatures who can choose their good, they must choose and cultivate that good for themselves. None can know the joy and suffering of another, especially another kind; no one can foster the good for another, certainly not the heterogeneous good of other kinds. Undertaking the good for another results in endless disaster. The work of cherishment presupposes autonomy, self-determination, the undertaking of the call of the good. We impose our understanding of others' good briefly at best and with infinite caution. We impose our own good upon the good of others as sacrifice, as injustice. Plenishment in the good serves for the most part, if not always, as a letting be. For we can never know the joy possible for another kind and must find a joy for ourselves in letting that other kind be in its joy.

6. Nothing can justify the sacrifice of any kind to the good, whether that kind include women, children, animals, Jews, or even the AIDS or smallpox virus. Cherishment demands sacrifice, but can never impose in the name of kindness the destruction or death of a kind, thereby reducing heterogeneity. Such a destruction is profoundly unjust, bears with it responsibility for endless restitution. The sacrifice of an individual, of many individuals, is terrible. But sacrifice is inescapable. Nothing can justify the destruction of a kind in the march of history. Yet history is the recurrence of such catastrophes.

7. In the places where we compose ourselves and others in proximity, face to face, we know our good to whatever extent it is knowable and we know of, grant, the good of others. Especially, we know the weight of our injustices in the struggle for the good. We are more effective agents, closer to heterogeneous possibilities of the good, able to undertake our endless responsibilities, face to face, in proximity with others. The work of the good is undertaken locally, face to face—in this sense, privately. The work of the good disperses in the general economy of goods in circulation—in this sense, publicly. The form in which goods circulate in public is by means of authority. Everything depends on the struggle between the rule of authority in restricted economies and the upsurge of sovereignty in general economy, everywhere in nature's plenitude. Everything depends on our capacity to struggle against our own injustices more than against the injustices of others. The call of the good is a responsibility for our unending injustices.

8. Heterogeneity works face to face, in proximity, in the indefinite dyad, arising in the face to face, the wounding and the joy of love, passing away into the general economy of goods, circulating everywhere. Heterogeneity complicates the identity of every kind in proximity, the indefiniteness and impurity of the dyad. What we find face to face, in proximity, are cherished bodies whose sufferings and joys plenish the earth. Authority, sovereignty, and the good all do their work upon bodies, work through representation upon material and embodied things.

(1) expresses place, locatedness among and with others, constituting our and their identities among kinds. I have spoken of such locatedness as locality, inexhaustibility, and ergonality, the general economy of goods and judgments circulating in multiple locales, which are multiply ingredient and compose environments and environments of environments, the general economy of kinds. (2) expresses cherishment as unconditional love, everywhere and for every thing. (3) expresses cherishment in relation to heterogeneity, giving rise to (4), which expresses the impossibility of fulfillment of the work of cherishment without loss, without injustice. (2), (3), and (4) together express cherishment and sacrifice together, that is, plenishment in the earth from which our acts and judgments emerge in response to our infinite responsibilities for the good. The call of the good includes all things toward which we bear an impossible responsibility.

(5) and (6) address nationalities and kinds, entail heterogeneity and autonomy. (5) expresses liberation and democracy, offers perhaps the strongest argument for democracy to be derived from plenishment. Of the forms of political sovereignty, of community, democracy reflects the possibility that those who act, for themselves and others, must suppose others to know something that I can never know, but that I must cherish. In return, democracy presupposes that others respect me and what I take to be my good, respect me and my kind. In this way, (5) entails shared proximity and cherishment without mutuality and reciprocity, without rule.

Against those who would suppress our pursuit of our good, I respond that they cannot know what we know of that good. Against the force of our own struggles toward the good, as if ours were the only good, I hope that we remember injustice and heterogeneity. Everything in nature knows and strives toward something that we must acknowledge but cannot know so as to override. The others whose heterogeneity the good calls upon us to respect are of different kinds, known and unknown, whom we encounter face to face and at a distance, whom we compose in our encounters. Face to face, the good calls upon us to cherish other kinds of people, creatures, and things in their impurity and heterogeneity, in possibilities of the unknown that we do not know and may never know, that are brought forth in our struggles to know. At a distance, the good calls upon us to take responsibility for, to struggle to know, our injustices, the wounds we have inscribed in our responses to the call of the good.

(6) represents collective identity in which our responsibility for our own good gives rise to an impossible monstrosity. For to foster one's own good, together with one's own kind, fails to represent the inexhaustible heterogeneity of goods, in proximity, the inexhaustible good of others, and leads to the abolition of alien kinds, other possibilities of the good. Nothing can sacrifice the destruction of a kind even where we compose that kind by our sacrifices.

(7) and (8) express the possibility of work toward the good, in proximity, where we are, face to face, inseparable from sexual difference and its excesses. Here heterogeneity is erotic, sexual difference, the kind of the other that we encounter face to face in an unknown and yet inescapable proximity, promising unknown intimacies. The dyads of proximity, where the work of the good takes place, echo endless songs of love. This dyadic proximity where we do the work of the good, wounds us repeatedly, yet it contains, together with its endless sorrows, a singular joy, joys of love we have known and the promise of joys we may never have known, face to face with others' unknown and unknowable joy. The circulation of such proximity is what we know as nature's music, plenishment in the earth.

(8) brings us face to face with something obscure in the Western tradition, yet of profound importance to the good, incorporating death and blood. The work of the good, where we respond to endless responsibility, is from within and directed toward, material bodies. We work upon and work by means of bodies. And our bodies, in their work, work differently for men and women, who bear different relations to blood, and for human beings and animals, perhaps, or members of natural habitats, who bear different relations to death. Spirit, here, expresses no higher ethical or hu-

man truth, but represents exclusion. We achieve the highest goods we can, undertake our responsibilities for the deepest thought, under the good, in and through our bodies. In return, the materiality of our bodies is inexhaustible and excessive, filled with endless promises. The greatest works of humanity work through material bodies in proximity. The most destructive works of humanity work upon material bodies, face to face. We understand the general circulation of bodies in the earth as rapturous and rhapsodic.

The joy of plenishment in the earth is a sonant, ethical joy, where the general circulation of the good, everywhere, resounds in musical harmony and disharmony, but where the musicality circulates through the rhythms and percussions of bodies. The joy at plenishment in the earth is a great and wonderful joy, a bodily joy, filled with tensions, unknowns, displacements. We plenish the earth in our ethical regard, filled with mourning and resistance to injustice, haunted by endless injustices, especially our own, but still a joy, a love and kindness, singing the *Stabat Mater.* Plenishment works in a kindness inseparable from mourning, grief, memories of injustice. We mourn the death of something so precious that we cannot bear its loss, yet must remember and mourn and tenderly feel that loss as cherishment. Nothing can heal the scar, replace the loss. We mourn impossible losses impossibly, others' losses as well as our own. That, incredibly, is our joy in the good, plenishment in the earth. If we did not so mourn, we would never know this plenishment. Our joy lies in our capacity to mourn, to remember pain and sorrow. And to love.

NOTES

CHAPTER ONE. PRELUDE

1. Leading Irigaray to say, of women's resistance to a reason that has enslaved them:

> Turn everything upside down, inside out, back to front. *Rack it with radical convulsions,* carry back, reimport, those crises that her "body" suffers in her impotence to say what disturbs her. . . . *Overthrow syntax* by suspending its eternally teleological order, by snipping the wires, cutting the current, breaking the circuits, switching the connections, by modifying continuity, alternation, frequency, intensity. Make it impossible for a while to predict whence, whither, when, how, why . . . something goes by or goes on; will come, will spread, will reverse, will cease moving. (Irigaray, *ATS,* p. 142)

This is what she says, in a striking voice; but she speaks in other voices, as I do here, hoping to resist, at least to question, the hold of Western reason upon us, with its exclusions, without excluding reason from the good.

See n. 2.

2. Luce Irigaray, together with Hélène Cixous, Catherine Clément, Julia Kristeva, and Monique Wittig, compose the "New French Feminists." They repeatedly examine an ethical relation to the Western canon whose exploration is part of my undertaking here. Many of their works, those addressed here, are listed in the Bibliography. The reference here to the question of sexual difference is from Irigaray, *ESD* and *ÉDS,* the focus of attention in chap. 3.

What "sexual difference" means, in relation to gender, culture, and sex, I take to belong to the question of sexual difference. Or rather, that question expresses a certain hesitation within the question of sexual difference in which we dwell.

Note: All textual references are indicated by abbreviations listed in the Bibliography.

3. The question of sexual difference, the preferred form in European discourse of the question of gender, leaves open the relations between gender and sexual difference, sex, sexuality, and gender, and the extent of sexual difference. The question of sexual difference addresses heterogenous excess directly as the question of gender may not. I understand the question of sexual difference as the question of gender, and more. It includes the excesses of sexuality and desire.

4. See n. 2. I am referring to Kristeva's *SM* and *WT.*

5. Levinas speaks of looking into the face of the other as *le regard.* See n. 7.

6. See chap. 2, n. 11, for a discussion of general economy. See also chaps. 5 and 6 and thereafter.

7. The language of radical alterity, of "otherwise than being," echoes in Emmanuel Levinas, for whom the call of the good imposes endless responsibilities toward the other, face to face. This face-to-face responsibility expresses something of the concern expressed here for heterogeneity.

See Levinas, *OB.*

CHAPTER TWO. REST

1. In conjunction with a chorus of words in French that echo the music of ethical difference, where our bodies meet the earth—*entre* and *antre, intervalle, enveloppe.* Irigaray speaks in French of "*reste*": "Il y a toujours un *reste*" (Irigaray, *ÉDS,* p. 20). My overture to ethical difference comes by way of *reste,* reminding us of the heterogeneous remains of ethical difference.

2. "For that which can foresee by the exercise of mind is by nature intended to be lord and master, and that which can with its body give effect to such foresight is a subject, and by nature a slave" (Aristotle, *Politics,* 1252ab). The head rules, the body—represented by slaves, women, and animals—obeys. See chaps. 3 and 7 for an extended discussion of these matters.

3. The hope for a new ethics, or ethics|politics, has arisen against the historical exclusions of ethics and politics. For some it arises in the form of questioning. "I intend to show that when the question of ethics governs a discourse, certain types of suppression and pain can be perceived with a depth and range that is not possible in ethical thought" (Scott, *QE,* p. 3). This institutes an opening onto inclusion of paramount importance. Yet we may hesitate at reinstituting another ethical sovereignty, another "governance." To the contrary: "The 'question of ethics' indicates an interruption in an ethos, an interruption in which the definitive values that govern thought and everyday action lose their power and authority to provide immediate certainty in their functions" (Scott, *QE,*

p. 4). They lose this authority in resistance to the cut of traditional ethics, between good and bad, high and low.

4. I hesitantly speak of blood to call attention to the association of both race and gender to mixed blood and especially to women's repeated and multiple associations with blood, to the theme of blood in war and in internment camps, and to the relation of blood to AIDS and sexuality. This huge subject cannot be addressed here except in relation to the theme of kinds, women, racial, and animal kinds, expressing natural plenitude, divided by blood and bloodshed.

5. Discussed in chap. 8.

6. "Into those things from which existing things have their coming into being, their passing away, too, takes place, according to what must be; for they make reparation to one another for their injustice according to the ordinance of time, as he puts it in somewhat poetical language." (Simplicius, *Phys.*, 24, 18 [DK 12 B 1] as quoted and translated in Robinson, *EGP,* p. 34) I translate *tisis* as restitution.

Here I speak of injustice as sexual difference, passing from the suffering of women to memories of their oppression.

See my *IR*.

7. "We must, therefore, reconsider the whole question of our conception of place [*lieu*], . . . " (Irigaray, *ESD,* pp. 11–12). "I will never be in a man's place [*place*], never will a man be in mine. Whatever identifications are possible, one will never exactly occupy the place [*lieu*] of the other—they are irreducible one to the other" (Irigaray, *ESD,* p. 13).

8. "Sexual difference is one of the major philosophical issues, if not the issue, of our age" (Irigaray, *ESD,* p. 5). The translations pull back from the radical thought that sexual difference might mark our time in the deepest possible way. See chap. 3.

9. Or gendered, or something else, but we do not know with assurance the distinction between sexual difference and gender or between sexual, ethical, and "ontological" difference. We do know of desire.

10. Responding to Lévi-Strauss.

11. This difficult notion of a general economy reverberates in Bataille.

> The science of relating the object of thought to sovereign moments, in fact, is only a *general economy* which envisages the meaning of these objects in relation to each other and finally in relation to the loss of meaning. The question of this *general economy* is situated on the level of *political economy,* but the science designated by this name is only a restricted economy, . . . The *general economy,* in the first place, makes apparent that excesses of energy are produced, and that by definition, these excesses cannot be utilized. The excessive energy can only be lost without the slightest aim, consequently without any meaning. It is this

useless, senseless loss that *is* sovereignty" (Bataille, *MM,* p. 233, n. 1; quoted in Derrida, *FRGE,* p. 271).

A restricted economy is where work is done, under the authority of law. Yet goods circulate excessively, beyond the possibility of work, disturbing the law of authority. This excessive circulation of goods and judgments is the plenitude of nature. It is repeated in the endless circulation of women without which there could be no civilization.

See chap. 5.

12. I speak of Andrea Dworkin and Catharine MacKinnon. I remind you of the deaths of women, the countless rapes inflicted on women, by Russian soldiers on German women, by Serbian soldiers on Bosnian women, by Croation soldiers on Serbian women, all in the name of life.

MacKinnon asks how we can distinguish sexual intercourse from rape where the former is obligatory and violent. "If violation of the powerless is part of what is sexy about sex, as well as central in the meaning of male and female, the place of sexuality in gender and the place of gender in sexuality need to be looked at together" (MacKinnon, *FU,* p. 6). Our discussion turns on this place where sexuality means violation.

Yet even this sexuality is *jouissance et souffrance.* If we will not forget the *jouissance* of sexual difference, we must not forget the *souffrance.* One question of sexual difference asks what lies between joy and suffering, sexual love and violation. Another asks what memory of violation.

13. Peter Strawson rejects the possibility that a world of sound might establish a ground for individuality. He asks, "Could a being whose experience was purely auditory have a conceptual scheme which provided for objective particulars?" (Strawson, *I,* p. 58). His answer is that such an experience would not allow for the identification and reidentification of particulars. I respond, with the question of sexual difference echoing around us, by asking whether identities (and envelopes, as Irigaray speaks of them) and identifications are excessive, exceeding individuals heterogeneously. I take seriously the possibility that a world of sound may compose a general economy in which something exceeds every work, every identification, especially every individuality.

Strawson offers no recognition that the envelope of identity that enfolds us, women and other subjects, chokes our lives away. "But what," Irigaray asks, "if the 'object' started to speak?" (Irigaray, *SOW,* p. 135). What indeed of the envelopes of objects of our desires? What of other kinds of envelopes?

14. Where he says: "The unlimited responsibility in which I find myself comes from the hither side of my freedom, from a 'prior to every memory,' and 'ulterior to every accomplishment,' from the non-present

par excellence, the non-original, the anarchical, prior to or beyond essence" (Levinas, *OB,* p. 10). The otherwise is anarchic.

15. That is the point of the passage quoted from MacKinnon in n. 12, this chap. But it is stated with greater theoretical force by Wittig. See pp. 33–34. Also see chap. 1, n. 2.

16. This is the point of Butler's *GT.* See chap. 9.

17. But who have souls. One form of the question of ethical difference is whether others—men, women, animals, inanimate things—possess precious souls. At least two major Western philosophers, Leibniz and Whitehead, thought that nature was filled with souls. And Plato speaks of *psychē* everywhere: "All soul has care of all that is inanimate, and traverses the whole universe, though in ever-changing forms" (Plato, *Phaedrus,* 246b). The song of ethical difference sings of the rests of the earth as nature filled with souls, filled with precious beings with souls included in our responsibilities.

CHAPTER THREE. LULLABY

1. Burke's and Gill's translation is somewhat different:

> Sexual difference is one of the major philosophical issues, if not the issue, of our age. According to Heidegger, each age has one issue to think through, and one only. Sexual difference is probably the issue in our time which could be our "salvation" if we thought it through. (Irigaray, *ESD,* p. 5)

Seán Hand's translation is even more remote:

> Sexual difference is one of the important questions of our age, if not in fact the burning issue. According to Heidegger, each age is preoccupied with one thing, and one alone. Sexual difference is probably that issue in our own age which could be our salvation on an intellectual level. (Irigaray, *SD,* p. 165)

2. "But might there not perhaps be a more primarily granted revealing that could bring the saving power into its first shining-forth in the midst of the danger that in the technological age rather conceals than shows itself?" (Heidegger, *QT,* p. 315).

3. Irigaray speaks of Diotima's speech as *l'amour sorcier* (Irigaray, *ÉDS,* p. 27.

4. "The Goddess has at last stirred from sleep, and women are reawakening to our ancient power. The feminist movement, which began as a political, economic, and social struggle, is opening to a spiritual dimension. In the process, many women are discovering the old religion, reclaiming the word *witch* and, with it, some of our lost culture" (Starhawk, *WWC*).

I think here of feminist women as witches, even (pro)feminist men, to emphasize that women were the predominant target of witchburnings in the West, and that witches, and women, inhabit the edges of social order, places of disturbance in the West and elsewhere, live in non-Western places. I think of witches as intermediary figures.

We will return repeatedly to intermediary figures.

5. "The hand is infinitely different from all the grasping organs—paws, claws, or fangs—different by an abyss of essence. Only a being who can speak, that is, think, can have hands and can handily achieve works of handicraft" (Heidegger, *WCT,* p. 357). See chap. 7, pp. 155–63, for the rest of the quotation and an extended discussion of *Geschlecht,* of how gender in German excludes animals.

6. As Plato suggests in *Phaedrus,* discussed here in chap. 2, n. 17.

7. See chap. 4, n. 7, for the full quotation.

8. Except for some who repudiate ethics, speaking against its safety. Heidegger is not alone in a post-Nietzchean refusal of ethics by those who do not suffer oppression. Caputo says repeatedly in *Against Ethics,* "I am against ethics"; "I am also against originary ethics" (Caputo, *AE,* pp. 1, 2). Yet Feyerabend, whose title recalls Caputo's, does not say that he is "against science," but "against method," pursuing an anarchistic science (Feyerabend, *AM*). What of an anarchistic ethics, of an ethics that knows no safety? Is that not the revaluation of all values?

> Ethics makes safe. It throws a net of safety under the judgments we are forced to make, the daily, hourly decisions that make up the texture of our lives. Ethics lays the foundations for principles that force people to be good; it clarifies concepts, secures judgments, provides firm guardrails along the slippery slopes of factical life. It provides principles and criteria and adjudicates hard cases. Ethics is altogether wholesome, constructive work, which is why it enjoys a good name. (Caputo, *AE,* p. 4)

I pursue an ethics far from safety, an inclusive ethics filled with danger, guided by questions of sexual difference. W|e must not forget that those who disdain safety but who do not suffer oppression and misery have little to lose in giving up the safety of rules.

9. Lyotard speaks of Heidegger and "the jews," those who were forgotten while Jews were gassed.

> [H]ow could this thought (Heidegger's), a thought so devoted to remembering that a forgetting (of Being) takes place in all thought, in all art, in all "representation" of the world, how could it possibly have ignored the thought of "the jews," which, in a certain sense, thinks, tries to think, nothing but that very fact? How could this thought forget and ignore "the jews" to the point of suppressing and foreclosing to the very end the horrifying (and inane) attempt at exterminating, at making us forget

> forever what, in Europe, reminds us, ever since the beginning, that "there is" the Forgotten? (Lyotard, *HJ*, p. 4)

Perhaps Lyotard himself forgets Jews.

10. A thought of the origins of Western philosophy, from the beginning and after, in Plato and Aristotle, Spinoza and Hegel. The question of sexual difference demands a re-traversal of the course of European philosophy. Even so, Irigaray regards first philosophy, *protē philosophia,* as resistance to sexual difference, resistance to any event that might involve "the production of a new age of thought, art, poetry, and language" (Irigaray, *ESD,* p. 5). The question of ethical and sexual difference unfolds an event to be resisted. Perhaps this resistance is the thought of the event, which may be thought "only" as ethical and sexual difference. *This* thought of the event of sexual difference is *protē philosophia!*

I hope to think of first philosophy as ethical by refusing the thought of "only," of exclusion. I hope to think of first philosophy as sexed; I hesitate in thinking of it as Western.

11. Also see Heidegger, *OBCP.*

12. "If the matrix [*matrice*: womb] is extendable, it can figure as *the place of place* [*lieu du lieu*]" (Irigaray, *ESD,* p. 34). The *chōra,* the receptacle, from which all space derives, has no place. The place of place is no place even as the womb.

13. I am not now speaking of his sympathy for Nazism, but of a certain refusal of the good, for example, in *LH.* Even so, how can we forget Rektor Heidegger?

14. I refer here to Bernal, *BA,* and others for whom the idea that first philosophy is Greek is a colonial event. Which is not to deny that in the period Bernal emphasizes in this volume, that is, eighteenth-century Germany, it was indeed a colonial event.

15. Compare the discussion of the canon in chap. 5, pp. 91–93.

16. Derrida refers to *Schlag,* appearing repeatedly, in *Geschlecht,* in *alles wiederum geprägt:* all struck by the duality of the sexes, and in the curse that has struck humankind.

17. The "bestial," through which we move our thought from sexual to ethical difference, following *entre* to *antre,* echoes in Heidegger after Georg Trakl. For the second stanza of Trakl's poem, "Autumnal Soul," is as follows (quoted from *LP* in Heidegger, *OWL,* p. 170):

> Fish and game soon glide away.
> Soon blue soul and long dark journey
> Parted us from loved ones, others.
> Evening changes image, sense.

Heidegger's words, in Hertz's translation, connect *Geschlecht* and animals, humanity and sexual difference, with two blows.

> What curse has struck this humankind? The curse of the decomposing kind is that the old human kinship has been struck apart by discord among sexes, tribes and races. Each strives to escape from that discord into the unleashed turmoil of the always isolated and sheer wildness of the wild game. Not duality as such, the discord is the curse. (Heidegger, *LP,* p. 170)

As Derrida says, sexual difference is struck two blows (perhaps three), duality becomes discord, *polemos.* As Derrida strongly suggests, but does not say, sexual difference is struck the blow of the beast. This monstrosity in sexual difference gives rise, repeatedly, to other questions of our age, perhaps the one (other) question of our age that if thought might bring us to salvation. It too would be one question that embodies endless questions, as it would have to be to be the question of our age. I am speaking of questions of animal difference, of differences in race and kind, also bodily and spiritual difference, where the latter, spirit, echoes less as Spirit, certainly not German Spirit, and possibly not Human Spirit. I am speaking of questions of soul—there is no contemporary, secular equivalent. What of animal soul, animal spirit? For whom is this a question, who would ask it, and toward whom could it be directed?

Could questions of sexual difference be multiple questions (however repugnant) of whether women have souls, full souls, whether there is a Woman's Soul, and whether souls are heterogeneous? Irigaray asks, "[h]ow are we to give girls the possibility of spirit or soul?" (Irigaray, *CD,* p. 47). She answers that, "[t]oday, only a mother can see to it that her daughter, her daughters, form(s) a girl's identity" (Irigaray, *CD,* p. 50).

Analogously, could questions of ethical difference be questions of whether animals have souls, whether there is a Human, Animal, or Other Soul, whether souls are heterogeneous? How are we to give animals and other creatures the possibility of soul? Can we be their mothers? And what of souls in dead matter, souls everywhere?

We may remember that the question of soul, in nature, is both very early Greek (and Hebrew), and later, through the Middle Ages and Renaissance, and returns in modernity, in Spinoza and Leibniz, for example, later in Whitehead. Western naturalism, away from the side of nature owned by science, grants nature its plenitude of souls. Foucault speaks of this in his own way in *OT.* The prose of the world sings the inexhaustible plenitude of souls and meanings in nature.

18. Discussed at greater length in chaps. 7 and 9.

19. The same theme is repeated and extended later, where she asks, "[s]o long as men claim to say everything and define everything, how can anyone know what the language of the male sex might be?" (Irigaray, *Q,* p. 128). This "everything," regarded as male, objective, truthful, is di-

vided by ethical and sexual difference. "Objectivity" is an invention to obscure ethical and sexual difference as indifference.

20. "Ce qui s'inverse dans la différence sexuelle ?" (Irigaray, *ÉDS,* p. 15); translated as "Which would be inverted in sexual difference?" (*ESD,* p. 7).

21. In *DL,* Krell speaks of "air," reading Irigaray's *OA,* restoring the elemental and bodily, the living, to the elevated height of Spirit. "What compels Irigaray is the thought of an *element* or a *material* in *physis,* which Heidegger thinks as upsurgence in presencing, and as domain, scope, or dimension" (Krell, *DL,* p. 309). Krell understands this incredible thought of another intermediary figure, the infinite breath of song, as the upsurgence of daimon life. "Being needs and uses the herring too, and not just for pickling" (Krell, *DL,* p. 316); "It would be worth our bestirring ourselves to recount something of their [daimon life] history. In another terrain, in other waters, breathing another air" (Krell, *DL,* p. 317). Yet he follows up with another quote, from Chief Seattle's letter in 1852: "The President in Washington sends word that he wishes to buy our land. But how can you buy or sell the sky? The land? The idea is strange to us. If we do not own the freshness of the air and the sparkle of the water, how can you buy them?" (Krell, *DL,* p. 317). The sky, the land, the air, the freshness, the sparkle, the water. Nature's plenishment.

What matter if this letter is feigned if it plenishes the earth?

22. The point of this difficult chapter is to show that the question of sexual difference evokes the most far-reaching and primordial questions of philosophy. There can be no philosophic thought without a deep thought of sexual difference, which opens onto fundamental questions of space and time, heaven and earth, embodiment, being, and the good.

23. *WT* was published in 1979, *ÉDS* in 1984.

24. She translates the passage from *Timaeus* 52, translated again into English, as "Indefinitely a place; it cannot be destroyed, but provides a ground for all that can come into being; itself being perceptible, outside of all sensation, by means of a sort of bastard reasoning; barely assuming credibility, it is precisely that which makes us dream when we perceive it, and affirm that all that exists must be somewhere, in a determined place . . . " (Kristeva, *WT,* p. 211).

A more conventional English translation of the same passage is: "which is space and is eternal, and admits not of destruction and provides a home for all created things, and is apprehended, when all sense is absent, by a kind of spurious reason, and is hardly real—which we, beholding as in a dream, say of all existence that it must of necessity be in some place and occupy a space, but that what is neither in heaven nor in earth has no existence."

I add two considerations, one the first appearance in *Timaeus* of the *chōra,* "the receptacle, and in a manner the nurse, of all generation" (Plato, *Timaeus,* 49b), the other Whitehead's interpretation of the receptacle. He speaks of "two metaphysical assumptions" in relation to the contemporary world (Whitehead, *PR,* p. 65):

> (i) That the actual world, in so far as it is a community of entities which are settled, actual, and already become, conditions and limits the potentiality for creativeness beyond itself. (Whitehead, *PR,* p. 65)
>
> (ii) The second metaphysical assumption is that the real potentialities relative to all standpoints are coordinated as diverse determinations of one extensive continuum. This extensive continuum is one relational complex in which all potential objectifications find their niche. It underlies the whole world, past, present, and future. . . . This extensive continuum expresses the solidarity of all possible standpoints throughout the whole process of the world. It is not a fact prior to the world; it is the first determination of order—that is, of real potentiality—arising out of the general character of the world. In its full generality beyond the present epoch, it does not involve shapes, dimensions, or measurability; these are additional determinations of real potentiality arising from our cosmic epoch. (Whitehead, *PR,* 66)

We observe two things, first that the receptacle, the place of all things together, is beyond measure. The place of place is for all things together, beyond measure. Second, this "beyond measure" is before sexual difference, though in Plato it is the "nurse, of all generation." There is no sexuality in *Process and Reality,* no male and female principles, no gender. But there is constant generation, engendering, Creativity. The home of all generation is the receptacle. The place of place is . . . the *hystera?*

I wonder if sexual difference silently echoes in Whitehead, as always, twice: as the place of generation, the mother that gives birth to all generation (female), and as sexual in-difference (male). Sexual difference, in Western metaphysics at its best, never appears as male and female, equal and together, but distorted twice in its origins, as the female principle before all becoming, and as her overcoming into indifferent time. With one important qualification in Whitehead: generation incessantly continues. If the generative principle is female, the world continues to be female, a Creativity (together) of inexhaustibly multiple things that are in place, and no place, and everywhere.

25. Continuing:

> these two types of temporality (cyclical and monumental) are traditionally linked to female subjectivity in so far as the latter is thought of as necessarily maternal. . . . (Kristeva, *WT,* p. 192)
>
> In return, female subjectivity [*le féminin*] . . . becomes a problem with respect to a certain conception of time: time as project, teleology, linear

> and prospective unfolding: . . . in other words, the time of history." (Kristeva, *WT,* p. 192)

26. See chap. 2, n. 15.

27. This essay presents another thought of the question of sexual difference that I find important to pursue as far as possible.

> What is woman? Panic, general alarm for an active defense. Frankly, it is a problem that the lesbians do not have because of a change of perspective, and it would be incorrect to say that lesbians associate, make love, live with women, for "woman" has meaning only in heterosexual systems of thought and heterosexual economic systems. Lesbians are not women. (Wittig, *SM,* p. 32)

W|e may doubt that lesbians escape the hold of heterosexual systems of thought, when so many inhabit heterosexual society, and so many are forced to work in it to survive. Perhaps the amazons of the island of *Lesbos* do so. But we must think, as hard as we can, of the possibility that lesbians are not "women." And we must think that thought without assuming that male homosexuals are not "men." Categories of oppression are not symmetric, even when complementary. That is the point of the "political" in the concept of opposition.

28. Spinoza follows the most infamous side of Aristotle, agreeing that authority's rule is by nature, that some kinds are by nature inferior to other kinds.

> Hence we see that is the nature and office of a slave; he who is by nature not his own but another's man, is by nature a slave; and he may be said to be another's man who, being a human being, is also a possession. (Aristotle, *Politics,* 1254a)

> Where then there is such a difference as that between soul and body, or between men and animals . . . the lower sort are by nature slaves, and it is better for them as for all inferiors that they should be under the rule of a master. (Aristotle, *Politics,* 1254b)

When Aristotle speaks of the rule of wisdom, he may not speak in such a contaminated voice. "[F]or the wise man must not be ordered but must order, and he must not obey another, but the less wise must obey [*peithesthai*] *him*" (Aristotle, *Metaphysics,* 982a), not at least where Peitho is the goddess of persuasion. See my *IR,* chap. 9.

29. I have discussed this in detail elsewhere. (See my *IR.*) The discussion here is an attempt to take questions of ethical and sexual difference into the ordinance of time.

30. "The good which every one who follows after virtue seeks for himself he will desire for other men; and his desire on their behalf will be greater in proportion as he has a greater knowledge of God" (Spinoza, *E,* Part 4, Prop. 37).

Also: "Nothing, therefore, can agree better with the nature of any object than other individuals of the same kind, and so there is nothing more profitable to man for the preservation of his being and the enjoyment of a rational life than a man who is guided by reason" (Spinoza, *E,* Part 4, Appendix, 9).

31. Spinoza appeals here to one of his most remarkable insights, that "The emotion of one person differs from the corresponding emotion of another as much as the essence of the one person differs from that of another" (Spinoza, *E,* Part 3, Prop. 57), to conclude that "Hence it follows that the feelings of animals which are called irrational (for after we have learned the origin of the mind we can in no way doubt that brutes feel) differ from human emotions as much as the nature of a brute differs from that of a man" (Spinoza, *E,* Part 3, Prop. 57, Note). Difference becomes a mark of authority, rule, and death. Yet how much does the nature of an animal differ from that of human beings? And how much does the nature of a woman differ from that of men?

He carries the difference between humans and animals to the most abominable conclusion.

> Except man, we know no individual thing in Nature in whose mind we can take pleasure, nor anything which we can unite with ourselves by friendship or any kind of intercourse, and therefore regard to our own profit does not demand that we should preserve anything which exists in nature except men, but teaches us to preserve it or destroy it in accordance with its varied uses, or to adapt it to our own service in any way whatever. (Spinoza, *E,* Part 4, Appendix, 26)

Anything but human beings may be used in any way whatever! And this despite the fact that every thing strives from within itself to persevere in its being as much as any other (Spinoza, *E,* Part 3, Prop. 4).

Could this be the extreme possibility in any ethic of exclusion, that anything whatever different from "ourselves" (whoever "w|e" may be) may ethically be used by us in any way whatever, if we do not cherish inclusion?

32. "The highest effort of the mind and its highest virtue is to understand things by the third kind of knowledge" (Spinoza, *E,* Part 5, Prop. 25).

33. "The intellectual love of God which arises from the third kind of knowledge is eternal" (Spinoza, *E,* Part 5, Prop. 33).

34. "Everything which the mind understands under the form of eternity, it understands not because it conceives the present actual existence of the body, but because it conceives the essence of the body under the form of eternity" (Spinoza, *E,* Part 5, Prop. 29).

35. "He who possesses a body fit for many things possesses a mind of which the greater part is eternal" (Spinoza, *E,* Part 5, Prop. 39). Yet infants and children possess "a body fit for very few things" (Note).

36. Irigaray speaks of ethical difference as a crossing, *à travers de,* inaudible in translation.

37. See pp. 11–12 and 91–93.

38. Irigaray, *ESD,* p. 7; see also pp. 30–31, this chapter.

39. Although "Who or what the other is, I never know" (Irigaray, *ESD,* p. 13).

40. This oblique reference leads to another marginal place inhabited by music. Sacks describes Dr P., who cannot recognize ordinary objects, who makes his way through life musically rather than visually. Sacks describes his pathology as "a profound visual agnosia, in which all powers of representation and imagery, all sense of the concrete, all sense of reality, were being destroyed" (Sacks, *MMWH,* p. 17). Concrete work is done to music.

> I often wondered about how he apprehended the world, given his strange loss of image, visuality, and the perfect preservation of a great musicality. I think that music, for him, had taken the place of image. He had no body-image, he had body-music: this is why he could move and act as fluently as he did, but came to a total confused stop if the "inner music" stopped. (Sacks, *MMWH,* p. 18)

We think of such displacement as dementia. Sacks offers us the possibility of understanding such displacement as the growth of other powers. See also Selfe, *Nadia,* and Curtiss, *Genie.* We wish to return to first philosophy, from the music of ethical|sexual difference, as envisaging (or musically listening to) inexhaustible unheard and heterogeneous powers.

41. Irigaray calls it a "trinity," but we have seen that it reverberates beyond any measure.

42. This may be a place for me to say that to read ethical and sexual difference as the displacement in the place of place, resisting the hold of place upon us, cutting us off from other places, is not to resist the call of place upon us, the call of places in the earth where we find ourselves. I mean to speak of feminist and other bioregionalisms, where we define our places in intimate relations to the earth. Yet the most loving, intimate relation to the earth is multiple displacement. The most precious place of rest is one of *reste,* with earthly remainders reaching different places in the earth. No place has irresistible limits. To be somewhere is to touch the lips of others, in other places, lips and other biological places.

More to the point, perhaps, sustainable development and respect for nature do not close nature's limits upon themselves, but represent awe in the face of nature's plenitude, the riches and excesses of every place. I speak of this awe as plenishment.

See Meyer, *LL,* and Plant, *GB.*

43. *Bordée:* another place–limit word.

44. And as animals continue their *dérangement.*

45. See n. 17, this chap.

46. "Le maternel–féminin demeure le *lieu séparé de «son» lieu,* privé de «son» lieu" (Irigaray, *ÉDS,* p. 18). Burke's and Gill's translation gives us "the *place separated from "its"* own place, deprived of "its" place" (Irigaray, *ESD,* p. 10). I prefer to read the "*«son»*" as somewhere between (*entre*) his, hers, and its, a figure of sexual difference. I also, in an extreme crossing of languages, wonder about the "son" of the maternal–feminine: the father, the mother (under the sign of the father, and the son, even the Holy Ghost).

47. The word *propre,* in French, rings throughout worlds only dimly echoed in English. See my discussions in *RR* and *IR*. I take up *le propre* here in the place of place.

48. Derrida speaks of ornamentation and the frame as the "parergon," as the at-the-very-limit-of-the-work (Derrida, "Parergon," in *TP*). Here, the very-limit-of-work is woman.

49. I read Derrida as showing us the envelope in every piece of work.

50. But see how this erotic truth of heterogeneity undergoes contamination, discussed in chap. 9, pp. 200–202.

51. " . . . l'homme entouré-enfermé dans l'horizon de son monde de travail."

52. How can we doubt that today—if not today especially, if we think of AIDS, of Ceaușescu's family policy, of the struggles over abortion, of Serbian soldiers raping Muslim women and killing Muslim men and women—that the universality of the law of sex remains firmly in place, ravaging every political *régime*. When we think of limit experiences where violence brings us to certain spheres of human bodies, we must think of the suffering of women as the carnal *reste* of all other violences. And we must think as well of exclusion by blood, carried to extremes, shedding blood.

53. These allusions to morning and dawn remind us of Heidegger and Nietzsche, profeminists both.

54. Foucault's reading of difference here alludes to Deleuze (especially *DR* and *LS*), but pertains so clearly to our discussion that I include it in relation to Heidegger. The question before us, the question I take from Irigaray, with difference everywhere undermining the domination of identity, escaping the law of the Same, is how profoundly this difference is sexual, difference in kind. The question we may ask Irigaray, once we have an answer to the first question, once we understand the domination of identity to lead directly to sexual difference, is where we may stop the movement. We must not, absolutely must not, dissolve sexual difference into difference in general. Heidegger tells us that dif-ference is not differ-

ence in general. If we must not dissolve sexual difference into difference in general, what then of other differences? Foucault's answer leads away from many, perhaps countable and measurable, differences to univocity. Our discussion of difference turns on its univocity. That is where we come to music. We listen to the music of the *Stabat Mater* and *Carnaval des Animaux*.

55. See Tannen, *YJDU*. And see this chap., pp. 22–23, in relation to animals. The force of this question is diminished very little by empirical evidence concerning men and women, even as we may and should pay close attention to such evidence. The question is of heterogeneity, exemplified by the number two. The number two, as Heidegger indicates, expresses heterogeneity. But the number two is displaced by heterogeneity, to three, or four, or more. This double heterogeneous displacement gives rise to an ethic—many heterogeneous ethics—I have called ethical difference. It should be clear by now why ethical difference is not an ethics of difference, where difference loses hold on the profusion of heterogeneity.

CHAPTER FOUR. REST

1. "Le corps qui m'a servi de lieu, où j'ai pu me tenir enveloppé(e), je le recherche à travers x corps, à travers la nature, à travers le Dieu [The body that served me as place, where I was able to envelope myself (man or woman), I seek to cross x bodies, to cross nature, to cross God]" (Irigaray, *ÉDS*, p. 41).

2. Which is not to deny that where they are, in their (improper) place, they and their places may be precious. A proper place excludes. Feminist bioregionalism speaks of the cherishment of place. I add that wherever we are is an intermediary figure.

3. At this point, I let myself speak freely in English of *reste*, speak of rest, in restitution.

4. However obscurely, this theme of economy, joining circulation and exchange, brings us to ecofeminism, bioregionalism, and gift economies. See chapter 5. Also see Plant, *HW;* and Hyde, *G.*

5. "Le maternel–féminin demeure le *lieu séparé de «son» lieu,* privé de «son» lieu" (Irigaray, *ÉDS,* p. 18). Does the woman remain separated from "her" place, or "his" place, even "its" place (see chap. 3, n. 46), and which of these places is properly human?

6. "I do deny that, on this account, it is unlawful for us to consult our own profit by using them [animals] for our own pleasure and treating them as is most convenient for us, inasmuch as they do not agree in nature with us, and their feelings are different from our emotions" (Spinoza, *E,* Prop. 37, Note).

7. Described by Plato as

> halfway between mortal and immortal. . . . A very powerful spirit, Socrates, and spirits, you know, are halfway between god and man. . . . They are the envoys and interpreters that ply between heaven and earth . . . . They form the medium of the prophetic arts, of the priestly rites of sacrifice, initiation, and incantation, of divination and of sorcery. . . . There are many spirits, and many kings of spirits, too, and Love is one of them. (Plato, *Symposium,* 202e–203)

8. See my *IR,* chap. 9, and Derrida, *PP:* "the *pharmakon* brings together all at once, in its strangeness, . . . *pharmakeia* as medicine, drug, madness, remedy, poison, potion, agent, dye, pigment, color; *pharmakos* as sacrifice, scapegoat; *pharmakeus* as wizard" (*IJ,* p. 223).

9. " . . . se retourne du dedans au dehors" (Irigaray, *ÉDS,* p. 85).

10.

> by *natura naturans* we are to understand that which is in itself and is conceived through itself, . . . that is to say God in so far as He is considered as a free cause. But by *natura naturata* I understand everything which follows from the necessity of the nature of God or of any one of God's attributes, that is to say, all the modes of God's attributes in so far as they are considered as things which are in God, and which without God can neither be nor can be conceived. (Spinoza, *E,* Part 1, Prop. 29, Note)

11. Whitehead says something similar of place, the place of every individual thing, not just God.

> Every actual entity in its relationship to other actual entities is in this sense somewhere in the continuum, and arises out of the data provided by this standpoint. But in another sense it is everywhere throughout the continuum; . . . Thus the continuum is present in each actual entity, and each actual entity pervades the continuum. (Whitehead, *PR,* p. 67; See also chap. 3, n. 24.)

We may hear "everywhere," as Irigaray hears God's "in itself," as a place, a proper place. The universe here would be the proper place for being, for man and God (but not for woman, who is no place). Such emplacements would silence Creativity.

> "Creativity" is the principle of *novelty.* An actual occasion [an event] is a novel entity diverse from any entity in the "many" which it unifies. Thus "creativity" introduces novelty into the content of the many, which are the universe disjunctively. The "creative advance" is the application of this ultimate principle of creativity to each novel situation which it originates. (Whitehead, *PR,* p. 21)

The universe is a many, a confused, blooming, buzzing many, unified here and there, various somewheres, but always everywhere as well. The universe is filled with events, doing their work, working out their identities, together, in various places, everywhere together, disjunctively and creatively. Creativity entails that each event is novel, different. The universe is an infinite succession of novel events infinitely repeating each other. The Law of the Same in Whitehead is the circulation of endless creation. Every entity, every being or event, is somewhere, but to be somewhere is to be everywhere, where everywhere is always somewhere else, in novelty and creativity. The plenitude of the universe, of being, makes every place another place, every somewhere somewhere else. Every place is other places, inexhaustibly. Every place is a place of rest.

Moreover, every place is an ethical place, of good and evil. "The nature of evil is that the characters of things are mutually obstructive. Thus the depths of life require a process of selection. . . . Selection is at once the measure of evil, and the process of its evasion" (Whitehead, *PR*, p. 340). The here and there of creativity give rise to ideals everywhere together with obstructions. Heterogeneity inhabits ideality and obstruction, good and evil, everywhere. The sense of the good everywhere is cherishment, a sense of the preciousness of things circulating everywhere, the endless call of the good. The sense of obstruction is sacrifice (a profoundly contaminated term), injustice and restitution, the work of the good in time, filled with endless losses, mourning, and destruction, of ourselves and others. Cherishment and sacrifice haunt every place in nature and experience as plenishment, responsibility for fulfilling the impossible task of the good. The song of their nearness, at rest, is ethical difference. We seek in ethical difference to plenish the earth in sorrow and joy. Plenishment, born of cherishment, instituted by our responsibility, supposes that all the others know something of their good, know something that we will never know. The good belongs to others.

12. Not unlike Foucault's view of power.

> Power is everywhere; not because it embraces everything, but because it comes from everywhere. (Foucault, *HS*, p. 93)
>
> —Power is not something that is acquired, seized, or shared . . .
>
> —Relations of power are not in a position of exteriority with respect to other types of relationships . . . but are immanent in the latter . . .
>
> —Power comes from below . . .
>
> —Power relations are both intentional and nonsubjective. (Foucault, *HS*, pp. 94–95)

See chap. 5, pp. 85–88.

13.

> 38. Some feel more grief over damages inflicted upon an animal than over those inflicted upon a human. This is because the animal is

> deprived of the possibility of bearing witness according to the human rules for establishing damages, and as a consequence, every damage is like a wrong and turns it into a victim *ipso facto*. . . . That is why the animal is a paradigm of the victim. (Lyotard, *DPD*, p. 28)

What is so important about bearing witness when we suppose that animals know their *jouissance*, know joy?

See chap. 7.

14. See chap. 1, n. 2.

15.

Die schmerzenreiche Mutter	La mère douloureuse se tenait
stand weinend am Kreuz,	en pleurs près de la croix
an welchem ihr Sohn hing. . . .	sur laquelle pendait son fils. . . .

(Text and translations of Antonio Vivaldi *Stabat Meter*, L'Oiseau-Lyre CD #414329.)

16. We may find the trace of ethical difference in Levinas: "The illeity in the beyond-being is the fact that its coming toward me is a departure which lets me accomplish a movement toward a neighbor [*le prochain*]. . . . Or, one may say, it is the fact that the others [*les autres*] show themselves in their face [*visage*]" (Levinas, *OB*, p. 13). Yet animals live as neighbors with human beings, sometimes more face to face than lovers. Responsibility face to face with the: "immemorial, unrepresentable, invisible" (Levinas, *OB*, p. 11); with "a passivity more passive than all passivity" (Levinas, *OB*, p. 14); in "a nudity more naked than all destitution" (Levinas, *OB*, p. 49); "a self uncovered, exposed and suffering in its skin" (Levinas, *OB*, p. 51); "vulnerability, enjoyment and suffering" [*jouissance et souffrance*] (Levinas, *OB*, p. 63). In the proximity, passivity, wounding, and obsession, there is *jouissance*. I wonder if passivity, nudity, vulnerability is rest, *jouissance* and *souffrance* in surplus, remaining, what remains, in rest. And what remains, for human beings, but nature, animals, insects, the rests of the earth? Could the hope of our ethic, of ethical difference, lie in our responsibility for the most Other *jouissances?* I profoundly hope to transmute *souffrance* into *douleur*, a sadness at inescapable sacrifice, never forgetting its injustice.

Ethics, in Levinas, against all the testimony of sexual–ethical difference, remains in proximity to reciprocity even as there is no reciprocity: substitution, equality, mutuality—"substitution as the very subjectivity of a subject, interruption of the irreversible identity of the essence" (Levinas, *OB*, p. 13). We may hear this "very subjectivity" as a reversal, in its irreversibility. Or, as many have hoped, we may hear the responsibility for the other to open up to another otherwise beyond subjectivity, beyond subjectivity in rest, to "All the others that obsess me in the other . . . " (Levinas, *OB*, p. 159). *Jouissance et souffrance. Jouissance et douleur.*

CHAPTER FIVE. CANON

1. Levinas speaks of "maternity" in relation to vulnerability, exposure, and persecution. "Maternity, which is bearing par excellence, bears even responsibility for the persecuting by the persecutor" (Levinas, *OB*, p. 75). Irigaray speaks of the maternal–feminine, in a very different voice.

2. Echoing in chap. 9, and more.

3. I postpone this difficult thought to chap. 11.

4. Again, see chap. 11.

5. We have seen that in "*Geschlecht* II," Derrida describes two blows that strike sexual difference through Heidegger's reading of *Geschlecht* in Trakl, one the *Schlag* within, the other "a *second blow* that comes to strike the sexual difference and to transform it into dissension, war, savage opposition. The primordial sexual difference is tender, gentle, peaceful; when that difference is struck down by a 'curse'" (Derrida, *G2*, p. 187; see chap. 3 here, p. 28). Sexual difference moves through the number two repeatedly from peace to war. Do we find that when we think of two we are led to *polemos?* Is our only hope of peace in All?

6. See my *IR*. The movement here is from injustice to restitution through the indefinite dyad. This archaic injustice does not belong to an oppositional dyad, knows nothing of justice. But still, work is done dyadically.

7. Derrida says this almost verbatim.

> Therefore, the "relation to the Being of the existent" cannot possibly dominate the "relation to the existent." Heidegger not only would criticize the notion of a *relation* to Being, just as Levinas criticizes that of a *relation to the other,* but also the notion of *domination*. Being is not elevated, is not the land of the existent, for elevation belongs to the existent. There are few themes which have demanded Heidegger's insistence to this extent: Being is not an excellent existent. (Derrida, *VM*, p. 138)
>
> Thus, the thought of Being could not possibly occur as ethical violence. On the contrary, without it one would be forbidden to let be the existent, and one would enclose transcendence within identification and empirical economy. (Derrida, *VM*, p. 142)

For us here, through ethical difference, nothing can escape ethical violence, nothing, nothing. That violence is immemorial injustice. Without this nothing that can escape, heterogeneity vanishes, reduced to . . . what? Being? Otherwise? Sexual difference inhabits the space of ethical violence even as we seek love.

8. See p. 54 for the full quotation.

9. See chap. 2, n. 11. Bataille follows the passage quoted there with the words, "En quoi le *souverain* comme le *solide* est une expérience

inévitable et constante [In which sovereignty like solidity is an inevitable and constant experience].” He opens *MM* with the words, “Mon ambition—dans les pages suivantes—est la plus lointaine que l’on ait eue [My ambition—in the following pages—is to go further than anyone has been]” (Bataille, *MM*, p. 211). And he opens the section in which the footnote appears, *Position Décisive*, with the words, “Si je le veux, *rire* est penser, mais c’est un moment souverain [If I wish it, *to laugh* is to think, but it is a sovereign moment]” (Bataille, *MM*, p. 230).

> Revenant sur une attitude (affirmée depuis longtemps), j’en dirai maintenant :
> —que je n’ai pas reçu (accepté) un monde subordonné qui me voulait moi-même subordonné . . .
> —mais tout cela d’autorité. (Bataille, *MM*, p. 231)

All that of authority, unquoted by Derrida, going further than anyone has gone, laughing at solidity’s sovereign authority.

10. Derrida denies both terms of this relation, in a certain way. “Insofar as it is a scientific form of writing, general economy is certainly not sovereignty itself. Moreover, there is no sovereignty *itself*. Sovereignty dissolves the values of meaning, truth and a *grasp-of-the-thing-itself*” (Derrida, *FRGE*, p. 270).

I have discussed “sovereignty itself” as authority, in relation to an immemorial injustice, before sovereignty and law. (See my *IR*.)

11. For the moment, we are face to face with number, measure, in particular the dyad of binariness and of gender before we face the canonicity of measure, the circulation of goods. We have seen that the language of irreducible alterity, of love as well as subjection, imposes a dyadic measure, however profuse and indefinite. Even as Levinas resists calculation and measure, as he resists reciprocity, he speaks in dyads: being and otherwise; the said and saying; most of all, I and the other, the one regarding the other. Responsibility for the other works as a dyad. We have felt its cut in a substitution that, while refusing reciprocity, repeats the sharpest edge of reciprocation. “Substitution is signification. Not a reference from one term to another, as it appears thematized in the said, but substitution as the very subjectivity of a subject, interruption of the irreversible identity of the essence” (Levinas, *OB*, p. 13). Irreducible alterity appears in a shared identity, a shared envelope, of subjectivity, between a pair of subjects, framed by substitution. A pair of subjects, two, divides the universe into another dyad, subjectivity and . . . : One subject and another; I and my neighbor.

A place in Levinas opens where this dyad falls apart, interrupted, a place where it breaks away from number to somewhere else, to a place without number, a place where place breaks down. "All the others that obsess me in the other do not affect me as examples of the same genus united with my neighbor by resemblance or common nature. . . . The others concern me from the first" (Levinas, *OB,* p. 159). From the beginning, in every dyad, in proximity with my neighbor, in every such face to face, all the others (univocally) obsess me, sing the rests of the earth without categories of resemblance or nature, without genus or kind. This "all the others," goes beyond the other in a way that even otherwise than being cannot say, than anything can say. This obsession is a responsibility for all the others, in plenishment and profusion, a responsibility to the other that breaks down the limits of the other's dyadic relation to my limits. I fall into the world, where all the others rest together, in general economy.

Even so, this movement in Levinas from the other to all the others, in obsession and with extraordinary responsibilities, an ethics that transports us from the one to the others, destroying any dyadic hold, occurs in virtue of a third, as if we move from ethics to politics, the good to law. "In the proximity of the other, all the others than the other obsess me, and already this obsession cries out for justice, demands measure and knowing in consciousness" (Levinas, *OB,* p. 158). The good, once it has broken the dyad, demands measure. It gives up two to subject itself to law. How can we doubt that this movement follows Hegel, with the proviso that the two is not master–slave, but responsibility and obsession? But still the number two obsesses us, when we are surrounded by countless others.

> In no way is justice a degradation of obsession, a degeneration of the for-the-other, a diminution, a limitation of anarchic responsibility, a neutralization of the glory of the Infinite, a degeneration that would be produced in the measure that for empirical reasons the initial duo would become a trio. But the contemporaneousness of the multiple is tied about the diachrony of two: justice remains justice only, in a society where there is no distinction between those close and those far off, but in which there also remains the impossibility of passing by the closest. (Levinas, *OB,* p. 159)

12. That is, in another place, demanding intermediaries.

13. As against "the gift" of language, Heidegger's *Geschlecht.* See pp. 155–63.

14. Lévi-Strauss, *ESK,* p. 36.

15. I reserve my return to "the randomness (?) of the animal kingdom" to chap. 7, with my own question marks [???].

16. Such an idea represents the intersection of exchange with gift economies, reminding us again of "the gift of the gods." Hyde speaks of a gift as "a thing we do not get by our own efforts. We cannot buy it; we

cannot acquire it through an act of will. It is bestowed upon us" (Hyde, *G*, p. xi). In gift economy, "whatever we have been given is supposed to be given away again, not kept. Or, if it is kept, something of similar value should move on in its stead. . . . The only essential is this: *the gift must always move*. There are other forms of property that stand still, that mark a boundary or resist momentum, but the gift keeps going" (Hyde, *G*, p. 4). Hyde also speaks of works of art as existing "simultaneously in two 'economies,' a market economy and a gift economy" (Hyde, *G*, p. xi). See also Mauss, *G*, and Cheal, *GE*.

To cherish everything in the earth as if each were precious as a work of art is to place it in gift economy, endlessly in circulation, endlessly placing and displacing it among the others, in general economy. Here works of art and everything else belong to restricted and general economy. Every place is elsewhere, circulates from here to there and elsewhere. We cannot stop the circulation even as we always make the effort.

Even so, a gift economy cannot serve the economy of gender, for we, men and women, do not own women to exchange or to give them away. To the contrary. With this thought, we see that even gift economy is a restricted economy.

17. And I say it between (*aentre*) Irigaray and Lévi-Strauss.

18. See chap. 3, pp. 54–55.

19. Foucault speaks of this displacement in relation to Bataille. "The limit and transgression depend on each other for whatever density of being they possess: a limit could not exist if it were absolutely uncrossable and, reciprocally, transgression would be pointless if it merely crossed a limit composed of illusions and shadows" (Foucault, *PT*, p. 34).

Irigaray speaks of thresholds. See chap. 3, pp. 53–54.

20. Including Ethiopia and Somalia.

21. It is not without interest that it is expressed in relation to sexuality.

22. That is the question of my *IR*.

Foucault contrasts power with Power in two more detailed ways. Specifically contrasted with power in general circulation, Power works negatively.

> These are some of its principal features:
> —*The negative relation*. It never establishes any connection between power and sex that is not negative: rejection, exclusion, refusal, blockage, concealment, or mask. . . .
> —*The insistence of the rule*. Power is essentially what dictates its law to sex. Which means first of all that sex is placed by power in a binary system: licit and illicit, permitted and forbidden. . . .

> —*The cycle of prohibition:* thou shalt not go near, thou shalt not touch, thou shalt not consume, thou shalt not experience pleasure, thou shalt not speak, thou shalt not show thyself; ultimately thou shalt not exist, except in darkness and secrecy. . . .
> —*The logic of censorship:* . . .
> —*The uniformity of the apparatus* . . . (Foucault, *HS,* pp. 84–85)

Exclusion, blockage, negation, rule, prohibition, logic, and uniformity represent the work of exchange economies, where law is ruled by the Same. We may think of exchange and substitutive economies as productive of the same relations as Power, masking its coerciveness. In this sense, our ethical agenda turns on viewing the movement from Power to general economy as an ethical|political movement. With one exception.

For sovereignty, power, and authority all belong to general economy. The power everywhere belongs to general, not restricted economy because it cancels equivalence repeatedly and at every level, cancels the hold of authority as it circulates it ever more widely. Replacing the five moments of Power's economy above are five very different moments of power, composing its general economy.

> —Power is not something that is acquired, seized, or shared, something that one holds on to or allows to slip away; power is exercised from innumerable points, in the interplay of nonegalitarian and mobile relations.
> —Relations of power are not in a position of exteriority with respect to other types of relationships (economic processes, knowledge relationships, sexual relations), but are immanent in the latter; they are the immediate effects of the divisions, inequalities, and disequilibriums which occur in the latter, and conversely, they are the internal conditions of these differentiations. . . .
> —Power comes from below; that is, there is no binary and all-encompassing opposition between rulers and ruled at the root of power relations, and serving as a general matrix. . . .
> —Power relations are both intentional and nonsubjective. If in fact they are intelligible, this is not because they are the effect of another instance that "explains" them, but rather because they are imbued, through and through, with calculation: there is no power that is exercised without a series of aims and objectives. But this does not mean that it results from the choice or decision of an individual subject. . . .
> —Where there is power, there is resistance, and yet, or rather consequently, this resistance is never in a position of exteriority with respect to power. . . . (Foucault, *HS,* pp. 94–95)

In the general economy of power, power cannot be held, slips away into innumerable points, yet is immanent, inseparable. One is never "outside" power. Power comes from below, occupies strategies, constellations, stabilizes in patterns of design, yet lies within no individual subject's control. In all these ways, power exceeds any hold that might be taken on it. In the same way, the will to power, in Nietzsche, like the will to truth, exceeds, escapes from, evades any hold that truth might be able to take on power. All of these excesses, joined with the constellations and strategies, indicate that power composes a general economy of excess, but does enormous work, makes an enormous difference. It does so through strategies and structures, but possesses no form itself. This is close to what Bataille means by general economy and its relation to sovereignty—authority and power—except that he denies its work.

But there is also resistance, and in this way power gives itself over to general economy and brings sovereignty to its cancellation.

> These points of resistance are present everywhere in the power network. Hence there is no single locus of great Refusal, no soul of revolt, source of all rebellions, or pure law of the revolutionary. Instead there is a plurality of resistances, each of them a special case: resistances that are possible, necessary, improbable; others that are spontaneous, savage, solitary, concerted, rampant, or violent; still others that are quick to compromise, interested, or sacrificial; by definition, they can only exist in the strategic field of power relations. . . . (Foucault, *HS*, pp. 95–96)

In its general economy, its endless circulation, power forms patterns of oppression and subjection and out of itself brings forth resistances. There is no rule of resistance, no locus of liberation. Power composes a general economy in which both its injustices and its resistances to injustice issue from its circulation. There is "only one" general economy of power in the sense that its forces and resistances work in the same circulation, on the same planet, in the same universe, interweaving and interwoven, endlessly permeated by plenishment and excess. All goods circulate, excessively, in a general economy of power, authority, desire, and truth. In the univocity of this general economy, you and I seek ethical difference. We pursue ethical difference in the general economy composing nature's inexhaustible places, the general economy of plenishment in the earth.

23. If that is not an oxymoron. I mean by it to emphasize the intermediariness of restricted economies.

24. Even within the circulation of gifts. See n. 16, this chapter.

25.

> Just as in the order of representations the signs that replace and analyse them must also be representations themselves, so money cannot signify wealth without itself being wealth. But it becomes wealth because it is a sign; whereas a representation must first be represented in order subsequently to become a sign. Hence the apparent contradiction between the

> principles of accumulation and the rules of circulation. At any given moment of time, the number of coins in existence is determined. . . . (Foucault, *OT,* p. 177)

This understanding of circulation gives us our understanding both that the circulation of goods, of coins, is general, immeasurable, everywhere, and in every thing, and yet, to be exchanged, measured, substituted, that the number of goods in existence must be determined.

26. This is the point of my *RR*.

27. I am speaking both of the gift of the gods and of gift economy.

28. This is the truth that Illich seems not to know in his division of sexual labor. See Illich, *G,* and here, chap. 9, pp. 215–23.

29.

> If the position of mastery culturally
> comes back to men, what will become of
> (our) femininity when we find ourselves
> in this position?
> When we use a master-discourse?
> Mastery–knowledge, mastery–power;
> ideas demanding an explanation from us.
> Other discourses?
> (Cixous and Clément, *NBW,* p. 136)

See chap. 1, n. 2.

30. As Irigaray says as well. See chap. 1, n. 1.

31. Summarized as follows:

> Feminism is a specialized pursuit, not part of the "mainstream" of philosophy. Philosophy is universal in scope, dealing with all mankind (sic), but feminism applies to a segment of the population. Feminist issues are trivial compared to the ultimate questions philosophers ought to address. Feminist concerns are transient, bound to a particular time and place; philosophy transcends particular time and place. Feminism is sociological, political, or anthropological; it asks no genuinely philosophic questions. Feminists haven't yet learned to argue properly; they have not learned to give proper evidence for their claims; no general principles, just vignettes and metaphors. Philosophy is neutral in its analysis. Feminism is a bias. (Singer, *DC,* p. 165; from Ruth, *MMBF*)

32. These three relations to the canon may be compared with the three relations described in chap. 3 to first philosophy. See pp. 25–26.

33. See n. 16, 24, and 27, this chap.

34. Gadamer similarly reimposes the number two in conversation, another, dialogic, exchange, as if one two were better than another. We cannot escape from the number two. We seem to require a partner.

> To conduct a conversation requires first of all that the partners to it do not talk at cross purposes. Hence its necessary structure is that of question and answer. The first condition of the art of conversation is to ensure that the other person is with us. (Gadamer, *TM*, p. 345)

> We say that we 'conduct' a conversation, but the more fundamental a conversation is, the less its conduct lies within the will of either partner. (Gadamer, *TM*, p. 345)

This duality of question and answer, speaker and interlocutor, this relation of conversation, dialogue and dialectic, to the other, is two throughout, whether we think of every dyad as binary or not. The first thing we might want to say of Gadamer's understanding of conversation is that, although it is proffered as an epistemology, an understanding of understanding, its structure is ethical|political. That is why Gadamer must speak of power, echoing Foucault:

> The concept of power has a central place within the historical world view because in it interiority and exteriority are held in a peculiar unity in tension. All power exists only in its expression. The expression is not only the manifestation of the power, but its reality. . . . But . . . power is more than its expression. . . . the offering of resistance is itself an expression of power. But even then it is an awareness in which power is experienced. Interiority is the mode of experiencing power, because power, of its nature, is related to itself alone. (Gadamer, *TM*, pp. 180–81)

Again, irresistibly, the number two reappears, between interiority and exteriority, power and resistance. Power is related to itself alone in virtue of falling between one dyad after another.

Even more, this power belongs to mastery, reshapes mastery as Gadamer hopes to reshape the number two around conversation rather than domination.

35. Baudrillard calls this "hyperreality." See Baudrillard, *FF*, pp. 51–52.

36. Some of this can be heard in Peirce, who links the number two with the number three. "[E]very genuine triadic relation involves meaning, as meaning is obviously a triadic relation. . . . a triadic relation is inexpressible by means of dyadic relations alone" (Peirce, "The Principles of Phenomenology," in *PP*, p. 91). Here two becomes three, must become three, because dyadic relations do not give meaning, either to two or to three. We may say, with respect to sexual difference, that the pair men and women, in dyadic relation, means nothing except under law and identity. The Law of the Father turns the dyad into three, thereby bringing sexual difference into meaning—a meaning that, whatever its other properties, has meant the systematic subjugation of women. In other words, subordination and subjection are thirds of law imposed on sexual difference.

Similarly, when Derrida speaks of the double blow visited on sexual difference, which should be loving and intimate but becomes oppositional and violent, both blows represent thirds.

So far so good. Two becomes three to come into presence. But Peirce says something more telling. "[A]nalysis will show that every relation which is *tetradic, pentadic,* or of any greater number of correlates is nothing but a compound of triadic relations" (Peirce, "The Principles of Phenomenology," in *PP,* p. 93). Our entire discussion of the indefinite dyad in relation to unlimit is devoted to this "nothing but," opening onto general economy.

37. Following Peirce, I move from the one of identity to two, the difference in which identity finds its limits, to three, to the law of their relation. In Peirce's phenomenology, Firstness is quality, Secondness is fact, Thirdness is law, a dialectical view of relation. I follow another way back to Socrates in *Philebus* and the gods:

> There then, that is how the gods, as I told you, have committed to us the task of inquiry, of learning, and of teaching one another, but your clever modern man, while making his one—or his many, as the case may be—more quickly or more slowly than is proper, when he has got his one proceeds to his unlimited number straightaway, allowing the intermediates to escape him, whereas it is the recognition of those intermediates that makes all the difference between a philosophical and a contentious discussion. (Plato, *Philebus,* 16e–17a)

The proper, we may observe, rests in the intermediates, and without them, without their measures, we cannot be philosophical, but sink into strife and contention. The number two, in sexual difference, wards off the danger that women will be violated as women, subordinated under the sign of the one, of man, as they have always in some ways been.

Peirce counters with a deep insight that is lost in many readings of Hegel, that two are nothing without a third. If no other third is present, that third will be violence and domination. But now, having discerned the thirds in the texture of phenomenological experience, knowing that nature and human experience require thirds as well as seconds, how do we let all of this pass away to unlimit? Certainly, we may suppose, not by insisting that unlimit is three. To the contrary, perhaps we must insist that three is unlimit. Let us hear this movement as surplus, supplementarity, excess. Within the hold of law upon us, within its exclusions, law moves in intermediary regions, expresses authority's excesses.

38. This is the burden of my *LL.* See also my *RR.*

39. In *IR,* chap. 9, I read *Phaedrus* as moving from *technē* to *poiēsis* through *erōs* and *mania* twice. The first movement is found in Socrates' two speeches. The first is blasphemous because it imitates Lysias's utilitarian view of love as a *technē;* the second is organized around the themes of

love and madness. Yet the second, great speech concludes about two-thirds of the way through the dialogue. On my reading, before Theuth's speech on writing, Socrates returns to *technē,* again to show under Pharmakeia's tutelage that a writing that lacks magic, madness, that is without the *pharmakon,* is lifeless, dead, without progeny. When Socrates speaks of the dialectical method Plato describes in *Statesman,* it may be read as *technē*'s measure, not as philosophy's *erōs*:

> The first is that in which we bring a dispersed plurality under a single form, seeing it all together. . . . (Plato, *Phaedrus,* 265d)

> The reverse of the other, whereby we are enabled to divide into forms, following the objective articulation; we are not to attempt to hack off parts like a clumsy butcher, but to take example from our two recent speeches. The single general form which they postulated was irrationality; next, on the analogy of a single natural body with its pairs of like-named members, right arm or leg, as we say, and left, they conceived of madness as a single objective form existing in human beings. . . . (Plato, *Phaedrus,* 266a)

For Socrates continues to describe other methods under the inspiration of Eros and Pharmakeia, especially music. One who knows music's *technē* may still lack musicality.

> "My good sir, it is true that one who proposes to become a master of harmony must know the things you speak of, but it is perfectly possible for one who has got as far as yourself to have not the slightest real knowledge of harmony. You are acquainted with what has to be learned before studying harmony, but of harmony itself you know nothing." (Plato, *Phaedrus,* 268e)

On my reading, *Philebus* bears the same relationship to *technē* and to music as *Phaedrus*. The circulation of goods in general economy circulates as the work of representation.

40. See pp. 98–99.

41. Nature's movement from itself toward itself expresses one understanding of excess and profusion, of general economy, brought under the rule of kinds. Aristotle's most frequently expressed concern about this rule echoes in terms of individuals. "The individuals comprised within a species, such as Socrates and Coriscus, are the real existences; but inasmuch as these individuals possess one common specific form, it will suffice to state the universal attributes of the species, that is, the attributes common to all its individuals, once for all . . . " (Aristotle, *Parts of Animals,* 644a). Our concern is with the profusion of kinds, the site at which hierarchy rules in Aristotle.

Foucault describes the corresponding Renaissance phenomenon, reducing nature's profusion to taxonomy. "According to this order, every chapter dealing with a given animal should follow the following plan: name, theory, kind, species, attributes, use, and, to conclude, *Litteraria*. All the language deposited upon things by time is pushed back into the very last category, like a sort of supplement in which discourse is allowed to recount itself and record discoveries, traditions, beliefs, and poetical figures" (Foucault, *OT,* p. 130).

Profusion, heterogeneity, and excess appear first as language, then as catastrophe and monstrosity.

> At the heart of this well-constructed language that natural history has become, one problem remains. It is possible after all that the transformation of structure into character may never be possible, and that the common noun may never be able to emerge from the proper noun. (Foucault, *OT,* p. 145)

> The monster ensures in time, and for our theoretical knowledge, a continuity that, for our everyday experience, floods, volcanoes, and subsiding continents confuse in space. . . . The monster and the fossil both play a very precise role in this configuration. On the basis of the power of the continuum held by nature, the monster ensures the emergence of difference. (Foucault, *OT,* p. 156)

Language's profusion echoes in its proper nouns, in the individuals of nature, and in the endless, inexhaustible common nouns that exceed, that are not reducible to, the repetition of individuals, proper nouns. Nature's profusion echoes in the monsters and fossils that disturb, displace, the taxonomy of categories and classifications, the common nouns and their order. The plenitude of nature bears a certain relation to the plenitude of kinds, genera and species, ordered by classification and taxonomy, but bearing underneath a certain Dionysian side, the general economy of nature. The good, ethical difference, passes here into kindred difference, differences in kind, passes but does not pass away.

42. Randall, Jr., understands Aristotle's view of nature as plenitude and plurality—"existence forms a many of things and processes, *ousiai* and *kinēseis* (Randall, Jr., *A,* p. 113)—and Aristotle's passion to know as noncoercive: "Aristotle's aim is to understand, to find out why things are as they are. It is not to control things, not to make them different from what they are" (Randall, Jr., *A,* p. 2). Randall also understands Spinoza as "the only other philosopher in our Western tradition who in this Aristotelian sense ever really tried to understand the world" (Randall, Jr., *A,* p. 3). Aristotle and Spinoza took nature as an unlimited plenitude, sought a knowledge that had no practical agenda. Even so, Spinoza excludes women and animals. And Aristotle's understanding of understanding imposes a taxonomy that works to subordinate and exclude. In Randall's words:

> The syllogism will operate in a world exhibiting "kinds" of thing, *eidē,* and more inclusive "kinds," *genē,* a world in which are to be found real species and genera, a world in which individual things are what they are because they are of a certain kind, because they belong to a certain species. (Randall, Jr., *A,* p. 49)

> It is to be noted, that a "nature," like an "essence," belongs not to an individual as such, but to individuals as members of a certain kind of species. Any individual, any *tode ti,* possesses an inexhaustible number of powers. Those powers that can be said to be "natural" to it are those powers that can be said to be "essential" to its being the determinate kind of thing it is: it is that kind that possesses a certain "nature." (Randall, Jr., *A,* p. 176)

Where things by nature, of a certain kind, dominate other things by nature, of other kinds. For Aristotle speaks of "human nature" as "not a private and individual possession" (Randall, Jr., *A,* p. 176). I resist the dichotomy of individual and kind, but understand heterogeneity to belong among the different kinds, in relation to kindred difference, the *aentres* of kinds and representations.

43. *Metaphysics,* Book VII, can be read in its entirety as struggling with the question of the identity of individuals that by nature belong to kinds. "Each thing itself, then, and its essence are one and the same in no merely accidental way . . . " (Aristotle, *Metaphysics,* 1031b); "when we come to the concrete thing, e.g. *this* circle, . . . of these there is no definition, but they are known by the aid of intuitive thinking or of perception" (Aristotle, *Metaphysics,* 1036a).

CHAPTER SIX. REST

1. See chap. 5, n. 36, 37.

2. Although I have always read *Process and Reality* as ethical, I never thought of reading it as an ethics, matching Spinoza's *Ethics,* until the suggestion was proposed in class by Deborah O'Connell-Brown that Whitehead's world is framed by obligation, value, and responsibility. In this sense, Whitehead finds the good, exceeding being, in being, everywhere. This everywhere is cherishment.

3. They remain two in Whitehead, the dyad rests. He speaks of "Ideal Opposites" (Whitehead, *PR,* pp. 337–41). This thought of two I bring to Peirce, who moves from one intermediate number to another, two to three, as if one number or the other could be the truth. I understand the movement from two to three to be a movement of unlimit, general economy, measure's circulation.

4. Coleridge, *BL,* p. 232. I take art to give us inexhaustibility by contrast. See my *TA.*

5. The expression "Third World" is Trinh's, in what I take to be a parody of "First World" discourse. For First and Third World defined another dyad, another restricted economy, even before the collapse of the Second.

6. A parergon. See chap. 3, n. 48.

7. " . . . each actual entity pervades the continuum" (Whitehead, *PR*, p. 67); for the full passage, see chap. 4, n. 11.

8. Prehensions are dyadic. Whitehead calls them vectoral: from the datum to the prehending occasion. Prehension is face to face, filled with feeling.

9. Hyde speaks of scientific knowledge circulating as a gift as well as a commodity (Hyde, *G*, p. 77) and of scientists' skepticism toward such a circulation (Hyde, *G*, p. 79). This closely approaches the idea of the general economy of truth, including science's truth.

See my *IR*, chaps. 9 and 10.

10. Lyotard as well, for example: "Repetition is a problem of time. And music is a problem of time" (Lyotard, *I*, p. 153, and throughout chap. 13).

11. Lyotard, *D*, p. 90; translated as "Reality entails the differend" (Lyotard, *DPD*, p. 55).

The sole meaning of *comporter* given in the *Larousse Dictionnaire de la Langue Française*, 1979, is "Avoir comme parties essentielles, avoir comme qualité naturelle," synonymous with "se composer de."

Reality is composed of *différends*.

12. As Peirce shows, again, the number two is the number three, and more, all the way to unlimit, and back.

CHAPTER SEVEN. CARNAVAL

1. The social contract, discussed in chap. 5, pp. 78–96. I return here to the animal kingdom.

2. *Sincérité*, perhaps better translated, with Heidegger in mind, as authenticity.

3. "Le tiers est autre que le prochain, mais aussi un autre prochain" (Levinas, *AÊ*, p. 245).

4. "Autrui est d'emblée le frère de tous les autres hommes" (Levinas, *AÊ*, p. 246). We remember Derrida's suggestion that the ethical–political–philosophical neighbor is always bound to us as friend, as male (Derrida, *PF*).

5. See this chapter, pp. 135–36.

6. The burden of chap. 9 is to trace the themes of proximity and alterity in relation to ecstasy and love.

7. See pp. 151–52, this chap., for the rest of this quotation.

8. Parts 3 and 4 of Spinoza's *Ethics* express this relation between emotion and the good, fulfilled, however we read it, in Part 5.

9. And let us not forget Bosnian women, and witches.

10. See pp. 163–65.

11.

> 2 And the fear of you and the dread of you shall be upon every beast of the earth, and upon every fowl of the air, upon all that moveth *upon* the earth, and upon all the fishes of the sea; into your hand are they delivered.
>
> 3 Every moving thing that liveth shall be meat for you; . . . (*Gen.* 1)

See pp. 163–65, this chap.

12. This is the appeal of bioregionalism, that where we are, in proximity to our local surroundings, we cherish these surroundings and plenish the earth. See chap. 3, n. 42; chap. 4, n. 2, 4.

13.

> There are several conventional theories as to why crows roost together during the winter: Perched in compact groups, they warm and insulate one another. It is virtually impossible for anything to approach a roostful of crows without being detected by some individuals who warn the others. Winter roosts may promote genetic diversity, functioning somewhat as singles bars, providing opportunities for members of opposite sexes to become acquainted. Congregating daily in the same place is, in effect, a share-the-wealth adaptation. In the fall and winter food resources are less evenly distributed than they are in the spring and summer. Having located rich foraging areas, smarter, bolder or luckier crows are subsequently followed to them by their roostmates. (Gilbert, "Crows," p. 110)

14. See p. 163.

15. Whitehead describes these qualities as belonging to the consequent nature of God; "the judgment of a tenderness which loses nothing that can be saved. It is also the judgment of a wisdom which uses what in the temporal world is mere wreckage" (Whitehead, *PR,* p. 346). The saving side, God's patience, can be read against its temporality. Yet Whitehead gives us two images of that patience. "He does not create the world, he saves it: or, more accurately, he is the poet of the world, with tender patience leading it by his vision of truth, beauty, and goodness" (Whitehead, *PR,* p. 346). He is a poet for whom the good in each rock and sparrow, in each thing, that would otherwise be merely lost, is saved—not preserved against time, but cherished, loved, remembered, mourned in the sacrifices of history.

Whitehead also speaks of something close to cherishment: he calls it "Platonic." "There is not just one ideal 'order' which all actual entities should attain and fail to attain. In each case there is an ideal peculiar to each particular actual entity . . . " (Whitehead, *PR,* p. 84). And although there is not an ideal order for all actual entities, the universe, however impossibly, fulfills itself in something like plenishment.

> Thus the universe is to be conceived as attaining the active self-expression of its own variety of opposites—of its own freedom and its own necessity, of its own multiplicity and its own unity, of its own imperfection and its own perfection. All the "opposites" are elements in the nature of things, and are incorrigibly there. The concept of "God" is the way in which we understand this incredible fact—that what cannot be, yet is. (Whitehead, *PR,* p. 350)

Elsewhere he speaks of "Peace":

> As soon as high consciousness is reached, the enjoyment of existence is entwined with pain, frustration, loss, tragedy. Amid the passing of so much beauty, so much heroism, so much daring, Peace is then the intuition of permanence. It keeps vivid the sensitiveness to the tragedy; and it sees the tragedy as a living agent persuading the world to aim at fineness beyond the faded level of surrounding fact. Each tragedy is the disclosure of an ideal:—What might have been, and was not: What can be. The tragedy was not in vain. (Whitehead, *AI,* p. 369)

The permanence of Peace is no guarantee, no measure, but a sense that within the injustices the ideal gives birth to music. We remember the *Stabat Mater.*

We also remember that Heidegger speaks of letting things be and *Gelassenheit,* speaks of something like plenishment (see chap. 13, p. 315). We ask again, how can the Heidegger for whom everything under the sun calls upon us to let it be exclude so much from the good under the name of *Geschlecht?*

16. Monstrosity echoes in Derrida in the dyad of *montre* and *monstre:* representation and excess, where monstrosity meets monstration and the demonic undergoes demonstration, proof.

> *Monstrer* is *montrer* (to show or demonstrate), and *une monstre* is *un montre* (a watch). I am already settled in the untranslatable idiom of my language, for I certainly intend to speak to you about translation. *La monstre,* then, prescribes the divisions of a line of verse for a melody. *Le monstre* or *la monstre* is what shows in order to warn or put on guard. In the past *la montre,* in French, was written *la monstre.* (Derrida, *G2,* p. 166)

Monstrosity, born of injustice, meets monstration, transforms itself into demonstration, the proper demon of evidence and proof, wherein we hope to hear the victims of *technē.*

17. I must add, in the midst of what some readers may regard as a harsh and unjust critique of Heidegger, that despite his denial that his

ontology is an ethics, I believe that his critique of modern technology, his attempt to rethink the relation between *physis* and *technē*, and his understanding of *Gelassenheit* are all profoundly ethical, an ethics that I and others seek to unfold beyond its call in Heidegger. (See Scott, *QE*, and Krell, *DL*, and chap. 13, n. 7.) Still, three things about this ethical truth in Heidegger must be kept in mind, however terribly, expressing the *aentre* of ethical difference. He never recognized the ethical nature of his own work, never took ethical responsibility for it. His work turns irresistibly around the gift of language, our *Geschlecht*. And he respected Hitler, joined the Nazis, and never understood the nature of such a crime.

Would that you and I may remain pure.

18. Described by David Krell as follows:

> Paul lists three principal meanings for *Geschlecht* (Old High German *gislahti*). First, it translates the Latin word *genus*, being equivalent to *Gattung: das Geschlecht* is a group of people who share a common ancestry, especially if they constitute a part of the hereditary nobility. Of course, if the ancestry is traced back far enough we may speak of *des menschliche Geschlecht*, "humankind." Second, *das Geschlecht* may mean one generation of men and women who die in order to make way for a succeeding generation. Third, there are male and female *Geschlechter*, and *Geschlecht* becomes the root of many words for the things males and females have and do for the sake of the first two meanings: *Geschlechts-glied* or *-teil*, the genitals; *-trieb*, the sex drive; *-verkehr*, sexual intercourse; and so on. (Derrida, *G2*, pp. 191–92; quoted from Krell, *IM*, p. 165)

"Kind" is an extraordinary word in English. See the ensuing discussion.

19. Returning in chap. 9.

20. Derrida continues:

> When returning to the originality of *Dasein*, of this *Dasein* said to be sexually neutral, "originary positivity" and "power" can be reconsidered. In other words, despite appearances, the asexuality and neutrality that should first of all be subtracted from the sexual binary mark, in the analytic of *Dasein*, are in truth on the same side, on the side of that sexual difference—the binary—to which one might have thought them simply opposed. Does this interpretation sound too violent? (Derrida, *G1*, p. 72)

Or does this interpretation remind us of the forgotten *Geschlecht* that undercuts the neutrality of both *Dasein* and Being, the beginning all over again of sexual difference? The thought within Heidegger of *Geschlecht* brings us face to face with Hitler on the right and the consumption of animals on the left.

21. " . . . als Hören der Stimme des Freundes, den jedes Dasein bei sich trägt" (Heidegger, *SZ*, p. 163).

22. Derrida traces a line from the (male) friend into two ethical spaces, never named ethical by Heidegger, into *philein*, but not *philia* or *philosophia*, and *polemos*, bringing us back to *Dasein*'s neutrality, sexual and specific neutrality, with a double and triple blow. For philosophy, thought, *Dasein*'s essence, bears a certain primordial relation to sexuality as well as to *polemos* (Derrida reading Heidegger, *WP*).

> *Sophon*—the being in being (*das Seiende im Sein*)—is now properly sought (*wird jetzt eigens gesucht*). Because *philein* is no longer an originary symphony with *sophon* (*nicht mehr ein ursprünglicher Einklang mit dem sophon ist*), but the particular tension of a searching *after sophon* (*sondern ein besonderes Streben nach dem sophon*), the *philein to sophon* becomes "*philosophia*." *Philosophia* whose tension (*Streben*) is determined [destined, *bestimmt*] by Eros (*WP* 14). (Derrida, *G4*, p. 191)

Erōs and *polemos* meet in the primordiality of *Dasein*, repeating for us the question of *Dasein*'s sex, being's and nature's sex, the sexual|ethical difference in nature I understand as kindred difference, pertaining to species and kinds, the profusion of species and kinds that composes nature's heterogeneity, the circulation of nature's general economy as the good. Nature's heterogeneity of inexhaustible kinds brings us face to face with sexuality, desire, *erōs*, and with animals in profusion, as well as with other natural kinds. But all in a certain *polemos, Streben, Kampf.*

I struggle with Heidegger, and with Derrida's reading of Heidegger, here, after a certain space, a place, of the "pre-," the primordial, the possibility that philosophy occupies a certain place before sex and kinds, a place of which, in *G1*, Derrida asks whether *Dasein* would be sexed in virtue of its neutrality, and in *G2*, described as falling under a double blow. "The primordial sexual difference is tender, gentle, peaceful; when that difference is struck down by a 'curse' . . . the duality or the duplicity of the two becomes unleashed, indeed bestial, opposition" (Derrida, *G2*, p. 193). The primordiality of *Dasein* is neuter, that is, not sexed, an indirect reference to sexual difference, on Derrida's reading in *G1*. Even so, in discussing Trakl, Heidegger speaks of the primordial sexual difference in relation to the *Schlag*, the blow, within, in *Geschlecht* and in sexual difference, in gender, the curse, the mark of gender.

23. See this chap., p. 156. Also, "*Dasein*'s going-out-of-the-world in the sense of dying must be distinguished from the going-out-of-the-world of that which merely has life [*des Nur-lebenden*]" (Heidegger, *BT*, p. 284).

24.

> Man is this night, this pure nothing that contains everything in its simplicity, a realm endlessly rich in representation and images. . . . In

phantasmagoric representations he is surrounded by night; suddenly a bloody head juts forth here, there another white figure, and just as suddenly they disappear. One glimpses this night when one looks into the eyes of another human—into a night, which becomes frightening; here each of us is suspended confronting the night of the world. (Hegel, *JR II,* pp. 180–81; quoted and translated in Agamben, *LD,* pp. 41–42).

The empty voice of the animal acquires a meaning that is infinitely determinate in itself. The pure sound of the voice, the vowel, is differentiated since the organ of the voice presents articulation as a particular articulation with its differences. This pure sound is interrupted by mute [consonants], the true and proper arrestation of mere resonation. . . . Language, inasmuch as it is sonorous and articulated, is the voice of consciousness because of the fact that every sound has a meaning; that is, that in language there exists a name, the ideality of something existing, the immediate nonexistence of this. (Hegel, *JR I,* p. 212; Agamben, *LD,* p. 44).

25. Agamben says something similar.

If language were immediately the voice of man, as braying is the voice of the ass and chirping the voice of the cicada, man could not be-the-*there* or take-the-*this;* that is, he could never experience the taking place of language or the disclosure of being. But if, on the other hand (as demonstrated by both the Heideggerian dialectic of *Stimmunt* and *Stimme* and the Hegelian figure of the Voice of death), man radically possessed no voice (not even a negative Voice), every shifter and every possibility of indicating the event of language would disappear equally. A voice—a silent and unspeakable voice—is the supreme shifter, which permits thought to experience the taking place of language and to ground, with it, the dimension of being in its difference with respect to the entity. (Agamben, *LD,* pp. 84–85)

Again, we note with pain and despair, shifting upon the corpses of animals, of other living creatures. We may compare Plato in *Phaedrus,* who in relation to writing and desire, to *erōs* and *philia,* and to death, has Socrates speak of the cicadas' song in different words, of music, music and death.

The story is that once upon a time these creatures were men—men of an age before there were any Muses—and that when the latter came into the world, and music made its appearance, some of the people of those days were so thrilled with pleasure that they went on singing, and quite forgot to eat and drink until they actually died without noticing. . . . to which the Muses have granted the boon of needing no sustenance right from their birth, but of singing from the very first, without food or drink, until the day of the death, after which they go and report to the Muses how they severally are paid honor among mankind, and by whom. (Plato, *Phaedrus,* 259c)

We may also recall that however "strange, pitiful, and ridiculous" (Plato, *Republic,* 620), many of the immortal souls described by Er, closing the dialogue, choose to come back as animals, swans and nightingales, eagles and apes, wild creatures and beasts. Every living creature bears within itself the possibility of an immortal soul.

26. We know it even when we are not philosophical. "Genocide, the deliberate and systematic destruction of an ethnic, religious, political or social group, is the ultimate crime against humanity" (Kazemzadeh, *SA,* p. 13). Perhaps the destruction of a kind is the ultimate crime against nature.

27. Returning to Heidegger in memory of genocide, shaping our contemporary history as a singular event, shaping our relation to other genocides, you and I may remember his service to Hitler within the memory of what he calls originary *polemos, Kampf.* Or rather, as Derrida carefully spells out, Heidegger speaks of *Kampf* along a difficult line that traces the entire thematic of the absolutely originary, from *Being and Time* to elsewhere, including the *Rectorate Discourse,* that traces the meeting of sexual difference with *logos* and *polemos,* with animal and kindred difference, here, in *G4,* with the voice of the friend, that is, with *philein* and *logos.* This play of sexual and ethical and kindred difference, the triangle of man and woman and animal, rings repeatedly in dyads of kinds, in English, of many and different kinds that make up nature, and of a kindness, a love, that inhabits the spaces between (*aentre*) *erōs* and *philia,* sexual–animal–kindred difference.

All of this is spoken of, in Heidegger, as *polemos, Kampf,* as strife, opposition, conflict, after Heraclitus, which I interpret in remembrance of Anaximander, who asks us to think of things in relation as injustice, fully and primordially ethical. The good rests on and in the plenitude of things together with their conflicts, their incompatibilities, together. Derrida traces, in *Being and Time,* the movement from the voice of the friend, *philein,* the friendship we think of as kindness and cherishment, to the close of *Being and Time* where *Kampf* is "the essential form of *Miteinandersein,* of community (*Gemeinschaft*), and of the people (*Volk*)" (Derrida, *G4,* p. 176). Then, through Heidegger's reading of *Dasein*'s originary and primordial neutrality, *Dasein*'s originary difference, still in *Being and Time,* as not sexual difference, we find a certain sexuality at the very heart of *Dasein,* the question of whether *Dasein* is sexed (Derrida, *G1*). I understand this question as whether being, nature, the earth is sexed, how sexual difference pertains to nature everywhere, to every thing, the question I understand to give rise to the question of ethical difference, sexual|ethical|kindred difference. This question, of *Dasein*'s sex, Derrida returns to *Kampf,* or rather *Schlag,* as the double blow that comes to *Geschlecht,* turning its peacefulness, the tenderness of *philein,* to war, *polemos* (Derrida, *G2*), to a battle for exclusion.

Now we trace the movement of *polemos* back to Hitler, to the *Rectorate Discourse*'s echoes of *Kampf,* of *Mein Kampf* and ours, We Germans, with an ear to music as well as to strife. For Heidegger speaks there of the *Kampf* of three services that "bind to the destiny of the State in a spiritual mission" (Derrida, *G4,* p. 197): labor, military service, and knowledge, all equally originary, all equally bound by *polemos* (Derrida, *G4,* p. 198). And with *polemos,* we return to Heraclitus, understanding this *polemos, Kampf,* as another absolutely originary event. "The *polemos* named here is a conflict that prevailed prior to everything divine and human, not a war in the human sense" (Heidegger, *IM,* p. 51; Derrida, *G4,* p. 204). Derrida explains,

> The *polemos,* the producer or the prevailing guardian that engenders gods and men, is neither a god nor a man. It is more originary than the human or the divine, precedes the opposition that places them face to face (Derrida, *G4,* p. 209).

> The struggle that precedes all then fights nothing, that is the very logic of this tautology. This *Kampf* does not yet have any contenders facing it. It does not make war with someone or something. It is not an "assault." (Derrida, *G4,* p. 210)

Derrida means that we hear, in the ear of the friend, that this *polemos,* which has no enemies, divides *Geschlecht* into the war of sexual difference, divides nature into the war of human and animal, that this *Kampf* without any enemies generates enemies out of *philia* and kindness. Or rather, in the form of the question before us, Anaximander's ethical question that pervades *polemos* to its heart: could the struggle, the strife, of justice, *dikē,* could the conflict in justice be injustice, an injustice that makes justice, truth, law, possible, possible as the call of, toward, responsibility toward the good? In this form, the *Kampf* that is not against anyone or any thing is cherishment toward things and kinds of things, heterogeneity, sexual and ethical and kindred difference, giving birth to sacrifice, to plenishment. In this form, we return again and again to resist the *polemos* that repeatedly, within our endless responsibility for the good, makes an enemy of women, of other people, of animals and natural things.

As Derrida says, Heidegger (almost) never names the enemy, and never names the relation to the enemy as hatred (Derrida, *G4,* p. 214), leaving us bereft of ethical regard. In Heidegger, "this originary enmity does not produce the exploding dispersion of contraries, rather it is their originary oneness (*ursprüngliche Einigkeit*). And that is why enmity would also have the characteristic of beatitude, bliss, *Seligkeit*" (Derrida,

G4, p. 214). "Conflict does not split, much less destroy unity. It constitutes unity, it is a binding-together, *logos*. *Polemos* and *logos* are the same" (Heidegger, *IM*, p. 51). Nature bears this enmity within, born by sacrifice, in a thought that seems so close to cherishment, and so far. "Conflict (*Kampf*) is *physis* inasmuch as it institutes but also inasmuch as it keeps what it institutes. It is institution itself, in the double sense of this word, instituting and instituted. When conflict stops, when one no longer hears what is unheard in the conflict, the being does not disappear, but is no longer kept, affirmed, maintained . . . , becomes an object . . . , an object *available* there where the world has ceased to become world . . . " (Derrida, *G4*, p. 212).

This institution is the event, bearing the full ethical gravity of the *arrive-t-il?*, holding in a certain ethical *regard* the being, the world, of beings. This regard is ethical in a way that Heidegger seems not to know, even as he comes so close to the ethical in a certain sense, that the unheard, the forgetting, suffers endless contamination, bears and suffers endless exposure, wounding, responsibilities, in Levinas's language, against the alleged neutrality of *polemos*. To the contrary, the ethical regard for immemorial strife, *polemos, Kampf* affirms, knows, struggles (another *polemos*) with their injustice, with endless injustices. The bliss of the ethical is within a regard that bears endless responsibility directed against our own contamination. And Heidegger's. Against the contamination of a *polemos* that has no enemy but enters a war in which women and animals and natural things suffer endless destruction.

Heidegger comes closer to an ethic of plenishment, on Derrida's reading, where the founding participants in the struggle for world—"creators, poets, thinkers, statesmen" (Heidegger, *IM*, p. 51) "vanish from the nation" (Heidegger, *IM*, p. 52) in an event thought of as *sacrifice* (Derrida, *G4*, pp. 212–13). "Ostracism and sacrifice, suppression, repression, foreclosure, the impossibility of tolerating the founding instance and authority, are structurally part of what is founded" (Derrida, *G4*, p. 213).

28. See p. 94 for the full quotation.

29. When will we stop sacrificing animals in the name of our *Geschlecht*, sacrificing women, animals, and other creatures and things? Paul Theroux writes of Gerard D'Aboville, who rowed alone across the Pacific in a small boat—a terrifying experience—who responds to the question "why." The voyage was terrible, far beyond its threat to d'Aboville's life. "The video of his last few days at sea, taken by a Coast Guard vessel, is so frightening that d'Aboville wiped tears from his eyes watching it with me" (Theroux, *SP*, p. 24). To the question why had he taken such an enormous personal risk, d'Aboville replies:

> I do not like to talk about it. Only an animal does useful things. An animal gets food, finds a place to sleep, tries to keep comfortable. But I

> wanted to do something that was not useful—not like an animal at all. Something only a human being would do. (Theroux, *SP*, p. 24)

This sense of the possibility that a human being might do something at the limits of thought and life, something incredible and wonderful, has to be told by denying that possibility to animals. Yet animals have traveled thousands of miles, through misery and pain, to find their loved ones, humans, animals, and birds. Animals may always be at the limit D'Aboville describes, at that limit and over, a limit that takes a human's immense will to pursue. Or they may not. We do not need to undermine animals and their capacities in order to amplify our own, as if we must prove our superiority by diminishing them, sacrificing them. We do not need to undermine the powers of women and animals, the preciousness of natural things and kinds, to undertake our ethical responsibilities. To the contrary.

30. These disclosures concerning Heidegger cannot serve to silence him, not within the gathering of ethical difference. Heidegger deserves to be cherished for more than one reason, in his humanity (despite his love for Hitler) and in his writing. For we may follow him in understanding the force of the Forgotten. And we may learn from him a compassion toward the writings that have given us our greatest dangers and truths, although we do not wish to join him in his lack of compassion toward animals and women and others.

31. Martha Nussbaum speaks of many of these things in *The Fragility of Goodness*. She also speaks of the impossibility of achieving the good as if it were within our control. Chance and monstrosity represent nature's plenitude for us, fundamental to ethical difference.

32. See my *IR*, chap. 3. See also Randall, Jr., *P*, pp. 162–63; and Nussbaum, *FG*.

33. And Spinoza says of anything "except men," we may "adapt it to our own service in any way whatever" (Spinoza, *E*, Part 4, Appendix, 27).

34. "There is nothing in nature that *belongs* absolutely and exclusively to anything else; belonging is always a matter of reference and distributive assignment, justified in any particular case as far as it works out well" (Dewey, *EN*, p. 234).

35. To consider a very Nietzschean passage:

> If classic philosophy says so much about unity and so little about unreconciled diversity, so much about the eternal and permanent, and so little about change (save as something to be resolved into combinations of the permanent), so much about necessity and so little about contingency, so much about the comprehending universal and so little about the recalcitrant particular, it may well be because the ambiguousness and ambivalence of reality are actually so pervasive. (Dewey, *EN*, p. 46)

36. "In . . . metaphysics, incompleteness and precariousness is a trait that must be given footing of the same rank as the finished and fixed" (Dewey, *EN,* p. 51).

37. How, you may wonder, can the Dewey who took the tradition to overemphasize unity and stability return to a union of stability and instability as the ethical goal? Here, his emphasis on error and delight inhabiting the places where unity and stability meet suggests less a union than a juncture, an *aentre.* For the union does not dispel the disturbance but enhances it. "[T]here can be no better except where there is shock and discord combined with enough assured order to make attainment of harmony possible" (Dewey, *EN,* p. 62). Again, we may understand the harmony as a vanishing of discord, but that would be unlikely. Rather, the harmony is a harmony of discord, expressing our musical economy.

Similarly, one would not interpret Nietzsche to mean that tragedy achieves a union of Dionysian and Apollonian elements, a synthesis in which each receives its due, for two reasons. One is that tragedy as such joins Dionysus and Apollo, as does art. We can flee Dionysus, but he continues to haunt us tragically. We can forget, but we cannot escape. The second reason is that the juncture of Apollo and Dionysus in tragedy is not a union, not a unity, but a disturbing, menacing movement. Rather, we are caught between Dionysus and Apollo, with tragedy the result, inhabiting the *aentre.*

Existence is perilous and secure, nature and the world, not just human experience, nor just for human experience. Ends belong to nature, where things exist in and of themselves.

> Empirically, the existence of objects of direct grasp, possession, use and enjoyment cannot be denied. Empirically, things are poignant, tragic, beautiful, humorous, settled, disturbed, comfortable, annoying, barren, harsh, consoling, splendid, fearful; are such immediately and in their own right and behalf. (Dewey, *EN,* p. 96)

> *Any* quality as such is final; it is at once initial and terminal; just what it is as it exists. It may be referred to other things, it may be treated as an effect or as a sign. But this involves an extraneous extension and use. It takes us beyond quality in its immediate qualitativeness. If experienced things are valid evidence, then nature in having qualities within itself has what in the literal sense must be called ends, terminals, arrests, enclosures. (Dewey, *EN,* pp. 96–97)

Things are means, but they are also ends, in their own right and behalf. Things in their own right and behalf are beginnings and endings. Referred to human experience, these beginnings and endings relate to processes of meaning, of use and activity, directed toward human enjoyment. Directed to nature, these beginnings and endings relate to natural plenitude. And the direction must be to nature: "nature is an affair *of* affairs, wherein each one, no matter how linked up it may be with others, has its *own* quality" (Dewey, *EN*, p. 97).

Dewey sings of qualities and individuality, but he describes the general economy of nature and human experience, understanding each, an affair of affairs, to circulate things inexhaustibly. In this circulation, things are linked with each other as means and circulate in relation. But things also, in circulation, are what they are, in their own behalf, are termini of circulation. Things circulate. That is the pervasive fact of ethical difference: that things circulate. As things, they bear promises and possibilities, evoke cherishment and concern. In relation, in circulation together, things bear causal and instrumental possibilities.

This circulation gives us the movement of means and ends, the rhythms of ethical difference.

> *Things* are beautiful and ugly, lovely and hateful, dull and illuminated, attractive and repulsive. Stir and thrill in us is as much theirs as is length, breadth, and thickness. Even the utility of things, their capacity to be employed as means and agencies, is first of all not a relation, but a quality possessed, immediately possessed, it is as esthetic as any other quality. (Dewey, *EN*, pp. 108–9)

Here two important understandings emerge in Dewey's account of natural ends, one that nature is filled with ends and qualities that can be, must be, known and cherished, felt, that nature is not a mechanical and lifeless movement. The second is that means have their qualities, are ends, as everything is an end, and everything is a means. The being of things in their own right is represented, expressed, in *poiēsis*. The movement of things in relation is expressed, represented, in *technē*. *Poiēsis* and *technē* together compose the working of the world together with ethical difference. Ethics is the working of means and ends in their means and ends.

CHAPTER EIGHT. REST

1. Warren elsewhere offers a somewhat different account of ecological feminism:

> (1) There are important connections between the oppression of women and the oppression of nature. (2) Understanding the nature of these connections is necessary to any adequate understanding of the oppression of women and the oppression of nature. (3) Feminist theory and practice must include an ecological perspective. (4) Solutions to ecological problems must include a feminist perspective. (Warren, *FEMC*, pp. 4–5; quoted in Sessions, *DEE*, p. 93)

I add a link to slavery, add antiracist and anticolonial perspectives. The privileging of a feminist perspective may work against a wider understanding of oppression. It may provide a sense of women who do not differ by race and class. It may impede plenishment everywhere in the earth.

What is at stake is the force of the "must," the possibility that it denotes an ethic of exclusion. For my entire discussion to this point has been to build the link between (but *aentre*) sexual and kindred difference. Ecological and feminist perspectives are linked, cannot be occupied except together.

I hope to pursue the link between the oppression of women and the domination of nature, from feminism to plenishment in the earth, without exclusion, remembering slavery, racism, and colonialism, remembering the exploitation of creatures in the earth, everywhere.

2. A word I consider to mark sexual difference in its sexual indifference.

3. Thomas Nagel, for example, claims that there are five "equally valid" moral perspectives: obligations, rights, utility, perfectionist ends, and private commitments (Nagel, *MQ*,). This number five is another intermediate number with a vengeance. I would resist it repeatedly, resist counting the number of ethical views in circulation at any time (five, or ten, or more) as destructive to general economy. None of the five seems to me to reflect my reading of Plato, Aristotle, or Spinoza on virtue and the good. I would also resist the idea of a certain number of possible ethical views. And it is here that I would interpose both ecological feminism and ethical difference, not as presenting another member of this list of five or ten or more, but as questioning the idea of competing ethical viewpoints.

4. Heidegger says something similar of technology in relation to *Gelassenheit*, releasement.

> We can use technical devices, and yet with proper use also keep ourselves so free of them, that we may let go of them any time. We can use technical devices as they ought to be used, and also let them alone as something which does not affect our inner and real core. We can affirm the unavoidable use of technical devices, and also deny them the right to dominate us, and so to warp, confuse, and lay waste our nature. (Heidegger, *DT*, p. 54)

We face the far more radical thought here that gender, dyadically, does affect our inner and real core, yet even so, we must deny it the right to dominate us. And so with every kind in the earth.

5. Curtin summarizes a number of ecofeminist arguments against some views of animal rights.

> First, it can be argued that views such as Rachels's and Regan's are too narrow to express feminist insights [defined by Curtin as "those that can be seen as arising from and expressing the conditions of women's

> moral lives." (Curtin, *TEEC,* p. 72, n. 3)] because they allow us to recognize only those rights-making characteristics that nonhuman animals have in virtue of being in some way *identical* to humans. . . .
>
> The second concern . . . is that the rights approach to treatment of animals is formalistic . . . committed to the idea that equal treatment based on a criterion of cross-species identity is the central concept of morality. . . . Feminist approaches to ethics, however, tend to be not only pluralistic but contextual. . . .
>
> Third, the rights approach is inherently adversarial. . . . Rather, a feminist understanding is more likely to be based in a pluralistic context that is dialogical and seeks mutual accommodation of interests.
>
> Fourth, . . . feminist moral thought tends to reconceptualize personhood as relational rather than autonomous. . . .
>
> Fifth, whereas the rights approach has tended to argue that ethical judgments are objective and rational and do not depend on affective aspects of experience, this has been questioned by feminist critics partly on the grounds that the conception of the purely rational is a myth, and partly on the grounds that this myth has tended to marginalize the experiences of women . . .
>
> Finally, as a result of the emphasis on the rational in traditional moral theory, feminist insights concerning the body have been missed. But as some feminist philosophers have argued, the identification of woman with body has been one pretext on which women's lives have been marginalized. (Curtin, *TEEC,* pp. 64–65)

In speaking of an ethics in which animals have rights only insofar as they are like human beings, a view like Singer's (discussed and criticized in chap. 7, pp. 133–34), Curtin is referring to Rachels, *WARL,* and Regan, *CAR.*

Roger King describes the same shortcoming as one of abstraction, constructing a "moral community on the basis of sameness rather than leaving space for a community of difference" (King, *CN,* p. 78). He comments that "[t]he ecofeminist criticism of this approach is that it excludes many beings in nature from moral consideration because no plausible argument can be made that their misfortunes make a claim on moral agents that is equal to the claims made by the misfortunes of humans" (King, *CN,* p. 78). We have seen that the result is far reaching and extends deep into nature, denying nature's inexhaustible plenitude. "In this way nature's difference, like women's, is excluded from consideration" (King, *CN,* p. 78).

This difference, taken into account insistently, is what I understand as ethical and kindred difference. In King's words, "[t]aking differences seriously . . . requires us to acknowledge the heterogeneity of the moral domain, of the kinds of things with which we can be in relationship" (King, *CN,* p. 79). Or in no relationship but one of awe or care. Warren gives us a version of such an acknowledgment.

> I felt an overwhelming sense of gratitude for what it [the rock] offered me—a chance to know myself and the rock differently, to appreciate unforeseen miracles like the tiny flowers growing in the even tinier cracks in the rock's surface, and to come to know a sense of *being in relationship* with the natural environment. . . . I felt myself *caring* for this rock. (Warren, *PPEF,* p. 135)

Even here, Warren insists on her relationship with the rock, on her ability to relate to and care for the rock available to her, rather than on a difference that withholds and refuses in its radical alterity.

Curtin's five considerations bear so close a resemblance, echo in such proximity, to my understanding of ethical difference that I cannot help but wonder at (and perhaps admire) the structure of her rhetoric. For she does not say that an ethic of rights is *wrong,* that all these other considerations are essential to a *correct* view of ethics, right and wrong, correct and incorrect, but speaks of feminist insights and women's experience repeatedly. Feminist insights arise from and express the conditions of women's lives. This seems to leave her open, despite every effort, to the same critique lodged against Gilligan's work that she examines women who live in an oppressive social context and cannot use that to say anything whatever about men or women or ethics.

6. These summarize Curtin's negative points quoted in this chap., n. 5.

7. Carol Adams similarly claims that "a structure of overlapping but absent referents links violence against women and animals" (Adams, *SPM,* p. 42), insisting that "[w]hat we require is a theory that traces parallel trajectories: the common oppressions of women and animals, and the problems of metaphor and the absent referent" (Adams, *SPM,* p. 47).

8. This is the burden of Nussbaum's *The Fragility of Goodness.*

CHAPTER NINE. TANGO

1. I will return to it in chaps. 11 and 12.

2. We have seen that neither Irigaray nor Aristotle seems to believe we can. "Who or what the other is, I never know. But this unknowable other is that which differs sexually from me" (Irigaray, *SD,* p. 171). "In the first place," according to Aristotle, "there must be a union of those who cannot exist without each other; namely, of male and female, that the race may continue . . . " (Aristotle, *Politics,* 1252a), and so that nature's order can be maintained.

> In like manner we may infer that, after the birth of animals, plants exist for their sake, and that the other animals exist for the sake of man, the tame for use and food, the wild, if not all, at least the greater part of

> them, for food, and for the provision of clothing and various instruments. Now if nature makes nothing incomplete, and nothing in vain, the inference must be that she has made all animals for the sake of man. (Aristotle, *Politics,* 1256b)

In the first place, where plants exist for the sake of animals (neither of whom we suppose to know, or love), and animals for the sake of man, there is sexual difference.

3. Not to mention other possibilities: womyn, wimmin, womin.

4. Dimen speaks of love and intimacy, notes how rarely they are discussed in feminist writing. In response to the myth of patriarchy in which the patriarch keeps all the women to himself until overthrown by his sons, she notes that "[m]issing in this myth are women, their subordination, and, indeed, all that they symbolize—personal life, reproductivity, alterity" (Dimen, *PSI,* p. 34). She asks the question for us here: "[w]here is there, in this talk of power and sex, room for intimacy, for the knowledge and expansion of self achieved through knowledge of the other?" (Dimen, *PSI,* p. 34). I hope to provide that room, the dance of intimacy, though perhaps not quite as she describes, when she adds, "perhaps the missing conceptual link in feminist theory is an engaged personal voice, saturated with feeling, values, and political protest, a voice such as emerges in feminist biography in which subject engages with subject" (Dimen, *PSI,* p. 35). Whatever the voice, a site at which sexual difference engages us with an ethics of inclusion is a site of intimacy, however we understand the relation between politics and intimacy, public and private, impure and pure.

5. Also: "You see then what this ancient evidence attests. Corresponding to the superior perfection and value of the prophecy of inspiration over that of omen reading, both in name and in fact, is the superiority of heaven-sent madness over man-made sanity.

"And in the second place, when grievous maladies and afflictions have beset certain families by reason of some ancient sin, madness [*mania*] has appeared among them, and breaking out into prophecy has secured relief . . . and in consequence thereof rites and means of purification were established . . . " (Plato, *Phaedrus,* 244e)

"There is a third form of possession or madness, of which the Muses are the source. . . . if any man come to the gates of poetry [*poiēsis*] without the madness [*mania*] of the Muses, persuaded that skill [*technē*] alone will make him a good poet, then shall he and his works of sanity with him be brought to nought by the poetry [*poiēsis*] of madness [*mainomenōn*]. . . " (Plato, *Phaedrus,* 245)

6. See my *IR,* chap. 9, for a detailed discussion of *Phaedrus,* also Derrida, *PP.* Here I read only the great speech at the center of the dialogue as a moment of heterogeneous sexual frenzy.

7. We may consider the first two references only. At the beginning, as Phaedrus and Socrates begin their walk outside the city gates, away from the *polis*'s law, toward *erōs*'s heterogeneity and heterosexuality, Phaedrus asks whether he and Socrates are close to where Boreas seized Orithyia from the river Ilissus, and whether Socrates believes the story. Socrates replies,

> I should be quite in the fashion if I disbelieved it, as the men of science [*sophoi*] do. I might proceed to give a scientific account of how the maiden, while at play with Pharmacia [*Pharmakeia*], was blown by a gust of Boreas down from the rocks hard by, and having thus met her death was said to have been seized by Boreas, though it may have happened on the Areopagus, according to another version of the occurrence. (Plato, *Phaedrus,* 229cd)

We find the story of Orithyia and its scientific understanding linked or joined by Pharmakeia.

The second reference comes where Phaedrus and Socrates arrive at their private spot for an erotic interlude. "You must forgive me my dear friend; I'm a lover of learning, and trees and open country won't teach me anything, whereas men in the town do. Yet you seem to have discovered a recipe [*pharmakon*] for getting me out" (Plato, *Phaedrus,* 230cd). Derrida discusses some of the ways in which Pharmakeia haunts writing and truth throughout *Phaedrus.* I add (in *IR*) the juncture of *poiēsis* and *technē.* Here I add the inexhaustible dyad of hetero|sexuality.

8. See my *IR,* chap. 9, especially pp. 222–23.

9. This is another reference to my *IR,* chap. 9.

10. Plato offers us repeated animal references, complicating the humanity of our reading of truth and Pharmakeia's heterogeneity. Two examples are "[a] hungry animal can be driven by dangling a carrot or a bit of greenstuff in front of it . . . " (Plato, *Phaedrus,* 230de) and in the multiple images of the wings of the soul (called "Pteros" [Plato, *Phaedrus,* 252b]) and the winged steeds in the climactic speech at the center of the dialogue (Plato, *Phaedrus,* 246–57).

11. Socrates names the goods that madness brings as prophecy, purification, and *poiēsis* (Plato, *Phaedrus,* 244–45b).

12. In both Heidegger, *BT* and Foucault, *CS.*

13. The Greek word *allōn* is translated in the Loeb edition as "other races," presenting us with another striking heterogeneity that we had no idea was present in the movement between the gods and humanity (Plato, *Phaedrus,* trans. Harold North Fowler, Loeb Classical Library, p. 470).

14. Later in the same speech, the steeds are described in much more heterogeneous terms and the human soul as far more impure. See this chap., pp. 211–12.

15. See chap. 3, p. 28.

16. Everything of which I speak here depends on the word "only," language's repeated mark of exclusion.

17. But not, perhaps, pure.

18. Socrates speaks in *Phaedrus* of living and dead discourse, of writing animated by soul, by madness and love. See my *IR*, chap. 9. I speak here of gender animated by *erōs,* by corporeal heterogeneity.

19. See chap. 2, p. 13, and chap. 5, pp. 78–79.

20. The theme is repeated in *Laws,* where sexual difference occupies the very core of the state (Plato, *Laws,* 839–41).

21. See chap. 3, p. 37.

22. "But what about the words 'just' and 'good'? Don't we diverge, and dispute not only with one another but with our own selves?" (Plato, *Phaedrus,* 263).

23. See pp. 232–37.

24. See also Harding, *IACFT.*

25. Nancy says something similar, reading Bataille, but does not understand the rupture as gender. "And so, Being 'itself' comes to be defined as relational, as non-absoluteness, and, if you will—in any case this is what I am trying to argue—*as community*" (Nancy, *IC,* p. 6).

See also chap. 10, p. 254.

26. I am echoing that "[t]he univocity of being, its singleness of expression, is paradoxically the principal condition which permits difference to escape the domination of identity . . . " (Foucault, *TP,* p. 192). See the full quotation, chap. 3, p. 54. I am reading gender as another univocity whose singleness of expression releases the hold of identity.

27. Especially those who inhabit impure kinds. See chaps. 11 and 12.

28. Derrida speaks of blood, but he is more interested in this essay, perhaps, in the hold of thought on *Geschlecht* and its reciprocation, the hold of *Geschlecht* on the very thought of thought, a hold he describes as "monstrosity." The "we" that *Geschlecht* authorizes decrees in an act of monstration, designating humanity and animals as monsters, following another line of thought directed at heterogeneity, at the other kind.

> What is *un monstre?* You know the polysemic gamut of this word, the uses that one can make of it, for example concerning norms and forms, species and genus|gender: thus concerning *Geschlecht.* I shall begin by privileging here another course (*direction*). It goes in the direction, the *sens,* of a less known sense, since in French *la monstre* (a changing of gender, sex, or *Geschlecht*) has the poetico-musical sense of a diagram that *shows* (*montre*) in a piece of music the number of verses and the number of syllables assigned to the poet. *Monstrer* is *monstrer* (to show or demonstrate), and *une monstre* is *une montre* (a watch). (Derrida, *G2,* p. 166)

In French, *monstrer* joins monstrosity, *Geschlecht,* with monstration and time, with showing, language and representation, in time. Two polyphonic themes resonate together producing something ethically different.

My concern is with the movement from this polysemic gamut that inhabits the public and abstract places of species and genera to the face to face, with the monstrosity in which we look into the face and eyes, for example, of an other, an other of an other kind, perhaps, but face to face, into the face and eyes for example of a woman (if I am a man) or an animal (if I am human), or the animal looking at me, *le regard* of the one for the other. For that is where Heidegger places us in the abstract neutrality of the gift, our *Geschlecht,* before the monstrosity of the animal.

In words I have already quoted in part:

> In the common view, the hand is part of our bodily organism. But the hand's essence can never be determined, or explained, by its being an organ which can grasp. Apes, too, have organs that can grasp, but they do not have hands. The hand is infinitely different from all the grasping organs—paws, claws, or fangs—different by an abyss of essence. Only a being who can speak, that is, think, can have hands and can handily achieve works of handicraft. (Heidegger, *WCT,* pp. 356–57)

Of which, Derrida remarks, "Here in effect occurs a sentence that at bottom seems to me Heidegger's most significant, symptomatic, and seriously dogmatic" (Derrida, *G2,* p. 173). It is dogmatic especially because "Heidegger takes no account of a certain 'zoological knowledge'" (Derrida, *G2,* p. 173) concerning whether animals can speak, whether, *in fact,* paws, claws, and fangs *are hands.* I have taken note of this dogmatism concerning animals in general, noted how in Heidegger as well as throughout the Western tradition, The Human defines itself by excluding The Animal dogmatically, even (or especially) where Man is Rational Animal. Reason here excludes animality, perhaps no differently from the gift of language.

My concern for the moment is not with this exclusion of animal monstrosity that shows us the essence of humanity, demonstrates for us *unser Geschlecht.* My concern is with the face to face of the animal dyad, first, let us imagine, toward companion animals, then other animals. Singer insists that we not understand our ethical relation to animals to rest on our love for them, on our attraction to cute and cuddly pet animals. My response was to ask what an ethic that did not love, did not cherish, animals face to face could mean, based on duty alone. I have followed Levinas into a proximity with the other that brought us face to face with ethical difference. But I have halted at Irigaray's understanding that Levinas does not know heterogeneity in this face to face. So I have turned back to *Geschlecht* to examine again the sexual difference and gender whose dyads, however inexhaustible and profuse, give us the hetero of heterogeneity and heterosexuality. I have understood that other to lead to the face to face of alterosexuality, to *erōs,* giving the latter a very different meaning from man and woman. Man and woman and . . . the other kinds.

Now we may imagine ourselves, in thinking, face to face with an animal, perhaps the lions we heard in the Kalahari Desert or the roosting crows, but most of us do not get close to wild animals except in zoos, separated by bars, where we disperse their strangeness. Let us imagine getting very close to an animal that stares us face to face, eye to eye, grips our hands with its paws, claws, or fangs. In this face to face, perhaps with a dog or cat or crow, I suppose that we know another heterogeneity, another kind than our own, know it in the sense that we know that we do not know it but suppose it known by the animal. Or put another way, in this face to face, in closest proximity with dogs and cats, birds and fish, even cockroaches—for this proximity need not be with pets—we encounter a radical alterity of kind, of truth and knowledge and kind, that moves us from our *Geschlecht* to another *Geschlecht,* animal *Geschlecht,* in such a way that the very force of the "our" in *Geschlecht* breaks open. In this movement of breaking apart, perhaps we know another sexuality, a hetero|erotic|alterity, closer to hetero or *AlterGeschlecht,* to *autremonstrosité,* closer to our fleshy embodiment than spirit tells us, but spiritual nevertheless, animal souls, soul in everything, heterogeneously, heteropsychically, heteroerotically. We find ourselves repeating in a different cadence the movement above from *Dasein*'s sex to color, from Our *Geschlecht* to animal monstrosity, as ethical difference, a movement in proximity.

29. Derrida takes us to this place from *Geschlecht,* from the genus to proximity. I pass over the gift of language as our *Geschlecht,* in Derrida's reading, to a different text, Heidegger's essay on Trakl, "Language in the Poem: A Discussion on Georg Trakl's Poetic Work ["*Die Sprache im Gedicht: Eine Erörterung seines Gedichtes*"] (Heidegger, *LP,* pp. 159–98). Heidegger connects the line from "Seven-Song of Death":

> O man's decomposed form: joined of cold metals,

with the stanza from "Autumnal Soul":

> Fish and game soon glide away.
> Soon blue soul and long dark journey
> Parted us from loved ones, others.
> Evening changes image, sense.

He adds the words, "The others—that is the cast of the decomposed form of man" (Heidegger, *LP,* p. 170), and continues (in Derrida's translation, keeping the relevant German):

> The word [*Geschlecht,* then] signifies the human species (*Menschengeschlecht*) in the sense of humanity (*Menschheit*) as well as the

> species in the sense of tribes, stocks, and families, all that struck again [*dies alles wiederum geprägt:* struck in the sense of what receives the imprint, the *typos,* the typical mark] with the generic duality of the sexes (*in das Zwiefache der Geschlechter*). (Derrida, *G2,* p. 185: [In Peter Hertz's translation: "The word refers to mankind as a whole as well as to kinship in the sense of race, tribe, family—all of these in turn cast in the duality of the sexes" (Heidegger, *LP,* p. 170).])

We have listened to the crossing of sexual difference with animal difference in Heidegger's reading of this stanza, the juncture of sexes, tribes, and races with wild game (see chap. 3, n. 17). My concern here is with the duality of the sexes, first "generic," then something else, in proximity. "The curse of the decomposing kind is that the old human kinship has been struck apart by discord among sexes, tribes and races. . . . Not duality as such [generically], the discord is the curse. Out of the turmoil of blind wildness it carries each kind into an irreconcilable split" (Heidegger, *LP,* pp. 170–71).

For on Derrida's reading, agreeing that "Heidegger does not say 'generic duality,'" (Derrida, *G2,* p. 185), still "'*Geschlecht*' first names the historial race, man, humanity . . . The word '*Geschlecht*' names at the same time, across all [*überall*] these distinctions, . . . the generic splitting in two" (Derrida, *G2,* pp. 186–87) of sexual difference. My concern, Derrida's concern, is with the "generic" duality of sexual difference, the way in which *Geschlecht* relates to gender through the generalities of sex, tribe, race, generation, and community. I am reading this generality here, through the flesh, as profoundly related to heterogeneity as alterogender. I am reading, through *Geschlecht,* through the traces of *Geschlecht* in other languages, heterogeneity as alterosexuality, resonating with other heterogeneities, other dualities, other kinds.

For Heidegger continues, after speaking of the curse of discord, the wildness of sexual difference, that "[i]ts proper cast is only with that kind whose duality leaves discord behind and leads the way, as 'something strange,' into the gentleness of simple twofoldness following in the stranger's footsteps" (Heidegger, *LP,* p. 171). Derrida describes this movement as "a *second blow* that comes to strike the sexual difference and to transform it into dissension, war, savage opposition" (Derrida, *G2,* p. 193; see chap. 3, p. 28, for the full quotation). However one might want to speak of sexual difference as tender, gentle, peaceful, primordial or emerging from "its proper cast," the "gentleness of simple twofoldness" is in proximity, face to face. *Geschlecht* as generic, as human kinship, moves to sexual difference, to gender, through opposition, bestiality, animals, monstrosity, in relation to the curse of nature's inexhaustibility, but arrives at a gentleness in proximity, face to face.

This turns us back into the circle we find ourselves tracing in this chapter, a circle of ethical difference that gathers in its unlimited responsibility toward heterogeneity all of nature's plenitude, of kinds and species and genera—"sex, race, species, genus, gender, stock, family, generation or genealogy, community" (all the movements of *Geschlecht*'s monstrosity)—all of these into a proximity face to face, evinced for us (we humans) and for many other living creatures as erotic, more compellingly, perhaps, as *erōs* and *philia,* where these are understood as face to face, as madly erotic, and as unknown, excessive desire. Here Derrida's reading of Heidegger's reading of *Geschlecht* meets my reading of *Phaedrus,* organized around the face to face away from the city, in a private place.

30. We may understand the double blow of which Derrida speaks in Heidegger's reading of Trakl's poem in two different ways (see n. 29). One is to resist the theme of decomposition as a curse, resist it doubly, first as a curse, second as something to be overcome. "What curse has struck this humankind? . . . the old human kinship has been struck apart by discord among sexes, tribes and races" (Heidegger, *LP,* p. 170). Heidegger does not add, as I have added throughout, the cleavage between human kin and nature's other kin. On this reading, I refuse the curse of an accord struck apart by discord, of a tender, gentle, peaceful primordial sexual difference struck down by a curse. And I especially refuse the curse its wildness or animality.

But my second reading turns back on our refusals to recognize—if in a voice of curses and discord, and especially in a voice that speaks of a "kind whose duality leaves discord behind"—that Heidegger understands *Geschlecht* as a place where accord meets discord. We may read this understanding to suggest that gentleness—understood as cherishment—is inextricable from duality, that is, from heterogeneity and sacrifice. Heidegger seems to forget that this heterogeneity and sacrifice are ethical, that difference is ethical, circulates in the places of injustice, in proximity. We move away from Heidegger, on this second reading, to the proximity of ethical difference. We encounter injustice and heterogeneity in the intimacy and proximity of alter*erōs,* rapture as erotic relation to an other. Ethical difference works in intimacy and proximity even where the project is political. For we have not given up the political in the ethical|political, in sexual difference, have not relinquished the political in proximity. We think of intimacy, proximity, and rapture as ethical|political, as forms of plenishment.

CHAPTER TEN. REST

1. All the passages quoted here can be found in MacKinnon, *TFTS,* sometimes in revised form.

2. "I know no nondegraded English verb for the activity of sexual expression that would allow a construction parallel to, for example, 'I am

working,' a phrase that could apply to nearly any activity. . . . Nor is there *any* active verb meaning 'to act sexually' that specifically envisions a woman's action. If language constructs as well as expresses the social world, these words support heterosexual values" (MacKinnon, *FMMS1,* n. 2, p. 517).

I would rather speak of passing the masculine off as the universal.

3. Despite his aversion to MacKinnon's conclusions, Ronald Dworkin shows a respect for her legal arguments concerning gender inequality rarely acknowledged by her other critics. In relation to abortion (discussed in this chap., pp. 255–56), before concluding with his own view that abortion represents conflicts over the meaning of the intrinsic value of human life, he acknowledges the importance of her argument from equality and the limitations of the argument from privacy. "The most characteristic and fundamental feminist claim is that women's sexual subordination must be made a central feature of the abortion debate. MacKinnon puts the point in a particularly striking way. If women were truly equal with men, she says, the political status of a fetus would be different from what it is now" (Dworkin, *FA,* p. 28). After expressing "important reservations," Dworkin concludes that "the feminist arguments of MacKinnon and others have added a very important dimension to the abortion debate" (Dworkin, *FA,* p. 28).

He acknowledges the strength of her argument from equality more explicitly and powerfully in relation to her attack on pornography. "MacKinnon . . . says that the way in which pornography is offensive—that it portrays women as submissive victims who enjoy torture and mutilation—contribute to the unequal opportunities of women in American society" (Dworkin, *OW,* p. 40). He acknowledges that this is a forceful argument, demanding respect and requiring a powerful rebuttal. His reply is:

> Exactly because the moral environment in which we all live is in good part created by others, however, the question of who shall have the power to help shape that environment, and how, is of fundamental importance, though it is often neglected in political theory. Only one answer is consistent with the ideals of political equality: that no one may be prevented from influencing the shared moral environment, through his own private choices, tastes, opinions, and example, just because these tastes or opinions disgust those who have the power to shut him up or lock him up. (Dworkin, *OW,* p. 41)

Yet Dworkin's reply lacks persuasiveness once he acknowledges the force of MacKinnon's claim that in a social life pervaded by gender and other systemic inequalities, private choices are political. The issue is not of disgusting others but of injuring women and members of minority groups. The issue collapses the space between private and public, showing that what may be regarded under some conditions as private decisions, such as pornography and abortion, like hiring decisions and memberships in groups, are deeply political and public under conditions of inequality. Private decisions perpetuate public and political inequalities. Social practices that would be mandatory in a social climate of equality might be intolerable under conditions of gender and ethnic inequality. Nothing less than this understanding inhabits MacKinnon's argument from gender inequality. Such a compelling argument calls for a political reply: societies that would restrict private freedoms have been more harmful to the same groups of people who suffer under unrestricted access to pornography. This is a powerful point, and I consider it plausible. But it is a very different reply from Dworkin's to the difficult issues MacKinnon and other feminist writers call to our attention.

4. See chap. 9, pp. 230–31.

5. "[Spirit] thus discovers this world in the living present to be its own property; and so has taken the first step to descend from the ideal intelligible world . . . " (Hegel, *PM*, p. 802). I read these words as describing a transitory stage, rather than the final stage at which Spirit relates to nature. Even so, that we have understood our relation to nature to be one of ownership, understood our own selves in the form of ownership, remains one of the most contaminated ethical understandings of our belonging to the natural world.

6. I speak here of that encounter with our general economy that Sartre calls "nausea [*nausée*]" (Sartre, *N*). Even so, Roquentin finds himself "face to face" with being.

7. Here is where I would place the truth of bioregionalism: that we meet nature face to face in our proximity, intimately connected to the earth around us. Sustainability is a local condition, in proximity. Bioregionalism is love for the earth, face to face in our proximity.

8. Ronald Dworkin also speaks of women's responsibility to the life within them and feminist arguments concerning the impossibility of forming and meeting that responsibility under conditions of gender inequality. (Dworkin, *FA*, p. 28)

9. Of domesticity, Lyotard says some extraordinary things despite an impoverished relation to sexual difference. "The *domus* gives the untameable a chance to appear" (Lyotard, *I*, p. 196); "Solitude is *seditio*. Love is *seditio*. All love is criminal" (Lyotard, *I*, p. 201).

10. Jacobs suggests that human life is divided into two moral "syndromes," after Plato, described as the "commercial" and "guardian" syndromes (Jacobs, *SS*). The first seeks to avoid fraud and violence, pursues novelty, inventiveness, and thrift, praises comfort and competition. The second pursues prowess, authority, loyalty, vengeance, deception, fortitude, and exclusiveness. Every human society requires both syndromes for its moral life; mixing them together promotes disaster.

I understand these as two restricted economies, halting the circulation of general economy, slowing down the movement of goods and ideas to promote an *ethos,* one good over another. I respond that both restricted economies are too slow, can offer no justification, no legitimacy for themselves, against the other or other others. Each exceeds the other; each marks the limits of the other. Political and commercial economies work against the mobility of time and the excessive circulation of unknown goods. Both assume that the good has finally done its work, that history has come to an end.

11. Some of this appears in Kafka, always in a strange and terrifying proximity to humanity. He writes of Gregor Samsa turned into an insect or vermin, and of dogs and unknown creatures.

> seven dogs stepped into the light. . . . They did not speak, they did not sing, they remained generally silent, almost determinedly silent; but from the empty air they conjured music. Everything was music, the lifting and setting down of their feet, certain turns of the head, their running and their standing still, the positions they took up in relation to one another . . . (Kafka, "Investigations of a Dog," in *CS,* p. 281)

> But the most beautiful thing about my burrow is the stillness. Of course, that is deceptive. At any moment it may be shattered and then all will be over. For the time being, however, the silence is still with me. For hours I can stroll through my passages and hear nothing except the rustling of some little creature, which I immediately reduce to silence between my jaws, or the pattering of soil, which draws my attention to the need for repair; otherwise all is still. (Kafka, "The Burrow," in *CS,* p. 327)

CHAPTER ELEVEN. WALPURGISNACHT

1. Goats, fireflies, jays, screech owls, plovers, salamanders, serpents, mice, bats, sows, farrows, bucks, snails, among many others, as well as vales, ramparts, rocks, fountains, fir-trees, streams, grasses, sand, boulders, gorges, evergreens.

2. "[N]ot once *I* swear to you will *I* utter your name" (Wittig, *LB,* p. 46). "*I* am she who holds the secret of your name. *I* retain its syllables behind m/y closed mouth even while *I* would rather cry them out over the sea so that they might fall and be sombrely engulfed therein" (Wittig, *LB,* p. 130).

3. For example, "the muscles all catch fire simultaneously the trapezii deltoids pectorals serrati obliques recti adductors artorii psoas" (Wittig, *LB,* p. 34).

4. Another, grander example:

THE AREOLAS THE ECCHYMOSES THE WOUNDS THE FOLDS THE GRAZES THE WRINKLES THE BLISTERS THE FISSURES THE SWELLINGS THE SUNBURN THE BEAUTY-SPOTS THE BLACKHEADS THE HAIR FOLLICLES THE WARTS THE EXCRESCENCES THE PAPULES THE SEBUM THE PIGMENTATION THE EPIDERMIS THE DERMIS THE CUTANEOUS NERVES THE INNERVATIONS THE PAPILLAE THE NERVE NETWORKS THE NERVE-ROOTS THE BUNDLES THE BRANCHES THE PLEXUSES THE MOTOR NERVES THE SENSORY THE CERVICAL THE PNEUMOGASTRIC

(Wittig, *LB*, p. 53)

LES ARÉOLES LES ECCHYMOSES LES PLAIES LES PLIS LES ÉCORCHURES LES RIDES LES AMBOULES LES GERÇURES LES CLOQUES LE HALE LES GRAINS DE BEAUTÉ LES POINTS NOIRS LES FOLLICULES PILEUX LES VERRUES LES EXCROISSANCES LES PAPULES LES SÉBUM LA PIGMENTATION L'ÉPIDERME LE DERME LES NERFS CUTANÉS LES INNERVATIONS LES PAPILLES LES RÉSEAUX NERVEUX LES RACINES LES FAISCEAUX LES BRANCHES LES PLEXUS LES NERFS MOTEURS LES SENSIBLES LES SENSORIAUX LES CERVICAUX LES PNEUMOGASTRIQUES

(Wittig, *CL*, pp. 50–51)

5. See my *RR*, chap. 8, "Embodiment."
6.

> There is no explanation of sexuality which reduces it to anything other than itself, for it is already something other than itself, and indeed, if we like, our whole being. Sexuality, it is said, is dramatic *because* we commit our whole personal life to it. But just why do we do this? Why is our body, for us, the mirror of our being, unless because it is a *natural self*, a current of given existence, with the result that we never know whether the forces which bear us on are its or ours—or with the result rather that they are never entirely either its or ours. There is no outstripping of sexuality any more than there is any sexuality enclosed within itself. (Merleau-Ponty, *PP*, p. 171)

7. This is far from the most violent, destructive intervention into the tissues, fleshes, of the beloved's body.

> Having absorbed the external part of your ear *I* burst the tympanum, *I* feel the rounded hammer-bone rolling between m/y lips, m/y teeth crush it, *I* find the anvil and the stirrup-bone, *I* crunch them, *I* forage with my fingers, *I* wrench away a bone, *I* fall on the superb cochlea bone and membrane all wrapped round together, *I* devour them, *I* burst the semicircular canals, . . . *I* apply m/y suckers to your delicious uvula. (Wittig, *LB*, p. 24)

And it is inseparably related to blood and death.

> You interrupt m/e, you sing with strident voice your certainty of triumph over my death, you do not heed m/y sobs, you drag m/e to the surface of the earth where the sun is visible. Only there at the exit towards the trees and the forest do you turn to face m/e with a bound and it is true that looking into your eyes *I* revive with prodigious speed.
>
> You are exsanguinated. All your blood torn forcibly from your limbs issues violently from your groins carotid arms temples legs ankles, the arteries are crudely severed, it involves the carotids brachials radials temporals, it involves the iliacs femorals tibials peroneals, the veins are simultaneously laid open . . . (Wittig, *LB*, pp. 20–21)

8. "*I* am laid under an interdict in the city where you live. *I* have no right to go there. The women loose your dogs on m/e when *I* approach" (Wittig, *LB*, p. 38).
9. And more:

> M/y fingers are spread out nails down, m/y palms are turned toward the sun, the metacarpals the phalanges are extended. M/y hands are like stars. *I* see at m/y wrists the blue veins, a broad network on the inside of m/y arms. You apply your new procedure to m/e to inoculate the sun, the veins and arteries of m/y wrists artificially dilated. You are obliged to hold m/e on the ground because of the shaking of m/y body. . . . At last

> our blackened skulls clash together, at last boneless with black holes to see you with without hands to touch you *I* am you you are m/e irreversibly m/y best-beloved. (Wittig, *LB*, p. 119)

10. Pagels describes the institution of a male and patriarchal God in early Gnostic Christian writings and practices as a religion that began ambiguously, bisexually.

> All the texts cited above—secret "gospels," revelations, mystical teachings—are among those rejected from the select list of twenty-six that comprise the "New Testament" collection. As these and other writings were sorted and judged by various Christian communities, every one of these texts which gnostic groups revered and shared was rejected from the canonical collection as "heterodox" by those who called themselves "orthodox" (literally, straight-thinking) Christians. By the time this process was concluded, probably as late as the year A.D. 200, virtually all the feminine imagery for God (along with any suggestion of an androgynous human creation) had disappeared from "orthodox" Christian tradition. (Pagels, *WBGM*, pp. 112–13)

Why, Pagels asks, did this rejection take place? The Gnostics answered that "he was a derivative, merely instrumental power, whom the divine Mother had created to administer the universe, but who remained ignorant of the power of Wisdom, his own Mother" (Pagels, *WBGM*, p. 113). This explanation, early as it was, represents an understanding of *technē*'s place within a far more archaic and immemorial divine production, including its blindness and forgetting.

Pagels calls these "mythical explanations," though I understand them to express something true about heterogeneity and the repressions that accompany it. Pagels prefers the more social and political understanding that what was at stake was the "domination of men over women as the proper, God-given order" (Pagels, *WBGM*, p. 116), repeating our traversal here through the Greek from Aristotle, a heterogeneous, plenitudinous view of nature (and divinity) with a hierarchy of sovereignty based on natural perfection.

Pagels rejects the interpretation that the Gnostic groups were suppressed "only because of their positive attitude toward women," that "the recognition of mankind as a male and female entity bore within it the explosive social possibility of women acting on an equal basis with men in positions of authority and leadership" (Pagels, *WBGM*, p. 115). I understand the explosiveness of this thought as something far deeper, more threatening, more far reaching.

If the masculinity of God repeats the subjection of women, then we may respond to the call of the Goddess. "The major difference between patriarchal religions and the evolving Goddess religions—perhaps even more central than the image of the divine as female—is the worldview that includes regarding divinity as immanent: in the world, not outside the world, as manifest in nature and in human beings, human needs and desires" (Starhawk, *EJGR,* p. 194). The transformation of God-The-Father into another spirituality, responsive to women, is already begun and far too late. Yet in the account of sexual difference as taking place in multiple dyads of heterogeneity, the Goddess threatens to repeat the mark of gender. Nor will the neutrality of God, ungendered, allow us to take up the spiritual task of enduring the weight of heterogeneity. If *Dasein,* if Being, and nature are sexed, alterogendered, then so is God, in enigmatic and difficult ways, more enigmatic perhaps than represented by the God|dess.

This enigma may vanish in the engendering of the (female) soul's affair with (the masculine) God in Irigaray's "*La Mystérique,*" repeating the privileging of heterosexual heterogeneity. The figure of the lesbian–witch may circulate an engendered|sexual body and self so far from heterosexuality and androgyny as to be entirely unthinkable. Yet that thought, of the unthought, expresses the call of the good.

11. A recurrent theme of feminist thought echoes the silence of women's experience in the canonical texts that define the West, sacred and other. For the moment, I leave to rest questions concerning cultures without texts and canons, concerned with what it might mean, once more, remembering the witches, their murders and their powers, to enter the reverberations of women's experiences.

> Men have actively shaped their experiences of self and world by creating the stories they have told. Their deepest stories orient them to what they perceive as the ultimate powers and realities of the universe. We women have not told our own stories. The dialectic between experiencing and shaping experience by storytelling has not been in our own hands. (Christ, *SQWE,* p. 229)

> Women have lived in the interstices between inchoate experiences and the shapings given to experience by the stories of men. In a very real sense, women have not experienced their own experience. (Christ, *SQWE,* p. 228)

I cannot easily accept this image of the absence of women's stories, for women have always told stories, always told each other stories, told their daughters and their sons. Men and women have been shaped by women's stories, everywhere, in every place, around every hearth. But perhaps not the revered, authoritative stories, the stories bearing the famous author's name. And perhaps not the authoritative stories of the ultimate, where men claimed God's and reality's authority.

In a growing feminist consciousness, women "will no longer be content to read ourselves sideways into stories in which 'the daughters do not exist' " (Christ, *SQWE,* p. 230). More important, my concern here, the concern for which I remember the witches, "we will begin to realize that the exclusion of our experience from the funding of sacred stories may point to a basic defect in the perception of ultimate power and reality provided by the traditional stories" (Christ, *SQWE,* p. 230). We seek, we find ourselves falling into, an "articulation of a new perception of the ultimate" (Christ, *SQWE,* p. 230). With all the reservations I can muster against falling back into God's Law, I understand this ultimate in two ways embodied in the witches, sideways and squinting. I understand this ultimate as heterogeneity, as sexed, specied, animaled, plenishment in the earth, as dispersed, profuse, plenitudinous, inexhaustible. The theme of "women's experience" does not represent another same, but another relation to heterogeneity than that defined canonically in the West, primarily by men. In this way, perhaps, in which the images of outcast women—witches, heretics, madwomen (Christ, *SQWE,* p. 23)—represent something profound of the ultimate, of the difference between heterogeneity and exclusion, "the feminine [that is, witches', heretics', madwomen's] perception of the ultimate . . . is fraught with potentially revolutionary implications for the human perception of the ultimate" (Christ, *SQWE,* p. 243), of the earth and its plenishment.

CHAPTER TWELVE. REST

1. Also:

> A "world" need not be a construction of a whole society. It may be a construction of a whole society. It may be construction of a tiny portion of a particular society. It may be inhabited by just a few people. Some "worlds" are bigger than others.
>
> In a "world" some of the inhabitants may not understand or hold the particular construction of them that constructs them in that "world." So, there may be "worlds" that construct me in ways that I do not even understand. (Lugones, *PWTLP,* pp. 9–10)

2. See my *IR,* chap. 11, for an African example of the juxtaposition of witchcraft and sorcery with sovereignty. Also see this chap., p. 293, and n. 7.

3. Compare the possibility that witches and sorcerers pervade daily life in many non-Western societies even though no one is accused of being a witch or sorcerer, an explicit expression of the witchery of life and nature, regardless of any associated craft or *technē.*

> In the course of listening to discussions about sorcery over several months, and observing the rancorous and often fiery debates on the topic that took place in village men's houses, two things soon became

> apparent: first, that people's interest in the subject was greatly heightened by particular events, notably serious illnesses, accidents and deaths; and second, that their responses to sorcery, or at least the illnesses that allegedly manifested it, were highly patterned. But there was another aspect of Kwoma sorcery that intrigued me, and that was that no one ever directly accused anyone else of practising it (although imputations were commonly made in private), and no one ever admitted in public or in private to knowing anything about how it was practised—at least not in any detail. (Bowden, *SISC,* pp. 183–84)

4. And further:

> When a man accedes to the kingship, he and his subjects know that he has one year within which to live up to the challenge of his office and bewitch three close relatives. One relative may be anyone in his matriclan; another relative must be someone in his immediate uterine family (often a sibling); and the third relative must be either his own child . . . or his sister's child. There are similar requirements for newly installed queens and male and female village chiefs. My informant assured me that the rule is carried out in every case. (Gottlieb, *WKS,* p. 254)

See also n. 7.

5. He has a disciplinary responsibility.

> In the Euro-American world view, there is a separation between the self and the nonself (phenomenal world). Through this process of separation, the phenomenal world becomes an Object, an "it." By Object, I mean the totality of phenomena conceived as constituting the nonself, that is, all the phenomena that are the antithesis of subject, ego, or self-consciousness. The phenomenal world becomes an entity considered as totally independent of the self. Events or phenomena are treated as external to the self rather than as affected by one's feelings or reflections. Reality becomes that which is set before the mind to be apprehended, whether it be things external in space or conceptions formed by the mind itself. (Dixon, *WVRM,* p. 55)

I understand this relation ethically not as a self–world relation, as if ethics circulates repeatedly and only around the self, but as a world–soul relation in which the self, besouled, finds itself surrounded by endless and inexhaustible others, all souled, individuals and kinds, where soul has care of all that is inanimate. But perhaps this difference is not as great as we may imagine on reading Dixon. Perhaps Dixon does not wish to go to the extreme in understanding the dispersion of the separation between self and nonself. The extreme disperses the self as the locus of ethical regard, so that every ethical relation is a relation to self. Worse, in Harding's words, offering her understanding of Dixon:

> The presence of "empty perceptual space" surrounding the self and separating it from everything else extracts the self from its natural and social surroundings and locates all the forces in the universe concerned with furthering the self's interests inside the circle of empty perceptual space—that is, in the self itself. Outside the self are only objects that can be acted upon or measured—i.e., known. (Harding, *CCFAM,* p. 301)

Dixon's own words are, "[t]he individual becomes the center of social space. There is no conception of the group as a whole except as a collection of individuals" (Dixon, *WVRM,* p. 58). We may hear Lugones speaking of different ethnic and socially constructed worlds. The subject again is natural kinds, ethnic and social kinds in human worlds.

6. We have heard such a sense in feminist writing, sometimes in places far from witchcraft.

> Touch is ambiguous and complex. As a symbol for power, it signals a range of intentions from coercion to persuasion, any one of which may further elicit a complex range of responses involving pain and pleasure. Touch as coercion may take the form of brutality or seduction. Whether brutality or seduction, the point is to exert control over others. By contrast, touch that signals an attempt to persuade presupposes recognition of respect for another, symbolized by a release of power. . . . Intentions are often not self-evident, nor are responses necessarily unmixed. (Cooey, *WF,* pp. 20–21)

7. See Gottlieb, *WKS,* p. 254; discussed in this chap., p. 293, and in my *IR,* chap. 11.

Gottlieb quotes a Beng informant: "Long ago, when it came matriclan X's time to contribute a member to be the chief of village P, the clan elders refused to do so because they did not want to have other clan members killed in witchcraft by the new chief. . . . The king of the region in which village P is located commented to me that P 'could not be a good village' until clan X reinstated itself back into the village chiefship rotation cycle." Gottlieb comments: "and, by implication, permits clan members to be killed through witchcraft by the new chief" (Gottlieb, *WKS,* p. 255).

8. She acknowledges that in virtue of the "important differences between the life worlds of Africans and Afro-Americans on the one hand and women of European descent on the other," it is no surprise that "feminist and Africanist accounts of our own realities are simply different" (Harding, *CCFAM,* pp. 302–3). The variety of experiences present here—among women, feminist and nonfeminist, Africans, and African–Americans, within each of the groups—is immense, lending little support to the overall opposition between European–American and African–American relations to nature. I have understood these different relations to nature as present throughout human experience and history, including

European–American culture, not just in the dyad self–world, but in our ethical regard toward nature. I do not understand ethical inclusion to be something alien to European experience, but to have been subordinated to rule.

9. Other dichotomies can be found in African writing about African philosophy. For example,

> Where Western man sits behind his desk, solving theoretical problems of life and of the world, the African creates his life in the world, concretely and with a vivid concern for the future as far as it is foreseeable. Where Western man puts down the result of his speculations in neat and tidy equations, which can never become a living part and parcel of the thinker, the African participates in the event which he expresses in the symbolism of his dance and of his complex ritual. To use a contemporary phrase in its full and literal meaning: The African is "with it." (Ruch and Anyanwu, *AP,* p. 106)

> The Westerner has a problem-solving mind whilst the African has a situation-experiencing mind. The Westerner has an aggressive mentality. When he sees a problem he will not rest until he has formulated some solution to it. He cannot live with contradictory ideas in his mind . . . he is rigorously scientific in rejecting solutions for which there is no basis in logic. . . . Africans, being a pre-scientific people, do not recognize any conceptual cleavage between the natural and the supernatural. . . . I think too, that the African can hold contradictory ideas in fruitful tension within his mind. (Ruch and Anyanwu, *AP,* pp. 209–10)

10. Harding understands the race, cultural, and gender distinctions she and Dixon discuss in terms of different cognitive styles and worldviews, based on different social roles and activities. "Thus, we should expect differences in cognitive styles and world views from peoples engaged in different kinds of social activities. And we should expect similarities from peoples engaged in similar kinds of social activities" (Harding, *CCFAM,* p. 310). Moreover, "[t]hose who participate in Africanist and feminist political struggles have far more ambiguous race and gender options, respectively, than the Africans and women whose emancipation they would advance" (Harding, *CCFAM,* p. 310). We may imagine that the emancipatory struggle itself introduces alternative and multiple forms of thought and experience, against traditional dichotomies, even against dichotomy itself, when disturbed and displaced by women of different races and cultures or by Africans who live in multiple cultures on a huge and fertile continent and who have been dispersed, some by choice, some by force, throughout the world.

For Harding does not address ethical difference as inclusion even as she addresses a question inescapable for ethical inclusion. The question of ethics in relation to heterogeneity is how we are to think of living and acting before the good when the form of our particular experiences has been oppressive. I have answered that difference inhabits the places of proximity, face to face, with heterogeneity, taking the forms of gender, race, and blood. Harding's question is how we are to think of inhabiting such places when our thoughts belong to historical oppressions. "We are different, not primarily by nature's design, but as a result of the social subjugations we have lived through and continue to experience" (Harding, *CCFAM,* pp. 311–32). She seems to understand nature's design as biological, to be resisted. I understand it as general economy, that circulation from which an inexhaustible plenitude emerges that disturbs every hegemony, displaces every instituted place, however oppressive, and imposes on those who can respond to it unlimited responsibility for ethical difference, unlimited responsibility to resist injustice and to care for, toward, and before heterogeneous others. The One, the Dichotomy, and the Plenitude all work to reduce heterogeneity. The question of ethical difference is how we may work refusing any such reduction.

11. An African expression of such a profusion is that

> The invisible world is symbolized or manifested by the visible and concrete phenomena and objects of nature. The invisible world presses hard upon the visible: one speaks of the other, and the African peoples "see" that invisible universe when they look at, hear or feel the visible and tangible world. This is one of the most fundamental religious heritages of African peoples . . . This religious universe is not an academic proposition: it is an empirical experience, which reaches its height in acts of worship. (Ruch and Anwanyu, *AP,* p. 122; quoted from Mbiti, *ARP,* p. 57)

> For African peoples this is a religious universe. Nature in the broadest sense of the word is not an empty impersonal object or phenomenon: it is filled with religious significance. Man gives life even where natural objects and phenomena have no biological life. God is seen in and behind these objects and phenomena: they are His creation, they manifest Him, they symbolize his being and presence. (Ruch and Anwanyu, *AP,* p. 123; Mbiti, *ARP,* pp. 56–57)

12. See my *IR,* chaps. 9 and 10.
13. See chap. 3, n. 21 and chap. 13, n. 5.

CHAPTER THIRTEEN. RHAPSODY

1. I ring the cacophony of the kinds of the earth within this triangle of locality, inexhaustibility, and ergonality.

> A *locus,* located and locating, in spheres of relevance: a *locale* of its *ingredients;* an ingredient of other locales.

> An ingredient, one among many other ingredients in a locale: as one, a *unison* with many *resonances,* the other ingredients relevant to it in that locale.
>
> A unison including many other unisons: a *superaltern unison* located in a *superaltern locale.*
>
> An ingredient with a superaltern unison in a superaltern locale *belongs* there, otherwise it *departs.* Every ingredient belongs to and departs from any of its locations in *harmony* and *disharmony.*
>
> An ingredient together with other alternatives ingredient in a locale: such an ingredient works there in *polyphony,* otherwise in *stillness,* lacking possibilities. Every ingredient echoes stilly and polyphonically in any of its locations. (Ross, *RR,* p. 13)

See my *RR* for the orchestration of these themes, and *IR* for their ethical and political reverberations. Here I am concerned with plenitude and plenishment.

2. Derrida speaks of friendship as measure's frame, perhaps against the disturbance of *erōs* marked by Socrates in *Phaedrus,* which can entail divine madness or *poiēsis.* See Derrida, *PF.*

3. See chap. 5, pp. 83–87.

4. Hyde locates art in gift economy (Hyde, *G*). I add the velocity of general economy, unworking every work, still gifted, cherished and cherishing.

We may also echo Heidegger's words concerning technology:

> We can use technical devices, and yet with proper use also keep ourselves so free of them, that we may let go of them any time. We can use technical devices as they ought to be used, and also let them alone as something which does not affect our inner and real core. We can affirm the unavoidable use of technical devices, and also deny them the right to dominate us, and so to warp, confuse, and lay waste our nature. (Heidegger, *DT,* p. 54)

This understanding of how we might use technology is close to plenishment, with the qualification that we abandon any inner and real core of our humanity, our kind, as belonging to our *Geschlecht.*

5. As air, even as blood, with hesitant memories of women.

> [H]ow can you buy or sell the sky? The land? . . . This we know: the earth does not belong to man, man belongs to the earth. All things are connected like the blood that unites us all. Man did not weave the web of life, he is merely a strand in it. Whatever he does to the web, he does to himself. . . . (Chief Seattle, quoted in Krell, *DL,* p. 317)

6. This is Taylor's language in *RN.* See chap. 7, pp. 147–51.

7. Rather, he speaks of it as freedom and truth. "Freedom for what is opened up in an open region lets beings be the beings they are. Freedom now reveals itself as letting beings be" (Heidegger, *OET,* p. 127). "Letting-

be, *i.e.*, freedom, is intrinsically exposing, ek-sistent. Considered in regard to the essence of truth, the essence of freedom manifests itself as exposure to the disclosedness of beings" (Heidegger, *OET,* p. 128).

Far more important, he speaks of letting-be [*sein lassen*] and *Gelassenheit* entirely in relation to humanity: human exposure, freedom, *Dasein*'s ek-sistence (Heidegger, *OET,* p. 129). "Evidently the nature of man is released to that-which-regions because this belongs to it so essentially, that without man that-which-regions can not be a coming forth of all natures, as it is" (Heidegger, *DT,* p. 83).

8. Whitehead calls them societies, and in a deep sense the world for him is composed of societies and societies of societies (Whitehead, *PR,* p. 90) "for each of its members, an environment with some element of order in it, persisting by reason of the genetic relations between its own members." But he also regards actual entities, however collective and public, as the "Final Realities" (Whitehead, *PR,* p. 22). Only in virtue of societies can "the problem for Nature" be posed and solved via "the production of societies which are 'structured' with a high 'complexity,' and which are at the same time 'unspecialized.' In this way, intensity is mated with survival" (Whitehead, *PR,* p. 101). The problem for Nature—on my reading, not a problem at all—is plenishment. The problem for nature is ethical regard, sexual and kindred, realized as plenishment. It bears a distant kinship to plenitude in Leibniz, where this "problem" is posed in a measured way.

> From the conflict of all the possibles demanding existence, this at once follows, that there exists that series of things by which as many of them as possible exist; in other words, the maximal series of possibilities . . .
>
> . . . We must say that God makes the greatest number of things that he can and [by means of the simplest laws of nature] to find room for as many things as it is possible to place together. (Leibniz, *EEE,* p. 92)

Leibniz speaks of maximal perfection, of as many things as possible. Whitehead speaks of the problem for nature and its solution. We may read neither as falling under measure, but to the contrary, as composing general economy, circulating the good in profusion. The maximal series of possibilities exceeds any measure, circulates whatever can be circulated together with the other goods in circulation. Nature solves its problem not by law but by judgment after judgment, by intensity, by plenishment and by plenitude. In the name of the good, we resist law's measure. Like Whitehead and Leibniz, we may understand Nature's plenishment to be the good, utterly without the trace of measure, requiring measure after measure to do its work.

That the work of the world is done by societies suggests, against Whitehead's explicit view, that societies, collectives, kinds compose the earth's ingredients, that plenishment pertains to them, to societies of societies, locales of locales, kinds of kinds, composites, without privileging an individual subject. Such a reading is closer to Whitehead's understanding of the relation between public and private. "The sole concrete facts, in terms of which actualities can be analysed, are prehensions; and every prehension has its public side and its private side" (Whitehead, *PR,* p. 290). Everything has its public and private side, but these do not mean collective and individual. I take public and private to pertain to general and restricted economy, to *poiēsis* and *technē.* I understand the public to be the general circulation of dyads, private and face to face, erotically and heteroerotically, one kind facing another. I understand cherishment here in kind, that is, in kindness related to kinds, the English language's *Geschlecht,* with a difference in kind, of kindness, these two quite different ideas meeting in Middle English, where the relation of one kind to another, of stock, race, genus, is given by nature a caring face. I understand cherishment's kindness to compose the meeting, the regard, face to face, in proximity, between heterogeneous and impure kinds, circulating excessively and endlessly in intermediary figures of representation.

9. "Truth and Beauty are the great regulative properties in virtue of which Appearance justifies itself to the immediate decision of the experient subject" (Whitehead, *AI,* p. 309).

"Beauty is the internal conformation of the various items of experience with each other, for the production of maximum effectiveness. . . . Thus any part of experience can be beautiful. The teleology of the Universe is directed to the production of Beauty" (Whitehead, *AI,* p. 341).

"Here by the last quality of Peace, I am not referring to political relations. I mean a quality of mind steady in its reliance that fine action is treasured in the nature of things" (Whitehead, *AI,* p. 353).

We may struggle with the idea of steadiness and effectiveness. But the play of these together composes something close to plenishment.

10. "But there can be intense experience without Harmony. In this event, there is Destruction of the significant characters of individual objects. When the direct feeling of such Destruction dominates the whole, there is the immediate feeling of evil, and the anticipation of destructive or weakened data for the future. Harmony is bound up with the preservation of the individual significance of detail, and Discord consists in its destruction" (Whitehead, *AI,* p. 339). Art brings a beauty in which individuality of detail is interwoven into harmony, resting on contrasts of kinds and kinds of kinds: "the interweaving of absoluteness upon relativity. In the work of art the relativity becomes the harmony of the composition, and the absoluteness is the claim for separate individuality advanced by component factors" (Whitehead, *AI,* pp. 339–40).

BIBLIOGRAPHY

Adams, Carol J. *The Sexual Politics of Meat [SPM*]. New York: Continuum, 1992.

Agamben, Giorgio. *Language and Death: The Place of Negativity* [*LD*]. Minneapolis: University of Minnesota Press, 1991.

Andolsen, Barbara Hilkert, Christine E. Gudorf, and Mary D. Pellauer, eds. *Women's Consciousness, Women's Conscience* [*WCWC*]. New York: Winston, 1985.

Aquinas, Thomas. *Summa Theologica* [*ST*]. Trans. Fathers of the English Dominican Province. London: Burns, Oates and Washbourne, 1912–36.

Arendt, Hannah. *The Human Condition* [*HC*]. Chicago: University of Chicago Press, 1958.

Arens, William, and Ivan Karp, eds. *Creativity of Power* [*CP*]. Washington and London: Smithsonian Press, 1989.

Aristotle. *The Basic Works of Aristotle.* Ed. Richard McKeon. New York: Random House, 1941. All quotations from Aristotle are from this edition.

Bataille, Georges. *L'Expérience intérieure* [*EI*]. Paris: Gallimard, 1954.

———. *Méthode de Méditation* [*MM*]. In *L'Expérience intérieure.*

Baudrillard, Jean. *Forget Foucault* [*FF*]. New York: Semiotext(e), 1987.

Bentham, Jeremy. *Introduction to the Principles of Morals and Legislation* [*PML*]. In Burtt, *The English Philosophers from Bacon to Mill.*

Bernal, Martin. *Black Athena: The Afroasiatic Roots of Classical Civilization.* Vol. 1, *The Fabrication of Ancient Greece, 1785–1985* [*BA*]. New Brunswick, N.J.: Rutgers University Press, 1987.

Bowden, Ross. "Sorcery, Illness, and Social Control in Kwoma Society" [*SISC*]. In Stephen, *Sorcerer and Witch in Melanesia.*

Bowles, Gloria. Conclusion to *Feminist Issues.* In Illich, *Feminist Issues.*

Burtt, Edwin A., ed. *The English Philosophers from Bacon to Mill* [*EPBM*]. New York: Modern Library, 1959.

Butler, Judith. *Gender Trouble: Feminism and the Subversion of Identity* [*GT*]. New York: Routledge, 1990.

In citing works in the text and notes, short titles have generally been used. These are given in brackets following the full title.

Caputo, John D. *Against Ethics: Contributions to a Poetics of Obligation with Constant Reference to Deconstruction* [*AE*]. Bloomington: Indiana University Press, 1993.

Card, Claudia, ed. *Feminist Ethics* [*FE*]. Lawrence: University Press of Kansas, 1991.

Cheal, David. *The Gift Economy* [*GE*]. New York: Routledge, 1988.

Cheney, Jim. "Eco-feminism and Deep Ecology" [*EDE*]. *Environmental Ethics* 9 (1987).

Christ, Carol P. "Reverence for Life: The Need for a Sense of Finitude" [*RL*]. In Cooey, Farmer, and Ross, *Embodied Love.*

———. "Spiritual Quest and Women's Experience" [*SQWE*]. In Christ and Plaskow, *Womenspirit Rising.*

Christ, Carol P., and Judith Plaskow. *Womanspirit Rising* [*WR*]. New York: Harper and Row, 1979.

Cixous, Hélène, and Catherine Clément. *The Newly Born Woman* [*NBW*]. Trans. Betsy Wing. Minneapolis: University of Minnesota Press, 1975.

Clark, Cedric X. "Some Implications of Nkrumah's Consciencism for Alternative Coordinates in NonEuropean Causality" [*SINC*]. In Ruch and Anyanwu, *African Philosophy.*

Clément, Catherine. "The Guilty Ones" [*GO*]. In Cixous and Clément, *The Newly Born Woman.*

Cohen, Rosalie. "The Influence of Conceptual Rule-Sets on Measures of Learning Ability" [*ICR*]. In Gamble and Bond, *Race and Intelligence.*

Cole, Eve Browning, and Susan Coultrap-McQuin, eds. *Explorations in Feminist Ethics: Theory and Practice* [*EFE*]. Bloomington: Indiana University Press, 1992.

Coleridge, Samuel Taylor. *Biographia Literaria* [*BL*]. Ed. John Shawcross. London: Oxford University Press, 1949.

Comstock, Gary. "Pigs and Piety: A Theocentric Perspective on Food Animals" [*PP*]. *Between the Species* 8, no. 3 (summer 1992).

Cooey, Paula M. "The Word Become Flesh: Woman's Body, Language, and Value" [*WF*]. In Cooey, Farmer, & Ross, *Embodied Love.*

Cooey, Paula M., Sharon A. Farmer, and Mary Ellen Ross, eds. *Embodied Love: Sensuality and Relationship as Feminist Values* [*EL*]. San Francisco: Harper and Row, 1987.

Curtin, Deane. "Toward an Ecological Ethic of Care" [*TEEC*]. In Warren, *Hypatia.*

Curtiss, Susan. *Genie: A Psycholinguistic Study of a Modern-Day "Wild Child."* New York: Academic Press, 1977.

Daly, Mary. "After the Death of God the Father: Women's Liberation and the Transformation of Christian Consciousness" [*ADGF*]. In Christ and Plaskow, *Womenspirit Rising.*

———. *Gyn/Ecology: The Metaethics of Radical Feminism* [*G/E*]. Boston: Beacon, 1990.

Deleuze, Gilles. *Différence et répétition* [*DR*]. Paris: P.U.F., 1969.

———. *Logique du sens* [*LS*]. Paris: Les Éditions de Minuit, 1969.

Derrida, Jacques. *Dissemination* [*D*]. Trans. Barbara Johnson. Chicago: University of Chicago Press, 1981.

———. "Force of Law: The 'Mystical Foundation of Authority'" [*FL*]. *Cardozo Law Review* 11 (1991).

———. "From Restricted to General Economy: A Hegelianism without Reserve" [*FRGE*]. In Derrida, *Writing and Difference.*

———. "Geschlecht: Sexual Difference, Ontological Difference" [*G1*]. *Research in Phenomenology* 13 (1983).

———. "*Geschlecht* 2: Heidegger's Hand" [*G2*]. Trans. John P. Leavey, Jr. In Sallis, *Deconstruction in Philosophy: The Texts of Jacques Derrida.*

———. "Heidegger's Ear: Philopolemology (*Geschlecht* 4)" [*G4*]. In Sallis, *Reading Heidegger.* Bloomington: Indiana University Press, 1993.

———. "Plato's Pharmacy" [*PP*]. In Derrida, *Dissemination.*

———. "The Politics of Friendship" [*PF*]. *The Journal of Philosophy* 85 (November 1988).

———. *The Truth in Painting* [*TP*]. Trans. Geoff Bennington and Ian McLeod. Chicago: University of Chicago Press, 1987.

———. *Writing and Difference* [*WD*]. Trans. Alan Bass. Chicago: University of Chicago Press, 1978.

———. "Violence and Metaphysics: An Essay on the Thought of Emmanuel Levinas" [*VM*]. In Derrida, *Writing and Difference.*

Dewey, John. "Context and Thought" [*CT*]. In Dewey, *Experience, Nature, and Freedom.*

———. *Experience and Nature* [*EN*]. 2nd ed. New York: Dover, 1958.

———. *Experience, Nature, and Freedom* [*ENF*]. Ed. Richard J. Bernstein. Indianapolis: Library of Liberal Arts, 1960.

———. "Nature in Experience" [*NE*]. In Dewey, *Experience, Nature, and Freedom.*

Dimen, Muriel. "Power, Sexuality, and Intimacy" [*PSI*]. In Jaggar and Bordo, *Gender/Body/Knowledge.*

Dixon, Vernon J. "World Views and Research Methodology" [*WVRM*]. In King, Dixon, and Nobles, *African Philosophy.*

Dworkin, Andrea. *Intercourse.* New York: Free Press, 1987.

Dworkin, Ronald. "Feminists and Abortion" [*FA*]. In *The New York Review of Books* 40, no. 11 (10 June 1993).

———. Review of MacKinnon, *Only Words* [*OW*]. In *The New York Review of Books* 40, no. 17 (21 October 1993).

Euripides. *Hecuba*. Trans. Edward P. Coleridge. In Oates and O'Neill, *The Complete Greek Drama*.

Feyerabend, Paul. *Against Method: Outline of an Anarchistic Theory of Knowledge* [*AM*]. Atlantic Highlands, N.J.: Humanities Press, 1975.

Foucault, Michel. *The Care of the Self* [*CS*]. Trans. Robert Hurley. New York: Pantheon, 1986.

———. *History of Sexuality*. Vol. 1 [*HS*]. Trans. Robert Hurley. New York: Vintage, 1980.

———. *Language, Counter-Memory, Practice* [*LCP*]. Ed. Donald F. Bouchard. Trans. Donald F. Bouchard and Sherry Simon. Ithaca, N.Y.: Cornell University Press, 1977.

———. "Nietzsche, Genealogy, History" [*NGH*]. In Foucault, *Language, Counter-Memory, Practice*.

———. *The Order of Things: An Archaeology of the Human Sciences* [*OT*]. New York: Vintage, 1973.

———. *Power/Knowledge* [*P/K*]. Ed. and trans. Colin Gordon. New York: Pantheon, 1980.

———. "A Preface to Transgression" [*PT*]. In Foucault, *Language Counter-Memory, Practice*.

———. "Theatrum Philosophicum" [*TP*]. In Foucault, *Language, Counter-Memory, Practice*.

———. "Two Lectures" [*2L*]. In Foucault, *Power/Knowledge*.

Freud, Sigmund. "Femininity" [*F*]. In *New Introductory Lectures on Psychoanalysis*. Vol. 22 of *The Standard Edition of the Complete Psychological Works of Sigmund Freud*. Ed. James Strachey. 24 vols. London: Hogarth Press, 1953–74.

Frye, Marilyn. *The Politics of Reality: Essays in Feminist Theory* [*PR*]. Trumansburg, N.Y.: Crossing Press, 1983.

Gadamer, Hans-Georg. *Truth and Method* [*TM*]. New York: Seabury, 1975.

Gamble, George, and James Bond, eds. *Race and Intelligence* [*RI*]. American Anthropologist, 1971.

Gilbert, Bil. "Crows by Far and Wide, but There's No Place like Home." *Smithsonian* 25, no. 5 (August 1992).

Gilligan, Carol. *In a Different Voice: Psychological Theory and Women's Development* [*IDV*]. Cambridge: Harvard University Press, 1982.

Goethe, Johann Wolfgang von. *Faust* [*F*]. Trans. Bayard Taylor. New York: Modern Library, 1950.

Gottlieb, Alma. "Witches, Kings, and the Sacrifice of Identity or The Power of Paradox and the Paradox of Power among the Beng of Ivory Coast" [*WKS*]. In Arens and Karp, *Creativity of Power*.

Graves, Robert. *The Greek Myths* [*GM*]. Baltimore, Md.: Penguin, 1955.

Hallen, Barry. "Phenomenology and the Exposition of African Traditional Thought" [*PEATT*]. In *Proceedings of the Seminar on African Philosophy/La Philosophie Africaine.* Ed. Claude Sumner. Addis Ababa, Ethiopia: Chamber Printing House, 1980.

Hallen, Barry, and J. O. Sodipo. *Knowledge, Belief and Witchcraft: Analytic Experiments in African Philosophy* [*KBW*]. London: Ethnographica, 1986.

Harding, Sandra. "The Curious Coincidence of Feminine and African Moralities: Challenges for Feminist Theory" [*CCFAM*]. In Kittay and Meyers, *Women and Moral Theory.*

———. "The Instability of the Analytical Categories of Feminist Theory" [*IACFT*]. *Signs* 11, no. 4 (1986).

Harrison, Beverly Wildung. "Our Right to Choose" [*RC*]. In Andolsen, Gudorf, and Pellauer, *Women's Consciousness, Women's Conscience.*

Hegel, G. W. F. *Jenenser Realphilosophie 1: Der Vorlesungen von 1803–1804* [*JR I*]. Ed. Johannes Hoffmeister. Leibzig: 1932. Quoted and translated in Agamben, *Language and Death.*

———. *Jenenser Realphilosophie 2: Die Vorlesungen von 1803–1804* [*JR II*]. Ed. J. Hoffmeister. Leipzig: 1932. Quoted and translated in Agamben, *Language and Death.*

———. *Phenomenology of Mind* [*PM*]. Trans. James Baillie. London: George Allen and Unwin, 1910.

Heidegger, Martin. *Basic Writings* [*BW*]. Ed. David Farrell Krell. New York: Harper and Row, 1977.

———. *Being and Time* [*BT*]. Trans. John Macquarrie and Edward Robinson. New York: Harper and Row, 1962. Originally published as *Sein und Zeit* [*SZ*] Seventh ed. Tübingen, Neomarius Verlag, 1953.

———. *Discourse on Thinking: A Translation of Gelassenheit* [*DT*]. Trans. John M. Anderson and E. Hans Freund. New York: Harper and Row, 1966.

———. *Introduction to Metaphysics* [*IM*]. Trans. Ralph Manheim. Garden City, N.Y.: Doubleday, 1961.

———. "Language" [*L*]. In Heidegger, *Poetry, Language, Thought.*

———. "Language in the Poem" [*LP*]. In Heidegger, *On the Way to Language.*

———. "Letter on Humanism" [*LH*]. In Heidegger, *Basic Writings.*

———. "On the Being and Conception of *Physis* in Aristotle's *Physics* B. 1" [*OBCP*]. Trans. Thomas J. Sheehan. *Man and World* 9, no. 3 (August 1976).

———. "On the Essence of Truth" [*OET*]. In Heidegger, *Basic Writings.*

———. *On the Way to Language* [*OWL*]. Trans. Peter D. Hertz. New York: Harper and Row, 1971.

———. *Poetry, Language, Thought* [*PLT*]. Trans. Albert Hofstadter. New York: Harper and Row, 1971.

———. "The Question Concerning Technology" [*QT*]. In Heidegger, *Basic Writings.*

———. *Was ist das—die Philosophie?* [*WP*], 1955. Quoted in Derrida, "Heidegger's Ear."

———. "What Calls for Thinking?" [*WCT*]. In Heidegger, *Basic Writings.*

Hoagland, Sarah Lucia. "Lesbian Ethics and Female Agency" [*LEFA*]. In Cole and Coultrap-McQuin, *Explorations in Feminist Ethics.*

———. "Some Thoughts about 'Caring'" [*STC*]. In Card, *Feminist Ethics.*

Hölderlin, Friedrich. *Friedrich Hölderlin: Poems and Fragments.* Trans. Michael Hamburger. Ann Arbor: University of Michigan Press, 1966.

———. "Patmos." In *Friedrich Hölderlin Poems and Fragments.*

The Holy Bible, containing the Old and New Testaments in the Authorized King James Version. Chicago: Consolidated Book Publishers, 1973).

Hyde, Lewis. *The Gift: Imagination and the Erotic Life of Property* [*G*]. New York: Random House, 1979.

Illich, Ivan. *Gender* [*G*]. New York: Pantheon, 1982.

———. "Toward a History of Gender." In *Feminist Issues* [*FI*] 3, no. 1 (Spring 1983). Includes symposium on his work.

Irigaray, Luce. "Any Theory of the 'Subject' has Always Been Appropriated by the 'Masculine'" [*ATS*]. In Irigaray, *Speculum of the Other Woman.*

———. "The Culture of Difference" [*CD*]. In Irigaray, *Je, tu, nous.*

———. *An Ethics of Sexual Difference* [*ESD*]. Trans. Carolyn Burke and Gillian C. Gill. Ithaca N.Y.: Cornell University Press, 1993. Originally published as *Éthique de la Différence sexuelle* [*ÉDS*] (Paris: Les Éditions de Minuit, 1984).

———. "He Risks Who Risks Life Itself" [*HR*]. In Irigaray, *The Irigaray Reader.*

———. *The Irigaray Reader* [*IR*]. Trans. Seán Hand. Ed. Margaret Whitford. Oxford: Blackwell, 1991.

———. *je, tu, nous: Toward a Culture of Difference* [*JTN*]. Trans. Alison Martin. New York: Routledge, 1993.

———. "*La Mystérique* [*M*]." In Irigaray, *Speculum of the Other Woman.*

———. *L'oubli de l'air chez Martin Heidegger* [*OA*]. Paris: Les Éditions de minuit, 1983.

———. "The Power of Discourse and the Subordination of the Feminine" [*PDSF*]. In Irigaray, *This Sex Which Is Not One.*

———. "Questions" [*Q*]. In Irigaray, *The Irigaray Reader.*

———. "Questions to Emmanuel Levinas" [*QEL*]. In Irigaray, *The Irigaray Reader.*

———. "Sexual Difference" [*SD*]. In Irigaray, *The Irigaray Reader.*

———. *Speculum of the Other Woman* [*SOW*]. Trans. Gillian C. Gill. Ithaca, N.Y.: Cornell University Press, 1985. Originally published as *Speculum de l'autre femme* (Paris: Les Éditions de Minuit, 1974).

———. *This Sex Which Is Not One* [*SWNO*]. Trans. Catherine Porter. Ithaca, N.Y.: Cornell University Press, 1985.

———. "When Our Lips Speak Together" [*WOLST*]. In Irigaray, *This Sex Which Is Not One.*

———. "Why Define Sexed Rights?" [*WDSR*]. In Irigaray, *je, tu, nous.*

———. "Women on the Market" [*WM*]. In Irigaray, *This Sex Which Is Not One.*

Isasi-Diaz, Ada Maria. "Toward an Understanding of *Feminismo Hispano* in the U.S.A." [*FH*]. In Andolsen, Gudorf, and Pellauer, *Women's Consciousness, Women's Conscience.*

Jacobs, Jane. *Systems of Survival: A Dialogue on the Moral Foundations of Commerce and Politics* [*SS*]. New York: Random House, 1993.

Jaggar, Alison M. and Susan R. Bordo. *Gender/Body/Knowledge: Feminist Reconstructions of Being and Knowing* [*GBK*]. New Brunswick, N.J.: Rutgers University Press, 1989.

James, William. *Essays in Radical Empiricism* [*ERE*]. New York: Longman's Green, 1912.

Kafka, Franz. *The Complete Stories* [*CS*]. Ed. Nahum N. Glatzer. New York: Schocken, 1971.

Kant, Immanuel. *Lectures on Ethics* [*LE*]. Trans. Louis Infield. New York: Harper and Row, 1963.

Kazemzadeh, Firuz. "The Slaughter of the Armenians" [*SA*]. *The New York Times Book Review* (25 April 1993).

Kheel, Marti. "The Liberation of Nature: A Circular Affair" [*LN*]. *Environmental Ethics* 6, no. 4 (1985).

Kierkegaard, Søren. *Fear and Trembling: The Sickness Unto Death* [*FT*]. Trans. Walter Lowrie. Garden City, N.Y.: Doubleday, 1954.

King, Lewis M. "On the Nature of a Creative World" [*ONCW*]. In Ruch and Anyanwu, *African Philosophy.*

King, Lewis M., Vernon J. Dixon, and Wade W. Nobles, eds. *African Philosophy: Assumptions and Paradigms for Research on Black Persons* [*AP*]. Fanon Research and Development Center Publication, Area 8, no. 2. Los Angeles, Calif.: Charles R. Drew Postgraduate Medical School, 1976.

King, Roger J. H. "Caring about Nature: Feminist Ethics and the Environment" [*CN*]. In Warren, *Hypatia.*

King, Ynestra. "The Ecology of Feminism and the Feminism of Ecology" [*EFFE*]. In Plant, *Healing the Wounds.*

Kittay, Eva Feder, and Diana T. Meyers, eds. *Women and Moral Theory* [*WMT*]. Totowa, N.J.: Rowman and Littlefield, 1987.

Krell, David Farrell. *Daimon Life: Heidegger and Life-Philosophy* [*DL*]. Bloomington: Indiana University Press, 1992.

———. *Intimations of Mortality* [*IM*]. University Park: Pennsylvania State University Press, 1986.

Kristeva, Julia. *The Kristeva Reader* [*KR*]. Ed. Toril Moi. Trans. Alice Jardine and Harry Blake. New York: Columbia University Press, 1986.

———. "Stabat Mater" [*SM*]. In Kristeva, *The Kristeva Reader.*

———. "Women's Time" [*WT*]. In Kristeva, *The Kristeva Reader.* Originally published as "Le temps des femmes," *Cahiers de recherche de sciences des textes et documents* 5 (Winter 1979).

Lacan, Jacques. *Feminine Sexuality* [*FS*]. Ed. Juliet Mitchell and Jacqueline Rose. Trans. Jacqueline Rose. New York: Norton, 1985.

———. "God and the *Jouissance* of The Woman" [*GJW*]. In Lacan, *Feminine Sexuality.*

Lahar, Stephanie. "Ecofeminist Theory and Grassroots Politics" [*ETGP*]. In Warren, *Hypatia.*

Leibniz, G. W. F. "The Exigency to Exist in Essences: Principle of Plenitude" [*EEE*]. In Leibniz, *Leibniz Selections.*

———. *Leibniz Selections.* Ed. P. Wiener. New York: Scribner's, 1951. All references to Leibniz are from this edition.

———. "The Monadology" [*M*]. In Leibniz, *Leibniz Selections.*

Levinas, Emmanuel. *Otherwise than Being or Beyond Essence* [*OB*]. Trans. Alfonso Lingis. The Hague: Martinus Nijhoff, 1978. Originally published as *Autrement qu'être ou au-dela de l'essence* [*AÊ*] (The Hague: Martinus Nijhoff, 1974).

Lévi-Strauss, Claude. *The Elementary Structure of Kinship* [*ESK*]. Trans. James Harle Bell, John Richard von Sturmer, and Rodney Needham. Boston: Beacon, 1969.

Lugones, María C. "On the Logic of Pluralist Feminism" [*OLPF*]. In Card, *Feminist Ethics.*

———. "Playfulness, 'World'-Travelling, and Loving Perception" [*PWTLP*]. *Hypatia* 2, no. 2 (Summer 1987).

Lyotard, Jean-François. *Le Différend* [*D*]. Paris: Les Éditions de Minuit, 1983.

———. *The Differend: Phrases in Dispute* [*DPD*]. Trans. Georges Van Den Abbeele. Minneapolis: University of Minnesota Press, 1988.

———. *Heidegger and "the jews"* [HJ]. Trans. Andreas Michel and Mark Roberts. Minneapolis: University of Minnesota Press, 1990.

———. *The Inhuman: Reflections on Time* [*I*]. Trans. Geoffrey Bennington and Rachel Bowlby. Stanford: Stanford University Press, 1991.

MacKinnon, Catharine A. "Feminism, Marxism, Method, and the State: An Agenda for Theory" [*FMMS1*]. *Signs* 7, no. 3 (1982).

———. "Feminism, Marxism, Method, and the State: Toward Feminist Jurisprudence" [*FMMS2*]. *Signs* 8, no. 4 (1982).

———. *Feminism Unmodified: Discourses on Life and Law* [*FU*]. Cambridge: Harvard University Press, 1987.

———. *Only Words* [*OW*]. Cambridge: Harvard University Press, 1993.

———. *Toward a Feminist Theory of the State* [*TFTS*]. Cambridge: Harvard University Press, 1989.

Manning, Rita. "Just Caring" [*JC*]. In Cole and Coultrap-McQuin, *Explorations in Feminist Ethics.*

Mauss, Marcel. *The Gift: Forms and Functions of Exchange in Archaic Societies*. Trans. Ian Cunnison. [*G*]. Glenco, Ill.: Free Press, 1954.

Mbiti, John S. *African Religions and Philosophy* [*ARP*]. London: Heinemann Educational Books, 1969.

Merleau-Ponty, Maurice. *Phenomenology of Perception* [*PP*]. Trans. Colin Smith. London: Routledge and Kegan Paul, 1962.

Meyer, Christine, and Faith Moosang, eds. *Living with the Land: Communities Restoring the Earth* [*LL*]. Gabriola Island, B.C.: New Society Publishers, 1992.

Morgan, Robin, ed. *Sisterhood Is Powerful: An Anthology of Writings from the Women's Liberation Movement* [*SP*]. New York: Random House, 1970.

Nagel, Thomas. *Moral Questions* [*MQ*]. Cambridge: Cambridge University Press, 1979.

Nancy, Jean-Luc. *The Inoperative Community* [*IC*]. Trans. Peter Connor, Lisa Garbus, Michael Holland, and Simona Sawhney. Minneapolis: University of Minnesota Press, 1991.

Nietzsche, Friedrich. *Basic Writings of Nietzsche*. Trans. Walter Kaufmann. New York: Random House, Modern Library Giant, 1968. All quotations from Nietzsche are from this edition.

———. *Birth of Tragedy* [*BT*]. In Nietzsche, *Basic Writings.*

———. *Ecce Homo* [*EH*]. In Nietzsche, *Basic Writings.*

Nodding, Nel. *Caring: A Feminine Approach to Ethics and Moral Education* [*C*]. Berkeley: University of California Press, 1984.

Nussbaum, Martha. *The Fragility of Goodness* [*FG*]. Cambridge: Cambridge University Press, 1986.

Oates, Whitney J., and Eugene O'Neill, eds. *The Complete Greek Drama* [*CGD*]. New York: Random House, 1938.

Oxford English Dictionary, Compact Edition. New York: Oxford University Press, 1971.

Pagels, Elaine H. "What Became of God the Mother? Conflicting Images of God in Early Christianity" [*WBGM*]. In Christ and Plaskow, *Womenspirit Rising.*

Parrinder, Geoffrey. *Witchcraft: European and African* [*WEA*]. London: Faber and Faber, 1970.

Peirce, Charles Sanders. *The Collected Papers of Charles Sanders Peirce* [*CP*]. Ed. Charles Hartshorne and Paul Weiss. 6 vols. Cambridge: Harvard University Press, 1931–35.

———. *The Philosophical Writings of Peirce* [*PP*]. Ed. Justus Buchler. New York: Dover, 1955.

Plant, Christopher and Judith Plant, eds. *Green Business: Hope or Hoax?* [*GB*]. Gabriola Island, B.C.: New Society Publishers, 1991.

Plant, Judith, ed. *Healing the Wounds: The Power of Ecological Feminism* [*HW*]. Philadelphia: New Society Publishers, 1989.

Plato. *The Collected Dialogues of Plato*. Ed. Edith Hamilton and Huntington Cairns. Princeton, N.J.: Princeton University Press, 1961. All quotations from Plato are from this edition unless otherwise indicated.

———. *Phaedrus*. Trans. Harold North Fowler. Loeb Classical Library. Cambridge: Harvard University Press, 1914. All Greek passages from *Phaedrus* are from this edition.

Pope, Alexander. *Essay on Man*. In *The Poetry of Pope*. Ed. Meyer H. Abrams. New York: Appleton-Century-Crofts, 1954.

Rachels, James. "Why Animals Have a Right to Liberty" [*WARL*]. In Regan and Singer, *Animal Rights and Human Obligations*.

Randall, John Herman, Jr. *Aristotle* [*A*]. New York: Columbia University Press, 1960.

———. *Plato: Dramatist of the Life of Reason* [*P*]. New York: Columbia University Press, 1970.

Reed, Alexander W. *Myths and Legends of Australia* [*MLA*]. Sydney: A. H. and and A. W. Reed, 1971.

Regan, Tom. *The Case for Animal Rights* [*CAR*]. Berkeley: University of California Press, 1983.

Regan, Tom and Peter Singer. *Animal Rights and Human Obligations* [*ARHO*]. 2nd ed. Englewood Cliffs, N.J.: Prentice-Hall, 1989.

Rigterink, Roger J. "Warning: The Surgeon Moralist Has Determined That Claims of Rights Can Be Detrimental to Everyone's Interests" [*W*]. In Cole and Coultrap-McQuin, *Explorations in Feminist Ethics*.

Roach, Catherine. "Loving Your Mother: On the Woman–Nature Relationship" [*LM*]. In Warren, *Hypatia*.

Robinson, John Manley. *An Introduction to Early Greek Philosophy* [*EGP*]. Boston: Houghton Mifflin, 1968. All Greek fragments are quoted from this edition unless otherwise indicated.

Ross, Stephen David. *Injustice and Restitution: The Ordinance of Time* [*IR*]. Albany: State University of New York Press, 1993.

———. *The Limits of Language* [*LL*]. New York: Fordham University Press, 1993.

———. *The Ring of Representation* [*RR*]. Albany: State University of New York Press, 1992.

———. *A Theory of Art: Inexhaustibility by Contrast* [*TA*]. Albany: State University of New York Press, 1983.

———. "Translation as Transgression" [*TT*]. *Translation Perspectives* 5. Ed. Dennis J. Schmidt. Binghamton, N.Y.: Binghamton University, 1990.

Ruch, E. A., and K. C. Anyanwu. *African Philosophy: An Introduction to the Main Philosophical Trends in Contemporary Africa* [*AP*]. Rome: Catholic Book Agency, 1984.

Ruth, Shelia. "Methodocracy, Misogyny, and Bad Faith: Sexism in the Philosophic Establishment" [*MMBF*]. *Metaphilosophy* 10, no. 1 (1979).

Sacks, Oliver. *The Man Who Mistook His Wife for a Hat and Other Clinical Tales.* Vol. 1, *Awakenings* [*A*]; Vol. 2, *A Leg to Stand On* [*LSO*]; Vol. 3, *The Man Who Mistook His Wife for a Hat and Other Clinical Tales* [*MMWH*]; Vol. 4, *Seeing Voices* [*SV*]. New York: Quality Paperback Book Club, 1990.

Sallis, John, ed. *Deconstruction in Philosophy: The Texts of Jacques Derrida* [*DP*]. Chicago: University of Chicago Press, 1987.

Sartre, Jean-Paul. *Nausea* [*N*]. Trans. Lloyd Alexander. New York: New Directions, 1964.

Scheper-Hughes, Nancy. "Vernacular Sexism: An Anthropological Response to Ivan Illich" [*VS*]. In Illich, *Feminist Issues.*

Scott, Charles E. *The Question of Ethics: Nietzsche, Foucault, Heidegger* [*QE*]. Bloomington: Indiana University Press, 1990.

Selfe, Lorna. *Nadia: A Case Study of Extraordinary Drawing Ability in an Autistic Child.* New York and London: Harcourt Brace Jovanovich, 1977.

Sen, Amartya. "More than One Hundred Million Women are Missing" [*MMWM*]. *The New York Review of Books* 37, no. 20 (20 December 1990).

Sessions, Robert. "Deep Ecology versus Ecofeminism: Healthy Differences or Incompatible Philosophies?" [*DEE*]. In Warren, *Hypatia.*

Singer, Linda. "Defusing the Canon: Feminist Rereading and Textual Politics" [*DC*]. In *Erotic Welfare: Sexual Theory and Politics in the Age of Epidemic.* Ed. Judith Butler and Maureen MacGrogan. New York: Routledge, 1993.

Singer, Peter. *Animal Liberation: A New Ethics For Our Treatment of Animals* [*AL*]. New York: Avon, 1975.

Slicer, Deborah, "Your Daughter or Your Dog" [*DD*]. In Warren, *Hypatia.*

Spelman, Elizabeth V. *Inessential Woman: Problems of Exclusion in Feminist Thought* [*IW*]. Boston: Beacon, 1988.

Spinoza, Benedict de. *Ethics* [*E*]. Ed. James Gutmann. Trans. William Hale White. Rev. Amelia Hutchinson Stirling. New York: Hafner, 1949.

———. *A Political Treatise* [*PT*]. Trans. Robert H. M. Elwes. New York: Dover, 1951.

Starhawk [Miriam Simos]. "Ethics and Justice in Goddess Religion" [*EJGR*]. In Andolsen, Gudorf, and Pellauer, *Women's Consciousness, Women's Conscience.*

———. "Witchcraft and Women's Culture" [*WWC*]. In Christ and Plaskow, *Womanspirit Rising.*

Stephen, Michele. "Contrasting Images of Power" [*CIP*]. In Stephen, *Sorcerer and Witch.*

———. "Master of Souls: The Mekeo Sorcerer" [*MS*]. In Stephen, *Sorcerer and Witch.*

———, ed. *Sorcerer and Witch in Melanesia* [*SWM*]. New Brunswick, N.J.: Rutgers University Press, 1987.

Strawson, Peter F. *Individuals: An Essay in Descriptive Metaphysics* [I]. *Garden City, N.Y.: Doubleday, 1959.*

Sumner, Claude. The Source of African Philosophy: The Ethiopian Philosophy of Man [*SAP*]. Stuttgart: Franz Steiner Verlag Wiesbaden GMBH, 1986.

Tannen, Deborah. *You Just Don't Understand: Women and Men in Conversation* [*YJDU*]. New York: Ballantine, 1990.

Taylor, Paul. *Respect for Nature: A Theory of Environmental Ethics* [*RN*]. Princeton, N.J.: Princeton University Press, 1986.

Theroux, Paul. "Self-Propelled" [*SP*]. *The New York Times Magazine*, 25 (April 1993).

Thomas, Elizabeth Marshall. "Reflections (Lions)" [*L*]. *The New Yorker* (15 October 1990).

Trinh, Minh-ha T. *Woman, Native, Other: Writing Postcoloniality and Feminism* [*WNO*]. Indianapolis: Indiana University Press, 1989.

Valiente, Doreen. *Witchcraft for Tomorrow* [*WT*]. Custer, Wash.: Phoenix, 1987.

Warren, Karen J. "Feminism and Ecology: Making Connections" [*FEMC*]. *Environmental Ethics* 9 (1987).

———, ed. *Hypatia* 6, no. 1 (spring 1991). Special issue on ecological feminism.

———. "The Promise and Power of Ecological Feminism" [*PPEF*]. *Environmental Ethics* 11 (1990).

Warren, Karen J., and Jim Cheney. "Ecological Feminism and Ecosystem Ecology" [*EFEE*]. In Warren, *Hypatia.*

Whitehead, Alfred North. *Adventures of Ideas* [*AI*]. New York: Macmillan, 1933.

———. *Process and Reality* [*PR*]. Ed. David R. Griffin and Donald W. Sherburne. Corr. ed. New York: Free Press, 1978.

Wittig, Monique. "The Category of Sex" [*CS*]. In Wittig, *The Straight Mind.*

———. *The Lesbian Body* [*LB*]. Trans. David Le Vay. Boston: Beacon, 1973. Originally published as *Le Corps Lesbien* [*CL*]. (Paris: Les Éditions de Minuit, 1973).

———. "The Mark of Gender" [*MG*]. In Wittig, *The Straight Mind.*

———. "One Is Not Born a Woman" [*OBW*]. In Wittig, *The Straight Mind.*

———. "The Straight Mind" [*SM*]. In Wittig, *The Straight Mind.*

———. *The Straight Mind and Other Essays* [*SME*]. With a foreword by Louise Turcotte. Boston: Beacon, 1992.

INDEX